Departing from Deviance

Departing from Deviance

*A History of Homosexual Rights
and Emancipatory Science in America*

Henry L. Minton

The University of Chicago Press   Chicago and London

HENRY L. MINTON is professor emeritus of psychology at the
University of Windsor. He is the author of *Currents of Thought in
American Social Psychology, Lewis M. Terman: Pioneer in
Psychological Testing,* and *Differential Psychology.*

The University of Chicago Press, Chicago 60637
The University of Chicago Press, Ltd., London
© 2002 by The University of Chicago
All rights reserved. Published 2002
Printed in the United States of America

11 10 09 08 07 06 05 04 03 02   1 2 3 4 5

ISBN: 0-226-53043-4 (cloth)
ISBN: 0-226-53044-2 (paper)

Library of Congress Cataloging-in-Publication Data

Minton, Henry L.
    Departing from deviance : a history of homosexual rights and
    emancipatory science in America / Henry L. Minton.
        p. cm.
    Includes bibliographical references and index.
    ISBN 0-226-53043-4 (cloth : alk. paper) — ISBN 0-226-53044-2
    (pbk. : alk. paper)
        1. Homosexuality—Research—United States. 2. Gay liberation
    movement—United States. I. Title.
    HQ76.3.U5 M56 2002
    305.9′0664′0973—dc21   2001027802

♾ The paper used in this publication meets the minimum requirements
of the American National Standard for Information Sciences—
Permanence of Paper for Printed Library Materials, ANSI Z39.48-1992.

To Jan Gay and Thomas Painter
for their courage and foresight

Contents

Preface   *ix*

1. Introduction: Emancipatory Science and
    Homosexual Rights   1

2. The Relationship between Homosexuals
    and Sex Researchers, 1870–1940   7

3. Jan Gay and the Sex Variants Committee,
    1935–41   33

4. Homosexual Life Stories, 1935–41   58

5. Henry and Gross and the Study of Sex
    Offenders, 1937–72   94

6. Thomas Painter and the Study of Male
    Prostitution, 1935–43   122

7. Toward Participatory Research on
    Homosexuality: Painter, Kinsey, and
    the Kinsey Institute, 1943–73   159

8. Evelyn Hooker, Frank Kameny, and
    Depathologizing Homosexuality,
    1957–73   219

    Epilogue: Beyond 1973   265

Notes   *275*

Index   *337*

Photographs follow page 158

This book is the product of a long intellectual journey. As a gay man who came out in the late 1970s, I was attracted to the new developments in social science that critically challenged the ways in which minority groups were studied. As a psychologist, I became interested in examining psychology's historical treatment of racial minorities. My first historical research dealt with the American mental testing movement and its biased investigation of racial and social class differences in intelligence. My approach was to study the work of one of the leaders in the mental testing movement, Lewis M. Terman. As I learned, Terman was not only interested in individual and group differences in intelligence, but also in emotional and personality differences. In this latter realm, he focused on gender differences and in the 1930s developed the first questionnaire to assess a person's gender identity on a continuum of masculinity-femininity.

In 1983, while working with the Terman Papers at Stanford University, I discovered a file, titled "The Committee for the Study of Sex Variants." Terman was a member of this interdisciplinary committee, which functioned from 1935 through 1941. He had been invited to join the committee because of his masculinity-femininity scale, which he attempted to validate by testing a sample of gay men and demonstrating that they had an inverted (feminine) identity. What especially intrigued me were the many references to a woman by the name of Jan Gay. She was not a committee member, but she had conducted case histories of lesbians and, as suggested in the committee minutes, the committee was organized to supervise and expand her research. Several questions flashed through my mind: Was she a lesbian? Was Jan Gay her real name? What was her relationship with the professional "experts" who constituted the committee? Through the committee file, I learned that her project was eventually translated into a 1941 published work, *Sex Variants: A Study of Homosexual Patterns*, authored by psychiatrist George W. Henry. This two-volume monograph contains the autobiographical voices of forty women and forty men. The committee file and the Henry volumes thus gave birth to the goal of this book—to demonstrate that before gay and lesbian liberation, homosexuals were not only the passive victims of scientific and medical inquiry, but also active agents in utilizing scientific research as a vehicle for homosexual rights.

The committee minutes also contained the name of another community, grassroots researcher, Thomas Painter. His project was a study of male prostitution and, as in the case of Gay, the committee was supervising his work. His research resulted in a two-volume manuscript that was never published but is preserved at the Kinsey Institute Archives. Because of other research projects that I had to complete, it was not until 1995 that I was able to examine his manuscript and papers. Up until that time, I believed that the major focus of my work would be Jan Gay and the Committee for the Study of Sex Variants. When I arrived at the Institute's archives and asked to look at the Painter Papers, I was led to a storage room that held a large two-door metal filing cabinet. Upon opening the doors, I found some thirty bound annual volumes of diaries as well as boxes that contained hundreds of photos of sex partners and various other assorted artifacts of Painter's life. I had struck a mother lode of archival riches and realized that Painter as well as Gay would play central roles in my narrative. And so this book is dedicated to their emancipatory spirit.

There are many people and institutions that have provided me with the resources to complete this work. In 1995 and 1999, I was granted six-month sabbatical leaves from the University of Windsor. In 1994 I was awarded a one-year research grant from the University of Windsor Research Board, and in 1995 I was awarded a three-year research grant from the Social Sciences and Humanities Research Council of Canada. My archival research was accomplished with the help of a number of libraries. I would like to thank Margaret H. Harter, Liana Zhou, and their staff at the Kinsey Institute Library; Roxanne Nilan and Linda Long at the Stanford University Archives; Adele Lerner at the Payne-Whitney Clinic Archives of New York Hospital-Cornell Medical Center; Elin L. Wolfe at the Countway Library at Harvard Medical School; Amy Hague at the Sophia Smith Collection at Smith College; Russell A. Johnson at the Department of Special Collections, University Research Library, University of California, Los Angeles; Jean Ashton at the Rare Book and Manuscript Library, Columbia University; Frank Gagliardi at the Burritt Library, Central Connecticut State University; and Nancy McCall at the Chesney Medical Archives of the Johns Hopkins Medical Institutions.

My research assistant, Scott Mattson, helped me in the qualitative analysis of the eighty case studies in the *Sex Variants* monograph. Brian Freeman, Jim Reed, Miriam Reumann, and Jennifer Terry kindly provided me with leads on archival resources. Through interviews, Bill Dellenback, Paul H. Gebhard, Canon Clinton R. Jones, Edwin S. Shneidman, and Clarence A. Tripp graciously shared their personal impressions of some of the individuals discussed in this book. The late Eric Garber shared his insights with me about some of the key figures in the lesbian and gay subculture of Harlem in the 1930s.

I owe a special debt to Jill Morawski for her interest and support in the early stages of this project. Doug Mitchell of the University of Chicago Press has given guidance and support throughout the long process of completing this book. My work has benefited from conversations with many research colleagues. I would especially like to thank Barry Adam, Betty Bayer, Jim Capshew, Larry Friedman, Ellen Herman, Darryl Hill, Ian Nicholson, Kathy Milar, Tina Simmons, and Leila Zenderland. I have also profited from the critical feedback offered by Barry Adam, Betty Bayer, Ellen Herman, and Tina Simmons, each of whom read portions of the manuscript, as well as two anonymous reviewers who read the entire manuscript. Finally, the love and support of my partner, Bob Martin, nourished this work.

Earlier versions of some parts of this book have appeared in several of my publications, which include "Community Empowerment and the Medicalization of Homosexuality: Constructing Sexual Identities in the 1930s," *Journal of the History of Sexuality* 6 (1996): 435–58; "Retrospective Review of *Sexual Behavior in the Human Male*, by Alfred C. Kinsey, Wardell B. Pomeroy, and Clyde E. Martin and *Sexual Behavior in the Human Female*, by Alfred C. Kinsey, Wardell B. Pomeroy, Clyde E. Martin, and Paul H. Gebhard," *Contemporary Psychology* 41 (1996): 975–77; "Deconstructing Heterosexuality: Life Stories from Gay New York, 1935–1941," *Journal of Homosexuality* 36, no. 1 (1998): 43–61 (with Scott R. Mattson).

Chapter 1

Introduction: Emancipatory Science and Homosexual Rights

> Oppressed people resist by identifying themselves as subjects, by
> defining their reality, shaping their new identity, naming their history,
> telling their story.
>
> —bell hooks, *Talking Back: Thinking Feminism, Thinking Black*

The social and political upheavals of the 1960s and 1970s reflected an intensification of the long struggle by oppressed people to resist domination by claiming the right to speak in their own voice. Rather than being treated as objects—defined and controlled by the dominant stratum of white heterosexual men—women, people of color, lesbians, and gay men strove to achieve subjective agency. As subjects, they could define their reality, mold their identity, rescue their history, and tell their stories—in essence, become cohesive politicized groups demanding social justice and political representation.

These liberatory social movements had far-ranging effects. Not only did they force political and social transformation; they generated change in intellectual spheres. In many universities by the early 1970s, programs in women's studies and black studies were created. In various fields of study, scholars became more sensitized to their own biases and the need to incorporate minority perspectives in their work as well as to deconstruct the categories through which certain groups are constituted as minorities. In the social sciences, which had a history of either ignoring or distorting minority experience, alternative forms of inquiry challenged established theory and research practice. These various strands coalesced into a perspective that became known as emancipatory or critical social science.[1]

Central to emancipatory social science is the idea that human knowledge is always *situated* within a framework of social relations. Thus, knowledge is based on the position that knowers or observers hold in society. This implies that there are multiple realities. Observers who occupy privileged positions in the social hierarchy have a perspective different from those who are marginalized. Being marginalized has the inherent advantage of being able to know the realities of both the oppressor and the oppressed. Blacks, for example, cannot escape the impact of white dominance and are thus aware of the norms and values of white society. But they are also aware of their own black world and its place in the larger society. On the other hand, whites have historically had little understanding of what it means to be black and oppressed.[2]

In the 1960s and 1970s, as more women, people of color, lesbians, and gay men entered the social sciences, the traditional white male heterosexist worldview within academia was challenged. Incorporating situated knowledge, women's experience was now interpreted from a feminist perspective rather than from the historically entrenched, androcentric viewpoint. In fact, a feminist perspective has not been limited to the social sciences. As Donna Haraway, commenting on primatology, has noted, feminist science in general acts to destabilize dominant accounts and explanations, and thus engenders a better science by providing a more complete, coherent version.[3]

By incorporating minority perspectives and hence challenging dominant views of reality, critical social science has emancipatory potential. Knowledge production that reflects the experiences and struggles of oppressed people undermines the biases and distortions that perpetuate the status quo of domination. Liberation and social transformation become possibilities when scientific knowledge contests the hegemonic assumptions, myths, and stereotypes that serve to rationalize and justify the inequitable treatment of the oppressed.

As part of the emancipatory social science of the 1970s, gay and lesbian scholars challenged the heterosexist ideology underlying the scientific treatment of homosexuality. The major target was the assumption that homosexuality was pathological, an assumption that was institutionalized by the American Psychiatric Association's (APA) official system of diagnostic classification. In 1973, as a result of a concerted effort by gay and lesbian activists and a group of psychiatrists and psychologists who dissented from the canonical medical model, homosexuality as a generic category was removed from the psychiatric nomenclature. The struggle to excise homosexuality from the psychiatric lexicon did not result in a complete victory since the APA introduced the new antigay category of "sexual orientation disturbance" to refer to homosexuals who were psychologically troubled by their sexual orientation. Nevertheless, 1973 marked a turning point in the movement for gay and lesbian rights. Removing the official blanket association of homosexuality with sickness enabled the social science of same-sex relations to gain legitimacy in academia. Parallel developments took place in the humanities and the arts. Gay and lesbian studies became a bona fide field of academic specialization.

But there is a much longer history of gay and lesbian studies. My purpose here is to tell that story, focusing on its scientific facet. From the origins of the first homosexual rights movement, which took place in Germany in the late nineteenth century, there has been an ongoing effort to use scientific knowledge as one means to emancipate homosexual men and women from the tyranny of moral ostracism, legal punishment, and medical treatment. Magnus Hirschfeld, the German sexologist and pioneer homophile activist, chose as the motto for his life's work "*Per scientiam ad justitiam*" (Through science to justice).[4]

Spurred by the liberatory climate of the gay and lesbian movement of the early 1970s, the last two and a half decades have witnessed an explosion of scholarly work in lesbian and gay history. As George Chauncey, Martin Duberman, and Martha Vicinus note in their introduction to *Hidden from History: Reclaiming the Gay and Lesbian Past,* this scholarly work has documented the history of homosexual repression and resistance. Not only has this work uncovered the extensiveness of homosexual victimization, but also in its revelations of homosexual resistance it has reclaimed the historical agency of gay men and lesbians.[5]

From the origins of the homosexual rights movement in Germany in the late nineteenth century, homosexual activists promoted their cause by writing about the nature of same-sex love. They created labels, such as the male "Urning," the female "Urningin," the "sexual intermediate," and, more concisely, the "homosexual," to reflect the group identity of people who experienced same-sex love. Ironically, with the emerging visibility of homosexuals, medical specialists expropriated the labels and medicalized the theories developed by the homosexual activists. Thus, homosexual activists who chose science as a means of promoting homosexual emancipation have had to engage in an ongoing struggle with medical and scientific authorities over who best understands the experiences of gay man and lesbians.

In this book I concentrate on the contested treatment of homosexuality in America by homosexual activist-researchers and medical/scientific authorities. By the 1930s there was an extensive sexological literature on homosexuality in America, Britain, and Europe. With some notable exceptions by homosexual activists and sympathizers, such as Magnus Hirschfeld and Havelock Ellis, this literature was driven by the assumption that homosexuality was a form of sexual pathology. In America two watershed events took place that undermined the hegemony of the pathology model. The first occurred in 1935 with the founding of the Committee for the Study of Sex Variants. This interdisciplinary committee comprised experts on sexuality and social deviance. In contrast with previous research on homosexuality conducted by physicians and scientists, homosexual activists played a major role in organizing and carrying out the committee-sponsored research. This grassroots involvement set the stage for a series of research studies of homosexuality that involved the active participation of homosexuals. It was this body of research that proved to be influential in the second watershed event to challenge the pathology model—the 1973 psychiatric declassification of homosexuality.

Central to the participatory research approach was the active strategy by homosexual activists to have gay and lesbian participants tell their stories. The goal was to establish a dialogue with sex researchers so that the investigators would understand the lived experiences and realities of homosexual people. It was thus hoped that the myths of homosexuality as a sin, crime, and sickness would be replaced by a social tolerance for sexual difference. For homosexual activists, life story narratives served as a vehicle for effecting social change.

My major objectives in this book are twofold. First, I want to reveal a hidden history of research production and collaboration on the part of American gay and lesbian activists who sought the right to speak for themselves and gain homosexual rights through the scientific enterprise. This history of gay and lesbian emancipatory research is a part of the history of homosexual resistance. Second, I want to present the substantive contributions produced by these gay and lesbian researchers. Much of this work is obscure because of the publication obstacles faced by these researchers. This body of work includes significant primary texts documenting the American homosexual world of the early and mid-twentieth century. Moreover, by revealing the lives of the researchers and their accomplishments, I hope to redress the suppression of their work and provide them with the recognition they deserve.

In the following chapter, I provide the historical background for the participatory research launched by gay and lesbian activist-researchers in the 1930s. Within the period of the late nineteenth and early twentieth centuries, I consider the relationship between homosexual research participants and sex researchers. There were also instances during this era in which gay men and lesbians carried out their own research and I examine the work of these early activist-researchers.

Several chapters are devoted to the Committee for the Study of Sex Variants and its role in spawning various research projects in the 1930s that involved the active participation of lesbians and gay men. Chapter 3 details the efforts of Jan Gay to publish her work on lesbian life histories. In order to achieve this objective, she required the sponsorship of recognized medical and scientific experts and she thus played a major role in the creation of the sex variants committee. Her research was expanded to include gay men. Unfortunately, her work was taken over by psychiatrist George W. Henry. The emancipatory potential of her project as well as her original contribution was thus subverted into a psychiatric treatise on homosexuality.

In chapter 4 I reclaim the substance of Gay's research by analyzing the lesbian and gay life histories from the perspective of the storytellers. Luckily, their narratives were preserved in Henry's published two-volume monograph, *Sex Variants: A Study of Homosexual Patterns*.[6] I also contrast the first-person accounts with Henry's psychiatric discourse. Chapter 5 deals with the collaboration between Henry and Alfred A. Gross, a closeted gay ex–Episcopalian priest. Henry and Gross focused their work on gay male sex offenders, and it was Gross who actually carried out the research. After World War II Gross directed the George W. Henry Foundation, a social agency devoted to helping gay men in trouble with the law.

The life and contributions of Thomas Painter are dealt with in chapters 6 and 7. Painter, like Gay and Gross, was associated with the sex variants committee in the 1930s. In 1941 he completed a two-volume manuscript on male homosexuality and male prostitution. The manuscript was never published, but it came to the attention of Alfred C. Kinsey. In 1943 Painter began a thirty-year unofficial association with the Kinsey Institute. Until Kinsey's death in 1956, Painter served as one of Kinsey's homosexual consultants, and more significantly, at the suggestion of Kinsey, he maintained a written and richly detailed "Life Record" of his sex life. I also deal with Kinsey's work on homosexuality and his relationship with other homosexual collaborators. Painter hoped that a biographer, a "Mr. X," would eventually extract his life story from his voluminous papers preserved at the Kinsey Institute. I have assumed that role and, as a gay man, have felt especially impelled to present his extraordinary contributions to gay scholarship and tell his remarkable story.

Chapter 8 focuses on the protracted struggle in the 1960s and early 1970s to challenge the official psychiatric classification of homosexuality as sexual pathology. The two key players in this challenge were psychologist Evelyn Hooker and homophile activist Frank Kameny. Hooker carried out a pathbreaking study in the 1950s that demonstrated there was no scientific basis for considering gay men to be psychologically maladjusted.

Her research was initiated through her friendship with a circle of gay men in Los Angeles. Kameny led the successful confrontation with the American Psychiatric Association.

In the epilogue I briefly consider the post-1973 emergence of gay and lesbian studies in academia, focusing particularly on the utilization of scientific inquiry in the interests of social justice for gay people. The liberatory climate of the last three decades has nourished the development of gay and lesbian studies and emancipatory social science. There is, however, a long history of achieving homosexual rights through scientific channels. This book seeks to place the modern era of a social science of same-sex relations within the framework of its historical antecedents.

Chapter 2

The Relationship between Homosexuals and Sex Researchers, 1870–1940

It occurred to me today with something of a shock how horrible it would be for this diary of mine to be pawed over and read unsympathetically after I am dead, by those incapable of understanding, who would be filled with disgust and astonishment and think of me as a poor demented wretch, a neurotic or a madman who was better off dead. And then the thought of the one thing even more dreadful and terrible than that—for my diary never to be read by the one person who would or could understand.

For I do want it to be read—there is no use concealing the fact— by somebody who is like me, who would understand. Yet Havelock Ellis is about the only person known to me, that is, known by name, to whom I could confidently entrust my life, my inmost soul at times.

—Jeb Alexander, *Jeb and Dash: A Diary of Gay Life, 1918–1945*, 14 April 1923

The pseudonymous Jeb Alexander was a gay man who was a government clerk in Washington, D.C. He started his diary in 1912, when he was twelve, and continued it until a year before his death in 1965. As his words suggest, he found sympathetic understanding in the work of sexual scientist Havelock Ellis. He most likely read Ellis's *Sexual Inversion* and discovered that others shared his own experiences. While Alexander had no intention of publishing his diary in his lifetime, like the respondents whose lives were recorded in Ellis's case histories, he wanted to leave a legacy of his life as a gay man. He thus willed his fifty handwritten volumes to his niece, Ina Russell, who in 1993 published selections from the years 1918 to 1945.[1]

By the late nineteenth and early twentieth centuries, there were gay men and lesbians who were attracted to medical and scientific experts of human sexuality. They sought clarification and explanation about their same-sex feelings through reading about homosexuality. In some cases they chose specialists for medical and psychological treatment and volunteered to be research subjects. In parallel fashion, as homosexuals became more visible in society, the medical and scientific community became increasingly interested in studying gay men and lesbians. In this chapter I deal with the motivations and goals of homosexual men and women in their relationship with physicians and sexual scientists. To set the stage, I briefly begin with a consideration of homosexual communities in Europe and North America and the development of sexual science. Beyond serving as research subjects, there were instances in which gay men and lesbians launched their own research, and at the end of the chapter, I examine the work by these gay and lesbian activist-researchers in America before 1940.

THE RISE OF GAY AND LESBIAN COMMUNITIES

Homoerotic relationships have been referred to throughout recorded history. In ancient Greece young men left their families to be socialized into manhood by forming affectional relationships with older men. In the medieval world, mythic stories were recorded about close friendships between men and between women, and same-sex marriage ceremonies were performed in Catholic and Orthodox churches. As early as the mid-sixteenth century, descriptions by explorers and missionaries surfaced about aboriginal North American men (*"berdache"*) who cross-dressed and coupled with masculine-appearing men. In the early and mid-nineteenth century, same-sex "passionate friendships" involved physical and verbal expressions of deep affection. Nevertheless, these relationships cannot be characterized as "homosexual" in the modern sense because they lacked any sense of a homosexual identity.

Gay male communities composed of individuals who possessed a homosexual self-awareness and group identity began to appear in Europe with the development of capitalism in the early eighteenth century. As new economic opportunities arose, men were no longer tied down to their agrarian roots and family networks. Reflecting this independence, meeting places for men seeking same-sex liaisons, known as "molly houses," were established in London and similar sites emerged in Paris and Amsterdam. At the start of the nineteenth century, a gay underground was in place in these cities, and as urbanization and industrialization spread, other gay communities emerged.[2]

In North America by the 1870s, a visible urban gay subculture was established. In a sexual advice manual for men, published in 1871, physician George Napheys exhorted:

> [If] we choose to draw the veil from those abominable scenes with which our professional life has brought us into contact, we could tell of the vice which called vengeance from heaven on Sodom practiced notoriously; we could speak of restaurants frequented by men in women's attire, yielding themselves to indescribable lewdness; we could point out literature so inconceivably devilish as to advocate and extol this utter depravity.[3]

Subsequent medical reports in the 1880s and 1890s pointed to the group identity of male "inverts" with statements such as "In many large cities the subjects of the contrary sexual impulse form a class by themselves and are recognized by the police."[4] Cross-dressing effeminate men, referred to as "fairies," were observed congregating in commercial "resorts," such as restaurants and beer gardens as well as masquerade or "drag" balls.[5]

Gay male communities comprised complex social networks. While effeminate fairies constituted the most visible facet of the gay subculture, their sexual partners were typically masculine-identified men. Many of these men did not think of themselves as homosexual even though they engaged in homosexual acts. In Newport, Rhode Island, for example, during the World War I era, large numbers of sailors engaged in homosexual relations with effeminate fairies without having it affect their self-image as "normal" men. Their sex acts conformed to masculine gender norms, such as taking on the active role in anal sex and the passive role in oral sex. They thus acted as "husbands" in relation to the "ladies" of the "inverted set." In gay communities in large cities, such as New York, there were also masculine-identified men who thought of themselves as homosexual, but because of the stigma of effeminacy distanced themselves from fairies. These men adopted the label of queer to reflect their nonconformist sexual object-choice of other men. For the most part, they preferred masculine men as sex partners.[6]

Women's experiences in forming same-sex relationships were quite different from those of men. Most women did not have the economic independence to pursue social arrangements outside of conventional family structures. Their economic security depended on marriage. Nevertheless, they were able to form close friendships among neighbors and relatives. By the second half of the nineteenth century, with the effects of industrialization, the rise of the first feminist movement, and the establishment of women's colleges, new opportunities emerged for unmarried working-class and middle-class women to enter the workforce and to choose to live with other women. By the first quarter of the twentieth century, such women were able to establish their own communities and develop a collective identity. Among the first generation of women college graduates, there were those who forged careers as teachers and administrators of women's colleges, leaders in the settlement house movement, and social reformers during the pre–World War I, Progressive era. Many of these women paired up with one another in same-sex households referred to as "Boston marriages." It is not clear to what extent these relationships were sexual, but they were clearly love relationships. Some of the most notable examples included social reformer Jane Addams and her partner of forty years, Mary Rozet Smith, and Bryn Mawr College president Cary Thomas and her lifelong partner, Mary Garrett.[7]

While women's intimate relationships based on romantic friendships persisted as late as the 1940s and 1950s, many women involved in same-sex relationships by the 1920s were aware of being sexually rather than spiritually attracted to one another. In order to understand this shift, it is important to consider the social changes that took place in American society between the 1880s and World War I. The industrialization and urbanization of American society in the late nineteenth century was accompanied by a growth of consumerism that, in turn, emphasized self-expression rather than sexual restraint. With respect to gender relations, the civilized morality of tender passion between spouses gave way to a new erotic consciousness. By the 1920s sex had become a source of motivation for both men and women. Women were now encouraged to find sexual expression with their husbands.[8]

During the 1920s and 1930s, as urban life opened up new opportunities for women in general, communities of lesbian-identified women began to emerge in bohemian and offbeat districts, most notably New York's Greenwich Village and Harlem, and San Francisco's North Beach. Harlem especially captured the new sexual freedom of the period, attracting both white and black women to its interracial lesbian and bisexual ambience. Its most popular entertainment venue for lesbians was the Clam House, where Gladys Bently, a 250-pound dark-skinned lesbian, attired in a white tuxedo and top hat, held forth at the piano with her infamous, obscene lyrics.[9]

Gay and lesbian communities were not necessarily confined to large cities. Salt Lake City was home to a close-knit community associated with a social organization. Salt Lake's Bohemian Club, founded in 1886, may not have been initially homosexually oriented, but it attracted many gay and lesbian members by the early twentieth century. Gay communities also sprang up around military training centers, like Newport, where there were ample opportunities for sexual encounters.[10]

Thus, in the late nineteenth and early twentieth centuries, there was a visible and diverse gay and lesbian subculture in Europe and North America. At the same time, sexual scientists became increasingly involved in studying gay men and lesbians. For these new sex experts, explaining the nature of homosexuality was viewed as integral to understanding the dynamics and varieties of human sexual functioning.

THE RISE OF SEXOLOGY

The formal origins of sexology began in 1906 when Iwan Bloch, a German dermatologist, proposed a science of sex that he labeled "*Sexualwissenschaft.*" Bloch conceived of the new sexual science as an interdisciplinary field, encompassing biological, psychological, cultural, social, and historical data. Subsequent steps in establishing the field were put forth by Magnus Hirschfeld, who instituted the first journal of sexology in 1908 and established the Institute for Sexual Science in Berlin in 1919, the first of its kind.[11]

Before the formal beginnings of the new sexual science, a preoccupation with the scientific study of sexuality had already existed by the late nineteenth century. The social changes produced by industrialization and urbanization increasingly turned human sexuality into a problem, as exemplified by the eugenic concerns about reproduction and the spread of sexually transmitted diseases associated with prostitution. The pioneering sexologists of the late nineteenth and early twentieth centuries set out to describe and analyze sexuality by detailing its normal expression and morbid variations. The classification of sexual pathology was thus viewed as the first step in constructing a sexual science, and homosexuality, the most visible deviation, became the prime example.[12]

Imbued with the Enlightenment faith in progress, the sexologists believed that science was closely connected with social reform. Despite the increasing rate of social change, antiquated sex laws persisted. Thus, most of the sexual scientists who turned their attention to homosexuality were concerned not only with scientific investigation, but also advocated the removal of laws criminalizing homosexual acts. The first sexologist to deal with homosexuality was the German lawyer, Karl Heinrich Ulrichs. Ulrichs, who was homosexual, published a series of twelve monographs (1864–79) on "love between men." He proposed that same-sex love was biologically based. He believed that if homosexuality was understood as biologically determined, then homosexuals should be accorded equal social and legal treatment. Ulrichs campaigned for homosexual rights, and in 1869 Karl Maria Kertbeny, who coined the term "homosexuality," joined him in these efforts. Ulrichs had used the labels of Urning and Urningin to refer to male and female homosexuals, respectively.[13]

Ulrichs's writings stimulated medical interest in the subject of homosexuality as a biologically based type of sexual pathology. Beginning with Karl Westphal's 1869 report of "contrary sexual feeling" and culminating in Richard von Krafft-Ebing's encyclopedic compendium of sexual pathologies, *Psychopathia sexualis,* first published in 1886, medical specialists espoused biologically based theories of homosexuality. Included among these writings by medical experts were Hirschfeld's theory of homosexuality as a congenital sexual intermediacy and Ellis's notion of inborn sexual inversion. Like Ulrichs, Hirschfeld used biology to justify the equal treatment of homosexuals. Moreover, he promoted "adjustment therapy," recommending that physicians encourage self-acceptance in their homosexual patients. Ellis, who was medically trained, was also a leading spokesperson for legal reform and social acceptance, but his views about lesbianism slanted toward the negative, as exemplified by his admonitions about assertive lesbians as seducers of heterosexual women. In treating congenitally inverted women, he therefore recommended the "ideal of sexual abstinence in so far as indulgence may be doing injury to others."[14]

Psychological explanations became increasingly popular with the appearance of Sigmund Freud's writings on sexuality in the early 1900s. While Freud believed that everyone had the capacity for homosexual feelings because of innate bisexuality, he viewed homosexuality as a form of arrested psychosexual development. The mature psychosexual object of desire was a heterosexual object-choice. To account for homosexuality, he pointed to a variety of environmental influences rooted in family dynamics, such as a seductive mother and weak father, which presented difficulties for a child's ability to become a heterosexually functioning adult. Beyond stressing the role of psychological factors, Freud's psychoanalytic theory was also influential in shifting the conception of homosexuality as a gender-role inversion to a sexual object-choice. As George Chauncey argues, this meant that homosexuality no longer incorporated the broader meaning of a sex-role deviation; instead, it referred specifically to aberrant sexual behavior.[15]

Sexology's legacy for homosexual rights was a mixed bag. On the one hand, it offered promise in terms of naturalizing homosexuality as a biologically based or developmentally determined variation of human sexuality. It therefore followed that homosexuals should be accorded equal rights. Indeed, medical specialists generally supported homosexual rights activists in campaigning for repeal of the penal laws against homosexuality. On the other hand, biologizing and pathologizing homosexuality established a distinct medical classification, akin to the categorization of physical and mental diseases. And medical nosologies were created to identify disease entities that, once differentiated, would lead to appropriate treatment. Unlike Hirschfeld, most medical practitioners believed in and applied various modes of treatment aimed at a cure, ranging from some who relied on relatively benign techniques of persuasion to others who utilized invasive physical interventions like castration. Moreover, biological and psychological reductionism masked the cultural, social, and historical contexts of homosexuality. The historical and anthropological works of writers such as John Addington Symonds, Edward Carpenter, and Edward Westermarck received little attention in comparison with the biological and psychological treatments of homosexuality.[16]

The sexological discovery of homosexuality was both a response to and a source of constructing gay and lesbian identities. Self-defined homosexual men and women existed before the sexologists labeled them. In fact, physicians appropriated the label "homosexuality" put forth by Kertbeny in 1869. The sexologists learned about homosexuality from what they observed in their patients and read about in police reports, judicial proceedings, and newspaper accounts. The medical classification, in turn, produced effects on the people who were the objects of inquiry. The very act of classification reinforced the grassroots sense of group identity among those who were part of the growing gay and lesbian communities of the late nineteenth and early twentieth centuries. Not only did the work of the sexologists reify existing identities and cultural patterns, but it also served as sources for redefinition and resistance. Sexual subjects used the scientific discourse for their own purposes.

The construction of the "mannish lesbian" illustrates the complex interplay between sexological definition and lesbian consciousness. By 1900 sex experts portrayed women who chose to live independent lives as aggressive, masculine, sexualized figures who constituted an "intermediate" sex. They drew upon existing cultural prototypes of mannish women, such as the independent "New Women" of the late nineteenth century. The well-publicized 1892 trial of Alice Mitchell, in Memphis, Tennessee, appears to have played an especially influential role in shaping both the sexologists' and the general public's image of the mannish lesbian. Nineteen-year-old Alice was tried for the murder of her lover, seventeen-year-old Freda Ward. The homosexual "love-murder" was sensationalized in newspapers across the country. The relationship between the two teenagers went beyond the recognized schoolgirls' romantic friendship of the time. The news reports revealed that Alice planned to marry Freda by cross-dressing and thus passing as a man named "Alvin." Apparently, Freda's vacillation over committing herself to Alice, coupled with Freda's attraction to several male suitors, sparked the murder. The news accounts played up the masculine/feminine difference between the pair—Alice, the male-identified suitor, and Freda, the feminine love object. In her analysis of the trial, Lisa Duggan notes that the sexologists were captivated by Alice Mitchell's love-murder. Ellis specifically pointed to Alice as the prototype of the female invert.[17]

The authoritative voice of medical discourse on the female invert was aimed at marginalizing women who challenged the conventional gender hierarchy. Yet the sexologists' image making was also appropriated by women who sought to create a lesbian identity. Many scholars of lesbian history have argued that the medical portrayal of the female invert was captured in lesbian self-representations in the early decades of the twentieth century. The most notable case is the English novelist, Radclyffe Hall, whose influential work, *The Well of Loneliness,* was published in America in 1928. But, as Duggan points out, Hall's depiction of the masculine protagonist, Stephen Gordon, and her feminine lover, Mary Llewellyn, not only mirrored medical renditions of female homosexuality, but also shared the structure of the Mitchell-Ward newspaper accounts. The origins of the mannish lesbian identity thus reflect a complex interplay of cultural and medical influences. Moreover Hall's construction of the mannish lesbian served her interests of challenging the social order. Masculinized women with sexual prowess could compete on equal terms with men, and female love was expressed in the face of sexual prohibitions.[18]

With the rise of sexology, an increasing number of gay men and lesbians became the subjects of scientific scrutiny. Understanding the motivations and goals of these research subjects sheds light on the varied nature of the relationship between homosexuals and sex researchers.

THE MOTIVATIONS AND GOALS OF RESEARCH SUBJECTS

Beginning in the 1870s in Europe and North America, men and women with same-sex desires came into contact with medical and scientific authorities who were interested in human sexuality. These homosexually inclined individuals became the subjects of medical case studies, sex surveys, prison studies, and investigations of homosexual communities. While many defined themselves as homosexual, the investigators labeled others if they showed signs of homoeroticism. Homosexual research participants played various roles in their relationship with sex researchers. In some cases, especially in medical or prison settings, they were captive subjects of research scrutiny and played a passive role. But in many instances, homosexual participants took an active part in medical and scientific inquiry. Some freely chose to be included in research projects. Even if they were not volunteers, many seized the opportunity to use their role as research subjects as a means of educating investigators about homosexuality and the lives of homosexuals. Thus, for many homosexual research participants, the research process became a proactive vehicle for changing public opinion and constructing more empathic and realistic understandings of homosexuality. Consequently, the motives of homosexual subjects ranged from seeking help and self-improvement to seizing opportunities for self-expression and social change. Male subjects tended to predominate, especially in the late nineteenth century, reflecting the greater visibility of gay men. There was also less interest in studying lesbians because, unlike gay men, they were not subject to legal persecution. Moreover, until the 1920s there were few women sex researchers, and their male counterparts found it difficult to extract sex histories from women. As American physician James G. Kiernan expressed it in 1884, in comparison with male "sexual perversion . . . a history of female sexual desire is much less easily obtained."[19]

The research reports of the late nineteenth and early twentieth centuries reveal a variety of motives among homosexual subjects. These included the search for a cure, an interest in seeking self-understanding, a desire to exercise self-expression, and educating and engaging researchers in effecting social change. With respect to cure, starting in the 1870s men and women, troubled by their same-sex feelings, turned to medical experts for help. Looking for sympathetic healers, they were drawn to specialists, most notably neurologists at first and then psychiatrists who had private practices in large cities. It is not necessarily clear that a cure was in the minds of the subjects described in the medical case reports. This, however, was often the assumption made by the reporting physician. Dr. William Hammond of New York, for example, in 1883 described a case of a man who was remorseful over engaging in anal homosexual relations and noted that his patient was "seriously desirous of being cured." In the same year, American physicians J. C. Shaw and G. N. Ferris similarly concluded that their male patient who had a "morbid desire" to embrace men was "distressed by his abnormal state, and wishes medicine to overcome it."[20]

These private patients, however, struggling with their same-sex erotic feelings, may well have been searching for self-knowledge as much as treatment. Many were unaware of others like themselves, which may have motivated them to turn to medical practitioners who could validate and offer explanations for their feelings. In several case reports, the medical authors referred to their patients' search for self-understanding. William Lee Howard, for example, a Baltimore physician, observed in 1906 that "sexual inverts . . . read all the literature on sex matters possible to obtain and many are better informed on this subject than the average physician."[21] Indeed, the published case studies provided a rich source of information for readers motivated to learn more about their homoerotic desires as well as discovering that there were others like themselves.

Sensing the value of the case studies in Krafft-Ebing's *Psychopathia sexualis,* a number of German-language readers submitted their own autobiographical accounts to Krafft-Ebing, which he added to his archival collection of case histories and in some instances published in later editions of his book. In 1890, for example, a young nobleman, "Von R.," prefaced his life story by stating, "I . . . trustingly turn to you, hoping that a layman might report something to the scholar that is not entirely without interest: even the most inconspicuous thing may gain importance in the right place and may be worth the researcher's scrutiny." Another writer expressed his gratitude to Krafft-Ebing for providing the opportunity to validate his own experiences, commenting, "Your book *Psychopathia sexualis* brought me much comfort. It contains passages that I might have written myself." The published case studies about homosexuality had the potential to serve the interests of homosexuals because they provided a body of knowledge that documented their lives and experiences. *Psychopathia sexualis,* although directed at medical and legal experts, became a popular book for laymen interested in extensive description of sexual experiences as well as discovering that there were others who shared their sexual outlook. As one of Krafft-Ebing's readers expressed his new sense of community, he had gained "the comfort of belonging together and not being alone anymore."[22]

Krafft-Ebing's work not only provided a source for self-discovery, but also served as a vehicle for self-expression. Respondents seized the opportunity to speak out and be recognized. Among the case histories are statements expressed in florid Victorian prose, such as "Our love . . . sprouts the most beautiful, precious blooms, develops all the more precious drives and encourages the mind, as much as the love of a young man for a girl." In another case history, Krafft-Ebing wrote, "He reports . . . with great contentment and remarkable cynicism that he has an innate contrary sexual sensitivity," adding a comment that the patient even stated that same-sex love was elevating.[23]

Other published studies also reveal that homosexual subjects were eager to speak out about homosexuality. One genre was the sex survey. Beginning in the 1910s, American physicians and social scientists constructed questionnaires to assess sexual behaviors and attitudes among the general population. The most ambitious of these endeavors was undertaken by Katharine Bement Davis. Based on a questionnaire that she mailed to twenty thousand women, most of whom were graduates of eastern women's colleges, she analyzed the responses of twenty-two hundred. Her results were reported in a 1929 monograph. What is especially noteworthy about her study is the extent of cooperation she received from her participants. Based on feedback she received, she reported that many were motivated to offer information about their private sex lives because they believed in the value of sex education as a means of preparing women for "life." Moreover, some women provided more than simple yes/no responses by writing open-ended descriptions of their experiences. These served as the basis for the liberal sprinkling of case studies among the voluminous pages of tabulated data.[24]

Reflecting the relatively high incidence of reported overt homosexual experience (25 percent for single women and 16 percent for married women), several case studies were included in the two chapters devoted to homosexuality. Among the single women, Davis labeled nine cases as "naturally" homosexual. These were women who generally accepted their homosexuality as natural and made a point of expressing their disdain for relations with men. Moreover, they took the opportunity to express their feelings. One woman, for example, proclaimed, "I have a woman friend whom I love and admire above everyone in the world and with whom life is perfectly happy because of our mutual love." Another woman speaking about her relationship noted, "It has arisen as an expression of love. . . . It has proved helpful and has made my life inexpressively richer and deeper."[25]

Studies of prison homosexuality also provided an opening for homosexual voices to be heard. In 1937 Samuel Kahn published *Mentality and Homosexuality,* a book based on his work as a prison psychiatrist in the 1920s for the New York City penitentiary on Blackwell's (Welfare) Island. The author focused on a sample of seventy-five men who were suspected of being homosexual because of their cross-gender characteristics. According to Kahn, even though he used a confrontational style of interviewing aimed at eliciting confessions, the homosexual men generally "seemed to enjoy being studied." Apparently, despite being questioned by an unsympathetic investigator, the men were willing to cooperate. Their willingness, at least in part, reflected their concerns that failure to cooperate would mean the threat of commitment to institutions for the "Mental Defective" or "Insane." After the respondents overcame their initial defensiveness, however, Kahn indicated that they "seemed to take great pleasure in discussing histories and other matters relevant to homosexuals."[26] They thus appeared motivated to educate their inquisitor. Indeed, the respondents offered rich descriptions of meeting places, drag balls, and sexual practices, as well as definitions of homosexual argot.

In a prison study of a different kind, Alexander Berkman, an American anarchist leader imprisoned in the 1890s in the Western Penitentiary of Pennsylvania, recorded his conversations with fellow inmates who spoke willingly about their homosexual experiences to a sympathetic listener. Apparently with the promise that Berkman would publish memoirs about his prison experience, which in fact he did in 1912, they readily talked about their homoerotic feelings. An imprisoned physician, for example, described his love for a young inmate. In the physician's words, "This boy . . . became so dear to me. . . . For two years I loved him without the least taint of sex desire. It was the purest affection I ever felt in my life. . . . But by degrees the psychic stage began to manifest all the expressions of love between the opposite sexes." Berkman acknowledged, empathetically, "I think it a very beautiful emotion. Just as beautiful as love for a woman. I had a friend here. . . . I felt no physical passion toward him, but I think I loved him with all my heart. His death was a most terrible shock to me. It almost drove me insane."[27]

Studies utilizing voluntary subjects drawn from urban homosexual communities served as yet another source for self-expression. During the 1920s and 1930s, there were instances in which American researchers successfully recruited self-identified homosexuals to participate in their investigations. The most significant example of this was psychiatrist George W. Henry's sex variants study involving both lesbians and gay men, which I discuss in the next chapter. In another study, begun in 1929, psychologist Lewis M. Terman of Stanford University enlisted a sample of gay men to participate in his study of gender identity. Reflecting the growing interest during the interwar years in the psychological impact of social and economic change on gender roles, Terman, a pioneer in the development of intelligence tests, turned his attention to developing a questionnaire measure of masculinity-femininity. Together with his associate, Catharine Cox Miles, a masculinity-femininity (M-F) test was constructed. In order to validate the M-F test, Terman wanted to collect test responses from samples of homosexual men and women, which he could compare with normative samples from the general population. While unable to draw lesbian volunteers, he was successful, through his graduate assistant E. Lowell Kelly, in recruiting a sample of fifty-nine gay men from San Francisco. These volunteers completed the M-F test and were also interviewed by Kelly about their life experiences and sexual practices. With the promise that such information would be published in a book, the willingness of the gay research subjects to be interviewed suggests that they viewed their participation as an opportunity to inform the general public about homosexuality. Indeed, after the Terman-Miles book *Sex and Personality* was published in 1936, Terman received several letters from young men concerned about their possible homosexuality. While these respondents received no support from Terman about their homosexual feelings, there were undoubtedly others who could validate their sexual identity by reading the case studies included in the book. And it seems likely that despite their negative portrayal in the book, Terman's gay volunteer subjects would gain some satisfaction from knowing that others like themselves could read about their lives.[28]

Some homosexual subjects sought more than simply speaking out about homosexuality. They used their relationships with sex researchers to promote the cause of homosexual rights. Several of Krafft-Ebing's respondents, perceiving him to be sympathetic to their concerns, contended that their problems stemmed not from their sexual orientation, but from the legal and social obstacles they faced. As one writer stated it, "Such a forcible repression of a deeply implanted drive primarily causes, in my humble opinion, the unhealthy phenomena that we can observe in many Urnings, but it is not necessarily a consequence of the Urning's disposition."[29] Several respondents criticized Krafft-Ebing for labeling homosexuality as an illness. As Harry Oosterhuis notes, by publishing such arguments and pointing out that they typified the sufferings of homosexuals, Krafft-Ebing made a powerful statement for those concerned. In fact, the continued input by Krafft-Ebing's homosexual patients and informants had a profound effect on his thinking. Through successive editions of *Psychopathia sexualis,* he increasingly included more extensive homosexual autobiographies and moved away from his initial equation of homosexuality with pathology. In place of viewing homosexuality as an illness, he considered it to be a biological and psychological condition that had to be accepted as a natural fate. His support of Hirschfeld's movement to decriminalize homosexuality was an outgrowth of his revised views.[30]

In cases where physicians were not sympathetic to the concerns of homosexuals, there were instances in which homosexual patients voiced resistance to the medical model. In America, where most physicians were unsympathetic, such resistance was noted in various case study reports. In 1912 New York physician Douglas C. McMurtrie, for example, cited the case of an effeminate man who "was very busy in arraigning society for its attitude toward those of his type, and was prepared to ethically justify his characteristics and practices." In the 1920s another physician, John F. Meagher, noted: "Some [homosexuals] want to be cured; others do not, but have a morbid, childish and psychopathic pride in their condition."[31] Homosexual rights activists also expressed resistance to the medical model. Edward I. Prime-Stevenson, an American writer who used the pseudonym Xavier Mayne, argued in his privately published 1908 book, *The Intersexes,* that because Uranianism (homosexuality) was "inborn," no "cure" was possible. Thus, if homosexuals sought medical help, it was the responsibility of the physician to offer sympathetic support and reinforce self-respect. Earl Lind, who had written a first-person account of his life in New York in the 1890s (published in 1918), published a response in the *Medical Review of Reviews* to physician Perry M. Lichtenstein's article in that periodical about "fairies." Challenging Lichtenstein's portrayal of fairies as "degenerates" who should be segregated from society in special institutions, Lind advocated that such individuals should not be prevented from expressing and acting on their natural sexual feelings.[32]

Homosexual resistance to medicalization met with some success in one notable instance. William J. Robinson, an American physician who eventually became an admirer of Hirschfeld and an activist in the sex reform movement, observed in 1914 that despite arguments to the contrary by some "sexologists," he was convinced that homosexuality was a sign of degeneracy and an abnormality. Moreover, he believed that homosexuals were generally dissatisfied with their condition. Eleven years later, based on his further contacts with homosexual patients as well as his visit in the early 1920s to Hirschfeld's Berlin Institute for Sexual Science, he modified his position by declaring:

> I have had occasion recently to converse with a number of homosexuals of both sexes. They told me their life histories, described to me their feelings, their aspirations. . . . I have met among them lovable, sympathetic types, some men and women of high intelligence. My attitude towards homosexuality of both sexes has undergone some change, has become broader, more tolerant, perhaps even sympathetic; but I am not yet ready to regard the homosexual with the same eyes that Dr. Hirschfeld or Edward Carpenter does.[33]

Despite his change of mind, Robinson was still not willing to give up the medical assumption of pathology.

In essence, homosexual subjects in their relationship with medical practitioners and sex researchers were motivated by a variety of goals, ranging from a need to seek personal help in struggling with their negative feelings to affirming their self-acceptance and promoting homosexual rights. In Germany and England homosexual activists, such as Hirschfeld and Carpenter, engaged in their own scientific writings wedded to the cause of homosexual equality.[34] In America, which had no homosexual rights movement until the 1950s, there were several isolated instances in which homosexuals undertook their own emancipatory research projects.

EARLY WORK BY AMERICAN GAY AND LESBIAN ACTIVIST-RESEARCHERS

In directing their own work, gay and lesbian researchers focused on presenting first-person accounts of the lived experiences of homosexual people. Around the turn of the twentieth century, Edward Irenaeus Prime-Stevenson and Earl Lind undertook the two most ambitious efforts. Prime-

Stevenson wrote a comprehensive book about homosexuality based, to a considerable extent, on his experiences as a participant-observer in the homosexual world. Lind wrote a series of books based on his life history and experiences as a male prostitute.

Born in 1868, Prime-Stevenson was a writer and music critic. Finding life in Europe more congenial to his homosexual interests, he became an American expatriate around the turn of the century. Little is known about his life, but he appears to have spent some time in Italy and he died in Switzerland in 1942. He authored three homoerotic novels, including two that were targeted for boys. In 1906, using the pseudonym Xavier Mayne, he wrote *Imre: A Memorandum* about the love between two men. In 1908, as Mayne, he privately published *The Intersexes: A History of Similisexualism as a Problem in Social Life,* although according to the author, this work was basically completed in 1901. While it appeared the same year as Carpenter's *The Intermediate Sex* and several years before Hirschfeld's 1914 *The Homosexuality of Men and Women,* it is apparent that Prime-Stevenson incorporated the views expressed by Carpenter and Hirschfeld in their earlier writings. *The Intersexes* was more similar to Carpenter's literary-oriented defense of homosexuality than Hirschfeld's scientific treatment. It was also much more sweeping in its historical coverage of literary sources from ancient to modern times than Carpenter's work or the earlier Symonds's treatises, which focused on classical Greek and nineteenth-century homoerotic texts.[35]

The Intersexes is significant both for its pioneering emancipatory viewpoint and as a historical record of homosexual life at the turn of the century. Prime-Stevenson's objective was to provide a readership of "intelligent laymen," such as social scientists and general physicians, with an informative sourcebook on homosexuality. As he notes in his preface, no summary in English existed for lay readers and what was available was typically restricted to medical specialists. While he did not include bibliographic citations (because of the publication delay), he quoted and paraphrased from a diverse array of sources, including psychiatric works, medical surveys, criminological studies, personal communications by "similisexuals" (homosexuals), biographies, histories, belles lettres, journals, and newspapers. In essence, he provided a voice for not only medical and scientific experts, but also homosexuals, both in the past and present.[36]

Prime-Stevenson's advocacy for social acceptance was best summed up by his statement:

> Happiest of all, surely, are those Uranians [homosexuals], ever numerous, who have no wish nor need to fly society—or themselves. Knowing what they are, understanding the natural, moral strength

of their position as homosexuals; sure of right on their side, even if
it be never accorded to them in the lands where they must live; for-
tunate in either due self-control or private freedom—day by day, they
go through their lives, self-respecting and respected, in relative
peace.[37]

Reflecting the theories of the time, Prime-Stevenson basically viewed homosexuality as an inborn sexual instinct, although he also indicated that it
could be acquired. Regardless of cause, his position was that homosexuals
should not be persecuted for feelings that they could not change, and he
was especially critical of the legal oppression of homosexuals in Britain and
America. Homosexuals were "intersexes" because, in contrast to the masculine and feminine sexes, they combined psychological elements of both
sexes—what we would today refer to as gender characteristics. He stressed
that homosexuals were psychologically rather than physically intermediate
between the masculine and the feminine. While all homosexual men and
women were intermediate in gender disposition, they varied in the extent
to which they leaned toward the masculine or the feminine. Among men,
there were not only the commonly recognized effeminate type, but also
those who were markedly masculine. Prime-Stevenson believed that there
was less variability among homosexual women, hence they all tended to be
"mannish." His sexist bias was revealed by his statement that homosexual
women were not as "finely-endowed . . . ethical . . . [or] interesting" as homosexual men. Consistent with Ulrichs, he did not divide sexuality into a
simple homosexual-heterosexual dichotomy, arguing that there were
people who were bisexual.[38]

He stressed that homosexuals could not be "cured" because they were
neither "pathological" nor afflicted with a "nervous disease." Thus, physicians were misguided in advising marriage as a "remedy" or in encouraging their patients to engage in "normal" sexuality. Instead, anticipating
Hirschfeld's adjustment therapy, he argued that physicians should provide
supportive counseling aimed at inducing the patient's self-respect. Prime-
Stevenson optimistically opined, "Ignorantly unjust sentiments of society
against legitimate satisfaction of similisexual instincts, the want of
equable laws for man, woman, and intersex, will slowly be bettered."[39] It
was thus the responsibility of physicians and psychiatrists to bring about
and bolster the resolve of their homosexual patients to carry their "burden
bravely." As examples of just and sympathetic treatment, he cited various
case studies by physicians, including Krafft-Ebing, to whom he dedicated
his book.[40]

Beyond depicting the characteristics and psychological state of homosexual men and women, Prime-Stevenson offered a rich survey of the in-

tellectual and literary contributions by such notable homophiles as Plato, Erasmus, Shakespeare, Byron, and Whitman. Nor did he restrict himself to the Western tradition, citing "Oriental" sources, such as classical Arabian and Japanese literature. Because of the social hostility homosexuals faced throughout history, he pointed out that literature was the most available outlet for expressing their sensibilities and experiences. Still, there were obstacles the homophile writer faced, such as "the comments of critics, editors, translators . . . to conceal or to ignore altogether, the personal homosexuality of . . . a writer and of his literary intentions." To demonstrate the extensiveness of homosexuality throughout history and across different cultures, Prime-Stevenson provided examples of homosexuals from different walks of life. He especially focused on the military to illustrate that not all homosexual men were effeminate.[41]

Of historical interest, he provided a relatively detailed look at the variegated homosexual subculture at the turn of the century in both Europe and America. In America he referred to several cities as "homosexual capitals." Among his entries were New York, Boston, Washington, Chicago, St. Louis, San Francisco, and New Orleans. In such cities there were various sites catering to homosexual men. These included "smart clubs," restaurants, and steam baths. He noted that in such "resorts," there was no police interference. In baths, for example, "each client has always a separate dressing room, usually with a couch. What 'goes on' is under the guest's own lock and key, and without surveillance."[42] According to Prime-Stevenson, male prostitution in various forms was common. There were "thousands" of boys and youths in large cities, either in the pay of male procurers or "working" for themselves. Men in "female costumes" solicited in parks, sidewalks, bars, and balls. In New York, as in many European and Egyptian cities, there were "houses" or brothels for male rendezvous. In India, China, and Japan "boy-houses" were popular. While prostitution by soldiers and sailors was more common in European cities because of the low military pay, there were instances in America, such as the young soldiers in San Francisco's Presidio who could be easily "had" for nominal prices.[43]

In contrast with Prime-Stevenson's historical and cultural survey, Lind wrote about homosexuality through the vantage point of his life history. He was born in 1874 and grew up in a small Connecticut town, about fifty miles from New York City. In 1899 he had finished writing his life story, *Autobiography of an Androgyne,* and finally succeeded in finding a medical publisher in 1918. His work was targeted for physicians as a means of enlightening them about the nature of homosexuality and the problems that homosexuals faced. He used his life story to illustrate the sufferings endured by gay men and, interwoven within his autobiographical framework, he mounted a defense of homosexuality. Lind believed in celebrating the uniqueness of homosexuality and the enriching contribution that homosexuals could make to a tolerant and diverse society. He promoted the need for homosexuals to challenge social convention by freely giving into their nonconformist modes of natural expression. For men, that meant to act out their effeminacy. Lind also went under the name of Ralph Werther and used "Jennie June" when he performed his "fairie" role as a street hustler. Both "Lind" and "Werther" were pseudonyms the author used when he sent his manuscript to various medical publishers. Reflecting his feminine and artistic temperament, he chose "Earl" to rhyme with "girl" and "Lind" for the nineteenth-century singer Jennie Lind. "Ralph" was for the painter Raphael and "Werther" for Goethe's hero. In his writings, he never revealed his real name.[44]

In recounting his childhood, Lind stated that for as long as he could remember, he was teased by his peers and criticized by his parents because of his effeminacy. His social ostracism resulted in a tormented and lonely childhood, although he was able to compensate for his suffering by excelling academically and finding solace in religion. By eleven he came to the realization that he was *"a girl imprisoned in the body of a boy."*[45] At sixteen he enrolled at a university in New York City. He continued to endure being teased but found that he was in love with his athletic classmates. Wracked by guilt and shame, he sought medical advice, hoping for a cure for his abnormal sexual urges and wishing that he could be made into a "complete male." By nineteen, after various medical treatments (drugs, electrical stimulation of the brain, hypnotism), he experienced an epiphany. With the support of an unnamed alienist (psychiatrist), he was determined to give in to his "peculiar instincts." He had "arrived at the conviction that while the voice of the world would cry 'Shame!' I was acting according to the dictates of reason and conscience."[46] It was at this point that he began to shape his alter ego, Jennie June.

In 1899, after about five years of leading a double life as a weekday graduate student/legal secretary-clerk and a Saturday night hustler, Lind decided to try and publish *Autobiography of an Androgyne,* which focused on his career as Jennie June. He had begun to keep a diary at fourteen and first thought of writing an autobiography in 1892 when he was told by one of his physicians that he was a "remarkable" case. He initially submitted his manuscript to Anthony Comstock, the anti-vice crusader who espoused sexual censorship, to determine if his work could be disseminated. Comstock, in response, railed that inverts were not "fit to live with the rest of mankind," and that they "ought to have branded in their foreheads the word 'Unclean.' "[47] Nevertheless, since he believed that Lind had no "evil intent," he returned the manuscript rather than destroy it.

While most people would have been discouraged by such feedback, Lind kept persevering in his attempts to get his work published by a medical publisher. Finally, after continual updating, he was able to convince Alfred W. Herzog, a physician and lawyer, to publish his autobiography. Herzog was the editor of the *Medico-Legal Journal,* and one thousand copies of Lind's autobiography were printed for sale by mail order to physicians, lawyers, legislators, and social scientists. Herzog was sympathetic to the cause of decriminalizing homosexuality for those in whom such practices were congenital rather than an acquired "vice." He shared Lind's view that the congenital "homosexuals" had the body of a male and the soul of a female. Herzog attempted to edit the manuscript, apparently prompted by its sexually explicit detail. He admitted that he had not enjoyed reading the contents, which at times "nauseated" him. In the end, however, he agreed to publish the manuscript, unedited, citing its value in lighting "a torch to show in . . . [the author's] own way the baser sex feelings of a sexual invert."[48] While the book did not quite meet the hoped-for sales, Herzog agreed four years later to publish an expanded version that was targeted to a more general readership. Lind felt strongly that his campaign for the humanitarian treatment of homosexuals had to reach a larger audience. Thus, in 1922 *The Female-Impersonators* appeared, which dealt not only with his own life, but also provided ethnographic renderings of New York's gay male subculture, as well as the lives of other effeminate hustlers and newspaper accounts of the sufferings of homosexuals, including suicides and murders.[49]

What stands out in Lind's writings is his emancipatory spirit. Reflecting his self-perception, he equated homosexuality with congenitally based physical and emotional characteristics of the opposite sex. "Androgynes" were thus men with male genitals, but with the souls of women. Although he mentioned women only in passing, "gynanders" were women sexually, but with the souls of men. Influenced by Ulrichs and Hirschfeld, he viewed homosexuals as intersexes (he used the term "bisexuals"), possessing attributes of both sexes as opposed to the "full-fledged" sexes of man and woman. Androgynes varied between those with "mild" cross-sex characteristics and those, like himself, who were "ultra-androgynes" because of their marked effeminacy. In contrast with Ulrichs, Hirschfeld, Ellis, and Prime-Stevenson, Lind did not believe that homosexual men included masculine as well as feminine types. Essentially, he celebrated the way in which homosexual men differed from other men. Anticipating the use of effeminacy as a confrontational strategy by the British activist-writer Quentin Crisp in the 1930s, Lind argued for homosexual emancipation based on the distinctiveness of homosexuality. He noted that it was not only morally wrong to persecute homosexuals for their nonconformist though natural

urges, but that society should embrace homosexuals for the unique contributions they could make. Pointing to historical examples, he observed,
"The emergence of androgynism is a sign of national health. The ultra-
brilliant Age of Pericles surpassed all other periods in the recognition and
influence of androgynism. . . . The androgyne, being a combination of
man and woman in a single individual, has a wider view of life than the
full-fledged man or woman. . . . Such duality is the reason artistic genius
crops up far more frequently among androgynes." Elsewhere, he proclaimed, "Surely, we androgynes who for two thousand years have been
despised, hunted down, and crushed under the heel of normal men . . .
have no reason to be ashamed of our heritage."[50]

In telling the story of Jennie June, Lind gave a richly detailed depiction
of the fairy subculture as well as his own sexual adventures. As Byrne Fone
points out, Lind was a master of the erotic confessional with its high op-
eratic pornography. He began his career as Jennie June at nineteen. On Saturday nights he went to Mulberry Street, an Italian working-class district
on New York's Lower East Side. Using feminine makeup and hints of
cross-dressing, such as white kid gloves and a flashy red neck-bow, he
sought out the young tough men who hung out on street corners near
neighborhood bars. He had little trouble in attracting sex partners who,
sometimes paying him, eagerly assumed the male role of being fellated or
performing anal penetration. These acts typically took place in dark al-
leyways. There were times when sex was followed by physical attacks.[51]

After a year's "apprenticeship" on Mulberry Street, Lind advanced to
the middle- and upper-class entertainment district on Fourteenth Street
near Union Square, known as the Rialto. As before, he had no trouble finding sex partners, although his clientele now included middle- and upper-
class young men as well as neighborhood working-class toughs. If he
picked up men on the street, he would take them to a room in a nearby hotel that he referred to as the "Hotel Comfort." He also frequented "Paresis" (Columbia) Hall on Fourth Avenue, not far from the Rialto. This was
an infamous bar and beer garden that catered to fairies and earned the so-
briquet "Paresis" because of the association of homosexuality with insan-
ity. Above the bar there were rooms for sexual liaisons between fairies and
their customers. Paresis Hall also provided a social space for homosexuals, and Lind became a member of a small social club of female impersonators, known as the Cercle Hermaphroditos. According to Lind, the
club was organized as a "defense against the world's bitter persecution of
bisexuals."[52] Although it appears to have functioned essentially as a social
club, it nevertheless represents the first effort among homosexuals in
America to organize for political objectives. Connected with his experiences at Paresis Hall, Lind offered several vignettes of other fairies, some

of whom spoke in their own voice, such as Frank-Eunice, who recounted his five years in prison resulting from being entrapped by a young detective.

Lind proudly claimed that he was the most famous female impersonator on the Rialto in the 1890s. His career as a fairy-hustler ended in 1899 when he left New York City to return to his parents' home. He had been recognized and denounced by a deliveryman who frequently delivered goods to his employer. Rather than jeopardize his reputation, he resigned from his position as a private legal secretary. He later learned that it was unlikely that his employer was ever informed by the deliveryman. Over the next six years, as a "French doll-baby," he acted out his fairy role weekly at a nearby military base. Once again he attracted many sexual partners and reported several romantic affairs, but unlike with his previous sexual experiences, he also suffered several bouts of venereal disease. Although there were times when he was robbed and blackmailed, the local police never arrested him. By 1905, at thirty-one, he felt that he was too old to continue his fairy career. By the time he published *The Female-Impersonators,* nearing fifty, he believed that his sex life in general was over. There were earlier signs reflecting increasing concerns about his sexual capacity. At twenty-eight he chose to be castrated as a cure for spermatorrhea, a condition involving frequent involuntary discharge of semen without an orgasm. His desire to be castrated may have actually satisfied a transsexual urge to become physically transformed into a woman, although he did not make this connection. He viewed himself as a woman psychically because he was sexually attracted to other men. And those men had to be physically opposite, that is, highly virile, masculine types. While he reported that there were some fairies who became romantically attached, he could not see this as a possibility for himself. He sought romantic involvement with virile men whom he referred to as "husbands"; that is, men who did not think of themselves as homosexual and assumed the masculine role in their relationship with a fairy. He had had some brief affairs with husbands and hoped that he could find a lasting relationship.

Lind is an especially significant figure in gay American history. Through his writings, he has left an indelible portrait of effeminacy as a cultural strategy and therefore illustrated how the role of the fairy served as a source of personal and collective identity. His bold liberatory message promoting tolerance for sexual difference anticipated the goals of the homophile movement in America that emerged in the 1950s and 1960s. As Fone suggests, his contributions need to be reclaimed as one of the early voices of gay liberation in America.[53]

In addition to Lind's work, there were other published autobiographical revelations of homosexual lives. Although more limited in scope, Claude

Hartland, in 1901, privately published his autobiography *The Story of a Life*. Hartland, a thirty-year-old teacher, dedicated his autobiography to physicians "who have at heart the welfare of their fellow man . . . with the one hope that it may furnish the key to a vast realm of human suffering, of which I find that they, as a body, are for the most part ignorant."[54] Thus, like Lind, Hartland was motivated to write about his experiences so physicians could become more knowledgeable about homosexuality. He spoke from experience since he described numerous visits to various physicians who were unable to help him. He was not able to adhere to their recommendations of abstinence and was particularly unhappy with a "nerve specialist" who prescribed sexual intercourse with a woman. In flowery but straightforward Victorian prose, he recounts his history of homosexual passion from childhood on a farm in the South to his experiences on the city streets of St. Louis. Written as a defense of homosexuality, his autobiography's message was that until (or unless) medical experts could discover a way of treating and eventually preventing homosexuality, homosexuals should not be punished or ostracized for acting on their natural sexual urges. Because of his own struggles and isolation, his defense falls short of the position espoused by homophile writers, such as Hirschfeld, Carpenter, Prime-Stevenson, and Lind, that homosexuality was not a pathological condition subject to cure.

In the 1930s several lesbian autobiographies were published. Hall's *The Well of Loneliness* appears to have provided the impetus for this genre because, as Julie Abraham notes, Hall's work was treated as if it were the author's own story. The pseudonymous Mary Casal's *The Stone Wall*, published in 1930, presented an exceptionally candid sexual and affectional life history. Published when she was sixty-six, the author recounts growing up in rural New England as a girl who preferred masculine activities. Beginning in grammar school, she had a series of emotional attachments to other females. After finishing college, she was briefly married and went on to become a successful businesswoman and commercial artist. As a young woman, she became coupled and wrote glowingly about her relationship with her lover, Juno. Reflecting the turn-of-the-century sensibility of lesbian couples, Casal idealizes the spiritual and romantic side of same-sex relationships, arguing that sex was selfish, while love was altruistic.[55]

In contrast with Casal, two other pseudonymous lesbian authors in the late 1930s, Elisabeth Craigin and Diana Frederics, focused on the sexual pleasure of lesbian alliances. Craigin and Frederics were younger than Casal, and their stories are set within the context of lesbian life in the 1920s and 1930s. Although purporting to be true confessions, these authors are rather vague about the details of their lives. Yet by appealing to the autobiographical authority of telling one's life story, these writers buttressed their position of revealing the true lives and experiences of lesbians. This objective was given further weight in Frederics's *Diana,* which contains an introduction by physician Victor Robinson, the son of Hirschfeld supporter William Robinson. Victor Robinson suggests the contribution that Frederics's work could make in correcting the "inaccurate and confused . . . knowledge on the etiology and prognosis of homosexuality."[56]

Unlike Lind's autobiographical writings, which took a radical, confrontational stance and appealed to a collective identity, the lesbian autobiographers limited their political viewpoint to an affirmation of lesbian relationships. In Craigin's *Either Is Love,* the author declares, "A so-called Lesbian alliance can be of the most rarefied purity, and those who do not believe it are merely judging in ignorance of the facts."[57] Yet Craigin and Frederics placed limits on who constituted real lesbians. They believed that mannish lesbians were not true women who could love other women. In describing her lesbian relationship, Craigin asserts, "My lover was a girl . . . with all the primary feminine capacities. . . . [O]ur pleasure in each other . . . was [a] sensuality between loving young women, and not of a loving young woman for the other gender in disguise."[58] Frederics was also hostile to masculine women because their calculated visibility threatened the closeted lives of lesbians. Expressing her displeasure, she declares, "I disliked them for using their abnormality as their claim to uniqueness as individuals. I disliked them for their defiance in making themselves conspicuous. . . . Male attire on a woman always struck me as a puerile gesture intended to appease one's self while thumbing one's nose at society, and ended only in smart-aleck unconventionality."[59] While shrinking away from the conspicuous challenge to gender roles that the mannish lesbian potentially represented, Craigin and Frederics may have been motivated, in their denouncements, to counter the medical appropriation of the stereotyped image. In essence, the lesbian autobiographers, like Lind and Hartland, were interested in contesting the taboos and misinformation about homosexual lives.

In a project quite different from the works by Prime-Stevenson and the gay and lesbian autobiographers, lesbian researcher Mildred Berryman set out to do an empirically based study on the lives of lesbians and gay men in a relatively small and provincial urban setting—Salt Lake City in the 1920s and 1930s. Berryman was the first investigator to study an American community of self-identified homosexual women and men. She began her study in 1918 when she was about seventeen and a student at Salt Lake City's Westminster College. The project was to have been an honor's thesis, and although her adviser discouraged her from pursuing it, she committed herself to the research for twenty years. She conducted interviews in a case study format with a sample of twenty-four women (including herself) and nine men, all of whom identified themselves as homosexual. The women and men were mostly in their twenties and thirties. All were white and most had a middle-class Mormon background. Among the women, three were married at the start of the study. The others worked, for the most part, in such traditional fields as teaching, nursing, and secretarial work. Berryman was a photographer.[60]

As in the case of the volunteer participants in Terman's San Francisco sample, the Salt Lake City volunteers had a community identity. Berryman recruited them from a pool of about one hundred homosexuals she was acquainted with, many of whom were members of the Salt Lake Bohemian Club, a homosexually oriented social organization. In her study she focused on the self-perceptions of her respondents, especially the women. Many of the women expressed pride in their sexual identity, as exemplified by a thirty-seven-year-old woman who stated that she "would not be happy in any other kind of relationship than homosexual, [and] wouldn't change if she could, unless it were possible to become wholly masculine physically." A twenty-year-old woman declared, "I know what I am and I'm not going on mak[ing] my life miserable trying to be what other people think I should be." Some women had a more negative view of themselves, as in the case of a thirty-five-year-old's comment, "In fact they [homosexuals] are all a little nuts, myself included."[61] Three of the women and one man reported suicide attempts. Berryman indicated that there was both fidelity and "philandering" among the women and men, but she emphasized the fidelity by pointing to the longevity of several lesbian and gay male relationships.

Influenced by Ellis's and Hirschfeld's defense of homosexuality as a congenital sexual inversion, Berryman categorized her female and male respondents according to their masculinity and femininity, both in terms of physical and psychological characteristics. Among the women, most fitted into one or the other type, but there were a few she judged to be fluctuating from time to time. She viewed herself as masculine and noted that masculine and feminine women were, in most instances, attracted to each other. Consistent with her use of the inversion model, Berryman portrayed masculine women as sexually dominant. For example, she described one of the female cases as "hyper sexed and dominating, [and] loves feminine types of girls." In complementary fashion, she characterized another woman as having a "deep-rooted feminine psychology—passive . . . attracted to dominating mas[culine]-type women."[62] In contrast to the cross section of gender types among the women, Berryman classified all but one of the nine men as effeminate. Because she idealized masculine attributes, she tended to denigrate the effeminate men. Describing one effeminate

man as being "emotionally unstable and vacillating in his affections," she
went on to generalize by indicating that she regarded such traits as "characteristics of many cases of male homosexuals." Her masculine bias was
also reflected in her female case studies, where she used masculine qualities, such as "practical and hard-headed with no emotional instability" to
underscore her positive assessment of particular women.[63]

The greatest concern expressed by the Salt Lake City respondents was
the fear that their sexuality would be discovered. This was especially manifested with the appearance in 1928 of Hall's *The Well of Loneliness,*
which created a climate of homophobia. According to Berryman, this produced an "effort . . . to classify [as homosexuals] every woman who wore
a suit and was seen in the company of a girl companion more than once,
and every man who had curly hair and might have a little more than a feminine walk or a flair for bright colored ties."[64] Yet no one was, in fact, discovered by the larger community. What is remarkable about Berryman's
study is that it demonstrated how homosexual women and men were able
to lead their lives undetected in the community in which they lived and un-
touched by the prying eye of physicians. This was a phenomenon that was
replicated in various American cities in the early twentieth century, such as
New York, San Francisco, and Chicago. It attests to Prime-Stevenson's
1908 observation that there were numerous homosexuals who "go through
their lives, self-respecting and respected, in relative peace."[65]

The voices of Berryman's respondents were not made public until after
her death in 1972. She was concerned about protecting their anonymity as
well as her own. Even in her manuscript, she disguised the locale of the
study as Seattle rather than Salt Lake City, and, as if to further protect the
respondents, there is a curious absence of information about religious
views or activities. Such material in Mormon Utah would have revealed
the actual location. Nevertheless, Berryman held on to her manuscript,
which was completed in November 1938, with the aim of having it published after her death so that there would be a public record of the lives and
experiences of homosexual women and men in a small community in the
1920s and 1930s. She willed her paper to Bonnie Bullough, the daughter
of Ruth Uckerman, who was Berryman's partner of thirty years. Bullough
and her husband Vern L. Bullough, both historians of sexuality, provided
a published summary of the study in 1977.[66]

Unlike the homosexual rights movements in Germany and England—
which were associated with notable, though controversial, writings by activists, such as Hirschfeld and Carpenter—emancipatory research efforts
by gay men and lesbians in America were sporadic and isolated. The two
most significant contributors, Prime-Stevenson and Lind, published pseu-
donymously and in very limited outlets. Their works were primarily tar-

geted for an audience of medical, scientific, and legal experts who would hopefully be enlightened by firsthand accounts about homosexual lives and cultural patterns. Published in such limited quantity, there is no indication that they had any meaningful impact on their intended audience or were accessible to gay and lesbian readers. The lesbian autobiographies undoubtedly reached a larger audience and profited from the impact of Hall's *The Well of Loneliness.* But the growing number of pulp novels characterizing lesbians and gay men as depraved, tragic figures compromised even their impact in the 1930s and 1930s.[67] Berryman's pathbreaking study of lesbian and gay lives remained unknown until after her death in the 1970s, a sign of the fear of personal disclosure.

On the other hand, like their European counterparts, these American emancipatory projects struck a common chord. They were imbued with the spirit that scientific knowledge as well as personal testimony could liberate gay men and lesbians from the myths and prejudices of public opinion that translated into legal and social oppression. These activist-researchers and writers also shared the liberatory objectives of some, perhaps many, of the homosexual participants drawn into the web of scientific research on homosexuality. Their emancipatory projects anticipated more coordinated grassroots efforts. What follows in the subsequent chapters is the story of how gay men and lesbians attempted to advance the cause of homosexual rights through scientific channels. A more concerted and ambitious emancipatory research effort by lesbians and gay men began in 1935 that required collaboration with medical and scientific experts. It is this project that I turn to in the next chapter.

Chapter 3

Jan Gay and the Sex Variants Committee, 1935–41

> Dr. Robert L. Dickinson . . . head of the National Committee on Maternal Health, secured for me from the funds of the Committee $1000 which we used to set the pattern for a medical and psychiatric study of homosexual men and women. He and I chose the names of a potential Committee on Sex Variants and sent out invitations to membership.
>
> —Jan Gay[1]

In 1937, in a preliminary published report of a study about homosexuality, psychiatrist George W. Henry presented a case study of "Mary Jones," a forty-nine-year-old black actress. The case, titled "Disillusioned in Marriage: Finds a Substitute in Homosexual Liaison," contained the following excerpt:

> Finally at the age of 41, while dancing with a woman, "something very terrific happened to me—a very electric thing. It made me know I was homosexual." . . . [F]or the past five years she has been living with a white woman. This woman is "one of the finest women I have ever known. She has come to be very, very dear to me—not just for sex alone—it's a very great love. . . . This last relationship affords a tenderness I have never known."[2]

In this case study, there is a juxtaposition of third-person psychiatric interpretation, as exemplified by the title, with first-person experiential narrative. This contrast in presentation was given fuller expression in Henry's 1941 two-volume monograph, *Sex Variants: A Study of Homosexual Patterns,* which was based on a volunteer sample of eighty "socially well adjusted homosexuals" living in New York City.

Henry's study was sponsored by the Committee for the Study of Sex Variants, a privately funded and incorporated body, established in 1935 by Robert Latou Dickinson. Dickinson was a prominent gynecologist who was also one of the leaders of the American birth control movement and a pioneer in sex research. The committee was composed of medical specialists and social and biological scientists who had expertise in human sexuality and deviant behavior.[3]

What is especially noteworthy about the committee's origins was the involvement of a lesbian activist-researcher. Dickinson had been in contact with a "Miss Jan Gay" who had collected three hundred case histories of lesbians over a ten-year period. Evidently Jan Gay did not hide her sexual identity from Dickinson since he and his professional associates knew that she was a lesbian. Louise Stevens Bryant, a Ph.D. biostatistician who worked closely with Dickinson on the National Committee on Maternal Health, referred to Gay, in private correspondence, as an "avowed intermediate."[4]

Gay's real name was Helen Reitman and she was born in Leipzig, Germany, of American parents in 1902. Her father was gynecologist Ben L. Reitman and her mother, May Schwartz, was a concert pianist. Apparently she never had any contact with her father since he abandoned his new family around the time of her birth. Reitman was a colorful and radical figure, best known as the lover and manager of anarchist leader Emma Goldman from 1908 to 1918. His background was highly unconventional. His father deserted him when he was a young boy and he became a hobo at age eleven. At nineteen, working in a Chicago medical clinic, he attracted attention from pathologist Leo Loeb, who paid his tuition for medical school. During his involvement with the anarchist movement, he campaigned for birth control and was arrested and imprisoned twice for distributing birth control pamphlets. In his career as a physician, he became known as the "Chicago Mafia doctor" because of his work as a "line doctor" examining women for venereal disease in houses of prostitution run by the Chicago crime syndicate. In his personal life, he had a reputation as a womanizer. In 1917 he fathered a son in a common-law marriage, and beginning in the 1930s, he had four daughters in his second legal marriage. He died in 1942 at the age of sixty-three.[5]

Growing up in the shadow of a publicly known father with a rather infamous reputation who had abandoned her must have been difficult for Gay, especially since she appears to have spent her formative years in Chicago. Yet her legacy of paternal desertion seems to have set the tone for her life as a self-made woman who embarked on a multifaceted career as a writer, language translator, public relations consultant, and nudist and lesbian activist. She graduated from Northwestern University and began her career as a reporter in 1922 for the *Chicago Examiner*. In 1927 she legally changed her name from Helen Reitman to Jan Gay—a move that reflected her lesbian pride since "gay" had become a popular code word among lesbians and homosexual men in the 1920s. But shedding her family name was also, most likely, an act of rebellion against the father she never knew. She appears to have kept her family name a secret; Thomas Painter, a gay man who knew her in the 1930s, thought her real name was Goldberg. Beginning in the late 1920s, she traveled extensively in Mexico, South America, and Europe in connection with her work as a secretary and translator for the National Railways of Mexico. Her 1932 book, *On Going Naked*, about nudism in Europe was banned in several states. Based on this book, she wrote the script for a 1935 film, *This Naked World*. As in the case of her commitment to advancing homosexual rights, her message in the film is that prejudice and fear about nudism could be overcome by familiarizing the general public about such a tabooed topic.[6]

During her travels in the 1920s, she visited Magnus Hirschfeld's Institute for Sexual Science in Berlin, where she learned how to conduct a survey on sexuality, based on Hirschfeld's exhaustive *Psychobiological Questionnaire*. This enabled her to launch her research on homosexuality, which involved interviewing three hundred lesbians in Berlin, Paris, London, and New York. The interviews were structured around Hirschfeld's questionnaire and covered topics including family background, childhood experiences, adult experiences, sexual development, health, interests, and views about society's attitude toward homosexuality. To supplement her interview data, she read the scientific and popular literature on homosexuality that was available in various libraries, including the Berlin Institute for Sexual Science, the Bodleian Library in Oxford, and the New York Academy of Medicine. A manuscript based on her interviews and library research was accepted by a British publisher, contingent on her ability to obtain medical data that would "validate" her research. With this goal in mind, she approached Dickinson.[7]

As an advocate for homosexual rights, Gay faced a dilemma that was to haunt activists until the 1960s, when a national gay and lesbian movement was strong enough to directly challenge the medicalization of homosexuality. In order to publish scholarly works that would serve the cause of homosexual rights, community activist-researchers like Gay were forced to obtain sponsorship and authorial cooperation from physicians and scientists who provided the legitimacy for such undertakings. Such alliances did benefit from common interests, most notably the goal of decriminalizing homosexuality. Moreover, as in the case of Havelock Ellis and Richard von Krafft-Ebing, homophile activists believed that forging dialogues with sympathetic medical experts would bring about a better understanding of homosexuality and the suffering homosexuals faced. Yet the interests of medical and scientific sexologists were often incompatible with the objectives of the homophile movement. Thus, while both groups campaigned for decriminalization, their ultimate goals diverged. Unlike the activists who viewed decriminalization as a source for empowering the homosexual community, medical and scientific specialists saw decriminalization as a means of wresting authority from the judicial system and consequently advancing their expertise and legitimacy as agents of social control.

Indicative of the regulatory objectives of the sexologists, Henry's first- and third-person split narrative style would, in the end, undermine Gay's hopes for forging a dialogue between the homosexual subjects and the medical/scientific researchers. Rather than opening communication and understanding, this discursive practice, with its medicalized overtone, served to further the subjugation of homosexual men and women to the scrutiny of the medical gaze. Nevertheless, the active involvement of homosexual research participants anticipated subsequent attempts at changing the power imbalance between subjects and researchers in investigations of homosexuality.

The sex variants study reflected a strong commitment on the part of both homosexuals and scientific investigators to carry out an investigation of homosexuality. My focus in this chapter is to examine the objectives sought by each group and to explore the nature of the relationship between them. I begin with an overview of the background and results of the sex variants study and then consider the broader context of this investigation by discussing how it is situated within the emergence of a grassroots community concern for homosexual rights and the medicalization of homosexuality.

THE COMMITTEE FOR THE STUDY OF SEX VARIANTS

Gay's selection of Dickinson as a potential collaborator seems to be connected with his apparent feminist and lesbian sympathies. Dickinson, who was seventy-three when Gay contacted him in 1934, was the leading medical advocate for birth control. In 1923 he had created the National Committee on Maternal Health, which was concerned with research on various issues of fertility. Within the medical community, he was a highly visible supporter of an issue that was of major concern to feminists. Moreover, Dickinson was in the vanguard of sex reformers who challenged the Victorian standard of sex for the sole purpose of procreation. He believed that marriage should be the ultimate form of human relationship and stressed the importance of sexual pleasure in marriage. He also believed that poor sexual adjustment was a threat to the stable family and thus viewed birth control as a means of strengthening the family. Reflecting his interests in changing sexual attitudes and identifying the mechanisms of marital adjustment, he had collected some five thousand case histories over the course of his obstetrical and gynecological practice, dating back to 1890. This rich source of data served as the basis for two monographs, coauthored with Lura Beam—*A Thousand Marriages* in 1931 and *The Single Woman* in 1934. Beam had a background in psychology and education, and she transposed Dickinson's case material into a finished product of analysis and interpretation. Although officially the junior author, she actually wrote the two books.[8]

The Single Woman includes an analysis of homosexuality, based on the homoerotic experiences of twenty-eight women as well as four men who were husbands or suitors of the women patients. This presentation tends to be sympathetic to the notion that homosexual expression is not necessarily a form of sexual maladjustment. Beam pointed out that it was premature to establish a homosexual "type" because the medical literature was primarily limited to men and to "psychopathic cases—sometimes observed in legal suits, in institutions or after serious collapse." In addition, contrary to the expectation of gender inversion, Beam noted that in the female cases, "homosexual interests were explained only in terms of femaleness, with no male types or behavior."[9] Consistent with Katharine Bement Davis's presentation of lesbian cases, the women's same-sex relations are candidly and nonjudgmentally described. Beam, however, did cite an example of the physician's (i.e., Dickinson's) advice giving, which was premised on the assumption that the ideal form of sexual expression could only be achieved through marriage. Furthermore, it is noted that most of the women experienced heterosexual relations after their homosexual encounters. The impression thus given is that lesbianism is a phase that some women go through in their sexual history.[10]

The tolerant perspective on homosexuality, expressed in *The Single Woman,* seems to have been clearly related to Beam's personal experience. She was involved in a long-standing, devoted relationship with Louise Stevens Bryant, who was the executive secretary of the National Committee on Maternal Health. The two women had lived together since 1923 and remained a lifelong couple. While it is not clear that their relationship was sexual, their bond was marked by deep feelings of affection and commitment, and reflected the kind of romantic friendship that characterized coupled women professionals in the early twentieth century.[11]

Thus, *The Single Woman,* with its relatively positive presentation of homosexual cases, might have caught the attention of Jan Gay and signaled to her Dickinson's seeming openness to homosexuality. In his own thinking, however, Dickinson viewed homosexuality as a form of arrested sexual development, biologically induced in some cases and in others the result of environmental influences. He placed particular significance on the effects that modern society had in blocking the normal course of heterosexual development, such as the gap between biological maturity and the economic feasibility of marriage. In contrast to the point that Beam made in *The Single Woman* that female homosexual expression is not associated with masculine characteristics, Dickinson connected homosexuality with gender inversion.[12]

Dickinson was excited about the opportunity Gay's work presented for conducting a large-scale medical investigation of homosexuality. He believed that it was important to study homosexuality because it could lead to a better understanding of heterosexual relations. Thus, when he read her manuscript notes, he was enthusiastic about supporting her work and extending it to include the medical data she needed. To help launch Gay's research, Dickinson had access to a research fund of $1,000 from an anonymous donor, described as a "private citizen, a man of outstanding breadth of vision and filled with enthusiasm for scientific research."[13] The anonymous donor was Sidney Gamble, an heir to the Proctor and Gamble fortune and the missionary brother of medical researcher Clarence Gamble, who was Dickinson's protégé and a major financial backer of the maternal health committee. The Gamble brothers were imbued with the cause of world population control through the use of contraception. Like his brother, Sidney Gamble also provided financial support for the maternal health committee. Apparently, at the end of 1934, he had some money left over from his commitment to pay for office expenses. Dickinson provided him with a list of the committee's planned research projects and Gamble chose to support the project on homosexuality. Gamble's wish to be anonymous most likely reflected the stigma attached to any public association with such a taboo subject.[14]

Gay's proposed study was further expanded to include homosexual men. This came about through her contact with Thomas Painter, a twenty-nine-year-old gay man who had graduated from Union Theological Seminary in the summer of 1934. He had begun a research project on male prostitution and, like Gay, was looking for medical sponsorship. Gay introduced Painter to Dickinson, who was impressed with Painter's work as well as his contacts with male homosexuals and male prostitutes. With the potential of Painter as a resource for obtaining male subjects, Dickinson encouraged Gay to expand her research to include males. By the fall of 1934, Gay and Painter began to recruit a sample of lesbians and male homosexuals, and Gay conducted preliminary interviews on personal and family background.[15]

With the funding and preliminary research in hand, Dickinson in December 1934 set out to gain the maternal health committee's sponsorship. He proposed that Gay and Painter, identified as "known inverts," be hired as committee staff members. Dickinson was the founder and honorary secretary of the committee and because of his status and reputation, most likely assumed that his personal support would ensure the committee's approval. As events turned out, however, a majority of the committee members, led by Bryant (the committee's executive secretary), voted not to support the project. She believed that the proposed research on homosexuality was divergent from the committee's mandate and approved budget and would thus jeopardize future fund-raising. After failing to interest the National Research Council's Committee for Research in Problems of Sex, Dickinson went about creating his own committee—the Committee for the Study of Sex Variants. Dickinson, apparently, chose the label "sex variants" because Hirschfeld had used a similar term, "sexual variants," to reflect the congenitally intermediate nature of homosexuality.[16]

Toward the end of January 1935, in consultation with Gay, Dickinson began recruiting members. Attached to each invitation was a proposal for creating the committee that included a brief description of Gay's study as well as Painter's study of male prostitution. Within two months a nineteen-member committee of medical and scientific specialists was constituted. The membership included seven psychiatrists, one endocrinologist, one gynecologist, one pediatrician, two anatomists, one physical anthropologist, two sociologists, and four psychologists.[17]

Three of the psychiatrists—Adolf Meyer, George W. Henry, and Eugen Kahn—played key roles on the committee. Meyer, the director of the Phipps clinic at Johns Hopkins, was the dean of American psychiatry. Through his collaboration with Clifford W. Beers, he was instrumental in organizing the National Committee for Mental Hygiene in 1909 and was influential in the mental hygiene movement's promotion of adjusting individuals to their social environment as the key to mental health. In the early 1920s, he conducted a "sex life" survey, based on a questionnaire he developed, which was never published. Meyer's major contributions to the committee were to act as a consultant for its organization and as a liaison with various funding agencies. Henry, a former student of Meyer, was associated with New York Hospital, where he engaged in a series of psychiatric research studies, including a study of homosexuality. On the basis of this research, Henry was asked by the committee to direct Gay's case history study. Kahn, a professor of psychiatry at Yale, was a leading exponent of the German constitutional school of psychiatry. While stressing the constitutional basis of homosexuality, he acknowledged the role of environmental influences and believed that through psychotherapy homosexuals

could successfully control their impulses. Reflecting his expertise on homosexuality, Kahn was elected committee chairman. Two of the social scientists—psychologists Lewis M. Terman and Catharine Cox Miles—were
also influential in the committee's activities. As noted in chapter 2, they
had collaborated on the development of a scale that measured masculinity-
femininity, which demonstrated that male homosexuals scored in the direction of femininity.[18]

The diverse membership of the committee reflected its mandate to act
as a coordinating body for the various scientific interests in the field of
sexual variation and to serve as a scientific sponsoring agency for the promotion of research on sexual variation. In addition to the two initial projects, several other studies were planned, including a hormonal study of the
blood and urine of homosexuals, an investigation of homosexuality
among delinquent boys, and a study of homosexuality among men in the
merchant marine and coast guard. To carry out the committee's ambitious
research objectives, committee members engaged in exhaustive efforts to
obtain funding. Reflecting its controversial focus on homosexuality, the
committee was unsuccessful in gaining support from any of the existing
foundations and none of its planned projects were begun. The committee's
only source of funding was the anonymous funds provided by Sidney
Gamble, which over the course of four years amounted to a total of
$7,500. This was used to support Gay's case history project, which came
to be known as the sex variants study.[19]

The prostitution study was carried out by Painter, who completed a
manuscript in 1941 that was never published. Henry also studied a small
sample of male prostitutes, which was part of a series of studies on sex offenders. He worked on these studies with Alfred A. Gross, a gay man who
was not publicly out to the committee. Henry and Gross published two
preliminary reports, but with no financial support from the committee,
their plans for a more extensive study were abandoned. With the publication of the two-volume *Sex Variants* monograph in 1941, the committee
ceased to operate.[20]

THE SEX VARIANTS STUDY

The *Sex Variants* monograph was published by Paul B. Hoeber, the medical book department of Harper & Brothers, with the stipulation that the
material was "prepared for the use of the medical and allied professions
only." According to Henry, physicians were especially targeted because
their professional training enabled them to be objective and free of the
common prejudice directed against sex variants. Thus, they possessed
the perspective to deal with the social ills and serve in the capacity of "the

mental hygiene leaders in the community."[21] In keeping with the objectives of the mental hygiene movement, mental health and social welfare were premised on the integration of the individual with the norms and values of the community. Sexual adjustment was one of the components of this ideal individual-society fit.

Throughout the study, Gay was employed by the committee to act as Henry's research assistant. She was responsible for recruiting the sample of homosexual women and men. Painter recruited a small sample of male prostitutes. If prospective subjects indicated a willingness to participate, Gay obtained personal and family histories as well as demographic data. It is likely that she had already interviewed some of the lesbians she recruited as part of her New York case history sample. After her contact with the participants, she introduced them to Henry under a pseudonym, which was a first name and the initial of a last name. The background information that Gay provided enabled Henry to have some familiarity with the subjects when he interviewed them at New York Hospital's Payne Whitney Psychiatric Clinic. These psychiatric interviews were open-ended with some "guidance" on Henry's part so that a standard series of topics would be covered, including family background, childhood and adolescent experiences, social and work patterns, sexual practices, and the participant's attitudes toward homosexuality. The sequence and coverage of topics that Henry utilized in his interviews closely followed the protocol Gay had adapted from Hirschfeld, which she employed in her research. Henry, however, acknowledged neither Gay nor Hirschfeld. Henry conducted follow-up interviews, based on a questionnaire, after a two-year interval to check on statements previously made and to provide supplementary information. For both interview sessions, Henry used shorthand to produce a verbatim record of each respondent's remarks, which he indicated had the effect of facilitating communication because it conveyed the impression that everything that was said was of value.[22]

Somewhat over two hundred individuals from New York's homosexual community, centered in Greenwich Village and Harlem, volunteered and were interviewed initially in 1935 and followed up two years later. The unusually large number of volunteers suggests that these men and women were eager to cooperate in a study that was organized by community insiders, that is, Gay and Painter. Not all of the volunteers labeled themselves as homosexuals. In addition to self-identified lesbians and gay men, there were also bisexuals, male transvestites, and male prostitutes. From the original subject pool, Henry selected forty men and forty women for the sample he used in the *Sex Variants* monograph. According to Henry, this selection was based on those who were particularly informative in the interviews. This final sample was, for the most part, made up of participants who were in their twenties and thirties, white, well educated, and in the professions, fine arts, and performing arts. There were five African Americans, four of whom were women. Some of the participants were affected by the economic hardships of the Depression, either having lost money or being unable to find steady employment.[23]

With Gay's assistance in scheduling, the participants were subjected to various medical examinations. Based on a general physical examination, a team of physicians searched for such physical signs of masculinity as "heavy" skeletal structure, large and firm muscles, and presence of body hair. Physical signs of femininity were at opposite poles and included "light" skeletal structure, small and soft muscles, and general hairlessness. Radiologists conducted X-ray examinations of the head, chest, and pelvis to assess morphological signs of "maleness" and "femaleness." To supplement the X-ray indices, about a third of the sample agreed to be photographed in the nude. Most of the women (thirty-one) agreed to have a pelvic examination, the results of which were analyzed by a team of gynecologists and obstetricians (headed by Dickinson). Some of the men submitted semen for a fertility analysis, but, interestingly, the women were not tested for fertility. As Jennifer Terry notes in her analysis of the sex variants study, while producing fertile sperm was associated with masculinity, giving birth was not a sufficient sign of femininity since several of the woman had given birth. Finally, most of the sample completed the Terman-Miles test of masculinity-femininity.[24]

Henry's monograph includes the first-person autobiographical narratives he obtained from his psychiatric interviews. He indicated that the personal accounts were composed "almost entirely of statements made by the subject which I have edited to make a connected history." Before each autobiographical statement, Henry provided a brief "general impression," in which he described the outstanding physical, behavioral, and emotional characteristics of the respondent, as well as a family (genealogical) chart with notations including the degree of aggressiveness and submissiveness of family members. Following each autobiography, Henry reported the findings of the medical examinations as well as the results of the masculinity-femininity test. Each case ended with a section in which Henry presented his own analysis. The male and female cases were subdivided into three categories—bisexual, homosexual, and narcissistic—reflecting, according to Henry, "the extent to which they deviate from heterosexual adjustment."[25] The "bisexuals" represented those individuals who had had some incidence of heterosexual experience, while the "narcissistic" category reflected those who revealed narcissistic tendencies or other psychosexual "eccentricities," such as male prostitution, male transvestitism, and female promiscuity (with both sexes).

The participants' narratives offer a rare glimpse into the shared experiences, sensibilities, and struggles of an underground subculture whose voices were typically silenced in medical and scientific discourse. Among the varied themes in these texts are expressions of positive self-identity, such as Alberta I., a thirty-year-old artist who proclaimed, "I have a great confidence in the future. . . . Homosexuality hasn't interfered with my work. It has made it what it is." Expressions of resistance are exemplified by Michael D., a thirty-two-year-old interior decorator who stated, "I have never seen any literature on homosexuality with which I have agreed." The struggle to achieve a positive homosexual identity against the force of social rejection is reflected by Ellen T., a thirty-eight-year-old artist who declared, "In the beginning I was very silly about homosexuality. Never for a moment did I think it was anything very wrong. . . . I know now that that is stupid."[26]

In contrast to these personal reflections of coping with a stigmatized identity, Henry steadfastly held to a medical model of homosexuality. In dissecting the etiology of homosexuality, he presented a loose, multidetermined perspective that encompassed the wide variety of explanations and hypotheses available in the medical literature. Both genetic and environmental factors were considered. With regard to hereditary influences, Henry and his team of medical investigators searched for structural and physiological characteristics that reflected atypical gender patterns. They found relatively little in the way of consistent empirical support. For example, contrary to the assumption that male homosexuals would display a high proportion of feminine physical characteristics, Henry reported that four-fifths of the male sample had an athletic body build, marked by broad shoulders and narrow hips. Among the female group, he found some support for masculine features because half of the women had an athletic body build. As a sign of a general abnormal pattern, Henry attributed the high incidence of athletic body build in both the homosexual men and women to an immature form of skeletal development. Dickinson, in his gynecological analysis, relied on his own clinical experience and looked for signs that would distinguish the lesbian sample from "normal women." Although acknowledging that the pattern he found could be the result of masturbatory or heterosexual experience, he nevertheless concluded that "there is *evidence in flush, wetness and clitoris erectility, plus large size of the prepuce and of the glans of the clitoris and the labia minora,* which would lead the examiner to bear in mind the possibility of homosexual methods of considerable duration and frequency."[27] Despite such flawed reasoning, he suggested that physicians use such guidelines in detecting homosexuality when they examined their female patients.[28]

While not dismissing the contribution of a hereditary predisposition,

Henry emphasized the nurturing role of the family. The most fundamental nurturing influence, according to Henry, was the gender discordant pattern of aggressiveness and submissiveness that emerged from his genealogical diagrams based on the family histories gathered in the interviews. Going back as far as maternal and paternal grandparents and including parental siblings and the respondents' siblings and their families, the most typical pattern was one of aggressive, dominant females and submissive or autocratic males. Family patterns of masculinity-femininity and dominance-submission were thus conducive to the generation of homosexuality in the offspring. Mothers who were masculine or fathers who were feminine, according to Henry, would each be detrimental to the nurturing of their children's heterosexual adjustment. He spelled out examples of each: "Masculinity in a female may be manifested in aggressive occupations, aggressive attitudes toward society, and through intolerance of the personal relationships involved in being a wife and mother. . . . Femininity in a male may be manifested directly as such through dependence upon a more aggressive male or female."[29]

In the case of men, the net result of these faulty socialization models was that mothers established abnormally close attachments to their homosexual sons, while fathers were either too weak or too punitive for their sons to identify with. Mother attachment also played a role for women, but it was not as ubiquitous an etiological determinate as it was for men. With his emphasis on homosexuality as a reflection of gender inversion, the case was more complicated for women. Mother attachment afforded a logical rationale for effeminate male homosexuals, but with the exception of cases where daughters displaced their fathers, the connection between mother attachment and masculine-identified lesbians was not apparent. Henry thus provided a wider array of explanatory considerations in accounting for lesbianism, including father identification, rebellion in the form of feminist protest, and unsatisfied sexual relations with men. Henry also found it more difficult to account for those cases that did not manifest gender inversion; that is, masculine-identified gay men and feminine-identified lesbians and bisexual women. In these instances, he resorted to explanations, such as a fear of the opposite sex, general insecurity, and the lack of maternal affection.[30]

Regardless of the specific cause, Henry viewed homosexuals as socially maladjusted individuals who could not adapt to social laws and conventions. Moreover, he believed that due to early environmental influences, which in some cases reinforced genetic predispositions, most homosexuals would not be able to achieve a heterosexual adjustment. In essence, they were developmentally damaged individuals, victims of poor parenting and the breakdown of the family in times of rapid social change. Consistent with these views, Henry voiced sympathy for homosexuals. They were often the unfortunate targets of community "witch-hunts," ending up as victims of a prejudiced judicial system. His goal in presenting and analyzing the lives of homosexuals was to make the medical community more aware and informed so that homosexuals could be helped by experts sympathetic to their plight. He conveyed this paternalistic attitude by acknowledging his indebtedness to the "courage" of his homosexual volunteers for submitting themselves for study.[31]

In his final conclusions about the study, Henry focused on prevention rather than treatment. Since he thought of homosexuality as a social maladjustment rather than a disease, he did not believe that homosexuals could be "cured," that is, achieve a mature heterosexual adjustment. The therapeutic goal was to enable homosexuals to control their sexual impulses. He believed that this could be accomplished through a combination of "occupational, psychiatric, and institutional treatment."[32] He recommended psychotherapy for those who could afford it and, in the case of men who were imprisoned for a sexual offense, psychiatric and follow-up services.

Henry was rather pessimistic about the potential for homosexuals to fit into society. The role of the physician was to help make society more tolerant, protect homosexuals from unjust legal practices, and provide help for homosexuals in controlling their sexuality so that they could conform, hence, adjust themselves to social mores. Reflecting his views that homosexuals were basically immature and limited in their capacity to become heterosexual, Henry often aired negative, sometimes even contemptuous views toward his individual respondents. He was especially critical of those who expressed no desire to change. Henry, for example, described Victor R., a twenty-three-year-old homosexual prostitute who ran a male brothel, as "a person of meager ambition," who was a "menace to society . . . through the seduction of adolescent boys who are often thereafter drawn to male prostitution. . . . [He] is unconcerned about this problem." Percival G., a forty-six-year-old former matinee idol of the stage and screen, "had no opportunity to learn the ways of conventional people . . . for he was at puberty already a confirmed worshipper of the phallus. . . . Thirty years of dissipation in sex and drink have left Percival with no regrets."[33]

Henry and the homosexual rights activists agreed on the goals of decriminalizing homosexuality and generating a more sympathetic public attitude toward gay men and lesbians. Where they differed was the issue of who should control the lives of homosexuals. Since Henry and his associates on the sex variants committee considered homosexuals to be psychologically and socially maladjusted, control was to be placed under the

watchful eyes of medical and scientific experts. For advocates of homosexual rights, the objective was for gay men and lesbians to be able to live
their lives in a sexually pluralist society; that is, without having to conform
to the social conventions of the heterosexual majority. I consider these
conflicting objectives in the following sections.

THE OBJECTIVES OF THE GAY AND LESBIAN ACTIVISTS AND RESEARCH PARTICIPANTS

Jan Gay shared Magnus Hirschfeld's commitment to science as a significant avenue to social reform, and her use of case histories reflected Havelock Ellis's belief that published histories could counter negative attitudes
about homosexuality. Through her ambitious and innovative research, she
undoubtedly hoped to produce a definitive study of lesbianism. When her
project was completed, her plan to write a book with the help of medical
specialists was diverted into Henry's monograph. As she reported, her
original 70,000-word manuscript was "assimilated" in the two volumes.
Nowhere in these volumes was there any reference to her authorship. In
fact, Henry provided no review of the extensive literature available at the
time to substantiate his conclusions. Gay's exhaustive library research was
obviously ignored. Moreover, she was not credited with conceiving and
initiating the research project. Henry simply acknowledged her role in recruiting the volunteers and obtaining personal and family histories. She
was also included among those recognized for their editorial help on the
final manuscript.[34]

In essence, the experts that Gay needed to legitimize her work, by
means of their professional credentials and their ability to generate the required medical and scientific data, robbed her of her authorship as well as
her objective of being an agent for social change through her research. In
fact, disillusioned over the fate of her project, she abandoned any further
involvement in research on homosexuality. While the oversight of Gay by
Henry and the sex variants committee may not have been deliberate, it reflected the gulf between the experts and the subjects of their inquiry. How
could a self-identified lesbian, a member of a pathological population, be
an expert in her own right? Yet the unfair and scientifically unethical treatment Gay received from the sex variants committee was not an isolated
episode. As Henrika Kuklick and Robert E. Kohler point out, scientists in
such field sciences as cultural anthropology and geography have historically often neglected to acknowledge the contributions of the informants
and technicians they relied on for their field research. Gay's case, however,
goes a step further, reflecting the problematics of gaining intellectual credibility when one is a member of a stigmatized and pathologized group. Her

sad experience was emblematic of the barriers faced by homosexual writers, researchers, and activists to have their voices represented and taken seriously.[35]

Alfred Gross and Thomas Painter, the other two activists involved in committee-sponsored research, fared somewhat better than Gay did. Based on Henry's dependency on Gross to make contact with sex offenders, Gross was able to gain coauthorship on a series of journal articles, as well as to work closely with Henry after World War II in establishing a social service agency targeted for male homosexuals in legal trouble. While Painter never published his research on male prostitution, he was eventually able to gain the support of Alfred C. Kinsey and became one of Kinsey's unofficial research consultants. Gross's and Painter's experiences will be revealed in subsequent chapters.[36]

Gross's and Painter's motives for generating their research appear to have been closely connected with the changing political atmosphere of the Depression years. In the early 1930s, New York state and city authorities began a campaign to exclude homosexuals from public gathering places. In contrast to the "pansy craze" of 1930–31 in which Times Square nightclubs featured drag shows, there was a crackdown to close bars and restaurants frequented by gay men. The political shift reflected a backlash against the moral looseness of the Prohibition era. By the late thirties, many bars were forced to close and gay men became increasingly vulnerable to police harassment and arrest. Adding to the concerns of gay men, there was an influx of male hustlers. These men tended to be young drifters, with little education or social opportunity, who were attracted to New York because of its reputation as "the capital of the American homosexual world." In the midst of the Depression, they were unable to find adequate employment and turned to prostitution as a means of survival. Their increasing presence constituted a threat, especially to those men who were not economically and socially established and thus, according to Henry and Gross, did not "have powerful friends who [were] . . . capable of dealing with blackmailers."[37] In Henry and Gross's study, the prostitutes admitted to victimizing sexual partners through blackmail threats, robbery, and physical assault. There was also the suggestion that some may have served as police informers. Gross and Painter, most likely, each believed that by revealing the vulnerability of homosexual men to victimization, published and scientifically sponsored studies of prostitution might result in a more sympathetic reading in legal, medical, and scientific circles. Moreover, they probably thought that such publications might serve as a practical source of information for gay men regarding the potential problems of prostitution.

The *Sex Variants* monograph also reveals that the research participants were committed to contribute to a scientific investigation. As Henry commented, "Most of them welcomed an opportunity to participate in a scientific and medical study of their development and of their problems. Through this study they hope for a better understanding of their maladjustments and as a consequence a more tolerant attitude of society toward them."[38] Some of the participants specifically associated their opportunity to take part in the research with the cause of homosexual rights. In his impressions of particular individuals, Henry noted instances of deep commitment. Will G. "is striving to improve the lot of the underprivileged sex variant. His interest in homosexual problems is manifested by unreserved submission of himself for investigation and by his frank exposition of himself and his family." Henry was an astute observer here, for "Will G." was Thomas Painter's pseudonym and Painter viewed himself as a spokesperson for the concerns of male hustlers. In describing Ellen T., Henry observed that she "is easily moved to tears . . . in speaking of what she feels is injustice to homosexuals. She is eager to help in this study and to know what progress is being made." Moreover, the participants expressed their own objectives in being a part of scientific research. Mildred B. declared, "I'm interested in having homosexuality better understood and in obtaining a more tolerant attitude on the part of the general public," and Virginia K. commented, "I believe the attitude of the general public toward homosexuality is unfortunate and unfair. They think that homosexuality is a degenerate thing and I don't think it should be considered abnormal."[39]

Other participants were drawn to the research in hopes of gaining a better understanding of themselves. Henry noted that Malcolm E. was "very much interested in this research study." In his own words, Malcolm stated, "I have had many theories about homosexuality but none is satisfactory." Sadie S. commented, "Many times I have wondered why my life is what it is." At the end of the interview, she revealed her satisfaction at having had the opportunity of self-exploration, declaring, "It's a big relief to talk to someone who will listen and understand." Some of the volunteers appeared to be motivated out of despair, looking at the interview with Henry as an opportunity to be helped. Salvatore N. confided, "The future looks dark because I have lost courage. I either want to be cured or to be able to live my life as I want," and Caroline E. stated, "The future looks pretty bad or I wouldn't be here."[40]

The objective of effecting social change, reflected in the work of the research activists and expressed by some of the research participants, was also manifested in a case of political activism. Consistent with the crackdown on bars catering to homosexuals, the New York State Liquor Authority promoted a campaign to prohibit bars from serving homosexuals. The argument was that such "undesirable people" would result in drinking establishments becoming disorderly. In 1940 one bar owner—a Mr. Schwartz of the Gloria Bar & Grill, who had his license revoked for failing to evict his homosexual patrons—appealed the decision on the basis that neither he nor the Liquor Authority's investigators had the expertise to identify homosexual men. In the petition, filed by his lawyer, it was noted that the investigators assumed that effeminacy was a sign of homosexuality in men. Yet, as the petition added, the investigators could not consistently agree on who was homosexual simply by observation and, if this was the case, how could the bar owner be expected to make decisions on whom to evict. Underscoring the invalidity of using effeminacy as a sign of homosexuality, the petition included a statement prepared by Henry, based on his forthcoming *Sex Variants* monograph. Henry asserted, "There is no necessary relationship between effeminacy in a man and his type of sexual desire and practice."[41] The petition played up this statement by ignoring Henry's qualification that there was still a somewhat higher proportion of effeminate men among homosexuals than in the "general community." Despite the attempt to use scientific research to counter public authority, the legal appeal failed and the bar remained closed.

It seems likely that Painter, who was familiar with the Gloria Bar, was responsible for drawing in Henry for the appeal. Henry presumably viewed his testimony as an opportunity to promote his research and the work of the sex variants committee. What is interesting is that Henry's statement of "no necessary relationship" between effeminacy and male homosexuality, even though hedged somewhat, was not reproduced in *Sex Variants*. In his published conclusions, he more emphatically associated gender conformity with heterosexual adjustment, stating, "Well-adjusted adult men and women usually have been predominantly male or female from early childhood."[42] Apparently, in the context of legal testimony in support of homosexual rights, Henry was more willing to qualify the stereotyped connection between effeminacy and male homosexuality. In *Sex Variants*, by signifying gender conformity as a means of preventing homosexuality, he was more interested in appealing to his medical readers and their role as reinforcers of normalcy.

THE OBJECTIVES OF THE SEX VARIANTS COMMITTEE

By the 1930s in medical and scientific circles, it was a well-established belief that homosexuality was pathological. Moreover, as a result of the new openness about sexuality and the rising visibility of gay men and lesbians in the interwar years, there was a significant interest in homosexuality in both the popular and medicoscientific literature. The opportunity of col-

lecting data on a large sample of self-identified homosexuals provided
Dickinson and his committee colleagues with an unusual chance to investigate a phenomenon that attracted so much social and scientific attention.
In contrast with previous research, which was limited to clinical cases or
surveys in the general population, it was now possible to undertake a more
definitive investigation of homosexuality based on a sample with a relatively long-standing history of homosexual experience.[43]

Committee chairman Eugen Kahn drew attention to the social significance of the committee's research, declaring:

> The Committee has the impression that the interest in research in the
> field of sex has broadened in the last few years and that the public
> welfare will be served by publication of the results of this research.
> Medical, psychological and sociological studies of sex are receiving
> some mention in the daily press. The public begins to realize that
> punitive measures alone in dealing with cases of "sex crime" are in-
> adequate and that the sex offender must be studied if progress in the
> prevention as well as in the treatment of sexual maladjustment is to
> be achieved.[44]

Kahn was referring to more than the new openness about sexuality. His
comments about "sex crimes" reflected the growing concern, which began
in the mid-1930s, about how to deal with the rise of sex crimes.

The primary objective of the Committee for the Study of Sex Variants
was to further the cause of establishing homosexuality as a medical and
social problem, thereby expanding the influence of medical and scientific
authorities. General medical practitioners were the audience especially
targeted for the *Sex Variants* monograph because once they were educated
about sexual pathology, they would be able to detect signs of such maladjustment in their patients. Committee members argued that it was especially important for the physician to be cognizant of homosexuality since
recent surveys revealed a higher incidence of homosexual experience than
previously thought. Dickinson, for example, in referring to Katharine Bement Davis's survey of twelve hundred unmarried women, stated, "*Half of
them had experienced emotional relations with other women,* and over
300, a *quarter of the total number, reported physical activities recognized
as sexual.*"[45] Henry was even more inclusive, declaring, "Few persons escape an overt homosexual experience at some period in life and desires are
universal. . . . Homosexuality is wide spread and involves all classes of society."[46]

Henry and Dickinson thus pointed to the strategic role that the physician could play in monitoring any suspicious signs of homosexuality. All
patients were potentially vulnerable to sexual deviation. Homosexuality

was not a distinct disease, but rather a problem of social adjustment or, as Henry phrased it, a failure of "adaptability to social laws and customs." In particular, homosexuals were a threat to the maintenance of "heterosexual adjustment" because of their inability to assume the familial responsibilities of child rearing and, as physician E. E. Mayer declared, their generalized "hostility to the family situation."[47]

While the general practitioner might contribute to initial surveillance, it was assumed that specialists had the skill to classify, treat, and prevent sexual pathology. Dickinson pointed to the role of the gynecologist in premarital counseling, whose goal should be to dissuade anyone who had an "ingrained homosexual pattern" from ever marrying. This reflected his belief that poor sexual adjustment was the main threat to family stability. Henry's role as primary investigator and author provided a particular boost for psychiatry as the most central specialty concerned with sexual deviation. He asserted, "Society must protect itself by classifying sex variants as soon as it is possible to do so,"[48] stressing that such a task could be carried out most effectively by psychiatrists who had the expertise in sexual psychopathology. Henry did not believe that most homosexuals could achieve a heterosexual adjustment, but he recommended psychotherapy to enable homosexuals to curb their sexual drives and thus evade such problems as arrest, imprisonment, or the threat of blackmail.[49]

It was in the area of prevention that medical and scientific specialists could have the greatest impact. Based on their clinical experience and/or research knowledge, specialists could provide the guidelines necessary to effect prevention. Drawing conclusions from the sex variants study, Henry argued that early environmental influences set the pattern for sexual development. The most significant of these influences was the gender-role behavior of parents. Henry pointed to the need for parents to adopt and maintain conventional standards of gender behavior. As he declared, "Under ideal circumstances the father should be an understanding, tolerant but virile and decisive male. The mother should have the gentleness, patience and passivity usually associated with womanhood. Any mixture such as an effeminate father and an aggressive, masculine mother is likely to be disconcerting to the child and accentuate homosexual tendencies."[50] He also noted the need for preventive measures beyond the confines of the family unit. Educational institutions had to assume the mandate for training children for "adult heterosexual life." This translated into girls gaining proficiency in "domestic activities" and boys being socialized to assume the role of family responsibility. Henry also warned about the dangers of sexually segregated educational environments because of their tendency to "favor a homosexual development."[51]

The discourse in the *Sex Variants* monograph reflected the broad historical changes that affected American society in the late nineteenth and early twentieth centuries. In particular, this discourse was responsive to three historical developments: (1) changes in the function of the family, (2) the emergence of a sexual identity based on sexual object-choice, and (3) medical and scientific professionalization. With respect to the family, Henry articulated his concerns about the breakdown of the family as a socializing agent by stating, "As our western civilization grows older homosexuality appears to be increasing. A century ago in this country children afforded the greatest security to the parents. With . . . [our] present mode of living children are among the greatest liabilities to the parents. As a result young people are driven more and more to find substitutes for adult heterosexual relationships."[52]

What Henry was voicing was consonant with the theme, expressed by many social scientists in the 1920s and 1930s, that as a result of urbanization and industrialization, the family no longer performed an economic function. Medical and scientific experts were thus needed to provide advice for the family that was no longer able to look after itself. These experts stressed the need for the family to develop bonds of affection and to provide a harmonious set of interacting roles. Medicoscientific discourse on marriage, sex, and child rearing expanded during this interwar period. Sex, in the form of heterosexual adjustment, took on new significance because it was viewed as an anchor of family stability. Dickinson and Henry each pointed to homosexuality as a symptom of marital breakdown. According to Dickinson, "The psychoanalytical literature is replete with examples of cases, in which frustration in marriage resulted in the adoption of homosexual relationship[s] to attain security and avoid anxiety."[53] In the sex variants case of Mary Jones, Henry stated, "Having the desires of a mature, healthy woman and with the fading chances of being satisfied by a jealous, unfaithful husband it is not surprising that she experienced a thrill from the embraces of a passionate woman."[54]

Complementing the medicoscientific discourse on marriage and family, sexuality as expressed through heterosexual relationships was extolled as a sign of mental health. As Henry commented, "The most harmonious unions result from affectionate relations between two persons whose inclinations are primarily heterosexual." Henry, however, did acknowledge that the quality of heterosexual relations could be improved upon by studying the success with which homosexuals maintain romantic feelings in their relationships, as well as their ability to make "full use of erogenous areas,"[55] often neglected by heterosexuals. In these comments, Henry was referring to the binary distinction between homosexuality and heterosexuality, in which sexual identity was defined by the direction of one's sexual interest. By the 1930s the medical and scientific literature had shifted from viewing homosexuality as sexual inversion to viewing it as sexual object-choice. This change reflected the influence of Freudian thinking as well as the cultural shift that began to emerge in middle-class society around the turn of the twentieth century in viewing the development of a heterosexual identity.[56]

For the members of the sex variants committee, homosexuality was therefore viewed in terms of sexual object-choice and in opposition to heterosexuality. Yet the inversion paradigm was not fully supplanted. Gender inversion was still appropriated as a sign of sexual identity because it was linked to the etiological determinant of faulty socialization. As Henry had concluded, cross-gendered identification among family members "is most likely to result in sex variants among the succeeding generations. . . . [These children] grow up with a distorted conception of and impaired emotional adaptability to masculinity and femininity." Reflective of the persistent cultural anxiety about threats to masculinity, Henry added, "The male child appears to be more vulnerable to distortion in psychosexual development than the female."[57] Nevertheless, despite the conflation of gender and sexuality, Henry promoted homosexuality as sexual object-choice by probing, at great length, the specific sex practices engaged in by the sex variants participants. His queries included preferences in physical contact; preliminaries, frequency, and duration of sex; and preferences in sexual role performance (active versus passive). As a result, he found that his homosexual respondents generally engaged in a variety of sex acts and, regardless of their gender identity, they could not be consistently classified as active (the male role) or passive (the female role).[58]

The expansion of medicine and the social sciences into the realm of sexuality reflected the professional changes taking place within these disciplines. Psychiatry, in particular, was beginning to move beyond its identity as an institution-based specialty concerned with mental illness as a somatic disease. Infused by the influence of the mental hygiene movement and psychoanalysis, psychodynamic psychiatry was gaining influence. In the psychodynamic school, it was assumed that there was a continuum of normal/abnormal behavior. This implied the need for outpatient psychiatric intervention and early treatment. While most psychiatrists continued to work in mental hospitals, there were increasing numbers involved with child guidance clinics, private practice, and the criminal justice system. Those in the vanguard of psychiatric reform, such as Meyer and others associated with the mental hygiene movement, advocated a shift from institution to community in order to enhance the legitimacy and prestige of psychiatry. Psychiatry's claim to the study and treatment of homosexuality, along with allied medical and scientific specialties, was consistent with the new community orientation of the field.[59]

The inclusion of sexual pathology within psychiatry meant that medical experts had the authority to challenge the view that homosexuality was a criminal offense. Sexologists in the late nineteenth and early twentieth centuries, such as Krafft-Ebing, had advocated that homosexuality was a medical, not a legal issue. Consistent with this discourse, Henry stressed the need to rescue homosexuality from the control of the legal system, arguing that "the treatment of the sex variant should be a medical and social problem . . . [whereas] the segregation of the sex variant in a penal institution is futile and undesirable."[60] Not only was it inappropriate to treat the homosexual as a criminal, but also according to Henry, viewing homosexuality as a medical problem would protect the parents, wives, and children of sex variants from the stigma of public scandal. The medical profession had not only the expertise to deal with homosexuality, but also the humane approach.[61]

Within the context of these social, scientific, and professional influences, the sex variants committee viewed their sponsored projects as a means of reinforcing marriage and the family against the disruptive forces of modern society. Homosexuality was symptomatic of marital and familial breakdown. Family members became more vulnerable to deviant sexual expression because of the increasing pace of social change. While Henry and Dickinson believed that constitutional predispositions contributed to some cases of homosexuality, the results of the sex variants study underscored the significant role of early family socialization in virtually all cases. Reflecting the economic and social gain women were making, the traditional dominance of husbands and fathers was threatened. The more parents deviated from conventional gender roles, the more vulnerable children became to the onset of homosexuality. Moreover, because the sex variants researchers conflated gender and sexuality, the most obvious signs of homosexuality they pointed to were instances of cross-gender identification, mannerisms, and behaviors. The sex variants study thus reinforced the utility of the Terman-Miles M-F test as a diagnostic barometer of homosexual inclination.[62]

The identification of pathogenic family patterns served as the rationale for preventive strategies. The insidious strain of dominant females and submissive males, which was prominent in many of the family histories of the sex variants cases, warranted strong recommendations for parents and marital couples to adhere to the traditional family pattern of male dominance and female subservience. Beyond the family, schools were cited as a significant source of acculturating children to conventional gender roles.

Not only was prevention necessary to contain the spread of homosexuality, but treatment was also paramount to the sex variants committee objectives of promoting marital and family health. The mental hygiene movement's philosophy of social adjustment pervaded the discourse on treatment. Reflecting the influence of his mentor, Adolf Meyer, Henry's therapeutic prescription centered on the goal of homosexuals achieving control over their sexual urges and desires. This objective was not only for the benefit of homosexuals, especially men (i.e., to keep them out of legal trouble and vulnerability to victimization), but also for the protection of the greater community. As Henry was to reiterate at length in his 1955 popular version of the *Sex Variants* monograph, homosexuals had to learn how to conform to community moral standards by developing the capacity for self-control. This would enable them to fit into the community and consequently enhance their acceptance. If homosexuals could not control their sexuality, they posed a threat to social stability. In the words of psychiatrist William Alanson White, who along with Meyer was a leader of the American mental hygiene movement, "The individual who manifests a kind of conduct that is calculated to tear down the existing conventions, to deviate greatly from the normal conduct of the community,—that person is an individual who has to be relegated to some place other than a position of free citizenship."[63] White was referring to the full range of psychopathological types he categorized as "socially inefficient." But it was this kind of thinking that was reflected in the objective of "homosexual adjustment" by Henry, Meyer, and the sex variants committee.[64]

Homosexual adjustment as a treatment goal was consistent with the role of the psychiatrist as an agent of social control. It was quite different than Hirschfeld's promotion of adjustment therapy, which was aimed at getting homosexual patients to accept their sexuality. Yet although it was simplistic and worked against the interests and needs of homosexual patients, the homosexual adjustment advocated by Henry was at least relatively benign when compared with the aggressive physical therapies, such as hormonal treatment and electroshock therapy, that some psychiatrists perpetrated on their unfortunate patients. And it was probably less invasive and harmful than the virulent version of psychoanalysis, practiced by most American analysts who sought a cure in terms of heterosexual adjustment.

THE SIGNIFICANCE OF THE SEX VARIANTS STUDY

The sex variants study represented a significant milestone in the appropriation of homosexuality as an object of medical and scientific inquiry. Following initiatives from the homophile movement in Germany and England, it was the first American investigation in which homophile activists and research participants attempted to engage in a collaborative relationship with medical and scientific investigators.

For the most part, however, this collaborative relationship was doomed from the start because the homosexual activists and the professional experts were working at cross-purposes. While both groups were committed to the goal of decriminalizing homosexuality, their overall objectives conflicted. The homophile activists/participants hoped for an opportunity to have their voices heard by entering into a dialogue with medical/scientific investigators. Such an authorial relationship would provide a rare opportunity to break through the censorship that restricted any expression of the lived experiences of homosexual men and women. If the lives of homosexuals could be made familiar, social tolerance would hopefully follow.

On the other hand, the medical/scientific investigators were eager to gain full authority over the study and management of homosexuality as a means of expanding their professional interests, which were intricately tied to their role as experts of personal adjustment and social efficiency. This professional status in turn legitimized medical and scientific specialists to function as agents of social control, and the control of sexual deviance was an integral component of the mental hygiene ideology during the Progressive and interwar eras. The ideal society was equated with the adjustment of individuals to the established social order. Moreover, defining sexual deviance as a medical and social problem attested to the belief that such deviancy could be controlled through therapeutic and preventive practices.

Scientific and community interests were thus at odds. The sex variants participants were willing to reveal their lives and experiences, and the professional experts were eager to have access to this rich source of sexual subjectivity. But it was the objectives of the experts that prevailed. They had the power to gather the physical, psychological, and narrative data and shape it to fit their preconceptions of homosexuality as individual pathology and social problem. The homophile activists and participants had no resources of power other than their own personal commitments to engage in a scientific endeavor that held the promise of social change. Grassroots efforts by homosexual men and women to successfully challenge social ostracism and legal persecution through emancipatory scientific projects would require a political movement. In America a national homosexual rights movement did not begin to take shape until the early 1950s, and, even then it would take another twenty-five years or so before the stigma of illness was stripped from homosexuality.[65]

At another level, the medical and psychiatric discourse perpetuated the conventional social-cultural understanding of homosexuality. The everyday realities of the sex variants participants were distorted to fit the medical model of pathology as well as the stereotypical views about homosexuals and the threat they posed to the community. The first-person narratives were reinscribed into authoritative third-person interpretations of "socially inefficient" and personally troubled individuals. Yet when the first-person narratives are uncoupled from Henry's psychiatric analysis as well as the report of medical and psychological indices, the personal agency of the storytellers emerges. In the long view, their stories of personal struggle in the face of social ostracism echoed the turn-of-the-century renderings by Earl Lind and Claude Hartland and anticipated the coming out stories of the post-Stonewall era of the 1970s.

The relative failure of the homosexual activists and research participants to successfully fulfill their intended mission does not diminish the historical significance of their effort. The fact that their life stories have been preserved through publication provides a window into the personal and cultural experiences of gay men and lesbians in the 1930s, a world that has been largely lost to sources of recorded history. Their narratives allow us to share and therefore understand their personal and collective struggles for self-validation. The sociohistorical context of these life stories is especially important with regard to time and place. The 1930s were a harbinger of what was to come in the next two decades. In the 1930s visible urban homosexual subcultures were becoming established and, as a consequence, were also vulnerable to sociopolitical backlash. The post–World War II era was a time of accelerated development in the flowering of the gay male and lesbian subcultures and a time in which a national homophile movement would emerge. It was also a period in which the homosexual panic of the 1930s would be given new life in the throes of McCarthyism. New York City in the 1930s was the largest and most influential homosexual community in America. The stories in the *Sex Variants* monograph provide an in-depth look at what life was like in this urban subculture. In essence, these life stories have a life of their own. Their historical significance as well as their capacity to inform us about the multifaceted ways in which history shapes how we construct identities validates the efforts of Jan Gay and the research participants. While medical authority appropriated Gay's research initiative and silenced her voice, the spirit of her activist legacy lives through the personal accounts contained in Henry's *Sex Variants*. In the next chapter, I present an analysis of these life stories.

Chapter 4

Homosexual Life Stories, 1935–41

> The homosexual should have the same position in society as the so-called normal person has. They wouldn't then be all running around to dives and getting persecuted. They wouldn't be so sorry for themselves. They wouldn't be so queer or fight people who didn't understand. They wouldn't have to be hiding more than 50 per cent of the time.
>
> —Virginia K., in *Sex Variants*

The life stories in George W. Henry's *Sex Variants* monograph revealed the variegated and complex subjectivity of gay men, lesbians, and other sexual minorities in the 1930s. These storytellers did not speak in one voice. Gender, class, race, and age shaped their experiences and perspectives. Moreover, even within these structuring categories, the autobiographical accounts exposed diverse subjectivities. Most significantly, these storytellers varied in the way in which they dealt with their sexuality. Some took pride, even defiance, in speaking about their homosexuality or bisexuality. These stories conveyed the proto-politicization that anticipated the homophile movement of the 1950s and 1960s. In marked contrast, other stories disclosed the despair and inner turmoil of struggling with a stigmatized identity. In these cases, there was often a plea to Henry to alleviate the suffering. In still other instances, there were tales that displayed contradictions between self-acceptance and feelings of shame and guilt. Here, the storytellers were in the throes of trying to make sense of who they were and how their sexuality defined them.

We might wonder if these varied revelations were consistent with what

Jan Gay would have expected. As an advocate for homosexual rights, she would, most likely, have reveled in expressions of personal pride and social resistance. Yet as we have seen with Earl Lind and even Richard von Krafft-Ebing, writers sympathetic to the cause of homosexual rights believed that it was necessary to disclose the pain and suffering experienced by homosexuals. Gay, in her earlier interviews with some three hundred lesbians, must have been exposed to a wide cross section of expressed feelings.

To understand these life stories, it is essential to be cognizant of the context in which they were produced—that is, being told to a physician. Henry's interview protocol, based on Gay's original work, shaped the pattern and content of what was disclosed. Yet because the interview approach was open-ended, the respondents had considerable liberty to reveal what they chose as well as to express their personal beliefs and attitudes. Their perceptions of Henry also influenced their discourse. Some of the respondents made a point of expressing their support for homosexual rights and thus appeared to see Henry as a conduit for disseminating such a political perspective. Others appealed to Henry to help them overcome unwanted sexual desires and consequently poured out their troubles.

Thus, the stories reflected the motivations, goals, and agendas of the respondents. This raises the question of how truthful or reliable the stories were in relation to the storytellers' lives. Life stories cannot be understood as objective accounts since they are always subject to the role that self-reflections play in interpreting one's life experiences and, consequently, they are continuously being rewritten. What Henry's respondents disclosed was how they constructed their pasts to fit in with their self-perceptions at the time they were interviewed. Rather than reporting the actual events of their lives, they were recalling and interpreting their past to give meaning to their present as well as projected future. The *Sex Variants* autobiographical accounts captured a particular time in the personal lives of the respondents. It is through that prism that I analyze their life stories.[1]

Before analyzing these stories, I also want to draw attention to the question of how accurately they were transcribed into the published version. Through various sources, a small number of the respondents can be identified. This makes it possible to check Henry's published first-person accounts with the known details of their lives. Among the men, Thomas Painter (Will G.) provides the best example for such a comparison. In an unpublished review of the *Sex Variants* monograph, Painter dissected Henry's presentation of him. He asserted that Henry falsely labeled his "reddened" face as a sign of "dissipation" when in fact it was a combined

effect of suntan and an irritation on his nose. Painter felt that this description cast a negative impression on the rest of the case presentation. In
the family history, he cited instances in which original statements were re-
worded in ways that gave an inaccurate and negative impression of what
was said about family members. In the personal history, Painter also cited
several inaccuracies that pointed to Henry's "telescoping" descriptions of
sexual episodes. Painter's evaluation points, at least in part, to what Henry
himself admitted; that is, that he did edit the respondents' statements "to
make a connected history."[2] Henry's predisposition to look for signs of
pathology may well have led him to seemingly false suggestions about conditions, such as "dissipation." Therefore, Henry's editing and observations
do represent instances of inaccuracy and distortion. Yet in looking at
Painter's case, Henry does appear to essentially reproduce the subject's life
story in the subject's own words. Painter's life story, based on his own papers as well as Henry's case presentation, will be dealt with in chapters 6
and 7. Painter also critiqued Henry's presentation of Leonard R., a friend
of Painter's who was a male hustler. Painter criticized Henry for showing
his negative bias by using such terms as "leering," "furtive," and "coy" in
describing Leonard.[3]

Among the other cases that can be identified, considerable biographical
information is available on Pearl M., who was the prominent African
American actress Edna Thomas. She was born in 1886 in Virginia and
raised in Boston. Married at sixteen and widowed at twenty-six, she came
to New York in 1915 and pursued an acting career by joining the Lafayette
Players, a Harlem repertory. She debuted on Broadway in 1926, but in
mainstream theater her career was limited to such stereotyped roles as
maids. In 1936 she appeared as Lady Macbeth in Orson Welles's Harlem
production of *Macbeth,* a highly publicized project. Her image is preserved in the 1951 film version of *A Streetcar Named Desire,* in which
she revived her stage role (the national touring company) of the Mexican
flower woman. In Henry's preliminary publication about the sex variants
project, her case study was one of the four included. She was identified as
a "successful negro actress," however, in *Sex Variants* her occupation was
given as "a successful negro singer." It seems likely that Henry made this
change in order to protect her anonymity. This illustrates that when necessary, Henry altered biographical details. His personal impressions of
Thomas were consistent with contemporary accounts. He described her in
the following terms: "Her soft, deep voice and her friendly attitude along
with an evident personal security have caused her to be sought after by
both white and colored people."[4] With respect to the impressions she
made on her contemporaries, Welles's biographer Simon Callow indicates,
"[Welles] treated [Thomas] with the deference due to a great lady of the

theater, and that is indeed how she was perceived by the company. . . . A discreet and rather statuesque lesbian, she stood apart from the company, but had great authority."[5] Thomas's lesbian partner, Olivia Windham, a scion of English nobility, was included in Henry's cases as Pamela D. Another well-known figure in Harlem's homosexual circles, Caska Bonds, was included as Walter R. Eric Garber, who has studied the Harlem homosexual subculture of the 1920s and 1930s, indicates that, based on his interviews with people who knew about the sex variants study, Henry's case presentations of those associated with the Harlem community are generally accurate.[6]

All in all, taking into account Henry's negative biases (more pronounced in those cases that departed from his own upper-middle-class background) and inaccuracies due to his editing, he does appear to have generally reproduced the life stories as conveyed to him by the respondents. The fact that statements asserting positive self-identities and resistance to the medical model often appear in the narratives attests to Henry's commitment to fully transcribe what his respondents stated. His earnestness appears to have been a reflection of Gay's research design, and, despite his failure to acknowledge her contribution, he was carrying out her intention to present comprehensive life stories of lesbians and gay men.

I deal with the male and female narratives separately, looking at the male stories first. I then consider the common patterns that emerge across both sets of stories. In looking at these patterns, I focus on the variations in the evaluative tone of the narratives, that is, how positive or negative the storytellers were about their lives. The chapter concludes with a consideration of how the stories, and the grassroots project that generated them, fit into the emergence of the American homosexual rights movement.

THE MALE NARRATIVES

Two themes stand out in these stories—sexual identities and "coming out." Regarding sexual identities, the majority of men thought of themselves as homosexual. Two men did not express a clear preference for men or women and had extensive experience with both. In addition, three men were heterosexual transvestites and two were homosexual prostitutes or hustlers. The hustlers did not consider themselves to be homosexual and stated that they preferred sex with women.

"Coming out" refers to the experience of discovering that one's sexuality differs from the norm. This was a common theme in the gay men's stories and typically signified a major developmental milestone around which these men constructed their life histories. Self-discovery was usually accompanied by introducing oneself into male homosexual society. In fact, the term "coming out" was appropriated from the upper-class ritual of the debutante's rite of passage into society. This meaning of coming out differs from the 1960s metaphor of the "closet" in which gay men revealed themselves to straight society. A coming out experience was not referred to in the cases of the bisexual men, hustlers, or transvestites. The bisexuals and hustlers talked about homosexual experiences as part of their sexual exploration with both sexes. The transvestites focused on their early attraction to cross-dressing and its connection with their sexual gratification. Only one of the three transvestites explored homosexual relations, and this was to test his sexual attraction to other men when he was dressed as a woman.[7]

I first discuss the male narratives from the point of view of sexual identities and follow this with a consideration of the coming out theme. I then move on to examine Henry's interpretations of the male cases to illustrate the ways in which he distorted the narratives to fit them into his medical model.

Sexual Identities

Among the gay men, there was a close association between sexual and gender identity. Consistent with what George Chauncey has noted about male homosexual society in New York during the interwar era, the gay men identified themselves either in terms of the inverted, effeminate "fairy" or the masculine-oriented "queer." "Queer" was not viewed as derogatory; instead, as one of Chauncey's respondents explained, "It just meant you were different."[8] Queer men generally dissociated themselves from the flamboyant fairies and eschewed the fairies' effeminacy. Like straight men, they considered themselves to be masculine, but unlike straight men their sexual object-choice was other men.[9]

Nine of the forty men showed signs of a fairy identity through their appropriation of a cross-gender role. Some of these men, looking back at their childhood, disclosed a long-standing desire to perform as the opposite sex. For example, Daniel O'L., a twenty-six-year-old unemployed Irish immigrant, stated, "I always liked to dress as a girl. . . . I was happiest when I was following Mother and my sisters around the house, sewing and cooking and doing all the things customary to girls." The behavioral expression of these engendered desires marked the budding fairy as different from other boys, often leading to harassment. According to Dennis C., a high school teacher in his mid-twenties, "I played all games like a girl, pitched and batted like a girl and played hopscotch with girls. The boys made fun of me . . . called me sissy." As these men entered the homosexual world, they internalized the role of the fairy. Julius E., a thirty-year-old interior decorator, described his coming out at drag balls, "I had become one of the 'belles' and for two or three seasons, whenever I could, I appeared in fancy dress, the petticoats, the shawl, and the fascinator of the Victorian period."[10]

The fairies expressed their sexual attraction to other men by typically acting the part women would play in sexual relationships. Signs of such role-playing were reflected in various ways. Many of these men viewed themselves as effeminate in manner or as possessing a feminine mentality. Malcolm E., for example, a twenty-four-year-old graduate student, reported, "I feel feminine in my mental traits." Most reported that they assumed the passive role of the female in their sexual relations and expressed a preference for masculine-appearing men. Gabriel T., an independently wealthy thirty-year-old, characterized his sexual role by commenting, "In all of my relations with men, I have the typically feminine emotions of being courted and conquered and of finally yielding to embraces." A history of cross-dressing was common, and some acknowledged that this was a lifelong practice they frequently engaged in. Victor R., a twenty-three-year-old proprietor of a male brothel, revealed that he often appeared and performed in drag at his establishment.[11]

Yet despite such unequivocal revelations of a cross-gender persona, some men with effeminate tendencies divulged signs of a gender duality, in which they appropriated both feminine and masculine attributes, thus defying conventional gender distinctions. Walter R., a forty-six-year-old black man who was prominent in Harlem homosexual society, reflected, "As I get older, I feel more like the protector, more and more like taking the feminine role."[12] Here, he appears to be folding in the conventional masculine role of the protector with what he considers to be feminine. This comment was made in connection with his recollections regarding a young black male of seventeen who he decided not to initiate sex with, seemingly to protect him from becoming involved in a sexual relationship. This incident also indicates that Walter, by being in control, assumed the active role. Walter also revealed that while he preferred the feminine role of passive sodomy, he also had engaged in sodomy in which he exchanged roles with his partner. Henry, in his conclusions about classifying homosexuals according to their sexual roles, acknowledged that "it is often difficult to classify sex variants as active or passive."[13] In another case, Antonio L. (Tony), a thirty-year-old laborer, also revealed a combination of gender characteristics. He had trained as a prizefighter and acted as a protector for his effeminate friend, Daniel O'L. Nevertheless, he assumed the role of housewife in his relationships with men, engaging in episodes of cross-dressing and performing sexually as a woman.[14]

As in the case of Victor R., some fairies engaged in prostitution for economic purposes and as a means of meeting sex partners. Daniel O' L., referring to his arrival in New York, where he lived in a boardinghouse in the Times Square district, said, "I soon became popular with the Greeks around the corner on Eighth Avenue. . . . They were quite generous as far as money was concerned and it seemed that this was an easy way of earning a living."[15] The fairies' preferences in sex partners varied from other effeminate men like themselves to virile, masculine types. Some had been involved in long-term relationships in which they performed the woman's role. Their partners, following the conventional marriage model, acted in the role of the "husband." In fact, this was the label used by such men who did not necessarily think of themselves as homosexual since they did not compromise their masculinity. Daniel eventually entered into a relationship with a baker who he had been living with for seven years. He described his partner in the following terms:

> He is well built, aggressive and domineering. . . . He works all week, draws his pay, brings it home, allows so much for household expenses and a certain amount for my clothes and recreation. . . . He likes to see me dressed as a woman. . . . When we go to parties I dress just like any other young girl. . . . I would like to work but . . . [he] doesn't ask me to. He makes enough to take care of both of us.[16]

For some of the fairy-identified men, the cross-gender appropriation was so marked that they expressed a lifelong desire to be a woman. Victor R., who was a cross-dresser, reminisced, "I still wish I was a girl. I used to envy my sisters. . . . My oldest sister . . . and her boy friend just kissed each other. I would sit on a bench near them. I wanted the man to kiss me too. This started when I was thirteen." Another cross-dresser, Daniel O'L., declared, "I've always wished I was a girl. If I was a woman I would like to have children. I've always thought I would like to have the hair taken out of my face. I would like to be castrated and made a girl now if it was possible."[17] These yearnings for a sex change reflect what we would today label a transsexual identity.

In contrast to those fairies who expressed a desire to be women, the three men who cross-dressed and wished to be the opposite sex did not reveal that they had a homoerotic attraction. Henry used the label "transvestite" to characterize these men. This label was coined by Magnus Hirschfeld in his 1910 book *The Transvestites*. Contrary to the conventional psychiatric thinking of the time, Hirschfeld argued that not all transvestites were homosexual. In fact, most of the cases he cited in *The Transvestites* were heterosexual. One of the transvestites in *Sex Variants*, Rudolph von H., a sixty-four-year-old businessman, corresponded with Hirschfeld and when Hirschfeld lectured in the United States in 1930, made public appearances as a "typical transvestite." In the 1920s he was castrated and underwent hormone treatment to develop his breasts. As a young man in Berlin, he was a member of a lesbian club in which he was accepted as a cross-dresser. Separated from his wife at the time of the interview, he revealed that his wife knew about his desire for women's clothes and at one time had made the dresses for him. His three children accepted his cross-dressing when they were young, but his son later became "ashamed" of it. Although he claimed, "I'm not homosexual," he reported two brief sexual experiences with other men that occurred when he was dressed as a woman. He described them as "very interesting but painful. . . . It was all from the point of vanity of being a woman. I have absolutely no taste for homosexuality itself."[18]

The other two transvestites, Howard N. (a fifty-five-year-old businessman) and Moses I. (a thirty-eight-year-old businessman), reported a strong interest in women's clothes beginning in early childhood. Both tried to satisfy their consuming desire to be the opposite sex by dressing in women's undergarments, and their wives were aware of their crossdressing. Like Rudolph, they were drawn to the homosexual subculture as a haven for those who did not fit into sexual or gender norms. In the 1930s there was no distinct transvestite community for these men to identify with. The fairy-transvestite distinction is a historicized one. With the 1970s emergence of a transgendered community (which includes crossdressers and transsexuals), some feminine-identified gay men might now choose transgenderism as their primary reference group.[19]

Regarding the motivations of the transvestites to be research participants, Rudolph apparently was interested in the sex variants study as a means of promoting a tolerant attitude toward transvestites. Howard and Moses did not use the term "transvestite" to identity themselves. They seemed drawn to the study as a resource for dealing with their severe depression and anxiety. Moses, for example, plaintively declared, "During the past year I've had spasms of hysterical crying. . . . Everything overwhelms me. . . . What is the way out for me? I wish I knew."[20]

Unlike the fairies, the transvestites' identity concerns were focused entirely on their gender and expressed as a desire to live as the opposite sex. The fairies' primary identity, on the other hand, was sexual, and their homosexuality was acted out by appropriating the feminine role. For those fairies who also had a desire for a sex change, such a desire was expressed as a means of attaining homoerotic satisfaction. Antonio L., for example, wanted to physically be a woman so that he could embody his sexual role. As he declared, "I would like to be a girl. . . . Being a girl I would be more satisfied. . . . In sex I act as a woman. I want to be the woman."[21]

Despite the complex and varied ways in which feminine-identified homosexuals constructed and defined themselves as gay men, there was a stereotyped image of the fairy as an outrageous caricature of the opposite sex. This image had taken hold in the 1880s, when the first visible homosexual communities emerged in American cities, and was embodied by Earl Lind's prototype of "Jennie June." By the turn of the twentieth century, however, some homosexual men began to break away from this stereotyped image. These men, who were mostly middle class, adhered to their middle-class preferences for privacy and self-restraint. They thus eschewed the exhibitionism of the fairy. Moreover, they viewed themselves as masculine. Some even professed that their love for other men was more masculine than the love for women. Reflecting their sexual difference from heterosexual men, these men labeled themselves as queer. As Chauncey points out, the fairies' desire for men was an extension of their gender persona. Because fairies saw themselves as feminine in temperament, they believed that it was natural for them to be attracted to other men. In contrast, the queers' same-sex attraction was based on sexual object-choice. They were "queer" or different from heterosexual men because their sexual desires were directed at men rather than women.[22]

By the 1930s, in contrast to the stereotype of the fairy in film, theater, and literature, queer became the most common form of male homosexual identity. The shift is reflected in the large number of queer-identified men in the Henry sample. Among the forty men, twenty-four revealed signs of a queer identity. Some as children had engaged in the same feminine activities that characterized the fairies. The interpretation of these behaviors, however, deflected an "effeminate" meaning. Michael D., a thirty-two-year-old interior decorator, noted that as a child, "I dressed in women's clothes for the benefit of showing somebody. I liked the performance of acting and it made more effect to dress in my mother's clothes. It was a playful masquerade. I didn't want to wear the dresses." Rodney S., a twenty-five-year-old actor, recalled that as a child he was "fond of acting, dressing up in girl's clothes and of dolls." At sixteen, however, when he became aware of homosexuality and its association with gender inversion, he attempted to control any signs of femininity. As he stated, "I read about homosexuality and I began to notice effeminate tendencies in myself and I tried to correct them."[23]

When these men began to deal with their same-sex feelings, they were aware of the stereotyped image of the fairy and many attempted to distance themselves from such an identity. Eric D., a teacher and architect, aged twenty-seven, recounted his first homosexual episode, "At the age of eighteen I came to New York. . . . I still wasn't aware that I had homosexual inclinations. . . . I did think that if I entered the theatrical profession I must avoid painted men. The following year an experienced homosexual man aged twenty-eight picked me up. He kissed me. This was very repulsive. I was disgusted. I accused him of being a painted man."[24] Such attempts to exorcise any association with effeminacy functioned to protect queer men from exposing their homosexuality. This motivation is revealed in another surviving document from the interwar era. Jeb Alexander, a masculine-identified homosexual man who was a government worker in Washington, D.C., wrote about his concerns regarding effeminacy in his diary. In 1927, at age twenty-seven, he expressed his feelings in referring to a sex partner: "I realize that effeminacy was born with him and sympathize with his handicap. I like gentleness, love it in a youth or man, but effeminacy repels me." Mindful of the danger of effeminacy as a sign of homosexuality, he added, "Thank God I have been spared that. Homosexuality may be curse enough (though it has its wonderful compensations and noble joy) but it is a double curse when one has effeminate ways of walking, talking, or acting."[25] The revulsion to effeminacy expressed by these men suggests not only a fear of their homosexuality being exposed, but also an underlying misogyny. To protect their masculinity, they had to distance themselves from feminine-associated attributes.

In some cases, the queers' antipathy toward fairies was driven more by political than personal concerns. The outrageous appearance and behavior of fairies was viewed as counterproductive to the objective of homosexuals gaining social acceptance. As Gene S., a twenty-five-year-old artist, declared, "I don't object to being known as a homosexual but I detest the obvious, blatant, made-up boys whose public appearance and behavior provoke onerous criticism." Expressing his interest in the sex variants study and implying its value by including nonstereotyped homosexual men like himself, he added, "I hope . . . [this study] will lead to an interpretation of sex deviates which will do something to remove the stigma from the homosexual."[26]

Like the fairies, some of the queer men recalled their childhood desire to be a girl. Gene S. recounted, "I always wanted to be a girl. . . . I loved wearing girls' clothes and I used to entertain the neighbor children. I did this until I was eleven." Similarly, Paul A., a twenty-eight-year-old worker in the advertising industry, revealed his childhood wish to be a girl and his cross-dressing, which he engaged in until the age of fourteen. Once Gene and Paul became aware of their homosexuality in adolescence and realized the sexual meaning attached to cross-dressing, they developed an aversion to any effeminate signs in homosexuals. Paul protested, "I . . . don't like effeminate men. Their manners and actions are very disagreeable, their way of talking and overdressing. Dressing as women is extremely objectionable."[27]

Consistent with their masculine identity and dislike of fairies, most queer men expressed a preference for masculine men as sex partners. Norman T., a professor of Latin in his early thirties, stated, "I prefer masculine men. . . . None of the men I like use perfume or powder very much and none dress in women's clothes. . . . If you like men why should you make them look like women? It doesn't seem to make sense." Some professed an attraction to other masculine-appearing homosexual men, as exemplified by Thomas B., a thirty-year-old librarian who declared, "I prefer men like myself." Others preferred heterosexual or bisexual men. In describing his "ideal sexual object," Will G., a twenty-nine-year-old theology student, included the following attributes: "He should preferably be . . . tall and lithe. . . . The muscles should be hard. . . . He must have no suggestion of homosexuality about him."[28]

Yet some men in wrestling with their homosexuality assumed a fairy persona as a phase in forging a queer identity. Irving T., a thirty-year-old fashion designer, described his progression from initially embracing the fairy subculture to moving away from it and assimilating the queer preference for privacy and self-restraint. As he stated:

> Gradually life started to change a little. I was twenty-seven and outwardly lived very conventionally in the circle of my family and their friends. I had acceded to my family's wishes to carry on the traditions of the family in the banking business even though I loathed it. I began to break away from these old associations, from the whole life of lying and fighting against myself. I went to the other extreme—designing dresses and associating constantly with obvious homosexuals. . . . I had needed an outlet to satiate my starved emotions but had had enough of it for the time being. I was glad to leave behind me the messy life in Paris and live in a new environment [the United States]. Few suspect my homosexuality . . . but I lead an active sex life.[29]

As in the case of Irving, David Johnson points out that the fairy was a transitional phase in his analysis of the male homosexual subculture in Chicago in the 1930s. For some young homosexuals, the fairy role was assumed to be the only way of expressing their homoerotic sensibilities. As they realized that the stigmatized fairy persona compromised their professional advancement, they made the transition to the more discreet queer identity.[30]

Even though queer-identified men eschewed the crude femininity of the fairies, it would have been difficult for outsiders to ascribe "masculine" qualities to these men. As Chauncey notes, queers, like fairies, were drawn to such unconventional masculine interests as the arts, fashion, decor, and mannered self-presentation. As Archibald T., a fine-fabrics salesman in his late twenties, proclaimed, "Some of the homosexuals I have known have a sensitiveness that usually doesn't go with the average normal. There is a certain understanding that goes with . . . homosexuality."[31]

Before moving on to the coming out theme, I want to briefly touch on the bisexual men and the hustlers. What distinguishes the two bisexual men from the other cases was their reported continuous sexual experience with both sexes. Donald H., who at age forty was still living on his family's income, spoke about his deep feelings for both his wife and his male lover, David. He referred to his ideal bisexual wish, saying, "I often daydream of some ideal combination whereby I could live equally with David and my wife so that it wouldn't hurt my wife's feelings."[32]

The two hustlers represented a growing number of working-class young men who migrated to urban centers in the 1920s and 1930s, seeking out the "sex trade" as a means of income. In talking about his sexual encounters with men, Leonard R., aged twenty-eight, declared, "Homosexual relations are just a means of earning money." As long as their masculinity was not compromised, they had no qualms about engaging in sex with other men. For example, Peter R., aged twenty-seven, spoke about his sexual practices, which were always consistent with the male role: "I like to have a sex party with a man every now and then. I have little desire for active sodomy and I'm never passive. . . . I prefer fellatio—always passive."[33]

Coming Out Stories
For the gay men, the coming out experience of acknowledging their homosexuality and entering the gay world marked a turning point in their lives. They constructed their stories around this epiphany. Thus, they recalled their childhood and youth from the perspective of critical events that signaled what they would later understand as homosexual desires and feelings. For some, the coming out experience was viewed as a natural outgrowth of these earlier tendencies and consequently led to an acceptance of their sexuality. For others, conflicting feelings and self-doubt marked the coming out phase of their lives. Some continued to be caught in the throes of conflict and despair, while others were able to resolve their conflict and gain self-acceptance. Among the tales with positive resolutions are revelations of a politicized awareness that telling their stories could contribute to the cause of homosexual rights. I will return to these signs of proto-politicization when I examine the common patterns across both the male and female narratives. Here, I focus on what the coming out stories reveal about the personal experiences of the storytellers.

Before these men talked about their coming out experiences, they reported earlier memories involving some form of sexual preference for other boys or men. Such a homosexual preference took the shape of a psychic reaction, such as being erotically stimulated, or engaging in some type of sexual behavior, such as mutual masturbation. The storytellers, however, recalled that they did not associate these episodes with a homosexual meaning. The timing of when these sexual experiences first began varied between childhood and early adulthood. For many, the first awareness of a sexual preference occurred in early childhood. Tracy O., a thirty-seven-year-old concert singer, recalled, "As a boy I was pure as far as sex was concerned although I did go swimming with a boy who was rather precocious sexually. He played with his organs after we came out and he would get an erection. I did the same thing but nothing happened. A year later I got an erection while wrestling with him in the nude." The lack of any homosexual signification associated with such events is exemplified by Tracy, who went on to report that at age fourteen, "I was attracted to a boy. . . . I felt a terrific devotion to him, a terrible feeling of love but I had no idea of homosexuality." Similarly, Eric D. declared, "In high school I got crushes on men. I wanted to caress an attractive male body. . . . I knew what homosexuality was but I had no idea that it had any connection with me."[34]

Several respondents reported that they had sexual encounters with both boys and girls, but preferred their same-sex experiences. Archibald T., in describing a "love affair with a girl" when he was twenty, declared, "We almost had sex relations but I just couldn't go through with it. There was something about it that nauseated me. . . . While going with her I had many intrigues with men. They intrigued me far more than she did." In other instances, a same-sex preference was contrasted with a lack of interest in the opposite sex. Will G., after telling about his first sexual experience of kissing a boy when he was in first grade, stated, "For a while I was attracted to a very nice girl, a tomboy . . . [but] I had no sex interest in her."[35]

In speaking about their coming out experiences, the storytellers often referred to the confusion and conflict they experienced. Eric D., for example, recounted that when he was twenty, "I went around with homosexuals for a year believing myself not to be one. . . . Then I went out to investigate and learn about actual sex relations. . . . By this time I was twenty-one and I had lost all scruples and prejudices. At first it was very degrading and disgusting but after I finally decided I was a homosexual it was all right."[36] Will G. recalled:

> While studying in England I took vacation trips on the continent. During these trips I visited public baths in order to continue my voyeur activities. I . . . went to homosexual cafés but was only slightly tempted. Finally a magnificent youth seduced me. . . . I said to myself, "This is what I've wanted all my life." . . . Immediately afterwards I was overwhelmed. I wept. While he was there I got down on my knees and prayed. I was still studying in the seminary and I couldn't be a hypocrite.[37]

Many men experienced the first signs of their sexual awareness through exposure to homosexual communities in New York, Hollywood, and other American cities. Daniel O'L., who was living in Boston, commented, "I had a few experiences with men there but was greatly interested in the tales I heard of the freedom and lively times to be had in New York." Two years later, at the age of twenty-one, he came to New York and was drawn to such meeting places as cafés and drag balls. Similarly, shortly after Julius E. came to New York, he attended his first ball. When Michael D. graduated from college and moved to a city in the South, he recalled, "I felt independent in a large city and was very naughty. . . . I discovered the Bohemian life . . . and I had innumerable affairs."[38]

Another source of coming out was connected with information seeking. Rodney S. reported that he first became cognizant of his homosexual tendencies when at sixteen he read about homosexuality. Norman T. had had affairs with men, but it wasn't until a friend gave him Havelock Ellis's volume on inversion that he realized he was homosexual. He reported, "I pondered over the content of this book and paid special attention to the overt homosexuals I encountered. . . . I then realized that I didn't have the usual interest in girls and that I must fall in the class of homosexuals." In some cases, sexual awareness was initiated by personal confrontation. Michael D., before he shed his homosexual inhibitions, recounted that at college, "I became attached to a girl. . . . We kissed each other but there was no sex. . . . She was the first one to introduce me to the word 'homosexual.' She suggested that I might be one." Nathan T., a thirty-four-year-old university instructor, stated, "In Paris I found out everything all of a sudden. I had heard about the Turkish baths and a friend finally took me to see one. He was not homosexual but he watched me and told me that I was."[39]

When the queer-identified men recalled their coming out experiences, they often spoke about their attempts to reject any signs of homosexuality. For example, when Nathan T.'s friend labeled him as a homosexual, Nathan stated, "I stayed up all night arguing with him and fighting against the idea." In another case, Michael D., in response to his girlfriend's suggestion that he might be homosexual, declared, "I wanted to join the best fraternity and . . . they were not interested in me. . . . I felt I was effeminate and I would say constantly to myself, 'Every day I'm getting more masculine.' Finally, I was asked to join the fraternity." An accelerated level of sexual exploration and forays into the homosexual world generally followed these negative reactions. For some, the sexual experiences included heterosexual as well as homosexual encounters. Once homosexuality became accepted, however, the heterosexual experiences ended. After describing an initial series of sexual escapades, Nathan T. stated, "When it became evident to me that my sexual preference was for men I broke off my engagement with the college girl."[40]

In contrast to the identity struggle expressed in many of the queer stories, the coming out phase in the stories by the fairies reflected a relatively conflict-free process of assimilating a newly recognized sexual identity that set them apart from other men. At the beginning of their stories, these men as children had connected their sexual preference for boys with a feminine identification. Their fairy identity was constructed along gendered lines, that is, as a natural extension of their femininity. Daniel O'L., for example, in describing his introduction to the homosexual world, declared, "I . . . started to mingle in male homosexual society, to use make-up and to give freer expression to my feminine instincts." Julius E. stated, "I'm more feminine than masculine in my attitude. I've never thought much about my homosexuality. It just seemed the natural thing to do."[41] The relative ease with which the fairies recalled incorporating their sexuality seems to be connected with their reports that as children they had experienced the alienation of being taunted for their femininity. Thus, apparently by the time they had to deal with their sexuality, they had already accepted their sense of being different.

The ending of the homosexual narratives reflected how these men coped with their sexuality at the time they were interviewed, that is, how successfully they were able to construct an identity that resisted the hegemonic metanarrative of heterosexuality. There was considerable variability in reported coping skills. Some men were caught up in an identity crisis, unable to move beyond the grip of ideological imperative. Others were relatively successful in constructing their homosexual identities.

Among those in a state of crisis, some sought escape in extreme terms. Rafael G., a Cuban immigrant of twenty-three who was financially supported by his family, revealed his despair by stating, "I go with girls now just to conceal my homosexuality. If I should get much older or poorer I would have no hesitation in trying suicide." José R., a thirty-two-year-old textile designer who also emigrated from Cuba, spoke about his drinking problem, "Drinking increases my desire for homosexual relations, but the next day I feel terrible. Sometimes I want to kill myself. Then I go with women but eventually I go back to men and I suppose I always will." Several men referred to family pressures to get married, as in the case of Thomas B., who talked about his parents: "They know nothing of my interest in men. They want me to get married and have children. . . . I suppose I will get married some day but I have had no tender feelings toward women."[42]

Stories ending on a positive note contain elements of psychological growth in the form of an acceptance of difference and openness to creating one's own life choices—in essence looking forward to continuing one's story. Speaking about his future and his hopes for adopting a child, Eric D. commented, "I have no regrets for my homosexuality. . . . I would have become neurasthenic if I hadn't adopted homosexuality because that is my normal. My future looks right unless I can't earn enough to adopt a child." Several men referred to the significance of long-term relationships in their lives. Michael D. referred to his relationship with Rodney S.: "Our relationship is physical, romantic, and intellectual. I think we are much more happy, considerate and tolerant of each other than the average seven-year married couple." Another facet of a positive ending is the incorporation of an appreciation for being different and having a special sensitivity. Gene S., who was an artist, proclaimed, "I don't want to be normal because I'm a creative person and I have a creative life."[43]

The coming out stories thus reveal the multiple ways in which the gay men came to terms with their sexuality. Through the prism of when they first acknowledged their homosexuality, they made sense of earlier sexual signifiers. The coming out process also set the stage for the various ways in which they managed and coped with their sexual identity. In contrast to these proactive revelations of personal struggle and acculturation into male homosexual society, Henry's case interpretations were filtered through a medical lens in which homosexuality was, by definition, pathological. The subjectivities of the gay man as well as the other male cases were thus subordinated to fit into his own prejudicial conclusions.

The Medicalized Interpretation

For Henry, in keeping with the presuppositions of the medical model, heterosexuality was the natural and thus mature expression of sexual desire. In his words, "The sex variant is a person who has failed to achieve and maintain adult heterosexual modes of sexual expression and who has resorted to other modes of sexual expression."[44] He thus held the heterosexual ideal of the stable family as a standard of comparison. In the case of Michael D., aged thirty-two, he seized the opportunity to contrast Michael's concerns with aging to this heterosexual value:

> Michael thinks it is unfortunate that he has become so much conditioned to homosexuals but he does not want to change now. He has grown to accept his homosexuality. Nevertheless he has a fear of age because it brings a waning of vitality, dependence and loneliness, especially as he knows that the chances of an enduring relationship between homosexuals are slight. In other words Michael is aware that many homosexuals are dependent on physical charm in the gratification of their desire and that there is no adequate substitute for the satisfaction derived from a home with children.[45]

In reaching this interpretation, Henry ignored the fact that Michael, in his two-year follow-up interview, no longer expressed his pessimism about the future. In fact, quite to the contrary, he reported, "Rodney still lives with me but he is going to Europe soon for three years. I don't think it should destroy our relationship. . . . He and I have a home. . . . I think we are much more happy, considerate and tolerant of each other than the average seven-year married couple." Henry heard only what he was predisposed to hear.[46]

Henry's predilection to distort assertions of personal pride is also evident in his comments about Noel W., a forty-year-old writer who spoke at some length about his current relationship. Noel declared, "I know that I have a lifelong attachment in my present lover. . . . It's been the most important affair in my life."[47] Henry viewed this relationship in terms of its pathogenic family origins by concluding, "Noel . . . combines the affection of his father, the appreciation of his mother and the passion of a lover." Reflecting his skepticism about the viability of long-term homosexual relationships, he translated Noel's commitment to his relationship as simply a wish, stating, "He hopes his present relationship will be permanent."[48]

Henry's biases were also reflected in his reactions to those men who expressed support and interest in the cause of homosexual rights. Despite his own acknowledgment about the unjust treatment of homosexuals, he interpreted such views voiced by his respondents as signs of personal deficiency. Will G.'s stated mission "to improve the lot of the underprivileged sex variant" was dismissed as "wistful determination" by an "impractical dreamer" whose homosexuality was "a by-product of [an] unsuccessful struggle for power" with his father and brother. Reginald M.'s "resentment over the unfair treatment of homosexuals" was part of a general contempt for social conventions, stemming from "being displaced by [a] younger brother in his mother's affection." Max N.'s declaration that "it's deplorable that there is so much lack of sympathy for homosexuals" was reduced to an expression of his misguided "alignment" with homosexuals.[49]

Henry reserved positive comments for those men who showed indications of controlling their sexuality through socially useful activities, in other words, sublimating their sexual energy into productive and creative channels. This was consistent with his therapeutic objective that homosexuals learn to control their sexual impulses. In the case of Norman T., a university professor in his early thirties, Henry commented that Norman had become so politically committed as "a champion of the downtrodden" (he fought in China with the "National" forces) that "his passion for young men . . . [is] less intimate and less personal." In his concluding impressions of Norman, Henry noted, "Sublimation of homosexuality as a teacher and protector of young men." Henry was especially impressed with Gene S., an artist who apparently had achieved recognition. Henry commented, "He is one of the few younger homosexuals astute enough to make sex the harmonizing chord instead of the chief motif of his existence." In a similar vein, Thomas B., a librarian, was extolled for being "fairly well adjusted in his work" and keeping his social life "with men of similar intellectual interests . . . comparatively quiet." Henry also observed that Thomas was "more aware of social problems and their implications than is the average homosexual."[50]

At least in one instance, the issue of sexual roles, Henry's preconceptions were revised. While most of the men consistently chose active or passive roles, there were cases in which sex partners exchanged these roles. Michael D., for example, in recounting his technique of lovemaking with his partner, described how they reversed roles, stating, "We both have a chance to be aggressive or passive. When I'm passive I feel like a woman. . . . When I'm aggressive I want to feel his submissiveness and relaxation." In his comments about Michael, Henry concluded, "He demonstrates the futility of rigid classification of sex variants."[51]

In general, however, the gulf between the storytellers' narratives and Henry's conclusions points to the conflicting objectives of the research participants and the medical and scientific authorities. Especially in the case of those respondents who wanted to inform and educate Henry about gay life and the cause of homosexual rights, Henry's preconceived medical model, for the most part, blocked any meaningful dialogue.

THE FEMALE NARRATIVES

As in the case of the men, the women's narratives focused on sexual identity and coming out. Also consistent with the men, the women's sexual identities were closely linked with gender. Not all of the women thought of themselves as exclusively homosexual. Eleven of the forty women identified themselves as bisexual. After looking at the themes of sexual identity and coming out, I examine Henry's conclusions about the female cases.

Sexual Identities
With the exception of some of the bisexual women, the women linked their sexuality to gender roles. Among the lesbians, nineteen considered themselves to be "masculine" or "mannish" and ten identified with being "feminine." These were the labels they used when describing themselves and other women. I will thus use "mannish women" and "feminine

women" to distinguish among the lesbians. This gender distinction became more accented with the "butch" and "femme" roles that characterized the working-class lesbian subculture of the 1950s. Masculine-
feminine couples were in evidence as lesbian communities arose in the
1920s and 1930s. Even earlier, at the turn of the century, the publicized
trial of Alice Mitchell generated a popular association between lesbianism
and gender inversion, and this association was given stronger weight with
the appearance in 1928 of Radclyffe Hall's novel *The Well of Loneliness*.[52]

In the case of the fairies, the mannish women had a noticeable cross-
gender identity. Henry's introductory descriptions pointed to their masculine attributes. If they were in their twenties, they struck Henry as
"boyish"; if in their thirties or forties, they seemed "aggressive" and
"business-like." They were "masculine" in posture and movement, and
some lacked a "feminine sweetness" or "feminine gestures." Many affected tailored clothes and "mannish" hair.[53]

In their own words, many of these women celebrated their masculinity.
Ursula W., a twenty-eight-year-old violinist, proclaimed, "I have masculine traits. . . . I like to do things for people and not have them done for
me. . . . I like tailor-made clothes. No frills for me. I enjoy sports and prize
fights and doing the things that men do." Mildred B., a twenty-eight-year-
old office worker, in describing her affinity for tailored clothes, noted that
she had preferred them "even when I was a youngster. I used to borrow my
brother's shirts. . . . I preferred boy's clothes because they didn't get in your
way." Yet these women did not necessarily eschew feminine qualities. Ursula also admitted to having "feminine traits," stating, "I love to have a
home and to cook and I love kids." As in the case of some of the men, Ursula viewed herself as androgynous. Her sense of gender duality was also
projected to her partner Frieda S., who she described as "tiny and very
feminine . . . very virile and aggressive."[54]

Masculine pride was also reflected in the role these women assumed in
their sexual relations. Most preferred to take the masculine-identified active role. Myrtle K., a thirty-year-old black woman who was a male impersonator on the black vaudeville circuit, phallicized her sexuality by asserting, "My greatest pleasure is to have a woman go down on me. . . . I
insert my clitoris in the vagina just like the penis of a man. The only way I
get satisfaction is from active sex. . . . While a woman is going down on
me I visualize myself as a man and I talk as if I was a man. I say, 'Ain't that
a good dick? O baby ain't that good.'" She boastfully added, "Women enjoy it so much they leave their husbands." Yet in taking on the active role,
these women did not necessarily give up their physical identity of being a
woman. Alberta I., a thirty-year-old artist, articulated a gender duality in
describing her sexual performance:

I'm active, I'm a very active lover, and I wouldn't dream of being passive. I have no inhibitions about any activity in love. I can stop an orgasm whenever I want to. If I let myself go I can finish in two minutes or I can wait hours. I can realize the physical experience of being a man. I can look at a woman exactly as a man does. I'm really both. I can understand a man better than most women. I feel so much like a man that I don't understand how a woman falls in love with a woman.[55]

In this statement, Alberta constructed her sexuality in ways that combined women's physical sexual gratification with a psychological internalization of men's sexual desires and performance.

Complementing their active role, most mannish women preferred passive feminine women as sexual partners. Anticipating the 1950s role of the "stone butch," which reflected masculine untouchability, many did not want their partners to touch them. Their satisfaction was derived from being able to sexually arouse their passive lovers. Kathleen M., a thirty-year-old artist, recalled the thrill of seducing her lovers by declaring, "I deliberately made conquests and I made every woman that I went after, . . . The affairs were not mutual. I didn't want them to touch me and wouldn't let them. I got some physical satisfaction and also an ego satisfaction out of it." Pamela D., a forty-year-old English heiress, presented a different slant on her relationship with her passive partner, stating, "I take the initiative. . . . She is completely feminine and passive. I wouldn't permit her to reciprocate because I feel she is too pure."[56]

Mannish women who were sexually dominant typically extended their dominance to other aspects of their relationships. Eloise B., a twenty-six-year-old German-born gymnastics teacher, accounted for her sexual preference for women in terms of its compatibility with her need to be dominant. In her words, "The only men to whom I have been attracted have been weaker and less assertive than I am. . . . However, as I take the dominant role in every relationship, it seems more suitable and satisfactory for me to have intimate relationships with a woman." Some mannish women, who were more flexible in their sexual roles, nevertheless adopted a masculine attitude in their emotional relationship with their partners. Ursula W. portrayed her lover as maternal, complementing her own paternal feelings. According to Ursula, her partner "loves to do things for me. She's quite maternal and makes a baby out of me pretty much as Mother did. Her desire is to take my mother's place. I feel paternal toward her." Marvel W., a thirty-eight-year-old literary researcher, conveyed a protective concern about her partner, described in Henry's words as "comfort and freedom from anxiety on the part of Ellen appeared to be Marvel's prime concern."[57]

In contrast with the mannish women's various expressions of masculinity, the feminine women projected femininity. In dress and manner, Henry described them as having a "feminine allure" or a "distinctly feminine bearing." Most expressed a preference for masculine-appearing women who were aggressive and assertive and assumed the active role in sex.[58]

Describing her preference for masculine women, Frieda S., a twenty-eight-year-old sculptor, stated, "Being small in stature myself I always admired women who were forceful, large, and masculine." She characterized her partner, Ursula, as "100 per cent masculine, both mentally and physically." The feminine women's attraction to mannish women was often accompanied by a desire for such women to be aggressive sexually. As Sara B., a twenty-eight-year-old divorced mother, declared, "Most of my women lovers have been more or less masculine in appearance, dress, and bearing. I like a woman who is aggressive sexually." In a similar vein, Pearl M., a forty-nine-year-old black actress, recounted her sexual relations with her partner, Pamela D., "She always takes the initiative and I'm always passive. She hugs me and kisses my lips, breasts, and genitals."[59]

There was also some diversity among the feminine women in the way they constructed their sexuality. In contrast to the typical preference for masculine women, Susan N., a black twenty-six-year-old muse for several gay Harlem Renaissance writers, preferred feminine women who allowed her to take the active role. She reported that in her affairs with women, "I took the active part. . . . They were feminine and willing to take the passive part." Susan, herself, had a feminine identity, indicating that she had never been a "tomboy" and usually wore "very feminine clothes." Frieda S. also stood out among the feminine women because of her strong feminist beliefs. She made a point of rejecting the conventional female role, revealing, "I had always been a great worshipper of virile women and women of achievement. . . . I made a compact with myself that I would be as strong as these women had been, that I would not be dependent upon men and that I wouldn't yield to them or lose my personality through wifehood and childbearing."[60]

The bisexual women were a varied group, some of whom expressed their lesbianism along masculine lines, others along feminine lines, and still others who did not have a gender-differentiated homosexual identity. They also varied in the strength of their bisexual feelings. While most of these women considered themselves to be bisexual because of their history of same- and opposite-sex attraction, others had only recently taken on such an identity through their heterosexual exploration.[61]

Some of the bisexual women made no differentiation in the strength of their attraction to both women and men. Olga R., a twenty-eight-year-old who was financially supported by her "bisexual" male companion, declared, "My bedfellows are ever changing and there is alternating attraction to men and women. I'm completely and thoroughly bisexual and I hope I never have to make a choice." Rebecca R., a twenty-five-year-old aspiring actress, proclaimed, "I'm pleased rather than confused by my bisexuality and just now any strong individual or influence could divert my energies into one channel or another." Other bisexuals drew a distinction between their same- and opposite-sex attraction. Some were attracted to men for physical sex and, in contrast, to women for love. As Blanche T., a thirty-nine-year-old entertainer, expressed it, "In . . . affairs with men. . . . I liked the idea of intercourse, the physical relation . . . but I couldn't fall in love with a man. . . . I want women because I adore them rather than for sex." Molly N., a forty-one-year-old dancer, confided that in the past she "enjoyed sex with men more than with women," but added, "I'm not as much thrilled now with a man. Love between women is so delicate and it is not the sex. It can exist without sex." She indicated some doubts about her bisexuality, stating, "I think I'm bisexual but I prefer women."[62]

The differentiated attraction to same- and opposite-sex partners took another form for other bisexual women. In the cases of Roberta H. and Fannie E., the attraction to men involved economic support and social acceptance. Both were involved in long-standing relationships with a male lover. Roberta, thirty-six, was the mistress of a married stockbroker. She reported, "I have sex with him and once in a while I enjoy it." Although she indicated that her "deepest pleasure" came from "holding a woman very close," she confided, "I don't know which sex I prefer." Elaborating on her mixed feelings, she admitted that while she admired women, she did not like to be seen publicly with them. In contrast, she stated, "Men can take me places." Fannie, although only twenty-three, had lived with several men and was at the time the mistress of a married physician. Reflecting on her heterosexual affairs, she remarked, "Sex with men is passively pleasant but there has been no romantic attachment to any of them such as I have experienced with women." She was torn between going off to California with her girlfriend or staying with the physician. Leaning toward the latter, she indicated, "I might marry him now because he understands me."[63]

As several of the above cases suggest, a bisexual identity could be fluid, in some instances giving way to a same-sex identity or in other instances being tenuously held as a compromised self-image encompassing both secretive lesbian expression and openly visible heterosexuality. Among the bisexuals, there were also some women who began to redefine themselves as bisexual after a history of unfulfilling lesbian experience. Rose S., a thirty-five-year-old businesswoman, had married when she was nineteen. Two years later she fell in love with a woman and left her husband and child. After her first lesbian relationship, which lasted only six months, she had another failed lesbian affair. When she left her husband, she had also taken on a markedly masculine identity. At the time she was interviewed, she revealed, "In the past few years I have gradually broken down the antagonism to men and I have grown to enjoy . . . men sexually." She noted that this change came about through her affair with a married man. She now felt that she wanted "to be a part of a man's life . . . to get married." Nevertheless, she indicated that she was still attracted to women, commenting, "Maybe I'll outgrow women, I don't know." Maria S., a twenty-five-year-old worker in the decorating field, spoke about her affair with fellow worker Yetta T. She was "madly in love with her," but eventually Yetta fell in love with another woman. Subsequently, Maria had her first heterosexual experience, which she described as "one of those beautiful accidents," and expressed the hope that "some day . . . I shall meet a congenial man and marry." She also revealed, "I think my homosexual relations have enriched me. . . . [I]t was a sort of coming out. It has matured me."[64] And yet despite her interpretation that her lesbian experience prepared her for heterosexual marriage, at the close of the interview, she still voiced a desire to live with Yetta.

Coming Out Stories

As in the case of the gay men, the coming out experience of identity awareness represented a turning point for the lesbian women. For the bisexual women, because their identities were more fluid, the coming out experience was not as marked. In looking back at their lives, most of the women revealed instances of their same-sex attraction prior to any self-defined sexual identity. For the mannish women, their childhood crushes on other girls were closely connected with their masculine inclinations. In recounting her attraction for a girl, Patricia D., a twenty-two-year-old who held various jobs as a nursemaid and waitress, recalled, "We just kissed and hugged each other but I wished I was a boy so I could make love to the girls." Most of the mannish women, in fact, referred to their long-held desire to be boys as well as early signs of a masculine identity. Myrtle K., for example, stated, "I always wanted to be a boy," adding that her parents had wanted a boy and "always treated me as if I were a boy." Betty E., thirty-five and recently separated from her husband, remarked, "I preferred to play with boys and it seemed that I could wish myself into being a boy." Regina C., forty-two, who left her husband some fifteen years before, typified the childhood recollections of cross-gender identity. She reminisced about growing up in Jamaica, "From the time I stopped crawling I was taught how to hold a cricket bat, throw a ball, swim, and jump. My father was pleased with my masculine tendencies. . . . I never wore girls' clothes if I could get hold of boys' things." These women's early masculine identity was shattered when they first experienced menstruation. They were now confronted with the reality of their female body. Irene K., a forty-seven-year-old businesswoman, stated, "I had always hated being a girl and I felt menstruation was an atrocious thing to foist on a human being." When Patricia D. had her first period, she recalled, "I felt so embarrassed and I wished still more that I was a boy."[65]

In contrast to the mannish women, most of the feminine women recalled that as children they felt comfortable with their gender. Aimee C., a thirty-five-year-old department store clerk, declared, "I didn't wish I was a boy and I played with dolls." Susan N. stated, "I wasn't a tomboy and I liked fluffy clothes and the typical girlish games and pleasures." With respect to menstruation, Susan added, "My periods started when I was fourteen. . . . I didn't resent it." For Angelina T., a twenty-six-year-old graduate student, menstruation represented a turning point. She recalled, "My periods started when I was thirteen. . . . I think I wished I were a boy when I was young but by the time I was thirteen I was satisfied with being a girl."[66] Among the bisexual women, masculine or feminine identity in childhood generally conformed to their masculine or feminine tendencies as adults.

Most of the women referred to childhood crushes, either with other girls or adult women they came in contact with, such as teachers or camp counselors. These attachments were not associated with any sexual meaning, as exemplified by Julia I., a twenty-four-year-old practical nurse, who commented, "I had many crushes on older girls and on teachers. . . . I knew very little about sex then and was unaware of the significance of attachments for girls. Our intimacies went only as far as kisses and embraces." Mae C., a thirty-two-year-old single mother, spoke of younger girls who had crushes on her in high school as well as her admiration for a teacher who, in her words, "liked me and was very nice to me but she didn't know about my interest. I was not aware of homosexuality at that time."[67]

As teenagers, sexual advances from boys generally turned off the mannish and feminine women. To please their parents or to be popular with other girls, many dated but found any physical contact to be repulsive. Nora M., a thirty-year-old who held a managerial position in a business firm, recounted, "I went out with boys, not because I liked them but because other girls did. . . . The boys wanted to kiss me but that seemed very stupid to me and it annoyed me very much." Sadie S., a twenty-nine-year-old office worker, remembered, "When I was sixteen I had a boy friend. I seemed to be very fond of him and I tried to satisfy his desires. He started to have intercourse with me but it hurt so terribly and I was so disgusted that I stopped him." In some cases, the women reported having sexual encounters with older men. According to Sara B., "Heckled and criticized by my mother [for showing no interest in boys], I did try to get interested in men and at eighteen I had intercourse with a man forty years old. . . . In sexual intercourse with him I was absolutely cold." Many of the bisexual women also reported negative heterosexual experiences as adolescents. For them, sex with men only became attractive when they reached their twenties. There were some, however, who did report positive heterosexual encounters. Olga R. stated, "When I was fifteen I began to have sex relations with . . . [a] man, aged twenty-four. I found him very attractive and he loved me very much." Maria S. confided, "When I was nineteen I met a very attractive young man. . . . I fell very much in love with him and was sexually aroused."[68]

The coming out process for the women, like the men, represented "coming out" into homosexual society, rather than breaking the silence of the "closet" to the straight world. Their lesbian acculturation encompassed varied patterns. For many, especially the mannish women, their first homosexual experience sparked an awareness of their sexuality. According to Myrtle K., "The first woman I was with was a white actress much older. She was twenty-five and I was thirteen. . . . It was about this time that I first realized I was homosexual." Marvel W. reported, "When I was twenty I had my first physical expression of homosexual love. . . . I was much aroused and had an orgasm. It seemed perfectly natural." After an unsatisfactory heterosexual affair, Alberta I. recalled, "When I was twenty-four . . . I went to a New Year's party and I was very bored until suddenly I saw a woman who simply made me feel faint she was so beautiful. . . . She knew what she wanted and I immediately knew what I wanted."[69]

Compared with the mannish women, the feminine women had more heterosexual experience. As adolescents, their femininity made them popular with boys. In their twenties, several had been married but left their husbands through divorce or separation. Pearl M. described her coming out, "Finally, at the age of forty-one and after having become disillusioned in my second husband, I had my first homosexual experience. It was a colored actress. She made no direct advances but we danced together and something very terrific happened to me, a very electric thing. It made me know that I was homosexual." Frieda S. confided, "The first liaison in which I had active sex was my sixteenth year. I was sleeping with a girl. . . . While I was married I dreamt about masturbating with this girl." Susan N. was repulsed by heterosexual experience at an early age. She reported being raped at thirteen by a boy two years older, adding, "By the time I was fifteen I was attracted sexually to women and I was conscious of them as possible lovers." The bisexual women also had considerable heterosexual experience but, unlike the feminine women, found it satisfying. In the case of Rebecca R., her liaison with a man made her doubt her exclusive homosexuality. In her words, "He was so clever in his attentions that I felt I would never want a woman again. I was satisfied so completely by him that I began to feel I was not a Lesbian." Rebecca, aged twenty-five, thought of herself as "typical of a most obvious group of young American woman who had homosexual tendencies."[70] She believed that most lesbians became bisexual by age thirty.

Some women experienced their coming out through exposure to lesbian communities in such places as New York, Hollywood, Berlin, Paris, and Capri. Patricia D. declared, "When I was eighteen . . . [I] went to Hollywood. Before this . . . I didn't realize what homosexuality was. I met some Lesbians and one of them was very fond of me." Eloise B. reminisced, "When I was twenty-one . . . I went to Berlin to study. Soon I was spending the evening in circles where there were only women and I found out more about homosexuality." Personal confrontation also sparked sexual awareness. Nora M. met a fellow office worker who confided to her "that he was worried because he loved men and I then said that I felt the same toward women. He told me that we were not supposed to be that way and gave me some books like Krafft-Ebing's on queer people. For the first time I realized what it was all about but I kept on having dates with girls." Betty E. remembered, "I was called to the office of the social director in college. She told me I was too much interested in girls and that I must stop or get out. She opened my eyes as to what I was doing."[71]

The first signs of lesbian self-awareness were easily accepted by some, such as Myrtle K. and Susan N., who, respectively at thirteen and fifteen, understood their homosexual feelings. Many of the women, however, were conflicted between their homosexual desires and the social pressure exerted by their families about marriage. As a result, they referred to a common pattern of seeking out heterosexual affairs, which turned out to be unsatisfying. Pamela D., for example, reported that while she was in a lesbian relationship, "I was having normal sexual relations with men. . . . [One] was . . . with an old friend. I liked him and wanted to please him. He wanted to marry me. Repeated sexual relations with him brought no satisfaction." Between lesbian relationships, Pamela continued to have sporadic affairs with men, which she described as "never emotional and not successful physically." This pattern stopped when she began her current five-year relationship with Pearl M. Some women, such as Sara B., gave into family pressure and got married. As she described her decision, "My sole desire was to escape the tyranny of my mother so at twenty I married the man I was engaged to."[72] She continued to have affairs with women, and when her husband found out, the marriage ended.

The ending of the women's stories represented how they dealt with their sexuality at the time they were interviewed. As in the case of the men, their coping skills ranged from an integrated acceptance of their sexual identity to pervasive conflict and anxiety. Among those struggling with negative feelings, Fannie E., a bisexual who was the mistress of a physician, confided, "Life is pretty unsettled. . . . I'm torn between . . . going off to California with Patricia and staying with the doctor." Earlier in the interview, she had noted, "I haven't been happy since I left school. Sometimes life is not worth living. I have often thought of suicide." Sara B. spoke about her desire to change in reaction to her family's persecution: "I have wanted to be different so I wouldn't have to be living a life of subterfuge. At home I was looked upon as a kind of freak and I was told how dreadful it was to be homosexual. . . . I have consulted several psychiatrists in order to change my life but I never get anywhere." Ellen T. attributed her homosexuality to the way her mother brought her up, stating, "I blame her for my whole development . . . but no matter how much you understand it now you can't turn around and be attracted to men." Resigned to her fate, she added, "You can turn . . . [homosexuality] into constructive fields if you are clear enough about it."[73]

On the positive side, many women expressed pride about their sexuality. Alberta I., an artist, proclaimed, "I have a great confidence in the future. . . . Homosexuality hasn't interfered with my work. It has made it what it is." Ursula W., a violinist, declared, "My sex life has never caused me any regrets. I'm very much richer by it. I feel it has stimulated me and my imagination and increased my creative powers." Reflecting the integration of her sexuality with her religion, Myrtle K. stated, "I go to church every Sunday. I don't think God would have made me queer if it wasn't right." Many women referred to their committed relationships as a validation of their positive sexual identity. Pearl M. commented, "I don't regret homosexual relations. This relationship with Pamela affords a tenderness I had never known," and Ursula W. recounted, "I'm so satisfied living with Frieda. . . . I would not trade places with any of the young married couples I know."[74]

The patterns revealed in the women's stories reflect the particular characteristics of the sex variants sample, a sample comprised primarily of working women in their twenties and thirties. With respect to their work life, most were connected with the arts or the theater, although several were in the business or commercial sphere. While some were dependent on husbands or male lovers, most were financially independent. The sex variants sample was thus a mainly middle-class cohort of women who were in many cases successfully competing with men in their work life. Moreover, in their social life, these women were a part of the cultural milieu of lesbian life in Greenwich Village and Harlem.

Noting the characteristics of this sample, it is possible to make comparisons with other samples of lesbians and bisexual women during the same
period. The pattern of masculine/feminine roles is consistent with other observations of lesbian life in various American cities during the 1930s. In
particular, the tendency for mannish women to view their sexuality as an
expression of gender inversion is consistent with what Elizabeth Kennedy
and Madeline Davis report in their study of working-class lesbians in Buffalo during this period. On the other hand, Esther Newton's analysis of lesbian life in the 1930s in the summer community of Cherry Grove, New
York, provides a markedly different portrait. These upper-class women,
who were part of the lesbian cultural elite of New York City, viewed the
masculine/feminine roles as esthetically repulsive. They had more in common with the literary and upper-class lesbian circles in Paris during the
interwar era, a group that fostered a distinctively elegant lesbian style. As
documented by Kennedy and Davis, the butch/femme culture itself went
through a metamorphosis by the 1950s. In this postwar period, women
moved away from the inversion model to a role-playing mode in which they
would try out the particular role that worked for them in attracting other
women. Moreover the butch/femme culture became increasingly associated
with working-class women. In the context of McCarthyism, many middle-
class lesbians were hesitant about advertising their sexuality.[75]

The Medicalized Interpretation

As in his medicalized analysis of the male case histories, Henry turned
statements of pride into signs of pathology. Kathleen M., for example, expressed her joy in being in a committed relationship and adopting a baby.
In her words, "Since we have been living together our lives are fuller and
happier. We create things together and we are devoted to our baby." Henry's reaction was to interpret these feelings as illusionary rather than valid.
As he expressed it, "She feels she has demonstrated that homosexuality
does not result in an empty life. . . . She seems inclined to feel that she and
her friend will remain faithful to each other." In response to Ursula W.'s
expression of deep satisfaction in her relationship with Frieda S. and
their desire to have children, Henry rather mockingly declared, "The original triangle of father and mother and child would then be complete. . . .
[Ursula] and Frieda live just as husband and wife." Henry's predilection to
view lesbian relationships as inherently pathological also led him to distort the personal significance of the passive/active roles. Thus, in commenting on Pamela D.'s union with Pearl M., he stated, "Pamela's happiness with the singer borders on the pathological: Pamela adored her and
believed she was too pure to reciprocate in their affectionate relations."[76]

Henry also turned expressions of social protest into symptoms of personal pathology. Marvel W.'s statements about the unfair treatment of homosexuals and the exploitation of women, Jews, and "negroes" was interpreted as "Marvel has come to project some of her own difficulties onto social and economic conditions." Ellen T.'s stated concern about the treatment of homosexuals was attributed by Henry to represent her "bitterness . . . projected on society."[77]

Paralleling his commentary about the male cases, Henry was pessimistic about the women's future. According to Henry, Molly N.'s two failed marriages predisposed her to prefer sex with women. As a result, she forfeited the benefits of being a wife and mother. In his words, "There is little evidence that Molly appreciates the emotional values of being either a wife or a mother." His prognosis for Betty E., who left her husband because he was "a poor lover," was "Betty still might be won over by a man who was virile enough to elicit a feminine response from her." Yet, he added, "her physical charm will before long be inadequate to maintain her popularity. Such comfort as she now gets from her companionship with girls is offset by her painful awareness of the stigma of homosexuality." Commenting about Marian J., a black woman in her fifties who expressed regrets about not having children, he stated, "Marian has lived long enough to learn that homosexuality is likely to end in loneliness, in ostracism." Finally, despite the feelings of fulfillment expressed by those women who were in committed relationships, Henry offered negative predictions. Referring to Ellen T. and Marvel W., Henry prognosticated, "They have achieved a 'married state' although they are not entirely compatible. . . . Both Ellen and Marvel may be able to compromise and adjust their individual needs but the records of other homosexual alliances indicate that a permanent relationship is unlikely."[78]

In general, Henry was insensitive to the importance most of the women placed on finding personal fulfillment through romantic attachments. Not only did he pathologize and downplay the experiences of those in committed relationships; he criticized those who experienced a series of relationships. Thus, for Olga R. and Angelina T., their homosexuality reflected a "futile search for affection." In the case of Alberta I., Henry focused on her masculine role in relationships in which she manifested "a desire to control and possess older, beautiful women." However, Alberta spoke about her series of monogamous relationships, acknowledging that she had yet to find the person she could commit herself to in a long-term relationship. She was, nevertheless, optimistic, expressing not only a "great confidence in the future" because of her work as an artist, but also because, as she stated, "I shall probably have a home of my own some day. I hope I can find a person I can share the rest of my life with."[79]

VOICES OF DESPAIR, VOICES OF RESISTANCE

Toward the end of their follow-up interviews with Henry, the participants responded to a series of questions about homosexuality, specifically, "What is your attitude toward homosexuality?" "Toward your own form of sexuality?" and "What should the attitudes of the general public be?"[80] The tone of their responses varied between expressions of despair about their personal situation and expressions of resistance against the way society treated homosexuality. These feelings were fairly evenly distributed within both the male and female samples; that is, about half the men and women voiced despair while the other half voiced resistance. Despair tended to be associated with signs of a negative self-image, and resistance was generally concomitant with positive self-assertions. In a few instances, respondents voiced both personal despair and social resistance.

The deepest level of despair was revealed in feelings of depression and suicidal thought. Although only thirty, Louis E. acknowledged a fear of aging, stating, "In recent years I am more inclined to get depressed. . . . [I]n ten years what will I be like? I'm not pursued by men now. Men used to pick me up. I want to attract." Betty E., conflicted about ending her marriage, revealed, "I dislike my inability to come to a decision and recently I've noticed a tendency to cry with little provocation. I'm apt to start crying at any minute." Depression combined with suicidal ideation is illustrated by Salvatore N., who confided, "The future looks dark. . . . I'm thinking more and more that I don't give a darn any more. Thoughts of suicide have entered my mind frequently." Similarly, Fannie E. declared, "I haven't been happy since I left school. Sometimes life is not worth living. I have often thought of suicide."[81]

Signs of anxiety also reflected despair. Blanche T., beset by financial problems and, at thirty-nine, concerned about her ability to attract women, reported, "In the last ten years I have become unnaturally concerned about my health. I'm frequently querulous and complaining and I have become almost a complete hypochondriac." Theodore S. voiced anxiety about his family finding out that he was homosexual, declaring, "I don't get along with normal friends and I don't see them as much as I used to. It's made me introspective and insecure. I'm afraid someone will find out. I'm afraid if they find out they would tell my family." For some, personal insecurity was transposed into hostility toward homosexuals. Paul A. commented, "The talk of the average homosexual is disgusting. They talk about conquests. . . . I really feel that homosexuals should not be in groups of more than three." Nora M. proclaimed, "The more I see of homosexuals the more I disapprove of them. . . . I can't understand why the average homosexual is incapable of telling the truth. My personal experience with them has been disillusioning."[82]

Among the men and women who revealed negative feelings, some expressed a wish to be cured and looked to Henry for help. Leo S., who had been arrested and briefly jailed for having "relations" with a man, stated, "I'm interested now in overcoming homosexuality. I think it has made me nervous. It makes me a social outcast." Henry, in fact, followed up on this case by agreeing to see Leo's sister, Bertha. According to Henry, Bertha was "anxious about Leo's chances of being cured." Henry indicated that the first step was "to help Leo re-establish confidence in himself," though he held no promise that Leo could be "cured." Caroline E. revealed her motivation for being in the study by stating, "The future looks pretty bad or I wouldn't be here. I would like to get married and have children. The whole idea of homosexuality seems useless. . . . [T]here is absolutely no future." According to Henry, her meeting with him produced "beneficial results." Rather than return for her follow-up interview, he reported, "a year later she indicated that she was reasonably contented in a heterosexual adjustment and she preferred not to recall her homosexual episodes." While not looking for a cure, Howard N., a transvestite, hoped that Henry could help him find the "right woman"; a woman who was sympathetic to his need for cross-dressing. When he realized he wasn't going to get any help, Howard angrily said, "You sit there and listen and offer nothing of yourself. It's like talking into a dictaphone."[83]

Resistance was reflected in declarations of personal pride, indications of interest and commitment to the research project, stated concerns about homosexual rights, and for the women, feminist attitudes. Exemplifying personal pride, Gabriel T. proclaimed, "I realize I'm different from the majority and yet I don't think I'm unique. I have been drawn to men as far back as I can remember but I have always felt normal and I have never wished to be different." Other instances include Kathleen M.'s defiant statement, "When Mother told me about homosexuality she told me it was abnormal, that there was no satisfaction and that the result was an empty life. I disagree, I don't care what people think and I avoid people who ask personal questions. My personal life is my own affair," and Alberta I.'s affirmation as an artist: "Homosexuality hasn't interfered with my work, it has made it what it is."[84]

Several of the participants revealed their deep commitment to the sex variants project, reflecting their desire to help Jan Gay accomplish her goal of accurately portraying gay and lesbian lives. This commitment was voiced not only in response to Henry's questions but also volunteered at the beginning of the first interview. For example, according to Henry, Michael D.'s "interest in the subject of homosexuality is such that he expressed a fear of not being included in the group studied," and in his own words, "I have been terrifically interested in this study. I feel it is a terrific benefit." Gene S. revealed, "I am greatly interested in this study and I hope it will lead to an interpretation of sex deviation which will do something to remove the stigma from the homosexual." Henry noted that Virginia K. and Marvel W. were pleased to contribute and be identified with the study, and even though Max N. demonstrated "no intellectual interest in the study, [h]e frankly states that he presented himself merely as a favor to the field worker" (an obvious reference to Jan Gay).[85]

In some cases, the commitment by participants to tell their stories was expressed in ways that revealed underlying tensions in their relationship with Henry. In the case of Julius E., for example, Henry noted that Julius was eager to cooperate but did not have enough confidence to volunteer information. Yet as the interview proceeded, according to Henry, Julius was surprised at his capacity to open up and remarked that he had "never before talked so much about himself." Several of the participants, especially the men, had mixed feelings about placing trust in Henry's ability to protect their anonymity. Nevertheless, they were willing to take the risk, as exemplified by Reginald M., who was anxious about revealing his homosexuality to professional associates, but as Henry observed, his cooperation in the study was stimulated by his "resentment over the unfair treatment of homosexuals." Marvel W., though motivated to participate, expressed initial apprehension about being interviewed, revealing, "I was afraid to have someone take me to pieces."[86]

Virginia K. succinctly voiced the case for homosexual rights by proclaiming, "The homosexual should have the same position in society as the so-called normal person has. They wouldn't then be all running around to dives and getting persecuted. They wouldn't be so sorry for themselves. They wouldn't be so queer or fight people who didn't understand. They wouldn't have to be hiding more that 50 per cent of the time." Frieda S. asserted, "I feel that a relationship between two women such as that of Ursula and myself is eminently proper. To me the usual distinction of normal and abnormal is baseless. I rebel against the narrow code of the world, the one that points a maligning finger at two people whose pattern of life does not accord with ordinary standards." Noel W., a writer, suggested that through his work he could contribute to the cause of homosexual rights: "For some time I have been interested in homosexuality as a cause. I had a feeling that through my writing I should do something about the homosexual cause, a sort of propaganda for those who could see what I meant."[87]

In support of homosexual rights, several participants referred to the strategic need to curb public displays of stereotyped behavior, pointing to the effeminate fairy and the mannish lesbian. Gene S., for example, made a point of distancing himself from the "obvious, blatant, made-up boys whose public appearance and behavior provoke onerous criticism" and expressed his hope that the sex variants research would contribute to eradicating "the stigma from the homosexual." Julius E., who was effeminate, nevertheless was mindful of discretion, noting, "It is nobody's business what a person does as long as he lives his life quietly. If he doesn't he deserves nothing but ridicule." Martha D. declared, "I can't see why people make all this fuss. . . . [I]t isn't terribly important how anybody gets their sex life. . . . I don't go around broadcasting. I detest people who are obvious."[88]

While those expressing support for the cause of homosexual rights were generally accepting of their own sexuality, there were a few who were struggling. Ellen T. was sensitive to the social hostility faced by homosexuals, stating, "Homosexuals are likely to turn out to be antisocial, disruptive people purely because of the attitude which society takes toward them." Nevertheless, she viewed her own homosexuality as the result of faulty psychological development, lamenting, "No matter how much you understand it now you can't turn around and be attracted to men." Will G. was committed to improving "the lot of the underprivileged sex variant," yet he stated, "I do not desire my homosexuality and keenly resent homosexuals and being classed with them." Will viewed himself as an advocate for the plight of hustlers, the "underprivileged" sex variants who engaged in homosexual relations as a means of economic survival. His real name was Thomas Painter, and in his role as a research assistant for the sex variants committee, he recruited the small subsample of hustlers. Painter's later career as an activist and his continued struggle with his homosexuality are dealt with in chapters 6 and 7.[89]

Among the women, many had expressed pride in appropriating masculine attributes and thus rejecting the conventional, submissive feminine role. Some translated these signs of gender subversion into explicit feminist attitudes. Frieda S., described by Henry as a "thorough feminist with intense sex bitterness," declared, "I made a compact with myself . . . that I would not be dependent upon men and that I wouldn't yield to them or lose my personality through wifehood and childbearing." Irene K., a businesswoman, commented, "In stories an ideal man is competent, dependable, two-fisted, can fight his way and protect the woman and at the same time be tender, sweet and thoughtful to her. As far as I am concerned there is no such person." She added, "I've always resented feminine helplessness and I get satisfaction out of doing a man's job better than he can. . . . It's marvelous to be a woman with a man's brain." Marvel W., anticipating the lesbian feminist position of the 1970s, asserted, "Being a feminist . . . might make a woman turn away from heterosexuality. It happened to be my only course." Virginia K., in speaking about the need for homosexual rights, alluded to the connection between a masculine identity and gender subversion. She noted that if lesbians were not persecuted, they wouldn't have the need to be "so mannish or on the defensive about things."[90]

Through their expressions of resistance to the prejudice and discrimination against homosexuals, roughly half of the sex variants participants shared the emancipatory objectives of Jan Gay's research project. Moreover, among the women, many voiced their protest against patriarchy. Even among those in the throes of despair, there was some understanding that their personal distress might be alleviated through medical treatment. They were thus motivated to contribute to a research project that could potentially enlighten medical specialists and sex researchers in the search for a cure. This is suggested by Archibald T.'s comment, "Homosexuality is very empty. . . . If there is a cure for homosexuality I hope it is found. That's why I am subjecting myself to all of this."[91]

In essence, Gay's research project and the active participation of homosexual, bisexual, and transvestite volunteers represented a grassroots collective effort to resist the mistreatment of homosexuals and other sexual minorities. The avenue chosen was to have their voices heard, to describe their own experiences, to erase the invisibility of their reality, to counter the imposed depictions of their lives by hostile and unsympathetic spokespersons. Indeed, this has been the path traveled by all oppressed groups in their liberatory struggles. As bell hooks states, "Oppressed people resist by identifying themselves as subjects, by defining their reality, shaping their new identity, naming their history, telling their story."[92]

To accomplish this mission of claiming subjective voice, Gay and the sex variants participants had to rely on medical and scientific experts to convey their stories and interpret them in an understanding and sympathetic way. Without the political leverage of an established national homosexual rights movement (only begun in the 1950s and not achieved until the late 1960s), the New York homosexual activists had no resources to draw upon other than to form an alliance with socially recognized spokespersons. The interests of the experts, however, undermined the success of their endeavor. The sex variants researchers thought they were helping the participants, but their assumptions of pathology meant that that help would take the form of therapy aimed at controlling desire. While some participants shared this goal and were thus willing to submit themselves to the authority of the experts, Gay and those participants committed to the cause of homosexual rights were interested in working with the experts as a means of gaining more control over their own lives. They needed the experts as allies in the struggle for social recognition and acceptance.

COMMUNITY EMPOWERMENT AND EXPERT AUTHORITY

In a generally favorable review of Henry's *Sex Variants,* anthropologist Ashley Montagu refers to the empowering potential of the autobiographical texts. In his words:

> The eighty histories in these two volumes are . . . the histories of the subjects as given by themselves. . . . In that lies their great value. Dr. Henry has performed the task of translating them from the shorthand record to the printed page most admirably. Except for the record of his "Impressions" in the Résumé at the conclusion of each chapter, and the half dozen pages of "Impressions" in Appendix I, Dr. Henry has kept his own views entirely out of the picture.[93]

Montagu believed that through such a record of self-presented life histories, homosexuals could obtain the just and sympathetic understanding they deserved. Yet even though he acknowledged the hostile social conditions homosexuals were subjected to, quoting from several of the participants' own statements, he uncritically accepted Henry's medical interpretation of homosexuality as a maladjustment primarily induced by psychological causes.

Granting the oppressed a voice in unequal power relationships does not lead to their empowerment. As Montagu's reactions indicate, Henry's voice of authority served to reinforce the social control of homosexuality exercised by medical and scientific experts. Kum-Kum Bhavani points out that empowerment involves the capacity of oppressed groups to influence the terms of their everyday life. For voice to be empowering it must lead to action, that is, positive change for powerless communities. While Henry and his sex variants collaborators acknowledged the unjust treatment of homosexuals by religious and legal authorities, they sought to improve the lives of homosexuals by identifying homosexuality as a medical problem to be solved by medical and scientific experts. Hence, the life stories by the sex variants participants were stripped of their empowering potential and transformed into objectified data to validate Henry's psychiatric interpretation.[94]

When the *Sex Variants* monograph was published in 1941, some of the participants did, in fact, express their disappointment. Gershon Legman, who worked as a bibliographer for Robert L. Dickinson and contributed the glossary of homosexual slang contained in the monograph, conveyed this. In his correspondence with Alfred C. Kinsey, Legman reported that several participants felt they were treated unfairly by Henry and also believed the two-volume book did little to shed light on the subject of homosexuality.[95]

Jan Gay was also unhappy with her experience in the sex variants project. She voiced her disappointment to Dickinson and Legman, each of whom conveyed her feelings to Kinsey. The ten years she had committed to producing a definitive study of lesbianism had been deflected into Henry's monograph. It's no surprise that her involvement in the sex variants study marked the end of her career as a homophile activist. Not only was she displeased with the results of her efforts, but also during the course of the project she suffered a bitter personal loss. Her partner, Zhenya Gay, who had adopted the same last name and was the illustrator for her children's books, left her for another woman. As a result, Gay's drinking problem worsened and she left New York in 1940 for Mexico, where she became director of public relations for the Latin American Institute. In 1946 she returned to New York and worked as a public relations consultant. By this time she had apparently overcome her alcoholism, and in 1950 she moved to San Francisco and became interested in doing research evaluating the effectiveness of Alcoholics Anonymous programs. There is no record of whether Gay was successful in this venture, but she continued her career in public relations and she did research editing for the University of California Medical School. In 1960 she died of breast cancer at the age of fifty-eight, survived by her partner of seven years, Marjorie Fritz.[96]

While the life stories of the sex variants participants fell short of their empowerment potential, they anticipated the genre of coming out stories in the post-Stonewall era. With the political impact of the gay and lesbian liberation movement, coming out stories contributed to the creation of a communal identity. By the 1970s, speaking on their own behalf, gay men and lesbians began to shape their own history. Before the 1970s it seems likely that the sex variants participants' accounts served as a resource for helping gay men and lesbians come to terms with their sexuality. In 1948 the *Sex Variants* monograph was reissued in a one-volume edition. Although still published by Harper's medical division, this edition went through more printings than its predecessor did. It therefore had a larger readership and was acquired by many college and university libraries. Just as the literature on homosexuality had helped some of the sex variants participants in their coming out, their personal narratives could be passed down in published form to future generations of gay men and lesbians seeking self-validation. And today, the preservation of their voices enables readers to reclaim a part of the history of gay and lesbian consciousness.[97]

Chapter 5

Henry and Gross and the Study of
Sex Offenders, 1937–72

> Segregation is the traditional form of treatment for known homo-
> sexuals in prison communities. . . . In too many cases it promotes the
> feeling of homosexual solidarity, and withdraws this group more and
> more from the conventional folkways. It separates them still further
> from the common life, and confirms them in their feeling that they
> compose a community within the community, with a special and arti-
> ficial life of their own.
>
> —George W. Henry and Alfred A. Gross,
> "The Homosexual Delinquent"

Beginning in the late nineteenth century, homosexuals had become the objects of medical and scientific scrutiny. They were not, however, necessarily passive victims. There were many instances, such as Richard von Krafft-
Ebing's and Katharine Bement Davis's respondents and the sex variants
participants, in which homosexuals took an active role, seizing the opportunity as research subjects to educate their interrogators and thus enlist professional experts as conduits for changing social attitudes about
homosexuality. Moreover, there were cases of active research collaboration between sex researchers and homosexuals, as exemplified by Jan
Gay's work with the Committee for the Study of Sex Variants. In this chapter I deal with the collaboration between homophile activist Alfred A.
Gross and psychiatrist George W. Henry. They worked together in studying and treating sex offenders from the late 1930s until Henry's death in
1964. The product of their collaboration increasingly reflected Gross's
voice, hidden behind Henry's printed words. After Henry's death, Gross
continued on his own through the early 1970s.

On 14 June 1970 Al Gross's seventy-fifth birthday was celebrated at an honorary service in Lower Manhattan's Episcopal Church of the Holy Communion. The church, on Sixth Avenue and Twentieth Street, was next door to the offices of the George W. Henry Foundation, which were housed in the church's parish house. Gross was the executive director of the foundation, an agency founded in 1948 to help young men charged with homosexual offenses. Gross's career as a homophile activist began in 1937 when he first became associated with Henry. A biographical sketch appeared in the church's program for the honorary service that charted Gross's career as a researcher and activist. No mention was made of how and why Gross embarked on his life's work. Indeed, this was not possible because Gross was a closeted gay man who began his endeavors after he had been removed as an Episcopalian priest.[1]

It is not clear what the exact circumstances of his defrocking were, but given his penchant for making sexual advances to young men, it seems likely that he was caught engaging in homosexual acts. Gross apparently took such risks because he moved in an underground gay ecclesiastical world in which clerics tended to feel protected by their revered status. Deeply troubled by his dismissal from the church in 1937, he sought help from Henry, who, as a result of his involvement with the sex variants study, had a reputation as a psychiatric specialist on homosexuality. During the course of treatment, Henry became aware of Gross's impressive educational background, which included a baccalaureate from the Yale Divinity School, a master's degree from Oxford, and a doctorate in philosophy from the University of Edinburgh. Apparently, with the promise of intellectual collaboration in mind, Henry suggested a form of work therapy in which Gross would function as his "contact man" for research on homosexuals and sex offenders. Gross took up Henry's offer and so began their three-decade collaboration. Gross officially joined the staff of the sex variants committee in 1938 as a research assistant. Over the course of his association with the sex variants committee and the Henry Foundation, Gross received a small monthly salary. His financial needs, however, were basically covered by the income he obtained from family investments.

HENRY AND GROSS'S RESEARCH ON SEX OFFENDERS

Gross's therapy with Henry in 1937 occurred at a time when New York City, under Mayor Fiorello La Guardia, was engaged in a campaign to stamp out sex crimes. La Guardia had been elected in 1933 as a reform candidate who promised to clean up the Prohibition era's legacy of corruption and vice during Mayor Jimmy Walker's tenure. Police crackdowns

on homosexual bars and cruising areas began early in La Guardia's administration. In 1937 the war on sex crimes was launched in response to
a series of shocking newspaper reports of sexual attacks on children. To
carry out this campaign, La Guardia established a Committee for the
Study of Sex Crimes, which was composed of psychiatrists, lawyers, and
criminologists. Based on the committee's recommendation, La Guardia instituted a policy that required sex offenders convicted of a felony (which
included consensual sodomy) to be examined at the psychiatric clinic of
Bellevue Hospital before sentencing. Custodial release was contingent
upon a psychiatrist's approval. Consistent with La Guardia's reform ethos,
the objective was to rehabilitate sex offenders.[2]

Sex offenses under New York State statutes included adultery, rape, incest, sex practices with a minor, indecent exposure, and "perverse" sex
practices. Homosexual offenses came under the last two categories. The
New York City Court of General Sessions dealt with the more serious
offenses (felonies), while the Magistrate's Court handled misdemeanors,
such as exposure and disorderly conduct. While psychiatric referrals were
made across the wide range of sex offenses, as Jennifer Terry notes, the
cases involving children and consensual homosexual acts between adults
received the most attention in published psychiatric reports.[3]

As a result of his work with the sex variants committee, Henry was a
member of the sex crimes committee and a consultant for the New York
City Department of Correction. Henry thus had access to sex offenders as
potential research subjects and, in view of his sex variants study, was especially interested in studying homosexual offenders. Consequently, sensing Gross's intellectual acumen, he enlisted Gross as his research collaborator. For their first project, Henry and Gross studied a sample of
homosexual offenders as well as a sample of homosexual men experiencing economic hardship. Since lower-class gay men were especially vulnerable to police arrest because they lacked social connections and were more
publicly visible, Henry and Gross thus constituted a combined sample of
one hundred "underprivileged" homosexual men.

Gross was given the assignment of studying the probation files of men
punished for homosexual offenses in the criminal courts. After several
months working with the court cases, he interviewed homosexual men in
public settings frequented by "drifters," such as parks, subway trains and
stations, the waterfront, bars, and restaurants. With respect to the probation files, Gross selected sixty-eight cases among the 1935 records of the
New York City Court of General Sessions and the Magistrate's Court. The
general sessions' cases were made up of fourteen men who were convicted
of sodomy (anal or oral sex) with a child (six to sixteen years of age). These
cases were described as "tenement-house sodomies," implying that the vic-

timized children and adolescents lived in the same premises as the convicted men. The fifty-four magistrate's court cases involved disorderly conduct in public places, such as subway toilets and movie theaters. For the sample of nonoffenders, Gross attempted to appear as a peer, by dressing "roughly" and showing up in public areas where he was likely to meet homosexual drifters. In these settings he gave the impression of being "an idler with a good bit of worldly knowledge" and consequently struck up conversations with the aim of getting the men to talk about themselves.[4] Suspicion was raised in only two instances. One man thought that Gross was doing a doctoral thesis and retreated from further conversation. Another man believed that Gross was a plainclothes policeman, but after being reassured to the contrary, he gave a satisfactory interview. Contacts were initially made with about eighty men, and of these Gross was able to produce thirty-two usable interview records.

Overall, the various subsamples produced a similar pattern. Most of these men were in their twenties and thirties, came from poor families often in "broken-home" situations, had limited education, and a spotty employment history. They were predominantly white—twenty-three of the one hundred were black. Henry and Gross noted that "despite the competition, the lying, the stealing, and the snobbery, there are observable signs of a certain camaraderie or solidarity among homosexuals." This, however, was not viewed as a desirable feature of homosexual life because it pulled homosexuals away from dealing with the realities of the larger community they had to function within. The underprivileged, because they frequented public places, were especially vulnerable to the risk of being caught by the police or victimized by extortionists. Consequently, according to the authors, they posed a high likelihood of becoming social liabilities, that is, creating a public nuisance, taxing the criminal justice system, and entering into a lifelong pattern of social delinquency. Henry and Gross concluded, "Thus far no effective medical, legal, or social means of dealing with the homosexual in an underprivileged social and economic situation has been discovered."[5]

Their published article about underprivileged homosexual men set the tone for their further collaboration. They were wedded to a project aimed at adjusting male homosexuals to society, especially those who came into conflict with the law. They spelled out the nature of the problem and then set about to study how convicted homosexuals, as well as other sex offenders, could be rehabilitated so that they would fit into the community. By early 1940 Henry and Gross had a research proposal, titled "The Study of the Sex Offender," which was sponsored by the sex variants committee. They proposed to study a sample of one hundred sex offenders once they were released from prison. The goal was to have a sample of ex-convicts who had been convicted of a variety of sex offenses, including sodomy, rape, incest, seduction, impairing the morals of minors, and indecent exposure. Based on their previous research, they expected that most of the subjects would be "underprivileged." Although they did not limit their sample in terms of age, their focus would be on the youthful offender (between the ages of sixteen and thirty) because of the greater therapeutic possibilities with such a group.[6]

The first step in the research plan involved the creation of the sample. This was to be carried out by Gross, acting in the role of a field-worker. He would conduct a preliminary survey of offenders who were about to be released from prison. Potential subjects would then be contacted with the aim of gaining their confidence. Once they agreed to participate, the research subjects would receive financial help to enable them to become established in the community. This procedure was introduced as a strategy to counter the long delays these men ordinarily faced in dealing with social agencies. Henry and Gross opined that it was because of such delays that the offender was tempted to repeat. The subjects were to initially receive a series of assessments, including a psychiatric interview (as in the sex variants study), psychological tests (the Rorschach, the masculinity-femininity test, and an IQ test), a physical examination, and an analysis of the male sex hormone (through assays of urine). The subjects were then to be followed up for two years, during which time they would receive prolonged supervision (in some cases, intensive psychiatric treatment), financial aid, and help in finding jobs. According to Henry and Gross, their study would be useful for the prevention of sex crimes, as well as providing guidelines for the rehabilitation of the sex offender.

Henry and Gross's ambitious proposal of a comprehensive after-care program for convicted sex offenders reflected the trend toward community care that was taking place in social welfare and correction. By the mid-1930s private social welfare agencies were affected by the economic reforms of the New Deal. Especially with the passage of the 1935 Social Security Act in which government took the responsibility for income maintenance, welfare agencies were free to devote their attention to offering direct services to individuals and families facing difficulties in psychological and social adjustment. By the 1930s in the field of corrections, probation had become commonplace and there was increasing interest in extramural treatment for former prisoners.[7]

As in the case of the other sex variants committee projects, Henry and Gross had no success in obtaining financial support from research foundations. They were, however, able to carry out two related research projects. The first was a general study of the social determinants of criminal behavior. This was based on a survey of case records of five hundred ad-

missions to the New York City Penitentiary on Riker's Island and interviews with a sample of two hundred first-offender young delinquents (between the ages of sixteen and twenty-one) in the "Tombs" Prison in New
York City. Henry and Gross concluded that all crime, including sex offenses, was a manifestation of personal maladjustment. Individuals prone
to crime suffered from a psychopathic personality disturbance, suggesting
a constitutionally based predisposition to antisocial behavior because of
poor impulse control. Henry and Gross, however, stressed the role of the
social environment as a breeding ground for young criminals. If youngsters
came from a background of poverty, they were especially disposed to a life
of crime because they lacked the social and economic resources that might
have deterred them from acting outside the law. The authors proposed an
ambitious ameliorative program involving such interventions as parental
guidance, improved vocational education, more effective social agencies,
and reforms in the criminal justice system aimed at reeducation and rehabilitation. Imbued with the New Deal ethos of reform, their rhetoric
was directed at establishing the case that sex offenders, like all criminals,
lacked impulse control (a manifestation of their psychopathic personalities), which could be effectively controlled through environmental manip-
ulation under the auspices of psychiatric supervision.[8]

Henry and Gross's second research project was a focused study dealing
with a group of imprisoned homosexuals. They gathered a sample of one
hundred inmates at the Riker's Island Penitentiary and indicated, once the
inmates were reassured of confidentiality, that there was little problem in
enlisting cooperation. Although not specified, it appears that Gross made
the initial contacts and Henry conducted the interviews. It is also possible,
as in the case of their study of the underprivileged homosexuals, that
Gross himself did the interviews. The chief objective of the study was to
compare the prison sample with the earlier report of the underprivileged
group. The prison sample was made up of homosexuals, most of whom
were first offenders, convicted of "homosexual disorderly conduct." Some
of the inmates were convicted of nonsexual crimes, such as larceny, for-
gery, drug addiction, and vagrancy. Nevertheless, because they were homosexual, they were housed in the segregated homosexual facility. Segre-
gating homosexuals was a common practice in prisons, going as far back
as the 1910s, the main purpose being to facilitate prison management. The
demographics across the two groups were highly consistent; that is, the
prison sample, like the previous sample, was composed primarily of young
men with limited education and a history of unemployment. The interviews focused on how the inmates perceived themselves and their crimes,
as well as what adjustments they proposed when released from prison.[9]

Henry and Gross played up the consistent pattern they found across the two studies, which indicated the particular vulnerability of lower-class homosexuals to get into trouble with the law and, if not given a rehabilitative environment, to repeat their sex offenses. The segregated experience of the prison sample was viewed as especially troublesome because it reinforced the feeling of homosexual solidarity and once released from prison, encouraged the ex-inmates to retreat further from society at large. Henry and Gross thus recommended a postprison intervention program in which the released homosexuals would receive psychiatric supervision, first in a penal hospital and then followed up during parole. This report was probably written before the research proposal on following up released sex offenders was completed, and so it lacked the details of financial and employment aid that became part of Henry and Gross's vision of a rehabilitative program. Central to their scheme was the role of psychiatric supervision— a role that fitted into the movement in the interwar period to expand psychiatry beyond the mental institution and into the community. This, obviously, suited Henry's professional interest, but Gross also built on this model in the postwar period to establish a community presence for the clergy in working with homosexuals.

Shortly before the war, Henry and Gross were able to attract preliminary interest in their work from the Society for the Prevention of Crime, an organization concerned with studying criminal behavior. They hoped to get the society's financial support for the rehabilitative program they had spelled out in their research proposal on the sex offender, a program they now referred to as a "research clinic." This funding possibility, however, was cut short by the society's decision to use its financial resources to support a project under the sponsorship of New York District Attorney Thomas E. Dewey. Thus, their rather ambitious plans for a research clinic would have to await the end of the war, when, in the spirit of postwar adjustment, they were able to attract interest from the Quakers. In the meantime, they became personally involved in the war effort.[10]

HENRY AND GROSS AND THE WORLD WAR II DRAFT

Henry, officially, and Gross, unofficially, played a major role in New York City in screening inductees for homosexuality during the wartime draft. Like psychiatrists in general, Henry was enlisted by the Selective Service System to carry out the policy of excluding homosexuals from the armed forces. Prior to World War II, homosexuals had never been systematically excluded from the military. As psychiatric screening procedures developed in the months before the war, homosexuality was included among the categories of mental disorder. This inclusion was more a function of the efforts of military officials than of the psychiatrists involved in drawing up the procedures for psychiatric screening. Henry, in fact, like many psychiatrists did not believe that homosexuality in itself should necessarily be a condition for exclusion from military service.[11]

When the war started, with the aim of speeding up the screening process, psychiatric examinations were no longer given at local boards. The screening was now relegated to nonpsychiatric examiners at army induction stations. In New York City the selective service referred any inductees suspected of homosexuality to psychiatrists for further screening. Henry was one of the major psychiatric consultants used for such cases. Some of his screenings were conducted at his Park Avenue office for private patients, but most took place in the offices he used as a consulting psychiatrist at New York Hospital's Payne Whitney Clinic. It was Gross, however, who actually carried out the interviews in both locales, and his work at the clinic raised controversy. Oskar Diethelm, the clinic director, was concerned about the fact that Gross, a nonphysician, was performing a role reserved for medical personnel. At first Diethelm tried to end the practice of having the screening interviews take place in the clinic, arguing that Henry was no longer associated with the hospital or the clinic. Henry had indeed ended his clinic affiliation in 1942 but still claimed a right to the use of the physical space because he was working on behalf of the sex variants committee, which had an agreement to make use of the clinic for its work. In effect, Henry and Gross were the only personnel to constitute the committee since, with the publication of the *Sex Variants* volumes in 1941, it no longer functioned.[12]

Diethelm was thus forced to tolerate Henry and Gross's work on the clinic's premises, but acting on behalf of the hospital's board of governors, he monitored their activities. In 1943 he became aware of complaints from some of the inductees about the screening practices that Gross was using. Of particular concern was the requirement that a "paramour" be physically present to serve as a witness for a man's stated homosexual behaviors. Another complaint dealt with the requirement that anyone suspected of homosexuality had to sign a written confession. These complaints were embarrassing to the hospital since they came through the wartime Committee of Neuropsychiatric Societies of New York City. Henry was apprised of the complaints and assured Diethelm that such screening practices would not continue. A few months after this controversy, Diethelm was informed of another problem. Word got around through the hospital that Gross was fraternizing with the men he was screening. The specifics involved two letters that he had written in which he tried to arrange "dates" with some of the inductees at the Stork Club, a prominent New

York nightclub. Gross was warned about such inappropriate behavior, and Diethelm continued to monitor his activities in the clinic until they were phased out toward the end of the war.[13]

Under Henry's authorization, Gross screened about two thousand men for the selective service, and, according to Henry, most were disqualified for military service because of homosexuality. In somewhat over half of these cases, Gross conducted extensive interviews aimed at adding to the case history database of Henry's research. When Henry published his popular version of the *Sex Variants* monograph in 1955, titled *All the Sexes,* he referred to the selective service cases as part of the extended research sample that he analyzed in the latter book. It is thus clear that Henry used his connection with the selective service as an opportunity to continue his research on homosexuality. Moreover, he apparently had no reservations in turning over all of the actual research work to Gross. As a result, Gross assumed a very powerful position. Through the authority of Henry's signature, Gross determined who should be disqualified from military service in thousands of cases in New York City. Since Gross was homosexual, Henry must have felt that Gross had the expertise to determine who was and who was not homosexual. In fact, according to Thomas Painter, Gross knew many gay men and offered to get them excused from service. This probably accounts for Gross's rather unusual practices of requiring a witness or a written confession from those men who he did not know and may have suspected of trying to pass as homosexual. His attempts to help gay men during the war anticipated his more extensive efforts after the war.[14]

As in the case of their collaboration before the war, Henry needed Gross to act as a contact person and carry out the interviews for their research. Gross, in turn, derived status and power through his association with Henry. This reciprocation characterized their relationship and it was to continue in the postwar years.

THE HENRY FOUNDATION

After the war Henry was approached by a group of Quakers to work with them in organizing a social agency concerned with helping young men arrested on charges of homosexuality. By the beginning of 1946, the Civil Readjustment Committee of the Quaker Emergency Service was established. Henry was appointed as psychiatrist-in-chief and Gross as executive secretary. As in the case of their selective service work, Henry was minimally involved. It was Gross who administered the day-to-day operations. The committee dealt with cases of arrested homosexuals who were placed on probation by the New York City Magistrate's Court. Its offices were located in the same building as the court. In each of the committee's first two years, it processed somewhat over two hundred cases. Most of the cases involved lower-class men who were detected in subway toilet episodes. These were men who were not typically enculturated into the homosexual subculture; that is, they either did not identify themselves as homosexual or purposely chose not to frequent homosexual bars, restaurants, and other public hangouts. The committee's major objective was to reeducate the men so that they would avoid future arrest by refraining from public sex. This was effected through the probationary casework carried out by Gross and, with a network of clergy and physicians (including Henry), religious counseling, medical assessments, and psychotherapy. Through these interventions, the men would hopefully learn to control their homosexual impulses and avoid frequenting the public places where they were vulnerable to arrest. The goal was to adjust the troubled homosexual to fit into society.[15]

Not only was Gross managing the committee, but he also appears to have actually written the official reports, which were signed and authored by Henry. According to Clarence A. Tripp, who had worked for Henry as a photographer during the war, the reports reflected Gross's rather than Henry's views. In fact, regarding the second (1947) annual report, Tripp confided to Alfred C. Kinsey that he doubted whether Henry actually bothered to read it. There does seem to be a difference in the tone of the 1947 report with respect to treatment goals and Henry's earlier statements about treatment. In *Sex Variants*, first published in 1941, Henry had suggested, rather vaguely, that if the homosexual "can afford treatment he may be helped in his adjustment by psychotherapy." Nor did Henry change his views since the same statement appeared in his 1955 *All the Sexes*.[16] In the 1947 committee report, the commentary about treatment goals included the following: "Psychiatric methods have not found the technique by which mass abstinence from homosexual behavior can be produced. . . . [The focus of treatment therefore] should be directed towards obtaining better and more effective methods of control, especially of public activity."[17] Thus, Henry's earlier general statement about adjustment was transformed in the committee report into a pronouncement that adjustment for the homosexual meant learning to control his sexual behavior in public. Abstinence from homosexual relations was generally an unrealistic goal and, by implication, so was a change to heterosexual behavior. The difference in language does strongly suggest that Gross was ghostwriting Henry's official reports. Consistent with this role is the fact that Gross later confided that he had written Henry's 1951 published article on pastoral counseling for homosexuals. Gross's views on treatment objectives did not necessarily contradict Henry's views since Henry never argued that homosexuals could achieve a heterosexual adjustment. On the other hand, Gross, by acknowledging that abstinence was not possible, defined adjustment strictly in terms of avoiding public sex. Homosexual behavior in private was acceptable. Indeed, this was the guideline that Gross tried to apply to his own sexual conduct. Whether he was consciously aware of it or not, his advocacy of homosexual relations in private mirrored his struggle to be active sexually without risking public disclosure.[18]

Essentially, the Quaker committee provided the opportunity for Henry and Gross to carry out their prewar plans to establish and administer a treatment program for homosexuals in legal difficulty. In the second year of the committee's functioning, however, Henry and Gross became involved in a conflict with the Quakers. It revolved around an article published in *Collier's* in February 1947. The author, Howard Whitman, had interviewed Gross about the committee's program. When the article appeared, it had a rather sensationalistic tone by playing up cases of women who were murdered and girls who were molested. Such cases were actually a small minority of the cases under the purview of the committee since its focus was on homosexual misdemeanors. Aside from its rather misleading description of the committee's work, the article also named some of the clergy who were involved with the program. One priest, in particular, objected to having his name publicly associated with the committee. Gross, acting on the priest's behalf, got into a fight with Whitman. Whitman, in turn, reported to Edgar Bromberger, the magistrate judge, that Gross was "fraternizing" with the men referred by the court. Bromberger then demanded that Gross be fired. Once again, Gross's difficulty in separating his private from his professional life got him into trouble. Nevertheless, as in the case of the selective service work, Henry came to his rescue and successfully interceded to keep Gross in his position, but the damage had been done. By early 1948 the Quakers pulled out their support of Henry and hired another psychiatrist, Frederic Wertham, to take over the committee.[19]

In response to the rupture with the Quakers, Gross took the initiative in organizing a new committee in the form of a nonprofit philanthropic foundation, which was named the George W. Henry Foundation. Gross's role as founder of the foundation reflected the increasingly dominant position he played in his association with Henry. Henry provided the stamp of authority and the cloak of respectability needed for a project directed at helping a stigmatized population. Gross, on the other hand, continued to function as he had in the Quaker committee by managing the day-to-day operations as well as ghostwriting much of Henry's official reports. Henry's interests were served through the prestige of having a foundation in his name, thus ensuring his reputation as an expert and a humanitarian with regard to the problem of the homosexual in society. Using Henry as a "front" enabled Gross to carve out a career for himself as a social worker devoted to helping homosexual men in trouble with the law. Moreover, Gross was utilizing Henry's attributed authorship to voice his own views and concerns.[20]

The George W. Henry Foundation began its operation in April 1948, with an office in the University Settlement House on the Lower East Side of Manhattan. Charles Cook, the director of the University Settlement, was on the foundation's board of directors. Not surprisingly, Gross was appointed as the executive secretary and Henry served as the psychiatrist-in-chief. In addition to Cook, the board included a number of other prominent figures involved in social reform, such as Edwin J. Lukas of the Society for the Prevention of Crime, Algernon D. Black of the Ethical Culture Society, and the Protestant Council's Leland A. Barnes, who was the board president. From its inception the foundation had a strong connection with the church, and throughout the years most of its board members were Episcopal clergy. In its close association with religious figures, the foundation anticipated the later movement in the 1960s in which liberal Protestant ministers became involved in the cause of homosexual rights. Since it was not attached to a particular court, as in the case of the Quaker committee, the foundation had more flexibility in drawing cases from a variety of sources. The major source of cases was court referrals of men who were on probation, but there were also men who were referred by social service agencies and the clergy. Moreover, as its reputation developed, the foundation drew a number of self-referrals through the "homosexual grapevine." These were men who were not necessarily in trouble with the law but wished to have psychotherapy or religious counseling.[21]

The foundation's statement of purpose, most likely written by Henry rather than Gross, presented a mandate concerned with rendering "practical assistance" for sexually maladjusted individuals who were suffering from emotional conflict or who were in trouble with the law. Such assistance was in the form of psychiatric, legal, and spiritual aid. The statement of purpose was couched within the medical model, as expressed by Henry: "In studying the problems presented by these [sexually maladjusted] persons . . . [the foundation] seeks to determine the causes of their maladjustment, the extent to which self-love and abnormal attraction to the same sex as well as the extent to which environmental influences have prevented mature sexual and emotional development." Consistent with Henry's previous writings, the statement of purpose stressed the "disorganizing" influence the sexually maladjusted had on society, specifically in their propensity for crime and mental illness and their disruptive presence in the family and school. It was also noted that the sexually maladjusted were mistreated because of the general public's prejudice and ignorance as well as deficiencies on the part of medical, legal, and religious agencies. The foundation therefore sought "to promote a better understanding of sexual problems and more rational methods of dealing with them."[22]

In line with its stated purpose, the foundation devoted its energies to rehabilitating gay men in trouble with the law so that they would become socially adjusted, that is, avoid being repeat sex offenders. Changing social attitudes about homosexuality was viewed as a contingent goal that could best be accomplished by disseminating the foundation's record of ameliorative work. To accomplish the foundation's treatment program, Henry and Gross appear to have been generally successful in recruiting the network of psychiatrists, psychologists, social workers, and clergy they had worked with in the Quaker committee. They also extended the network of support staff to include lawyers who could provide legal aid, and with the appointment of Betty Falek of the Vocational Foundation to the board, they instituted a program of vocational counseling. Since Gross ran the day-to-day operation, it is likely that he played the major role in overseeing these various projects and in forming liaisons with agencies and influential people in the community.

The foundation was unsuccessful in its attempts to obtain funding, something that was not unusual in the context of the postwar McCarthy homophobic climate. As a tax-exempt nonprofit organization, it thus depended on charitable contributions and the good graces of the various agencies it worked with as well as the members of its board. Stationery and printing needs, for example, were met by the donation of paper by one of the board members and collections for money conducted at board meetings. In exchange for using the physical facilities of the University Settlement House, Gross conducted group counseling sessions with neighborhood college-age youths concerned with economic and social issues. The professionals who worked with the foundation did so largely on a voluntary basis, while Gross, as a full-time administrator, received a small monthly salary. Individual clients were expected to pay for their treatment, if it was judged that they could afford the expenses. Most of the clients, however, were limited financially, so individual fees brought in relatively little income to the foundation.

In a 1951 article in *Pastoral Psychology* under Henry's authorship, but actually written by Gross (with Henry's approval), the foundation's strategies and objectives of successful treatment were articulated. The overall aim was to produce social adjustment. After an orientation interview, clients were placed in contact with a religious counselor, typically a minister or Episcopalian priest because of the foundation's connections with the Protestant Council. The objective of pastoral counseling was to build up the client's self-respect. This was accomplished by relieving the client of his guilt feelings and holding out the promise that he could learn to control his sexual urges and thus avoid getting into trouble. Since homosexuality was viewed as an immature, "deep-rooted" personality disorder, pastoral counseling was the first step in enabling the homosexual client to overcome his psychological insecurity. The client would then be directed to psychiatric treatment, which would strengthen his sense of personal "security." Consequently, the client would no longer have the need "to express himself as immaturely as he does in the psychosexual field."[23]

Henry and Gross were never explicit in their writings about how such vague therapeutic breakthroughs as strengthening personal security could be effected. In practical terms, the objective was to get gay men to lead a more discreet life by establishing enough impulse control to enable them to avoid having sex in the public settings that made them vulnerable to getting caught. Although never specifically stated by Henry or by Gross (at least before Henry's death in 1964), there was a subtext in the foundation reports that homosexual encounters in private were acceptable. The problem, however, was the assumption that most homosexuals did not know how to stay out of trouble. Given his own troubled history of indiscretions, Gross ironically opined, "Homosexuals have a positive genius for getting into hot water."[24] Particularly problematic was the tendency of homosexuals to ghettoize themselves. According to Gross, "As contact with the real world becomes more difficult to the homosexuals . . . [t]hey tend to retreat more and more from the real world into one peopled almost exclusively by such [as themselves], and contact with the world of real things and people becomes increasingly difficult."[25] Consistent with this attitude, Henry and Gross made a point of not making the foundation a membership organization for homosexuals. In words attributed to Henry in the foundation's 1953 annual report, he asserted, "It has been my consistent policy to refuse to countenance such societies, and I have pointed out the dangers lying in wait for those who operate them. . . . Lacking effective control, such groups inevitably deteriorate into places of assignation."[26] Henry was taken to task for this view in the homophile press. In *ONE Magazine*, homosexual rights activist Bill Lambert chastised Henry for his ignorance of homophile organizations as well as his sweeping and unfounded statements that homosexuals lacked self-discipline.[27]

In addition to pastoral and psychiatric counseling, and consistent with the postwar focus on follow-up programs for ex-prisoners, the foundation offered various support services, including job placement and financial and legal aid. The goal of these support services was to enhance the financial security of the clients and hence prevent them from becoming recidivists. In some instances, the foundation assumed an advocacy role in representing the rights of individual clients. For example, one client was a former medical officer in one of the armed services. He voluntarily admitted homosexual "interests" and possible "activity" in the course of a routine psychiatric examination and, rather than face court-martial, chose the only option open to him—a less than honorable discharge. Most likely prodded by Gross, Henry and a consulting psychiatrist associated with the foundation appealed the decision before a review board but were unsuccessful. In another case, two homosexual men were arrested for flaunting their "idiosyncrasies" on a beach at Fire Island, a summer colony on Long Island frequented by homosexuals. With the foundation's support, the two men, rather than face serious charges of public scandalous behavior, were allowed to plead guilty to a minor charge. In such cases, Henry noted that the source of the problem was the community's hostility toward homosexuals. Thus, although Henry's focus was on getting his homosexual clients to adjust to social mores, he also recognized the unfair treatment they received because of public prejudice and was willing to intervene on their behalf in such instances.[28]

Gross, for his part, often assumed an advocacy position for homosexual rights. In his own authored reports and public addresses to groups of Protestant clergy, he referred to homosexuals as constituting a minority group. In a 1947 address, he declared, "The problem of the homosexual is the problem of a minority group."[29] Defining the problem as such, he asserted that with respect to job discrimination, "homosexuals have just as much justification as any minority group to call themselves 'the last hired and the first fired.'"[30] He therefore seemed sensitive to the stigmatized and powerless position of homosexuals in society and the need for social change in this regard. Yet he also stressed the need for homosexuals to adjust to society by not openly flaunting their sexuality. He therefore believed that such ghettoizing institutions as gay bars were counterproductive to fitting into the larger community. As an alternative to the search for sexual liaisons in public settings, such as bars and parks, Gross acted as a matchmaker by using his position as Henry's research associate to ingratiate himself with the social network of homosexuals. Painter noted this in commenting that Gross liked to play "Cupid." It may have been this role that led to Gross's "fraternization" problems at the New York Hospital and with the Quaker committee. And, while some of his social advances appear to have been directed at satisfying his own sexual needs, these activities suggest that he was attempting to manage a discreet dating service as an alternative to the promiscuous sexual encounters in public places that made homosexual men vulnerable to arrest.[31]

Gross's efforts with the Quaker committee and the Henry Foundation in the late 1940s anticipated the emerging homophile movement of the

1950s. Under the rubric of social service, he launched public resistance to discrimination against homosexuals. His focus on adjustment as the key to survival for homosexuals in the larger society was also consistent with the dominant philosophy that defined the 1950s homophile movement. Although there were various homosexual social organizations in the post-war era of the late 1940s, such as the Veterans Benevolent Association in New York, the first group to attempt a national political presence for homosexuals was the Mattachine Society, organized in Los Angeles in 1951. The Mattachine's founder was Harry Hay, who had strong left-wing political views. He therefore had a radical homophile agenda regarding civil rights issues and advocated collective strategies of empowerment. Within two years, however, as the group grew in membership, Mattachine retreated from its radical stance of affirming a distinct gay identity to a position that argued for accommodation to social norms. This meant that homosexuals had to act discreetly and minimize any outward differences between themselves and heterosexuals. As a result of this political shift, Hay left the organization. Consistent with the notion of social adjustment, the new Mattachine leaders viewed medical and scientific experts as strategic allies who could teach homosexuals about self-presentation as well as speak to the broader society about homosexuality. As John D'Emilio notes, this conformist retreat seemed a necessary defense against the gathering right-wing attack of the McCarthy years.[32]

Although sharing the adjustment aims of the mainstream homophile movement of the 1950s and early 1960s, Henry and Gross avoided any association with homophile groups. In part, this reflected their homophobic attitudes and distrust of homosexuals acting as a collective force. Yet it was also politically necessary for the credibility and effectiveness of the foundation's work. As Gross confided to homophile activist Edward Sagarin in the mid-1960s, any connection of the foundation with the homophile movement would have been "the kiss of death." Alfred Kinsey and Evelyn Hooker, who were far more sympathetic toward the homophile movement and had close friendships with homosexuals, nevertheless avoided any official association with activist groups or known homosexuals because of the fear that the credibility of their work would be compromised.[33]

The Henry Foundation carried on its program throughout the 1950s and 1960s. Attesting to Gross's authorship, the annual reports were sprinkled with biblical references and Latin phrases. In 1964 Henry died at the age of seventy-five and the foundation was reorganized. As a more accurate reflection of his role, Gross's title became executive director and board members now included individuals with homophile connections, such as board members of the Mattachine Society. Ruth P. Berkeley, a former student of Henry's in the 1930s and associated with the foundation from its beginnings, succeeded Henry as the psychiatrist-in-chief. The foundation continued its mandate of dealing with problems encountered by gay men, and its work continued to be disseminated in addresses and publications sponsored by social welfare and church organizations. A Hartford, Connecticut, chapter was established in 1965 when the local council of churches became familiar with Gross's work. The Hartford council had begun to explore the issue of homosexuality in 1963 with the aim of developing an educational and counseling program. Once established, the Hartford chapter, unlike the New York Henry Foundation, was more amenable to working with homophile organizations.[34]

By the mid-1960s the homophile movement had moved away from its adjustment objectives and began to radically challenge the various strands of oppression. Included in this new direction was a campaign to extricate homosexuality from the medical model. The radicalization of the homophile movement meant that the foundation fell out of step with the increasingly militant objectives of homosexual emancipation. Yet in its 1965 report (coauthored by Berkeley and Gross), the foundation did, for the first time, publicly state its support for the acceptance of homosexual activity between consenting adults conducted in private, citing the recommendations of the British Wolfenden Report. In the early 1970s, however, against the tide of the gay and lesbian liberation movement, the foundation's reports continued to enunciate an adjustment position for those in trouble as a middle ground between the reactionary repression of moral traditionalists and the gay liberationists' advocacy of an "anything goes" view of sexual gratification. Moreover, these reports viewed the "Apartheid" objectives of the "gay" world as counterproductive to the need for homosexuals to become integrated into the greater community. Such discourse reflected Gross's continued distrust and concomitant distortion of the goals of the radicalized homophile movement. Missing in his diatribe was any recognition of the gay liberation movement's political agenda aimed at achieving sexual liberation. Gross suffered a heart attack in 1969, and after turning seventy-seven in 1972, resigned as executive director of the foundation. By the time of his resignation, the foundation's paternalistic purpose of helping gay men in trouble with the law had become anachronistic and, consequently, its financial viability was in jeopardy. Recognizing the inevitable, the foundation's board did not seek a new director and agreed to dissolve the organization. Gross died in 1987, two weeks shy of his ninety-second birthday.[35]

HENRY'S *ALL THE SEXES*

All the Sexes, published in 1955, was Henry's popularized version of the *Sex Variants* monograph. While the eighty cases in the original source served as the core of Henry's illustrative material, he also relied on subsequent clinical data, based on his psychiatric contact with somewhat over four thousand men. Most of the men in this sample were either interviewed in conjunction with the World War II selective service screening process or were referral clients of the Henry Foundation. The remainder of the sample comprised voluntary clients at the foundation and private patients. A small number of women who were private patients were also included. Almost all of the additional cases were homosexual or bisexual (94 percent) and the others were categorized under one of the following: exhibitionism, immature narcissism, transvestitism, and voyeurism.[36]

Henry's description and analysis focused on homosexuality, and his conclusions were consistent with those expressed in his earlier book. In fact, with the exception of some minor editorial changes, his "General Impressions" chapter at the end of the 1955 book is the same as the version that appeared in the 1941 monograph. While acknowledging that no two homosexuals were alike and that it was inaccurate to classify individuals as exclusively masculine or feminine, he asserted that homosexuality (and by implication, all forms of sexual variance from heterosexuality) reflected a distorted imbalance between masculinity and femininity in the form of gender inversion. As a result of this gender imbalance, mature heterosexual functioning could not be achieved. Henry, once again, stressed the need for preventive measures based on gender-appropriate socialization both within the family and at school. With respect to treatment, he was more emphatic than he had been earlier in arguing that psychosexual development could not be radically altered. Thus, cure in the form of a heterosexual object-choice was not realistic. The goal for treatment with homosexuals was to enable them to adjust to their condition by learning to control their sexual drives and, as a consequence, live their lives in harmony with the norms of the greater community.[37]

Henry's view that homosexuality was an irreversible condition was out of step with the shift in psychiatric thinking that began in the 1940s. While Freud had also believed that homosexuality was untreatable, American psychoanalysts like Sandor Rado were hopeful about a cure. Rado theorized that there was no innate homosexual drive, and thus homosexuals acted out because they had a phobic response to the opposite sex. The therapeutic goal was therefore to treat the sexual phobia. In a highly influential clinical study published in 1962, Irving Bieber followed Rado's lead by concluding that every homosexual was a "latent heterosexual" and voiced optimism that psychoanalytic treatment could produce a hetero-sexual "cure." Henry's 1955 book with its therapeutic focus on adjustment through impulse control, rather than a heterosexual cure, was thus incon-sistent with mainstream psychiatric thinking and practice.[38]

Aside from its departure from mainstream thought, Henry's book was unusual in two other respects. First, in his attempt to provide a rich de-scription of the homosexual subculture, he included a written contribu-tion by a gay man and another by a lesbian. He also elaborated his 1941 commentary, at considerable length, on the nature of homosexuality as a social problem.[39]

Revelations about Gay and Lesbian Life

Henry's unnamed male collaborator was identified as a "male homosex-ual who is also a well-trained psychologist."[40] In his contributed piece, the psychologist described the dress codes and mannerisms of gay men and how they develop an ability to recognize one another. Regarding the ritu-als of recognition, the psychologist declared:

> We know that a woman must develop a sensitivity and appreciation of her social environment because she does not have the ability to be as aggressive as her male companion. She must rely on many cues to which men, absorbed in their careers and specific occupations, do not pay much attention. Likewise, the homosexual, living in opposi-tion to a hostile social code, must develop in high degree his ability to recognize a fellow homosexual.
>
> Homosexuals always scrutinize another male. They do not pay at-tention to him after this first searching appraisal unless he is attractive or reveals some inclination to kinship. The follow-up is a search for additional identifying characteristics. If the individual is homosexual and interested in the observer, he too will "stare" and the two will "know" without verbal communication. But even when the other per-son appears to be uninterested or tries to cover up his homosexuality, how frequently the observer later finds evidence to confirm his first im-pression! This keen sensitivity is not innate, but one of the mechanisms the homosexual learns and employs in order to survive.[41]

This brief glimpse into gay life in the 1950s was relatively unique for its time. Aside from novels about homosexuals, the reading public had no ex-posure to such description. The one exception was the 1951 publication of *The Homosexual in America* by Edward Sagarin, who used the pseu-donym Donald Webster Cory. This book, which became popular among homosexual readers, had a limited circulation, owing to its publication by a small firm (Greenberg) that specialized in nontraditional genres, including gay novels.[42]

What was even more unusual in Henry's book was the inclusion of an extensive portrayal of lesbian life, which, with the exception of lesbian-themed novels, was not available to the reading public. In this case, the writer was introduced as a college faculty member who was "intimately acquainted . . . with all sorts of persons, including lesbians."[43] Although not identified as such, it is obvious from the rich description and the use of the vernacular that the writer was a lesbian. According to the anonymous author:

> The "gay girls" are pretty much divided into two groups—"them that do and them that don't." Don't let any of them get upstage and try to tell you there's a different classification such as "those who are and those who aren't." Any female homo will bust a gut for a toss in the hay if she thinks she can get it—or get away with it. In this enlightened age, it's a pretty backward number who pretends she doesn't know what it's all about. She may not know all the finer points, but she's dying to learn, and any bright teen-ager could wise her up. And in the meantime, she can dream—can't she?
>
> In fact, all of them have been dreaming of one thing or the other since half-past diapers. The soft babes dream of being "taken," and the tough ones dream of doing that little thing for them. Almost without exception, the female homo can recall the emotional highlights of her youth with vivid clarity. There was an overfond mama demanding constant attention or service, or a nurse or a governess who was seductive at bath or bedtime, or an angel of a teacher who loved the adulation and gifts of the younger girl. All of them can remember loving some female or other with varying degrees of intensity up to and including an absolute state of idolatry. Any gal who had gone to boarding school in the past fifty years is wise, whether she's gay or not. If she didn't do it herself, she will remember a schoolmate who had a terrific crush on some teacher or other girl. She will recall the notes, gifts, lovelorn looks and personal attendance that was danced upon the loved one and that all of it was often so intense and extreme it appeared quite ludicrous.[44]

The significance and description of schoolgirl crushes echoes what many of the lesbian sex variants storytellers recalled about their school days. The author also referred to the butch/femme distinction that was so prevalent during the 1950s and went on to describe, at great length, the differences between these types in dress, mannerisms, and sexual behavior. Moreover, she noted their courtship pattern in which the "aggressive

lesbian" (butch) pursues her desired "bitch" (femme), seeking a relationship where she would play the dominant role of the "husband."[45]

In the following passage, the author suggested the importance of finding relationships for self-validation:

> Many lesbians say they early learned about themselves and their sex-
> ual deviation from books, magazines and in school studies such as
> psychology—if they hadn't already learned about it from other
> women. They say frankly that they just decided to face reality and
> make the best of it—get what fun and satisfaction they could from
> an irremedial [sic] condition within themselves. One such honest
> young lesbian recently said, "What the hell—I like a home, I like to
> love and be loved. I've no intention of spending my young life alone
> in a furnished room. I want friends who understand and accept me.
> If I can find some sweet bitch to help with those plans—why not? I'm
> not hard to take—my body's clean and I am strong. I could make
> somebody a damn fine friend—and I'll find someone someday I can
> take to my heart's content." This girl will diligently search for her
> partner at work, among her friends or in bars and restaurants. She
> may "take" several before she finds the one she wants to stick with.[46]

Addressing the question of how successful lesbians are in maintaining
long-term relationships, the author opined:

> In the last analysis, the chances of satisfactory homosexual adjust-
> ment or a permanent lesbian marriage are slim. Whether the gay girl
> is of the quiet, subdued type or the frankly aggressive type, which is
> thought to be in the majority, the alliances—on high plane or lusty
> low level—are comparatively short-termed. The gals keep on trying,
> but sooner or later they learn that just physical sexual satisfaction is
> not, after all, the prize desired. The nameless and gnawing hunger
> stemming from the lacks in early emotional structuring are [sic] sel-
> dom stilled and satisfied through homosexual "marriage" and al-
> liances. With the more intelligent and mature women, this is quickly
> recognized. They stop straining at the gnat and effect a satisfactory
> compromise of companionship, mutual respect and sharing of life's
> experiences. This type of lesbian usually has the capacity for devel-
> oping a level of relationship which is socially acceptable, productive
> for society, and personally gratifying, no end.[47]

These sentiments point to the expectation in lesbian circles that committed relationships were attainable. Yet, as Lillian Faderman notes, there
were pervasive class and age tensions in the lesbian subculture of the
1950s. Middle- and upper-class as well as older lesbians were wary of the
visibly outrageous butch/femme pattern of working-class and younger lesbians. At a time in which social survival depended on conformity, public

signs of gender and sexual subversion were perceived to be dangerous. Henry's lesbian collaborator, though tolerant of the butch/femme subculture, appears to have viewed lesbian life through her middle-class lens.[48]

In his follow-up comments to the description of lesbianism, Henry underscored the need for homosexuals to be "socially acceptable" and "productive for society." He pointed out that homosexuality did not necessarily constitute a sexual maladjustment. There were some homosexuals who were reasonably well adjusted by virtue of their ability "not to impose their personal affairs upon the general public."[49] According to Henry, wealthy and socially prominent homosexuals, particularly lesbians, were more likely to succeed in keeping their sexuality discreet. They had the social and economic resources that enabled them to keep their sexual lives private. With respect to lesbians generally, Henry appeared to recognize that compared with gay men, they were more successful in staying out of public trysts. In terms of his examples, it was gay men who posed a social problem because most of them were publicly conspicuous in their sexual behavior. Although he did not refer to his own work in this context, he viewed his foundation's mandate as helping to resolve this problem.[50]

Homosexuality as a Social Problem

Alluding to gay men, the core of the problem, as Henry viewed it, was the fact that most homosexuals were "hedonists—concerned only with a search for pleasure."[51] As a consequence, they resented the standards of normality imposed upon them, and, in turn, society rejected them because they did not conform to acceptable standards. Moreover, in attempting to fulfill their sexual needs, homosexuals were under the constant risk of exposure. In order to alleviate social pressure, they sought support by forming their own communal networks. Yet, as Henry opined, such segregation only intensified the risks for homosexuals because the support they received insulated them from the negative attitudes and stigmatization of the larger society.

Henry was, nevertheless, optimistic that through new types of treatment a solution to the problem could be found. Before offering his own intervention strategy, he pointed to the failure of existing legal and medical practices. Laws had little value in achieving social control over sexual deviance since the majority of sex offenders managed to avoid arrest. Those who were arrested were not helped because they faced the dangers of public disgrace, and if they were imprisoned, their deviant behaviors were strengthened as a consequence of being segregated with their own kind. Regarding medical treatment, he dismissed the commonly held belief among physicians that homosexuality could be cured, declaring, "There is no medicinal agent, no form of sex hormone therapy, and no method of

physical treatment by which an habitual homosexual can become heterosexual."[52]

In place of these ineffectual interventions, Henry proposed a therapeutic approach that required close supervision of homosexuals. Possibly
influenced by the postwar movement to relocate juvenile offenders to residential centers, Henry proposed relocating homosexuals to rural communities where they would be removed from the distractions and temptations inherent in the homosexual ghettos of urban centers. To avoid the
danger of encouraging new ghettos, only small numbers of homosexuals
would be assigned to particular communities, where they would be given
assistance in finding living arrangements and work. Once settled, they
would be "kept under psychiatric supervision."[53] Psychotherapy would be
employed according to the needs of each case.

For such interventions to be effective, Henry stressed that the attitudes
of both the variant and society had to be considered. In the concluding
paragraphs of his book, he declared:

> The variant should have a sincere desire to conform to social stan-
> dards. Various forms and degrees of social pressure may have to be
> employed in supporting this desire. Society must be educated and
> kept informed so that it may deal with this problem objectively.
>
> Objectivity requires mutual recognition of and respect for the
> needs of the variant and of society. Standards of normality in a com-
> munity cannot be valid for all members simply because they have
> been established and imposed by the majority.
>
> If we were completely objective in dealing with the problems of
> sex variance we would recognize the inevitability of individual vari-
> ation of psychosexual adjustment and we would work together to se-
> cure such modifications as would contribute to the welfare of all con-
> cerned. We would temper our feelings and impulses with the
> realization that psychosexual variance is[,] after all, a manifestation
> or possibly a by-product of human evolution.[54]

Henry should be given credit for his call for social tolerance and understanding, a position in contrast with the intemperate and hostile attitudes toward homosexuals often expressed by his fellow psychiatrists. Yet
there are disturbing elements of social control and paternalism in his remarks. In his highly impractical scenario of rural resettlement, he gives
psychiatrists the police powers of a fascist state in which the lives of homosexuals are under constant regulation and scrutiny. And although he
acknowledged the inevitability of a sexual pluralism, brought into sharper
focus by the modern industrialized society, he nevertheless believed that
there were ways to stem the tide of sexual variation. As in his earlier book,
he devoted considerable attention to prevention.[55]

The key to prevention, according to Henry, was strengthening the factors that contributed to mature heterosexual modes of sexual expression. Well-established patterns of heterosexuality insured their historical continuity across generations. This objective implied a program of surveillance and close supervision in the way that children were socialized. Henry thus advocated that all childhood and adolescent emotional attachments had to be carefully scrutinized. Sex education should begin as early as infancy. Parents had to be "well-adjusted" and serve as appropriate gender role models. Servants, siblings, other relatives, and friends had to be watched to make sure that they did not contribute to the "psychosexual distortion" of children. Gender-appropriate curricula in the schools would further reinforce socialization.

Not only did the nature of face-to-face interactions influence the historical course of sexual expression and practices, but social movements could also be significant determinants. Henry was especially concerned about feminism, which he viewed as an insidious movement undermining the traditionally well-defined distinction between masculinity and femininity. Although he acknowledged that feminism had produced some beneficial effects, he expressed pessimism about its future impact:

> The rebellion of women . . . in the form of feminism . . . [in] the United States . . . has resulted in equal suffrage and virtual elimination of the double standard of morals. Women now own more property than do men, they outlive men, and if united they could control the government.
>
> All living beings are relatively masculine or feminine in response to circumstances under which they live; civilization and culture, as we understand them, are dependent upon characteristics and capacities which cannot be dissociated from masculinity and femininity. The present Occidental trend is in the direction of a matriarchal system, with increasing masculinity on the part of women. This ascendancy of women has been fostered by political and industrial competition between the sexes, the increasing tendency on the part of both sexes to avoid parental and homemaking responsibilities, and the destruction of masculine males and preservation of feminine males by modern warfare. This gradual change may foreshadow for Western civilization a decline and fall such as that of the Roman Empire.[56]

Henry's bitter attack of feminism and his fears of its subversive threat to patriarchy and heterosexuality reflected his uncritical assimilation of the prevailing political and social conservatism of the 1950s. In the cold war era, any nonconformity to traditional family life was viewed as a danger to national survival. Despite signs of enlightenment in his relative tolerance for homosexuality, he was essentially a political and social conservative, imbued with the prioritization of the need for social control and the role of psychiatry and the allied mental health professions in contributing to that objective. In this sense, he was in the mainstream of psychiatric thought and practice. It was not until the 1960s that there was a visible shift toward social criticism and activism among psychiatrists and psychoanalysts.[57]

THE HENRY-GROSS COLLABORATION AND GROSS'S MISSION

Before the 1960s Henry was among a small minority of American medical specialists who acknowledged that social hostility and unjust legal treatment contributed to the problems homosexuals faced. He did not go as far as more liberal practitioners, such as Clara Thompson, in interpreting homosexuality as a nonpathological form of sexuality. On the other hand, he was unique in associating himself with a program of social support, and at times advocacy, for homosexuals in trouble with the law. His relatively enlightened orientation appears to have been partly shaped by his long career of clinical work with male homosexuals. Attesting to this record, he was introduced at a 1951 professional conference by fellow psychiatrist Robert W. Laidlaw as "the man who has had more clinical experience with problems of H [homosexuality] than any psychiatrist in America today."[58]

Henry's association with Gross, however, seems to have been the catalyst propelling him in his social service work. Their relationship was a symbiotic one; neither could have forged their personal accomplishments without the other. Collaborating with Gross accorded Henry the opportunity of extending his work on homosexuality beyond the sex variants study. In fact, he virtually relied on Gross to do the actual work in their various endeavors. Through his fieldwork and his knowledge of the male homosexual subculture, Gross essentially carried out the research projects with sex offenders. When Henry was a consultant for the Selective Service System during the war, it was Gross who engaged in most of the interviewing. In the social service program, first initiated with the Quaker committee and then more ambitiously promoted through the Henry Foundation, Gross directed the services and wrote the official reports under Henry's name. Henry gained much out of this working relationship. While Gross did the work, Henry received the professional recognition. Moreover, his time was freed so that he could continue to devote his efforts to his private clinical practice in New York and the private sanitarium he ran in Greenwich, Connecticut.[59]

The above scenario suggests a rather exploitative relationship in which Gross was taken advantage of. Indeed, Henry had exploited Jan Gay in the

sex variants study and assumed credit and authorship for what had originally been her research project. Gross, however, was a shrewd operator
who opportunistically envisioned a place for himself through his association with Henry. As a defrocked cleric and a gay man, he needed Henry as
a "front." Making use of Henry's official authority, he etched out a personal career as a specialist in homosexuality, first as a researcher, then as
a medical assessor, and finally as an activist–social worker. The net result
was that he was given and exercised relatively free rein and considerable
responsibility in engaging in scientific, medical, and social service work.
Especially through his position as executive secretary for the Henry Foundation, he wielded influence with homosexual clients and with other community agencies. In essence, Gross resurrected his lost ministry by helping
young gay men in trouble with the law find a safety net through a social
support system.

Gross also seems to have had a profound influence on Henry. Since he
ran the day-to-day affairs of the foundation, he may well have initiated the
instances of Henry's role as an advocate for homosexual clients who were
dishonorably discharged from the military or unjustly arrested. Aside from
these particular cases, Gross's plight as a defrocked clergyman and his continual struggle with his sexuality may have shaped Henry's ideas about the
need to change society's attitudes toward homosexuals. Henry was quite
limited as a scholar. His two books on homosexuality contain virtually no
references to the literature on homosexuality. There is no mention of
Hirschfeld or Ellis, for example, and only passing general references to
Freud. His gender-inversion model of homosexuality, especially as it was
expanded in *All the Sexes*, was simplistic, and his clinical interpretation
was guided more by folk wisdom than coherent theory. It is thus likely that
Gross was the source of much of Henry's seemingly original ideas about
studying and working with sex offenders. Whatever the contribution of
each may have been, they basically agreed on the importance of social control for solving the problems surrounding homosexuality. Henry's take on
this came from the mainstream psychiatric view of equating mental health
with social conformity. Gross believed, as did most homophiles in the
postwar era, that the stigmatization of homosexuals could best be overcome by leading discreet lives, that is, keeping their sexuality private.[60]

The accomplishments of the Henry-Gross collaboration are mixed.
Their greatest success, the Henry Foundation, was a pioneering step in the
postwar homophile movement's campaign to fight injustice and intolerance. The foundation was an early example of a community-support network used to help gay men in trouble with the law. Unfortunately, it was
embedded in a culture of paternalism and welfare mentality. Homosexual
clients were kept in dependent relationships with community authority

figures, such as psychiatrists, social workers, and clergy. Collective action on the part of homosexuals themselves was discouraged, as was any association with homophile organizations. By the Stonewall era, with the reduction in the police harassment of gay men, the foundation had outlived its usefulness.

Henry's obvious hopes to become the leading expert on homosexuality were unsuccessful. Alfred Kinsey overshadowed his work. In 1948 Kinsey's male volume appeared. This was the same year that Henry's more accessible one-volume edition of *Sex Variants* was published. Henry did leave a significant legacy, one that he never intended. In his reliance on clinical case material to support his arguments, he preserved in his publications the voices of gay men and lesbians. We can learn from these firsthand accounts what it meant to be homosexual in midcentury America.[61]

As for Gross, what is most intriguing about his life is how he managed to exercise his voice as a closeted gay man. Unlike Gay, whose voice was stifled and then taken over by Henry and the sex variants committee, Gross used whatever opportunities were available, limited as they were, to project his views. Utilizing his role as executive secretary of the Quaker committee and the Henry Foundation, he spoke before various groups of clergy and divinity students and wrote articles in church-related periodicals. His mission was to make influential members of the religious community aware of the problems faced by homosexual men. He also used these occasions to advertise his efforts, through the foundation, to help homosexuals adjust to society. Under Henry's authorship in foundation reports and published articles, he voiced his philosophy of social adjustment. As he confided to Canon Clinton Jones, who organized the Hartford chapter, "Dr. Henry's paper called 'Pastoral Counseling for Homosexuals' . . . [a]ll he had to do with it was to have his name at the head of it. The hands were Esau's hands but the voice . . ." And he seems to have believed that the people he worked with knew, for he added, "I thought that was an open secret."[62]

Unfortunately, Gross often voiced homophobic views in which homosexuals were castigated as psychologically deficient individuals beset by problems of self-discipline. These attitudes may have reflected some degree of self-hatred, but they also reveal the dilemma of functioning as a closeted gay man. Indeed, although Henry and possibly some of the foundation's staff and board members knew that Gross was gay, any public acknowledgment would have jeopardized his position. Working within the system, he had to choose the path of voicing accommodation rather than resistance. In 1962 he published a book, *Strangers in Our Midst,* directed at the clergy, in which he reiterated the arguments in his previous talks and papers. By the mid-1960s in his speeches and writings, he took note of the changing political climate and championed the British legal reform movement, spurred by the Wolfenden Report. In a 1964 address to divinity students, he boldly advocated that homosexuals should be allowed into the ministry. Nevertheless, consistent with his gradualist philosophy, he also became increasingly virulent in the 1960s in his attacks against the militant shift of homophile politics. By the early 1970s, however, he grudgingly acknowledged that the "Homophile Movement is with us. It will probably be with us for a long time to come. We will have to make what we can of it."[63]

Chapter 6

Thomas Painter and the Study of Male Prostitution, 1935–43

> I feel that it is proper for me to complain—if not for myself, then for the millions of others, and if not for them then for the generations yet to come. . . . [F]or the homosexual there is not one voice, not one little agency, not a printed word. Some one must do something, and that apparently must be I, as no one else seems to be willing.
>
> —Thomas Painter, "Male Homosexuals and Their Prostitutes in Contemporary America"

Like as for Alfred A. Gross, the Committee for the Study of Sex Variants enabled Thomas Painter to launch his career as an activist-researcher. Tom Painter's life is significant in a number of ways. Through his association with Alfred C. Kinsey and the Kinsey Institute, he has provided an extensive collection of personal papers and artifacts that furnish an in-depth view of the life and times of a gay man in the pre-Stonewall era. As Wardell B. Pomeroy of the Kinsey Institute commented, Painter's contributions probably constitute "the most complete record of a human sexual life ever compiled, and much of it written with grace and style as well as factual accuracy."[1] Moreover, Painter's documents provide far more than a personal sex history because as a grassroots community sex researcher, he was a participant in the homophile movement. As such, he moved in the world of medicoscientific sex researchers, establishing significant working relationships, first with Robert L. Dickinson of the sex variants committee and then with Kinsey and his colleagues at the Kinsey Institute. Thus, his experiences as an activist-researcher shed light on the nature of the relationship between sex experts and "lay" researchers. His research connections also point to the considerable contribution that he made to the homosexual rights movement. Finally, he was a committed and talented ethnographer of the male homosexual subculture in general and the world of male prostitution in particular. Through his life story and specific research contributions, I hope to further illuminate the nature of the relationship between the homosexual and medicoscientific communities in the four decades before Stonewall.

When Painter commented in 1941, "I feel it is proper for me to complain—if not for myself, then for the millions of others, and if not for them then for the generations yet to come,"[2] he was attempting to be a spokesperson for a group that had been historically denied the opportunity to speak on its own behalf. He thus became engaged in the ongoing struggle of the homosexual emancipation movement to wrest control from non-gay-identified individuals over who speaks for homosexuals. In Michel Foucault's terms, his project was directed at shifting the discourse about homosexuality from the objective control of others to the subjective agency of individuals seeking the right to speak for themselves. He played an influential role in this discursive shift through his collaboration with Kinsey, a sex researcher who shared Painter's liberatory objectives.[3]

In an autobiographical manuscript, written toward the end of his life, Painter identified the dominant theme of his life as the "long search . . . for love and companionship."[4] He also referred to a complementary theme of transformation, in which his alter ego, a free spirit named "Will Finch," became his self-identity. Unlike Tom, Will acted on his homosexual desires and thus ultimately found his "companion." This search, however, had its costs, for it resulted in social rejection and consequently living a life as a social "outcast." Nevertheless, Painter viewed his search as a triumphant journey in which he was able to become the "proto-hippie," the outsider who defied the dominant norm of heterosexuality. It is this theme of resistance that I would argue is the most significant aspect of Painter's life and as such it reflects what queer theorists, like Eve K. Sedgwick and Judith Butler, conceptualize as a queer identity. Such an identity serves as a site for challenging heterosexist hegemony because it focuses attention on how heterosexuality is constituted by what it is opposed to—that is, homosexuality. In taking on the role as a spokesperson for homosexuals, Painter was demanding attention for a group marginalized and hence silenced for its difference (queerness) from heterosexist society.[5]

I frame Painter's life (1905–1978) within the historical influences that shaped his career as an activist-researcher. In this chapter I deal with his early life and his personal and research connection with the world of male prostitution in the 1930s. In the next chapter I explore his relationship with Kinsey and the Kinsey Institute and, in his later years, his final search for self-fulfillment.

EARLY LIFE (1905–35)

In a series of autobiographical essays, written between 1970 and 1973, Painter recounted his childhood and youth. These brief memoirs were concise versions of the detailed case history that appeared in George W. Henry's *Sex Variants* under the pseudonym of "Will G." The case history was based on Henry's interview of Painter in 1935, when Painter was around thirty years old. The tone of the later memoirs was consistent with the earlier recollections. In essence, Painter consistently thought of his childhood as an unhappy time, marked by the absence of any close relationships with family or peers. He thus seemed to believe that his lonely formative years shaped his lifelong quest for "love and companionship."[6]

Painter was born in 1905 in New York City and grew up in a world of wealth and social privilege. His father, Henry McMahon Painter, was an obstetrician, a member of the Social Register who counted among his patients members of the Vanderbilt, Rockefeller, and Morgan families. His mother, Carrie Stevens Painter, had been a schoolteacher before marriage. Both his paternal and maternal families could trace their lineage to the earliest generation of English settlers in the American colonies. Painter's father became professionally successful after an early struggle to establish himself. His success apparently led to marital strains because, as Painter observed, his mother was unable to keep up with the new demands of mixing in prominent social circles. Painter's parents were in their early forties when his older brother Sidney was born. Three years later, when Painter was born, his father began an extramarital relationship with Loraine Wyman, a woman in her twenties. Throughout Painter's childhood, this love triangle created disharmony, and his mother eventually agreed to a divorce the year that he entered college.

Painter's sense of family estrangement is captured by his characterization of his mother as cold and "egocentric" and his father as distant and "preoccupied."[7] His limited social contact with peers of either sex added to his feelings of isolation. He went to first grade at a private school in New York, but because of various bouts with childhood diseases, he spent the next three years at home, tutored by his mother. In 1914 Painter moved with his brother and mother to the family's country estate in Hawthorne, New York. Outside of the public school he attended, he had no contact with peers.

His sense of alienation was deepened at age thirteen with his first awareness of a same-sex attraction. As he described it, he had his "first love af-

fair with a very handsome Irish boy of the same age."[8] This "affair," however, was one-sided since the object of his affection ignored him. To deal
with the frustrations of his sexual awakening, he sought refuge in a rich
fantasy life based on the homoerotic images of free young men portrayed
by Walt Whitman and Joseph Conrad. These prototypes became the foundation for constructing an idealized self-identity in the form of Will Finch.
He portrayed Will as "an intellectual, gently reared, who ran away . . . to
sea as a youth and lived as a common sailor," a strong man among "half-
naked" men in the South Seas.[9] Painter's hero worship of rugged, independent masculine figures mirrored the idealized view of masculinity that
became popular in the early decades of the twentieth century. As further
evidence of his hero worship, Painter thought of Theodore Roosevelt as an
idol. As he recalled, when he was about thirteen, his father, knowing how
he felt, arranged a personal visit for him at Roosevelt's home in Oyster
Bay, New York.[10]

From the first recognition of his sexual desires, Painter strove to take on
the identity of Will Finch. Looking back in 1970, at age sixty-five, he
wrote, "So perhaps I did become Will Finch, became what my earliest sexual urges wanted me to become, modified by realities. Why did I want to?
Because I was a proto-hippie. I revolted against my parents, and the whole
establishment they represented."[11] Painter thus viewed his homosexuality
as emblematic of a general revolt against society. Will Finch represented
not only sexual freedom, but also social rebellion. Throughout his life
Painter struggled with the attraction of living as a rebel, by being openly
gay, and the negative consequences he had to endure as a result of his
openness. His need to split his identity reflected the political subjectivity
of gay men in the pre-Stonewall era. To be accepted in society, they had
to hide their sexuality. To reveal their authentic inner self to the straight
world was an act of social confrontation. The British writer E. M. Forster
focused on the theme of homosexuality as social rebellion in his novel
Maurice, written in 1913, though not published until 1970. Like the protagonist in *Maurice,* Painter openly acted on his inner self and thus chose
to contest social convention.[12]

When he was thirteen, however, Painter was unfamiliar with the concept of homosexuality. Will Finch signified a vague notion of sexual freedom and even this was threatening. In writing about this period, he stated
that he "sublimated" Will's rebellious sexuality by immersing himself in
religion when he went away to prep school and college. According to
Painter, his interest in religion was a form of revolt since his family was not
religious. He became president of the Christian youth associations at both
Taft prep school and Yale. Greatly influenced by Tolstoy and Ghandi, he
became a pacifist and developed his own theology based on Jesus as a fig-

ure personifying love. His search for sexual expression was fulfilled by religious activities that involved close spiritual relationships with boys and
young men, many of whom he was sexually attracted to. Yet there were
also some instances at school and college when he believed that he had
come close to having an overt sexual experience. These episodes took the
form of "roughhousing" or "wrestling" while almost nude with various
roommates. While in prep school, these encounters apparently prompted
him to read about sex, and, as a result, he decided that he was homosexual and confided this to his father. In response, his father sent him to see
Dr. Stoddard Kennedy, a neurologist who concluded, after two sessions,
that Painter's homosexuality was a passing adolescent phase.[13]

After two postgraduate years as graduate secretary of Dwight Hall, the
Yale University Christian Association, Painter went to Oxford in the fall
of 1931 for a year of theological study with the goal of starting to prepare
for a career in teaching biblical history. It was at this time that he had his
first orgasms by masturbating while fantasizing about sadomasochistic,
homoerotic experiences. During vacations on the Continent, he began to
explore the homosexual world. In Vienna at a men's bath, he was seduced
by a "muscular, naked young prostitute."[14] This first overt sexual experience produced conflicting feelings. According to Painter, "Two nights later
I asked him to take me to his room. I got on top of him and had an emis-
sion on his body. I said to myself, 'This is what I've wanted all my life.' Immediately afterwards I was overwhelmed. I wept. While he was there I got
down on my knees and prayed. I was still studying in the seminary and I
couldn't be a hypocrite."[15]

Shortly after this sexual epiphany, Painter revealed his overt homosexual experience to his father, who was "shocked to the core."[16] His father,
who was in France at the time, sent him home to New York to see the neurologist he had previously seen, who in turn referred him to treatment with
the eminent psychotherapist Alfred Adler. Over the next two years, while
continuing his graduate education at Union Theological Seminary, Painter
spent seventy hours in therapy with Adler. According to Painter, Adler ascribed his homosexuality to sibling rivalry for his father's attention and a
"hatred" for his mother. When therapy was concluded, Adler declared
that Painter was too "obstinate" to be cured. What Painter gained out of
treatment was getting rid of his guilt feelings.[17]

Coincidentally, as his guilt was being abated, Painter began to seek out
sexual partners. Toward the end of his first year at Union, in March 1933,
he had several encounters with known homosexuals but found these unsatisfying and started to look for male prostitutes. While he had formed
close friendships at Yale with several homosexual classmates, he was not

sexually attracted to them. After his unsatisfactory encounters in New York, he realized that he needed "butch" partners, but he did not have the physique to attract them. To satisfy his desires for young muscular men, he had to "buy" them. Looking back on how his preferences for sexual partners developed, Painter commented that he felt a sense of shame with his social peers because of his feelings of sexual inferiority. With hustlers, he felt more comfortable because they preferred sex with social superiors, that is, men who were older and had money.[18]

In the fall of 1933, Painter began to explore the Times Square area, looking for hustlers. As he recalled, it took a long time for him to understand how to identify them. In November he met his first hustler, Jack Flaherty, a tall, well-built blond who fitted his idealized sexual type. Painter followed Flaherty into a movie house, and after the initial contact was made, they had sex in a hotel. They continued their relationship for several months and Flaherty served as a mentor for Painter, teaching him how the Times Square hustler subculture worked and introducing him to a number of young hustlers. When Flaherty returned home to Chicago, Painter met another hustler, George, who was even closer to his ideal type. He fell in love with George and was enthralled by his wild, rebellious lifestyle, which for Painter was the embodiment of Will Finch. This relationship lasted for a few months until Painter's money "ran out."[19]

In March 1934 Painter's father died, apparently under the impression that Painter was being "cured" through his treatment with Adler. From the time that he began treatment, Painter felt compelled to be honest and open with his friends and acquaintances and thus revealed to them that he was an "overt homosexual." In the fall of 1932, he had gone up to visit his friends at Yale and agreed to lead a religious discussion group. However, when the new graduate secretary of the Yale Christian Association found out that Painter was homosexual, Painter was banned from the Yale campus. Nevertheless, by the time he was ready to graduate from Union in the spring of 1934, he made a decision, which he later regretted, that he would be thoroughly frank with everyone at the seminary. As a consequence, he was informed by the authorities that he would receive no recommendations for a teaching or ministerial position. His theological career was finished before it ever began.[20]

Reflecting back on his naive idealism of indiscriminately "coming out," Painter insightfully interpreted it as representing his need to rebel, especially from his father's values and social expectations for him. As he declared, "I wanted to shock . . . Father and defy his whole Establishment."[21] This was a turning point, one in which Painter was beginning to transform himself by assuming the identity of his alter ego, Will Finch. But he was to pay a heavy price. He could no longer function in the privileged world he had been reared in, and he had to give up his dream of becoming a spiritual leader and teacher within religious institutions.

STUDYING MALE PROSTITUTION (1935–43)

Ostracized from the academic and "respectable" world, Painter decided that his mission in life was to do research and write a book about homosexuality. He set out to use his own experiences and contacts with hustlers as a foundation for his work. In the fall of 1934, after sharing an apartment for about a month with a graduate student from Union, he set himself up in an apartment on West 109th Street. At a male brothel, he had met Blackie and engaged him as a live-in cook as well as a live-in sex partner. Blackie was a member of a group of Forty-second Street hustlers, and the apartment at 109th Street, known as the "ranch," served as an open house for this group of homeless prostitutes. These youths were typical of the kind of hustler who came to New York during the Depression and chose prostitution as a means of economic survival. Painter thus had a constant supply of sex partners in his apartment and also spent time with these hustlers in Times Square.[22]

Within about two months, he ran out of money from his family allowance, which forced him to give up the apartment. By this time he had become infatuated with a particular hustler from the apartment, Willie O'Rourke, with whom he lived for six months in a furnished room on West Fifty-fifth Street, the same block where he had been raised as a child in his family's town house. According to Painter, O'Rourke was a "tough character" with a criminal record of burglary and an addiction to heroin. Painter fell in love with him, and for the first time in his sexual relationships, he found that the feelings were mutually shared. Painter took it upon himself to "reform" O'Rourke and succeeded since O'Rourke, who had been a merchant seaman, returned to sea. As Painter recalled thirty-five years later, "This experience convinced me of the power of love, a conviction I have retained ever since."[23] When O'Rourke left, Painter returned to his promiscuous sex life.

While Painter was getting himself established for his participant observational research on male homosexuality and prostitution, he began to seek out professional and financial support for his project. In the fall of 1934, he had met Jan Gay and learned about her planned research with Dickinson. Gay introduced Painter to Dickinson, who was enthusiastic about Painter's research plans. Apparently at Dickinson's suggestion, Painter was enlisted to help Gay with her case study project and thus to expand it to include a male sample. It was also understood that Painter would pursue his own project on male prostitution. Dickinson hired Painter as a nonsalaried employee of the National Committee on Maternal Health, and when this committee rejected Dickinson's proposed sponsorship of the research on homosexuality, the sex variants committee hired Painter in the same capacity. With respect to securing financial support, Painter persuaded a wealthy Yale friend, Luther Tucker, to help. Tucker had been a year behind Painter at Yale and they were active at the same time in Dwight Hall, the Yale Christian Association. Tucker's mother had been very grateful to Painter because he had been such a good influence on her son. In the fall of 1935, Painter had received $500 from Tucker, a sizable fund in the Depression, which enabled him to get another apartment for himself and more seriously begin his field research. However, when Tucker's family found out about the purpose of the grant, the money stopped coming.[24]

In early 1935 Painter began his association with the sex variants committee. For the sex variants study instituted by Gay, he recruited the subsample of hustlers and volunteered to be a participant, using the pseudonym of Will G. What is unique about the published transcript of his interview in the *Sex Variants* monograph is the inclusion of a written essay in which Painter delineates his "ideal sexual object." Among the desirable physical attributes, he listed, "tall and lithe," well tanned, well-developed biceps and abdominal muscles, slender hips, and a smooth hairless body. With respect to the sexual relationship, Painter indicated that he had to be dominant and active, preferring his partner to be passive with "an almost statuesque lack of cooperation." It was also important that his ideal type had a pleasing personality, that is, "a clear eyed laughing, ebullient youth, not too worldly wise and cynical, not too stupid, not too innocent and afraid." Moreover, his object of desire had to be some one who had "no suggestion of homosexuality about him."[25] Here, Painter was expressing his distaste for the fairy stereotype of the effeminate homosexual. The idealized image Painter was describing was his alter ego, Will Finch, who was personified by the hustlers he pursued. Indicative of the rebellious nature of his Will Finch prototype, Painter included the following capsule description:

> In general: A person defiant of convention, ruggedly individualistic, independent, frank, slightly coarse, even slightly brutal, outspoken, strong minded, virile in every way is preferred. A casual defiance of convention as to wearing of clothing is intensely exciting—i.e., wearing too few, too light, or too much *en deshabille* clothing to suit the place or occasion is most erotic. A very "tough" youth in dress and manner, if otherwise physically desirable, is more exciting than one more conventional.[26]

Painter's search for Will Finch seemed to be epitomized by his immediate attraction to someone who signified rebellion and defiance through mode of dress and manner. As for his own quest of becoming Will Finch, he revealed that he was far from reaching his goal, declaring, "This sexual object is clearly in physique and character the epitome of what I wish to be myself—and fail in being."[27]

Painter's portrayal of his ideal sexual type, with its attention to physical attributes and appearance, was notably narcissistic. In fact, in later revelations about his homoerotic preferences, he described how he was sexually aroused by visually inspecting the muscular development of his sex partners while they were in a passive, resting position. This appears to explain why he preferred his partners to be passive. More generally, Painter's narcissism suggests the subjectivity of gay men in the early twentieth century, which focused on external appearance and manner. In an underground sexual subculture, the search for partners was dependent on using one's appearance as a source of homoerotic attraction.[28]

At the same time that Painter was contributing to the sex variants study, he wrote a preliminary report about the prostitution study that was submitted to the sex variants committee at its first meeting, which took place in March 1935. At the committee's next meeting in October, Maurice R. Davie, a committee member who was a sociologist at Yale University, reported that he had studied what Painter submitted and "felt that it was impressionistic and full of presumptions, and far from scientific in its approach."[29] Moreover, Davie added that because of Painter's "lack of training," he would require very close supervision in his further work. Over the summer Painter had apparently consulted with Robert W. Laidlaw, the secretary of the committee, and Laidlaw indicated at the October meeting that Painter was eager to work under the committee's guidance. It was therefore decided that Davie would chair a supervisory subcommittee, which also included Laidlaw and Henry. The sex variants committee had hoped to find sources of funding for the supervisory work, but this proved to be unsuccessful. Painter was thus left to work on his own until Dickinson assigned Gershon Legman to provide editorial help when Painter was in the final stages of his writing. Legman was employed by Dickinson to serve on the maternal health committee as a bibliographical researcher and undertook various projects assigned by Dickinson, including the glossary for the *Sex Variants* monograph.[30]

Established in a new apartment with the Tucker money, Painter proceeded with his field research in the fall of 1935. As he later admitted, it was difficult to legitimize the use of his research funds since he was an active participant in the sexual scene he was attempting to study. As he recalled, "It was a confused period. . . . [I] believed I was conning trusting and idealistic friends, e.g. Tucker, to finance my having a ball—in the name of field research."[31] Nevertheless, because he shared his new apartment with Al, a flamboyant homosexual who was especially well connected with both the homosexual and hustler subcultures, Painter had a rich source of ethnographic observation. By throwing large parties in his apartment, Painter was introduced to a wide cross section of New York homosexual society. In describing the scene, he recounted, "The place leaped with H's [homosexuals] and hustlers every moment of the day and night. . . . We staged big parties of over seventy people. In short we lived in a madhouse of confusion, 'camping,' liquor and sex."[32]

Between 1936 and 1940, Painter had a number of personal diversions that compromised his research and writing and probably accounts for, in part, his limited contact with the sex variants committee. At his mother's request, he spent the winter of 1936 with her in Florida. This served as an opportunity for him to meet hustlers in various parts of Florida and Georgia. Soon after Painter returned to New York, he met Tony and had his first serious relationship, which lasted for three years. When Painter first met Tony at the beach in Coney Island, he invited Tony to live with him. At the time, Tony was eighteen and had been on his own for four years, having left his home in Pottstown, Pennsylvania. On the road he had supported himself at various times by becoming a "casual hustler." He fitted Painter's idealized image for a sex partner—muscular with an outgoing personality. This was not a monogamous relationship and often they would bring hustlers home in each other's presence. Shortly after they met, Painter found a job for Tony at a Ford Plant in suburban New Jersey. In 1938 Painter's stepmother, who was living in France, died. Painter and Tony went to Paris to settle the estate. Painter now had a substantial inheritance from his father, which was supplemented when his mother died in 1940. Apparently because Painter and Tony had gone to France together, Painter's mother and brother now knew that he was homosexual. By this time Painter gloried in being able to show off his partner to his Yale friends and was especially proud of how he had transformed Tony. In describing their visit to Paris, Painter declared:

> How incredible the idea . . . [that] this rough, uncouth, ignorant, backward, underprivileged tramp boy, son of an illiterate Lithuanian coal minor and a drunken mother, would perfectly dressed, suave, polished, at ease, lead me with a protective and proprietary air into one of the most exclusive restaurants of Paris, order the dinner in French, debate various wines and hors d'oeuvres with the waiters, pay the bill and smile across the table at me, stuffed with roast goose, strawberries and cream, and champagne.[33]

This burst of paternal joy anticipated a quality that characterized Painter's subsequent long-term relationships. He reveled in his ability to transform poor, uneducated youths into the manners and sensibilities of his own upper-class heritage. Moreover, in intimately connecting with social inferiors, and thus transcending the class divide, he was defying the social order and living out his role as a rebel.

Unfortunately for Painter, his relationship with Tony was to last only another year. During their time together, Tony made frequent visits to Pottstown (financed by Painter) and became romantically involved with a woman whom he married in 1939. Within a short time after Tony left, Painter met Peter. Peter, like Tony, came from Pennsylvania and had left home when he was seventeen. After two years on the road, surviving with odd jobs and hustling, he arrived in New York, shortly before Painter met him through a prostitute "procurer." Peter had the physical and personal attributes Painter was looking for—a well-proportioned physique, golden blond hair, and a gentle, refined, yet "virile" personality. Painter was sexually enthralled with Peter and believed, as in the case of Tony, that he had fallen in love. Painter realized that Peter preferred women sexually, but he valued Peter's admiration and affection for him. Nevertheless, he also realized that Peter's stay with him would be, inevitably, temporary. Indeed, within a year Peter left to join the coast guard. Looking back, Painter described his Tony-Peter period as one of "false love and companionship . . . [with one-sided] infatuations [on his part] plus too much money and available sex."[34] Painter came to recognize that it was his money that was the primary source of their attraction to him. In other words, he felt that they were "kept boys."[35]

In reaction to the cumulative effect of two failed relationships, Painter immersed himself in his research and began working on his book manuscript. When he had a completed draft in the summer of 1941, he sent it to Dickinson, who assigned Gershon Legman to provide Painter with editorial and secretarial assistance. With Legman's assistance, the manuscript was completed in the fall of 1941. The working relationship between Painter and Legman, however, had been difficult. Painter resisted Legman's persistent attempts to make substantive changes. Moreover, Legman initially believed that he deserved coauthorship but dropped his claim when Painter refused to incorporate his recommended revisions. In the manuscript, Painter thus felt compelled to assiduously delineate Legman's contributions by stating, "The writer should like to acknowledge . . . his special indebtedness to G. Alexander Legman for the analysis of the epigraphs, the compilation of the glossary—originally a word-list of about one hundred and fifty terms compiled by myself—and of the bibliography, and in general for assistance practically to collaboration in writing and preparing the text."[36] The glossary referred to appeared under Legman's name in Henry's *Sex Variants* monograph. The bibliography, which was unfinished, was not included in the manuscript.[37]

In March 1942, a few months after he had completed his manuscript, Painter enlisted in the army. Much to his surprise, despite his age (thirty-seven) and heart and hearing problems, he was accepted. He served in Intelligence, achieving the rank of staff sergeant, and generally was very pleased with the type of work he was assigned. During his three and a half years in service, he was stationed in Miami, Amarillo, and Dayton, and was discreet about revealing his homosexual identity. As he commented, "[I] had given up telling everyone . . . [I] was homosexual."[38] He developed a friendship with another sergeant, Leonard Schwartz, and shared with him the work he had been doing for his book. Painter was indebted to his friend's tolerance, and, for his part, Schwartz was appreciative of Painter's acceptance because he was a target of anti-Semitism.[39]

While in the service, Painter had hoped to obtain a position that would make use of his expertise on homosexuality. He therefore asked Dickinson to write on his behalf to senior officials in the army and navy. Dickinson gladly agreed to support Painter's wishes. Although these efforts proved to be unsuccessful, they attest to Dickinson's high regard for Painter's work. In his letters he noted that Painter was well informed about the history, literature, psychology, and social incidence of homosexuality, and had unusual firsthand knowledge about the homosexual world and male prostitution. He added that Painter possessed tolerance, determination, and conviction.[40]

During Painter's army service, Dickinson made attempts to promote his manuscript for publication as a "medical book." While Dickinson was supportive of the work by homosexual researchers like Painter and Jan Gay, his goal was to insure that such work would be under the control of medical and scientific experts. He also recognized that publishers would only be interested if there was some form of legitimate medicoscientific sponsorship. Dickinson was eventually able to interest Kinsey in Painter's project. Even before he had seen the completed manuscript, he informed Kinsey about its scholarly potential in a June 1941 letter. In fact, this was Dickinson's first communication with Kinsey, prompted by an article Kinsey had written that was critical of the hormonal explanation of homosexuality. Dickinson commended Kinsey on his article, and this letter initiated a close relationship between the two men, one in which Dickinson served as a mentor and avid supporter for Kinsey's sex research. Dickinson's support was given at the very beginning of Kinsey's career as a sex researcher as this was his first publication on sexuality. Dickinson's letter also introduced Kinsey to Painter's work and Kinsey, in his reply, expressed great interest.[41]

When Kinsey learned that Painter's manuscript was completed, he eagerly looked forward to seeing it, noting, "We have much need to see the manuscript in order to correct our own thinking."[42] It took two years, however, for Kinsey to obtain the manuscript because Henry had possession of it. Painter, who had had problems with Legman about authorship, was even more concerned about Henry. As he confided in a letter to Dickinson, "I do not trust him [Henry]. He may be stealing my book."[43] Painter had a very negative opinion of Henry's scholarly abilities and integrity. Through Dickinson's efforts, the manuscript was recovered and sent to Kinsey in May 1943. Based on his initial impression, Kinsey commented to Legman, whom he assumed to be the coauthor, "You have done a very important thing in bringing these data together. It gives a picture of a certain aspect of the homosexual in much better detail . . . [than] anything that is in print."[44] In October, after he had had an opportunity to read the manuscript more thoroughly, Kinsey wrote to Painter, informing him about his own research on male sexuality and expressing the hope that they would be able to meet. In his letter Kinsey declared, "You could be of tremendous use to us, and I think you would find our approach objective and sympathetic to a degree which you have not met in your previous contacts."[45] In response, Painter replied, "It is with the greatest difficulty that I restrain my enthusiasm within the bounds of convention. Your letter is the only encouraging thing I have heard for ten years."[46] Painter also expressed his keen interest in working with Kinsey and asked about employment possibilities. Kinsey did not hold out the hope of adding Painter to his staff but suggested that Painter could be useful in making contacts for sex histories as well as being a consultant on research planning. He added that the exact nature of Painter's involvement would have to await their personal meeting. As Kinsey stated, "It is difficult to say much more, until I know you personally and I urge that you make a point of coming out here [Indiana University] as soon as you can."[47] It took several months for Painter to get enough leave time to visit Kinsey, but he finally arrived in August 1944. In the meantime, he had agreed to donate his personal library of books on homosexuality and the bibliography Legman had worked on to a very grateful Kinsey.[48]

After Painter's public coming out at Union in 1934, the start of his relationship with Kinsey in 1943 marked a turning point in his life. Through the encouragement and efforts of Dickinson, which were greatly appreciated by Painter, he had met the individual who "was doing the work . . . [I] had wanted to do."[49] Painter thus entered into an intellectual relationship that sustained him and gave meaning to his life. Dickinson had expected that Kinsey would take over the editorial revision, but Kinsey declined, indicating that he could not "undertake to criticize a manuscript in detail of such size, and of such importance."[50] While Dickinson and Kinsey had hopes that the manuscript could be put into publishable form, this objective was not realized, in part because of the failure to find medico-scientific sponsorship. And even if his work was legitimized through such an arrangement, it seems unlikely that in the postwar McCarthy era a publisher would be willing to produce a manuscript with graphic details about homosexuality. Furthermore, it appears that Painter himself had lost the will and interest to see it to completion. After his discharge from the army in 1945, he had no institutionalized base to support such an effort. He placed his faith in homosexual rights through scholarship in the hands of Kinsey. For Painter, working with Kinsey would fulfill his life's mission. Before continuing his life story in the next chapter, I turn to a consideration of the contents of his 1941 unpublished manuscript.

PAINTER'S RESEARCH ON MALE HOMOSEXUALITY AND MALE PROSTITUTION

Painter's manuscript title, "Male Homosexuals and Their Prostitutes in Contemporary America," conveyed his intent to analyze both male homosexuality and prostitution. The title also highlighted what Painter considered to be a major facet of homosexual life—the strong attraction that male homosexuals had for hustlers. Moreover, the title revealed Painter's binary conception of homosexuals and prostitutes; that is, male prostitutes were not themselves "homosexuals." Indeed, that had been his experience with hustlers. They had sex with him for money but were sexually attracted to women.

The typescript of close to six hundred pages (about half, single-spaced) was divided into two parts: "The Homosexual" and "The Prostitute." Painter's detailed ethnographic analysis of the male homosexual subculture of the 1930s was unique for its time. In American homosexual literature, it updated the turn-of-the-twentieth-century productions by Edward Prime-Stevenson and Earl Lind. It anticipated the 1951 book *The Homosexual in America,* by the pseudonymous Donald Webster Cory. Cory's work, however, was more impressionistic and contained relatively little on male prostitution.[51]

In addition to its ethnographic analysis, the manuscript exposed Painter's reflections about his own life around 1940–41 as well as his political stance regarding homosexual rights. In an essay entitled "De Profundis," which was withdrawn from the original manuscript and placed in an appendix, Painter poured out his personal feelings. He prefaced his essay by declaring, "This sincere, if somewhat naive and pathetic effusion is the production of a cultured and highly educated homosexual of a not at all effeminate type, in whom a deep but rather nebulous religious impulse is the most important inhibitory mechanism."[52] Painter freely expressed his deep suffering and the agony and futility of his life. He captured the source of his misery by declaring:

> I love a boy. . . . I love him as finely, cleanly and wholly as I hope some girl will some day. It is heaven when I am with him. It would be seventh heaven if he could love me in return as I love him. But he cannot, because he is "normal" sexually. And we are both of the same sex. It is absolutely impossible for him to respond to me, sexually. He likes me, respects me and even admires me. . . . But never can he *love* me. Never can he do what I so long to have him do—accept or proffer the physical caresses of love which are the same, the fulfillment of life to which every human, every animal, is entitled by nature, by birth.[53]

These words reflected Painter's despair and bitterness over his own plight of unrequited love. His search for the Will Finch object of his desire did not lead to the love he was yearning for. Generalizing from his own plight, he did not feel that it was possible for male homosexuals to find mutual love since, for the most part, they restricted their search for a partner to virile heterosexual men. Moreover, because homosexuals had not been allowed to communicate their suffering to society, he was going to use his authorial voice as a platform for speaking about the plight of this "afflicted" group. His goal was not to ask for pity, but rather that homosexuals be "tolerated, not persecuted" and that prevention and cure be found.

Throughout his manuscript, Painter incorporated the medical model of homosexuality. He did not, however, view homosexuality as a "psychosis" or a "disease," preferring to define it as a "psycho-physical condition" or even a "peculiarity." Nevertheless, male homosexuality was an "affliction" that he estimated affected some 2 million men in the United States. As a medical problem, the need was for research, both from a "medical" and "sociological" perspective. He viewed his own work as a preliminary sociological study, which set the stage for further research because it revealed, in depth, the life experiences and culture of male homosexuality. In order to further research on homosexuality, he advocated the establishment of a "Committee for the Promotion of Sexual Research." The committee's mandate would be to encourage and coordinate research, educate the public, and generate funding. He considered his own book as an example of how, with committee sponsorship, the public could be enlightened about homosexuality. He recommended that affluent homosexuals would be a significant target group for fund-raising and that an individual, like himself, who was "intimate at first hand with the homosexual world,"[54] be included in the committee structure. Painter's broad vision for

a committee devoted to promoting sex research appears to have anticipated aspects of what Kinsey was attempting to accomplish through his
own research center, which would eventually become the Kinsey Institute
for Sex Research. Kinsey, in fact, acknowledged that the financial support
and scientific backing he had for his own research was in keeping with
what Painter had envisioned in his manuscript.[55]

Painter's uncritical acceptance of the medical model is rather paradoxi-
cal. It appears that by 1940 he had retreated from the defiance he exhibited, several years earlier, when he indiscreetly announced his "overt homosexuality." Moreover, he had undergone medical treatment through his
therapy with Alfred Adler, which resulted in relieving his guilt rather than
curing him of his homosexuality. Painter's apparent drift toward a pathologized view of homosexuality reflected the social ostracism and mounting
personal despair he experienced once he proclaimed his sexual identity. As
Sedgwick argues in *Epistemology of the Closet,* coming out constitutes a
double bind of gaining control over one's gay identity, but at the expense
of risking social rejection. Indeed, the effects of heterosexism and homophobia were reflected in the self-hatred that was often expressed in the
coming out stories of the pre-Stonewall era. Nevertheless, in assimilating
a medicalized view of homosexuality (or it may have been more of a re-
affirmation of his previously held view), Painter framed it within the cause
of homosexual rights. He appealed to the common interest in decriminalizing homosexuality by medicoscientific experts and homosexual activists,
and he underscored the need for the homosexual community to be collaborators in funding, promoting, and carrying out research on homosexuality. If homosexuality was recognized as an "involuntary psychosexual condition" rather than a crime, the social stigma could be eradicated and the
unenforceable laws governing sodomy could be repealed. And, at the very
end of his manuscript, he held out the possibility that meaningful research
could demonstrate that homosexuality was "neither curable nor preventable . . . [and thus] society should rethink and revise its position in relation
to the homosexual, arriving at a more sane, just, efficient, and reasonable
attitude."[56]

In outlining the scope of his study, Painter pointed out that it dealt with
male homosexuality and, especially, with prostitution in the United States
between 1920 and 1940. Its particular focus was on the time and place in
which the writer had carried out his field research, that is, the years between 1935 and 1940 in New York City. He also referred to Legman's ongoing work on a bibliography of homosexuality, which when completed
would consist of some six thousand titles. He made a point of indicating
that female homosexuality would not be treated at any length because of
his lack of familiarity and the inappropriateness of his gender. He did,

however, include a brief commentary, which amounted to a rather sexist dismissal of lesbianism. He opined, for example, that lesbianism tended to be "faddish," appealing to women among the "intelligentsia" and in the arts, and he argued that even women who had homosexual impulses were basically bisexual, pointing to their protracted periods of "sexual normality." He observed that in contrast to the sexual nature of male homosexual relationships, lesbian attachments were primarily emotional. In addition, he indicated that lesbianism was not as sociologically significant as male homosexuality because there was no lesbian prostitution in America. His understanding of lesbianism led him to conclude, "Female homosexuality . . . is . . . too much female, and too little homosexual, to require treatment here."[57] In general, Painter was not sensitive to women's issues, and throughout his life he had no close women friends, either lesbian or straight. Moreover, his sexism reflected his distaste for effeminacy in homosexual men.

Male Homosexuality

The first volume of Painter's manuscript was devoted to an analysis of male homosexuality, based on his field research and the published literature. His literature review included a thorough survey of American medical and sociological publications from their inception in the 1880s through the 1930s. This was a significant contribution since such a review did not exist. Each study cited was summarized and general comparisons were made with the European literature, which Painter considered to be vastly superior. Unfortunately, his review did not include a list of references and the citations were not always completely or consistently indicated. This deficiency was due to the delayed (and never completed) bibliography being compiled by Legman, which was to be attached to the manuscript. Nevertheless, his literature review is quite remarkable in terms of its scope, thoroughness, and critical scholarship, and he added a number of incisive insights about the male homosexual and male prostitution subcultures of the interwar period.[58]

Painter began his volume with a consideration of historical trends, tracing the first signs of homosexual relations in America to the mid-nineteenth century. The discovery of gold, the westward thrust of the frontier, and the Civil War each created conditions in which large groups of men were thrown together without the availability of women. As evidence, he pointed to the observations recorded by social historians of the stag dances that were popular among frontiersmen. He continued to trace the development of segregated male sociality with the rise of the "hobo" and "tramp" in the post–Civil War period. By the 1880s, he observed, the growth of capitalism and the decline of religion had eroded the hold of Victorian morality. The new sexual openness was conducive to the development of a male homosexual subculture. He cited published accounts, such as Earl Lind's works, of the thriving male homosexual subculture of New York's Union Square district in the late nineteenth century. According to Painter, however, it was the effect of World War I that proved to be the major turning point in the increased visibility of male homosexuality. The new bohemianism and new affluence of the 1920s appreciably accelerated the availability of sex generally and male homosexuality in particular. Moreover, these postwar conditions produced a new type of male prostitution, that is, the prostitution of "normal" (heterosexual) men to homosexuals. Painter observed that by the mid-1920s, heterosexual male prostitutes, for the first time, overshadowed the traditional effeminate (fairy) homosexual prostitutes. The effects of the Depression in the 1930s served to strengthen this new form of prostitution because it became a means of survival for young men migrating to the cities. As he asserted, this trend was ignored in the contemporary medical literature because medical researchers were "unable to believe that boys and men who would prostitute themselves to homosexuals could be personally free from all or any homosexual condition."[59]

Painter also noted that there was a trend toward greater "tolerance" of homosexuality over the past fifty years (from the 1890s through the 1930s). He cited a decline in victimization through blackmail and robbery, a reduced threat of violence, and a greater likelihood of acceptance if one's identity was revealed. Yet he failed to note the increased extent to which gay men were affected by legal crackdowns and police harassment in the 1930s. It seems somewhat surprising that he was so optimistic about social attitudes, given his own experience of banishment from religious institutions when he came out publicly. He appeared to view religion as an exception to the trend toward greater tolerance by pointing out that "certain avenues of endeavor—such as church work—may be regretfully closed to the discovered homosexual."[60]

Moving beyond historical trends and the literature review, Painter divided his treatment of "The Homosexual" into "Who?" (classification and etiology), "Where?" (cultural patterns), and "What?" (sexual practices). Regarding classification, he viewed homosexuality as a category on a continuum, with heterosexuality as its opposite. In fact, anticipating Kinsey's heterosexual-homosexual rating scale of 0–6, he proposed seven categories, with bisexuality at the midpoint. Painter cited Karl Ulrichs as his source for proposing a continuum. Kinsey based his scale on the empirical data he collected for his study of male sexual behavior. While Kinsey did not cite Painter's classification scheme, he was undoubtedly aware of it because he had read Painter's manuscript and it seems likely that it would have influenced his thinking about a continuum of sexual behavior. Using his own notion of a continuum, Painter distinguished the homosexual, the bisexual, and the heterosexual on the basis of what a person seeks sexually. Thus, the object of desire for a homosexual male was another man. However, he went on to argue that some homosexuals if presented with a woman (although not their first sexual choice), would find heterosexual relations pleasurable. Such homosexuals, then, would be categorized as predominantly homosexual bisexuals, in contrast to "true" (exclusive) homosexuals. True bisexuals would be equally attracted to both sexes. This line of reasoning allowed Painter to point to cases of heterosexual men who because of circumstances, such as living in sex-segregated conditions like the military or prison, would pleasurably tolerate sex with other men. He also gave the example of heterosexual men who engaged in male prostitution because of economic necessity.[61]

In the context of sexual desire, Painter pointed out that homosexual men did not fit Ulrichs's assumption that they possessed a "woman's soul in a man's body." This was because the sexual urge of a homosexual man for another man was not the same as the sexual urge of a woman for a man. In contrast to heterosexual women, homosexual men were promiscuous and unfaithful as well as aggressive in their sexual practices, characteristics they shared with heterosexual men. He also observed that homosexual men, like heterosexual men, focused on the physical attributes of their sexual partners as well as the physical sexual act itself. Women, on the other hand, were primarily concerned with the emotional rather than the physical relationship with their lovers. With respect to nonsexual characteristics, however, he observed that male homosexuals possessed many of the traits associated with heterosexual women, such as being neat, domestic, emotional, and generally nonaggressive. He also revealed his sexist attitude by adding that male homosexuals are "generally rather prone to the typically feminine intellectual superficiality and confusion . . . and . . . to women's slavish acceptance of, and obedience to, transient and stupid fads and vogues, especially in clothing, beliefs, and amusements."[62]

With respect to etiology, Painter indicated that the cause of homosexuality was unknown but suggested that it was most likely a combination of biochemical, psychological, and sociological factors. He pointed to the innate basis of homosexuality because exclusive homosexuals were typically aware of their sexual urges when they were very young and these feelings persisted despite growing up in an atmosphere that assumed and rewarded heterosexuality. He also observed that environment played a significant role, pointing to social class differences. There was greater tolerance for homosexuality among the poor because of their general acceptance and practice of sexual promiscuity.[63]

In discussing sexual categories and etiology, Painter made a point of demystifying assumptions about homosexual identity. He argued that many homosexual men did not fit the commonly held caricature of the fairy. In fact, he noted that many homosexuals concealed their identity by deliberately presenting a facade of heterosexuality. Also contrary to stereotyped views that homosexual men feared or were hostile to women, he observed that most homosexual men enjoyed close social relationships with women. He also pointed to the social diversity of homosexuals with respect to professional status. One characteristic that he felt was widespread among homosexual men was loneliness. This was because of the unavailability of a lover, someone who could become a life partner. Unlike heterosexuals, who had the freedom and social approval to search for opposite-sex partners, homosexual men were forced to defy society in their search for same-sex partners. Moreover, because most were sexually driven to rugged, straight-appearing males, their choices were generally limited to male prostitutes. Alluding to his own frustrated experiences of searching for love, Painter observed that even if the homosexual finds the man of his dreams, "his final tragedy is that he cannot hold him, for at best more than temporarily."[64]

Painter's observations on loneliness reflected his own experiences. To what extent did they represent the typical experiences of homosexual men in the pre–World War II era? This is a difficult issue to resolve. Consistent with Painter's sexual predilections, early observers of the male homosexual culture, such as Ulrichs and Hirschfeld, had noted that homosexuals were especially attracted to virile young men who were not necessarily homosexual themselves. In the social circle that Painter moved in, he was not sexually attracted to other homosexuals and described his homosexual friends as sharing his preference for hustlers. But Painter, himself, was not consistent in his argument that homosexuals were primarily attracted to male prostitutes. In his manuscript, he described settings in which homosexual men sought out one another for sex, as in the case of bars and bathhouses. Yet these locales, with their focus on immediate sexual gratification, would be unlikely sources for combating loneliness. Another way of dealing with the dilemma Painter raised about the unavailability of committed partners is to look for examples of long-term relationships in the male homosexual community. As can be ascertained from the male autobiographies in Henry's *Sex Variants* monograph, there were instances, although not typical, of long-term committed relationships. Nevertheless, until the Stonewall era, it has been difficult to document committed gay male relationships. The relationships that existed were not very visible in the homosexual culture. With the relative absence of relationship models and the focus on physical sex within the male homosexual world, Painter's

observations about loneliness may very well have been quite representative. What may have countered the loneliness for the gay men of Painter's
era was the importance of homosexual friendships. Although Painter had
several close homosexual friends, this apparently was not enough to coun-
teract his feelings of social alienation.[65]

In depicting the homosexual subculture of the interwar period, Painter
provided a rich source of information, which, with the exception of the gay
novels of the time, was not disseminated in print. He began by describing
how homosexuals recognized one another. The starting point was in the
movement of the eyes. He elaborated:

> When normal men pass each other in the street they may glance at
> each other, but if their eyes happen to meet they both flash their
> glances away quickly. It is not conventional to gaze intently into the
> eyes of a stranger of the same sex—nor is there any reason for it. But
> when a homosexual passes a male in whom he feels any interest, he
> looks at him, and usually looks him in the eye . . . intently. . . .
> "[L]ooking" is not done entirely with the eyes; there is the cast and
> slant of the head, the directness or obliqueness of the glance, and im-
> portantly, the concomitant expression of the mouth—pleasant or
> forbidding, smiling or scornful, tight-lipped with anger or relaxed
> with indifference.[66]

From this beginning phase of eye contact, if the signs were mutually acknowledged and the observer was interested, he would quickly check
other details, such as the style of walking:

> The homosexual, typically, has a peculiar walk, a feminine walk. It
> is not the exaggerated, tip-toeing, swivel-hipped mincing weave at-
> tributed to the homosexual on the vaudeville stage, but a more or
> less subtle modification of it. It may best be described as walking in
> hypothetical high-heeled women's shoes—walking so that the ball of
> the foot, and not the heel, strikes the ground first and then the heel,
> as if one were almost walking on tip-toe, but came down lightly on
> the heel at every step. With the resulting hip-swinging and shoulder-
> swaying motion of the body, this is the typical homosexual glide.
> Add to this the taking of short, mincing steps, hold the elbows
> against the body while the forearms and hands are held flipper-
> fashion, and the sway of the shoulders and swing of the hips are ac-
> centuated. The result is "swishing," which can range from a mild ef-
> feminacy of gait to a grotesque caricature of femininity very similar
> to the vaudeville exaggeration.[67]

Painter noted, however, that many homosexuals, in order to avoid detection, shunned such obvious mannerisms. Yet an observer in the know
could still "spot" a fellow homosexual by looking for signs of eye contact.

In addition to physical characteristics, clothing and language were significant signs. With respect to clothing, he pointed to the French use of a green necktie and the American affectation of a red necktie. In general, the homosexual preferred color, looseness, softness, and informality, qualities that sharply contrasted with the conservative male fashions of the time. If all else failed in trying to ascertain if a man was homosexual, one could rely on the use of certain key words that had distinctly homosexual connotations, as Painter illustrated:

> For instance, supposing one met a stranger on a train from Boston to New York and wanted to find out whether he was "wise" or even homosexual. One might ask: "Are there any gay spots in Boston?" And by slight accent put on the word "gay" the stranger, in "wise[,]" would understand that homosexual resorts were meant. The uninitiated stranger would never suspect, inasmuch as "gay" is also a perfectly normal and natural word to apply to places where one had a good time. Such words as "queer," "trade," cruise," "fish," and many others may be used with similar double meaning. The continued use of such *double entendre* terms will make it obvious to the initiated that he is speaking with another person acquainted with the homosexual argot.[68]

The search for recognition among homosexuals also served as a basis for their general gregariousness. As Painter noted, in socializing with one another, homosexuals did not have to be on guard, protecting themselves from the social rejection and hostility they might receive from heterosexuals. Moreover, the forbidden sexuality they shared in common bonded them together and destroyed many social barriers. Central to the search for sexual partners and social interaction were the institutionalized gathering places where homosexuals could meet one another. As Painter pointed out, they had to be public places where people would naturally congregate, yet they could not be visibly identified as exclusively homosexual, as in the case of clubs, lodges, or meeting halls. He provided descriptions of homosexual bars, "drag" shows, cocktail parties, cultural events frequented by homosexuals (such as the ballet, theater, and concerts), movie theaters, baths, public toilets, YMCAs, and drag balls.

Among homosexual bars, Painter distinguished between those that included hustlers and those that did not. The former type was discussed in his volume on prostitution (see the next section). His characterization of the strictly homosexual or "gay" bar was colored by his personal dislike of such establishments because, in his view, they were places driven by sexual furtiveness and competition. Unlike the later portrayals of gay bars by

Donald Webster Cory and Evelyn Hooker, which pointed to both the sexual and social functions of bars, he downplayed the social facets of camaraderie, communication, and acculturation. According to Painter, the typical gay bar was a place in which

> the atmosphere is quiet, though pregnant, yearning glances are cast from table to table. Just what pleasure these homosexuals find in such funereal surroundings it would be hard to say. . . . One enters a cheap bar of this type and finds it noticeably crowded. Usually one has to search for sometime to find a place at the bar, not to mention a table at which to sit. . . . Everyone turns—if there is room to turn so much as one's head—and stares at anyone who comes in; and he tries to be nonchalant and to stroll up to the bar . . . just as if he were not being observed, and mentally undressed, disected [*sic*], analysed, and classified by practically everyone in the place. For a while he will look strictly at the drink he orders when he got to the bar. . . . Then, after the others have looked him over to their satisfaction, he may slowly start inspecting them. This is what everyone is doing to everyone else.[69]

If such cruising was successful, one man might invite the other to his room or, more likely, one would follow the other to the men's toilet, where sexual contact would take place. In the toilet there was the danger of being caught, but as Painter observed, "the danger being not so much the legal aspect of the matter, but the gossip and jealousy that might be started."[70]

Painter did point out that the bar served social purposes, but in his view the social interaction did not stand apart from the sexual undertone. He captured the social scene with the following description:

> Conversation flies back and forth, sometimes very shrilly. The typical homosexual's voice is at times accentuated to the point of caricature by its owners. Scandal is retailed, and repartee and insults are exchanged wholesale. People call each other by feminine names— this is considered quite proper. People rub up against each other and feel each other's genitals, seldom bothering with an elaborate pretense of accident. The conversation drips with *double entendre*. "Swinging" and "rimming" and "reaming" are everywhere to be heard mentioned, along with "meat" and "baskets" and "sprayed tonsils." One homosexual adjures another to "tell Mother all about it"; or cries, "Mary!" or "But, my *dear*!" in mock-shock at some bit of ignorance or bizarrerie. A trifle noisier and more self-consciously attempting to attract attention, and this becomes "camping." But even in its milder forms this sort of thing makes the air electric with sex in such places; perhaps a better description would be "heavy" with sex, because there is something very gross and yet timid, lustful but covert, refined yet extremely animal about it all.[71]

For Painter, the gay bar, despite its atmosphere of sexual playfulness, had a pervasive feel of sadness. He noted, "There is nothing hearty or even healthily vulgar about it; nothing at all frankly open. One hears no hearty laughter; what laughter there is is strained and shrill. . . . There is no song-singing, no convivial drinking, and drunkenness, no simple enjoyment. Such things would be inconceivable in these places."[72]

In contrast to the typical gay bar, he described some bars that produced a more upbeat, "campier" tone. They usually had a "drag" floor show with female impersonators who performed with a mock "strip-tease," or rendered songs with double entendre lyrics. The police did not always allow male entertainers to dress in women's clothes, but it was usually possible in bars that were away from the central districts of cities. Private cocktail parties and commercial "cocktail hours" shared some of the same features as bars, but especially in the case of private parties, the guests felt freer to "let down their hair."[73] These events provided the opportunity to show off one's lover, or search for someone new, or simply to "dish" the latest "dirt." The private parties also afforded the opportunity for private sex since guests would often retire to available bedrooms.

Painter pointed to the baths as a prominent place for homosexuals to meet. Sexual contact could take place in the steam rooms or the dormitories. Some Turkish baths were especially favored by homosexuals, and although they were raided from time to time, they continued to be popular. These places of homosexual assignation were generally off limits to hustlers. As Painter commented, "'Hustlers' cannot afford them, and anyhow it is not convenient to try to collect a fee from a naked man."[74]

Drag balls were richly pictured in the following fashion:

> While theoretically innocent masquerades, such balls are actually just transvestist carnivals, with all of the participants and most of the spectators homosexual or lesbian. Elegant and showy costumes of precisely the type loved by homosexual transvestists are worn, and the masqueraders "swish" and promenade before judges in competition for prizes for the "beauty" of their costumes and the perfection of their make-up as females. The homosexuals "in drag" dance with other males, and the Lesbians present dance with other women. . . . At "drags" there is much "groping" done on the dance floor, but the police stationed around the ballroom usually try to keep the out-and-out sexuality in the toilets. . . . There is also much jollity involved in deciding who should use which toilet room, and it does seem incongruous to watch a homosexual in a flamboyantly decorative gown go into the men's room, and to watch a Lesbian in slacks, tweed coat, and slouch hat stride into the ladies' room.[75]

The police were invariably present at these balls because a permit was needed to operate them. At times the police attempted to suppress the balls. One method was "planting" a number of "handsome" detectives who induced homosexuals to accost them. Another method was to seize homosexuals "in drag" and make them walk across the street from the door of the ballroom to a police van. They would then be arrested for the offense of publicly wearing the clothing of the opposite sex. Ballroom participants learned to avoid this trap by coming to the ball in taxis or cars. Although Painter did not refer to it, there was an increasing level of police suppression during the 1930s, and by the end of the decade, the drag balls were no longer permitted to operate.[76]

In rounding out his volume on male homosexuality, Painter provided an extensive section on homoerotic sexual practices. He believed that for his manuscript to be comprehensive and meaningful, such a presentation was necessary. If his work turned out to be a "manual of instruction" to homosexuals, that could not be helped. While his work was targeted as a vehicle for informing a medical and scientific readership, he undoubtedly knew that if his manuscript reached publication, there would be homosexual readers. He argued that the details of homosexual intercourse were "the whole point and crux of the matter. It is surely easier to keep such a book as this out of 'improper hands' than for readers whose hands are proper to be forced by the author's reticence to go a-seeking other less reticent writings for the elucidation of crucial details." He added that while many details of human behavior were grim and unsavory, a marshaling of all the facts was necessary if progress was to be made. Consistent with his incorporation of the medical model, the hope that homosexuality could be prevented required that every aspect of the phenomenon had to be probed, studied, and analyzed. His elucidation of homosexual practices was organized according to three broad types: masturbatory, oral, and anal. He included an extensive analysis of each type. With respect to oral sex, for example, he discussed such psychological and "aesthetic" factors as the appearance of the genitals, the olfactory sources of attraction, the mouth as an erogenous zone, and the sense of "conquest of the most personal area."[77] He also described the technique of fellation, including positions, mutual fellation, preliminary physical excitation, and the disposal of semen. Such graphic detail was unprecedented in the scientific literature on homosexuality.

Male Prostitution

In 1962, twenty-one years after he wrote his volume on male prostitution, Painter added an editorial note that qualified the generalizability of what he had written. He pointed to several aspects of prostitution that he had omitted or not fully dealt with because of his lack of knowledge at the time. For example, while he had included some discussion of homosexual prostitutes who offered their services to other homosexuals and, in some cases, to heterosexual men, he had underestimated their numbers. He also noted that he had omitted young boy prostitutes (some beginning as early as nine years old), older men (over thirty-five), and the extensiveness of "casual" prostitution among the Hispanic, African American, and muscle boy/male model subcultures. He thus acknowledged that his volume dealt with young, professional, heterosexual, white, male prostitutes in New York. His work is, nevertheless, significant in its in-depth treatment of this new form of male prostitution that emerged in American cities during the Great Depression. The group of young heterosexual men who migrated to the cities in search of economic survival and thus resorted to hustling was especially attracted to New York because of its reputation as a homosexual center. Painter's rich, textured portrayal of Depression-era heterosexual male hustlers provides an analysis of a cultural microcosm that would otherwise be unknown. Indeed, this was his intent, to produce research that revealed the nature of a hidden world and in so doing to gain public recognition of the experiences and struggles of the men who inhabited this demimonde. His work added to the earlier writings by Earl Lind on fairy prostitution and anticipated the later research on male prostitution, beginning in the post–World War II era.[78]

Painter began his treatise with a definition and classification of prostitution. Prostitution was "the indiscriminate, unemotional, and more or less habitual and public offering of one's sexual services to other persons for money, support, or other valuable considerations."[79] Prostitution did not necessarily have to be resorted to for a protracted period or be the prostitute's sole means of livelihood. This broad definition pointed to differences between female and male prostitution. Unlike women, men had the social freedom and independence to easily enter into prostitution on a temporary or partial basis. Painter distinguished between the professional, casual, and private hustler. The professional was engaged in prostitution for a protracted period of time without any other appreciable means of support. Some spent as much as ten years, beginning in their late teens. Most were involved for a period of three to five years. For some, retirement came after their youth had faded, or they became so familiar to their homosexual customers that they were no longer successful. Many professionals would travel between cities to enhance their prospects of picking up new customers. The professional hustlers who initially migrated to New York usually came from poor families in the industrial and mining areas of the East or from Appalachia. Among the casual or temporary hustlers were teenagers or young men who might spend only a few weeks until they earned enough for a specific purpose, such as spending money on a girl, or as a means of livelihood between jobs. Some casual hustlers came from economically privileged backgrounds and engaged in prostitution for temporary novelty. The private hustler, sometimes referred to as a "lover," "boyfriend," or "kept boy," became involved in a relatively protracted "affair" with a homosexual who provided financial support, which sometimes supplemented what was earned on a job. Painter stressed the fact that by the 1930s most male prostitutes were predominantly heterosexual; that is, they would tolerate homosexuality, but they had a marked preference for sex with women. In fact, they tended to denigrate their homosexual clients, referring to them as "queers," "freaks," or "half-men."[80]

The locales where hustlers functioned were described in considerable detail. In New York, the "capital of the homosexual world," there were a number of street areas frequented by hustlers. These spaces shifted over time. In the 1920s, for example, Riverside Drive, Fifth Avenue, and Battery Park were the centers of hustler activity. By the 1930s the scene had shifted to the Times Square area and was closely connected to the location of bars that were known hangouts for hustlers. With the increased pace of bar closings during this period, the specific areas changed. In the mid-thirties the most popular spot was the north side of Forty-second Street between Seventh and Eighth Avenues because the Barrel House bar was situated on this block. When the police closed the Barrel House, the scene shifted to the south side of the block, centered on another bar. Painter noted that seeking out hustlers in Times Square had associated dangers because the district was a haven for pickpockets and a focal point for vice and crime. Hustlers also hung out in parks. Painter referred to New York's Central Park and identified specific locations, such as the southeast end, where the benches would be solidly lined up with homosexuals and hustlers.[81]

The bars frequented by hustlers varied according to class and racial dynamics. The Keg on Forty-second Street, for example, attracted a drunken, coarse, and often-violent type of hustler. As Painter stated, these "boys in dungarees and polo shirts responded to signals to drink with wealthy bankers and play-boys." Marco's on Fifty-second Street between Fifth and Sixth Avenues was "exclusive" and catered to mostly homosexual hustlers who were sought by wealthy homosexuals. In this atmosphere, male prostitution functioned "at its most refined level." Hustlers were often paid with gifts rather than cash. Relationships had to appear more like "love" than sex; hence sexual denouement had to be delicately maneuvered. In contrast, at the Whoopee Club, the homosexual crowd tended to be so cheap that only a few hustlers would drop in. The Cosmopolitan Club in

Harlem was a large ballroom with tables accommodating four hundred. Homosexuals and lesbians, white and "colored," all mingled with one another, and same-sex couples danced with one another "in the most amorous, close-hugging, and ecstatic manner." Black hustlers, both heterosexual and flamboyantly homosexual, responded to suggestions to "dance" or visit the men's toilet. At midnight, when the "Cosmo" closed, some of the customers would stop at a nearby unostentatious "street-bar," full of homosexuals and black hustlers, most of whom were homosexual. White hustlers were a rarity in Harlem because of the prejudice "against a white boy selling himself to a Negro."[82]

In discussing bars, Painter described how they got started. Whether it was a "gay" bar, which catered to homosexuals, or one that also attracted hustlers, the "host" was often homosexual. Such an individual might get a financial backer, or he might go to a bar owner and persuade him that his business could improve with a homosexual clientele. Once established, the bar's popularity would spread by word of mouth. The police could easily close these bars, although the police were often paid off. Eventually all such bars would be closed because their liquor licenses were taken away.[83]

Painter pointed to public toilets and movie theaters as other sites for hustler activity. The toilets were a focal point for clients with a "penis fetish," which meant that they were looking for oral sex. Hustlers would be attracted to a potential client if he left the stall door ajar or lingered at the urinal with his penis exposed. Toilets were convenient locales for homosexual and hustler advertisements, but they were also dangerous because homosexual clients could easily become victims of robbery or extortion. Movie theaters served as places to meet hustlers or other homosexuals. For the hustler, movie theaters provided rest and warm shelter and they were spaces where one could easily be propositioned and sex (groping and fellatio) could be performed on the spot. A scandal arose at New York's Capitol Theater because it had love seats for two and male couples were discovered using them.[84]

Unlike female prostitutes, male hustlers generally worked alone and were not dependent on houses of prostitution. Nevertheless, some hustlers did work in male brothels. There were two types—the "slide" and the "peg house." The slide was a rarity in America and Painter identified only one, which was in New Orleans, a city long noted for its prostitution. The term originated from the argot used by female prostitutes. In this type of bordello, the hustlers were effeminate homosexuals ("faggots") who dressed as female prostitutes and solicited male clients. The clients were either aggressive heterosexual men ("wolves") who sought active pedication, or other homosexuals ("ki-ki queens"). Along similar lines, when specially requested by clients, some of the more expensive houses of female prostitution would supply a boy acting as a woman. Such a house of female prostitution was known as a "benny house." Painter noted that in Cuba most female brothels had a boy or two on hand.[85]

Peg houses catered to homosexual clients who preferred the virile, straight-looking male hustler, and the hustlers were predominantly heterosexual and in some cases bisexual. The term was appropriated from British India and referred to brothels furnishing young boys to pedicators. Between sexual acts, the boys were kept sitting on benches studded with upright pegs for the purpose of keeping their anuses distended to a size large enough to accommodate anal penetration. Most people who used the term "peg house" were unaware of its origins, and many of the hustlers in such establishments simply referred to them as a "house for men" or a "whore house" and referred to themselves as "hookers." There were about eight peg houses in New York, and one in each of a few other cities, including San Francisco and Los Angeles. The peg houses in New York were usually identified with the pseudonym used by the person or "madam" who ran the establishment. This was necessary because in order to avoid police detection, the locations shifted every few months. According to Painter, the best-known New York peg houses were those run by "Matty Costello," "Danny Rodgers," "Miss Fox," and "George." Painter frequented Matty Costello's and recruited Matty as a participant (Victor R.) in the sex variants study. George was Gustave Beekman, whose house in Brooklyn, near the Navy Yard, was raided in 1942 because it was suspected that German spies were among his clients. This led to the scandal involving a prominent Democratic senator, David I. Walsh, who was a client at George's and had contact with the spies.[86]

The typical peg house, according to Painter, was an apartment of three to five rooms. In one of those rooms, anywhere from one to ten hustlers would be entertaining themselves by talking, playing cards, or reading magazines or comic books. The radio would be playing with the lights fairly dim, perhaps tinted blue or red. The hustlers were generally dressed in street clothes, although in some peg houses if they had good physiques, they were encouraged to remove their shirts. They tended to range in age from eighteen to twenty-eight, although most were in their early twenties. They were quite diverse in appearance, but they generally displayed a lack of education and refinement. Most arrived early in the evening and stayed until about two in the morning. Often the proprietor would choose three or four as residents of the apartment.

The "madam" who owned and ran the establishment was homosexual. He recruited his hustlers by going to the street locales where they congregated. Once they agreed to work in his peg house, they were free to come and go and to refuse offers, which was seldom done. One of the hustlers was usually the madam's favorite and became her "husband." Some of these relationships lasted as long as two years. The husband was usually available to customers and was often given those who were considered to be the best. He had some supervisory duties and might get a share of the profit. Some peg houses also had a "maid" who was homosexual and did the housework, served drinks, and ran errands. The madam devoted himself to business and entertaining customers, sometimes in drag. Matty Costello was known for his rendition of the dance of the seven veils.[87]

In various other sources, Painter provided considerable background about the two peg house proprietors he knew well—Matty Costello and Danny Rodgers. According to Painter, Matty, at the age of eight, emigrated with his family from Italy to America. As a child he had a strong feminine identity. As a teenager he had his first homosexual experiences and subsequently was attracted to strong, masculine partners. By the time he was seventeen, he became a prostitute, assuming the effeminate "fairy" identity of "Deloris Costello." A few years later he met a sailor and became involved in a relationship with him. At his partner's suggestion, they started a peg house in which "Deloris" became "Matty" and his partner assumed the role of "husband." This relationship broke up after two years, but Matty continued to run the peg house on his own. By the late 1930s he also began an antique business, and when the police closed down his peg house in 1942, he devoted himself to antiques. Danny had a similar background, starting off as a hustling "drag queen" who also acted in drag shows under the name of "Molly King." He took the name "Rodgers" from his "husband" with whom he lived for many years. Painter noted that he ran one of the most successful peg houses, carefully screening his customers and being very selective in his choice of hustlers. During World War II he was a cook in the navy and was stationed at an Italian POW camp, where he freely chose sex partners among the prisoners in exchange for granting them the opportunity to work in his kitchen. After the war, he ran a "call house," in which arrangements for hustlers were made by phone.[88]

Many of the homosexual clients of the peg houses were quite wealthy. They preferred going to peg houses rather than finding hustlers themselves for a variety of reasons, including not having the time or energy to find boys, lacking the courage to do so, or, especially if they were socially prominent, fearing being recognized. Some were well-known actors and writers; many others came from the professional and business world. In some cases, in order to insure privacy, clients would make arrangements for the madam to bring a group of hustlers over to their homes. Peg houses also had advantages for hustlers. Unlike public spaces, they were safe and comfortable and there was an opportunity to meet wealthy homosexuals who could provide long-term security.

Peg house clients were admitted either by recognition or through another client's introduction. Often customers telephoned first to make sure
that there was no threat of a police raid and to find out which hustlers were
around. If the customer was known, he was admitted and directed to the
room where the hustlers were. The madam, using only his first name or a
pseudonym, would introduce him. The madam would then offer him a
drink and engage him in conversation. During this exchange, the customer
would covertly eye and appraise any of the hustlers he found desirable.
Even if he was a steady client, he would find many new boys because of the
rapid turnover among the hustlers. The madam would also help in the selection process since he was aware of the various tastes of his customers.
Once the customer had made a tentative choice, he and the madam would
go to a private room to confer. Here, the client would make various in-
quiries about the hustler in question, such as what sexual acts he would
and would not perform, what his price was, what his naked physique was
like, and what the size of his penis was. These questions were often
phrased in terms of the homosexual argot, such as, "What kind of meat
has he got?"[89] When these matters were satisfactorily settled, the madam
would send the boy into the room. Sex was usually performed on the premises, but some customers preferred to take the hustler to a hotel or back
to their home. The fee was usually split between the hustler and the
madam—in the late 1930s, it was $5 to the boy and $5 to the house. If the
customer wanted to spend the night with the hustler, then the price would
be higher.[90]

What was most noteworthy about the hustler selection process, as
Painter later commented, was the attitude of the hustlers. Unlike female
prostitutes, there were no acts of seduction and, with a few exceptions,
they were not dressed in an erotically revealing manner. The boys did not
consider themselves to be "'whores.' . . . They weren't going to half strip
like women in a whore house. They weren't going to act alluring like a
woman."[91] Gender distinctions were also significant for hustlers when it
came to sexual practice. Although the proprietors urged that the hustlers
should be open to all forms of sexual activity, the hustlers generally preferred not to engage in the "feminine" acts of fellating their partners or being the recipients of anal penetration. As a result, many charged a higher
price for these acts. They could then rationalize having their masculinity
violated.

Peg houses institutionalized certain practices of male prostitution that
were already widespread. The male "madam" was a development of the
"procurer," who, for a price, would match up a homosexual with a hustler. As Painter noted, "Many homosexuals assist other homosexuals—for
a consideration—in 'making' a boy or in being introduced to a desired

boy."[92] In fact, some homosexuals enjoyed the pursuit and seduction of hustlers and thus had a number of boys "on the line." Moreover, at private parties some hosts would invite a number of hustlers to entertain the homosexual guests. The host, guests, or both would pay the boys. The informal patterns of procurement continued after peg houses ceased to exist. In the early 1940s, as a result of the war hysteria, the FBI closed them down. After the war, with the housing shortage, it was impractical to operate male bordellos because they could not be easily relocated when it became necessary to avoid a police crackdown. Some ex-madams, such as Danny Rodgers, instituted "call houses" whereby customer-hustler arrangements were made by phone through the person running the call house.[93]

Homosexuals who chose to find their own hustlers would go to public areas in large cities, such as streets, parks, and bars, where male prostitutes were known to gather. In these settings, hustlers used such signs as dress, posture, and eye contact to attract potential customers. For their part, homosexuals looking for hustlers would be alerted to these recognition factors as well as other unintended giveaways. With respect to dress, professional hustlers assumed either the rough dress of jeans, cowboy outfits, riding boots, or sailor caps, or the "smooth" dress of well-coordinated sports and dress clothes. Beyond either style, there were signs homosexual customers would be cognizant of. Jeans, for example, would be tight fitting and suits would be especially well matched with accessories. Often there would be unintended signs, such as suede shoes or frayed shirts, items that former customers would give away. Hustlers were generally good-looking and well built physically. Their facial expressions typically signified a sense of cynicism and disillusionment. The most notable sign was eye contact. Just as in the case of homosexuals trying to attract one another, hustlers would stare back when looked at. Added to this were such signs as an inviting expression in the gaze and the position of the mouth—"intently closed or lasciviously drooping."[94] On the street, the most common approach strategy on the part of the homosexual customer was to ask for a match. In the bar, eye contact might be followed by the hustler and potential customer each proceeding to the men's toilet or striking up a conversation and agreeing to go a hotel or movie theater.[95]

In his field research Painter had made observations of sixty-seven hustlers, and in his manuscript he provided an analysis of this group as well as brief biographical sketches of a subsample of twenty-two. Most of the hustlers, according to Painter, came from very poor families who lived in urban slums or depressed rural areas and small towns. As children they had little supervision and, as a result, engaged in a considerable amount of sexual exploration, including homosexual experience. To counter their drab surroundings and sense of hopelessness, they craved adventure. They were therefore open to the idea of hustling when they first learned about it, either through what they heard from friends or from their own experience of being accosted. Because of poverty and broken families, many of these boys left home by the time they were fifteen. With the difficulty of finding steady employment, hustling proved to be a strong incentive for economic survival. They were attracted to large cities, especially New York because of its reputation as a center for homosexuality.[96]

The day-to-day life of the hustler was scheduled around his working hours, which were generally between ten at night and eight in the morning. While some hustlers lived in rooming houses, most depended on finding a night's lodging at a customer's hotel room or apartment. Paying a weekly rent for a room was therefore viewed as a waste of money. Hustlers without a room of their own often ran the risk of "carrying the banner," that is, spending a homeless night walking the streets or sleeping on a bench in the park or subway. Without having received any money for a night's work, flophouses or cheap hotels might not be affordable. After a homeless night, some hustlers would try to "bum" or steal food or cigarettes. Some were able to catch up on their sleep the following day by using a friend's room and thus be ready for the next night. Money earned was often quickly spent on gambling or sex with women. Generally, the hustler's income was quite low and unpredictable. The one exception was the case of "kept boys," the private hustlers who were supported by a homosexual for a period of time. Many kept boys, however, were improvident and ended up without any money.

The attitudes that hustlers had toward homosexuals depended on the way they were treated. What was most important for the hustler was to be treated with self-respect. They objected to being thought of as objects and resented being described by their clients with such terms as a "number" or a "piece of trade." In response, they would refer to their clients as a "score" or "trick," or even worse, a "fag" or "queer." The type of homosexual that the hustler preferred as a client was one who was thoughtful, considerate, and generous. Taking into account the needs of hustlers and the risks involved for homosexual clients, Painter provided a set of guidelines, entitled "advice to a homosexual who likes rough trade."[97] Among his recommendations, he suggested that the homosexual be direct and open about what is to be paid; generous, offering if needed food, clothing, or shelter; and engaging in as little effeminate behavior as possible in bed, such as kissing, which would threaten the hustler's masculinity. Correspondingly, he also recommended that the homosexual be as "manly" as possible in walk, actions, and speech. Moreover, Painter pointed to a number of cautions that homosexuals needed to take, including not carrying large amounts of cash or valuables; not getting drunk unless sure of one's companion; avoiding going back to a hustler's room, where one could be victimized; and never submitting to blackmail. In essence, homosexuals had to be aware of the dangers of robbery, extortion, and blackmail. Such threats were a fairly frequent part of the hustler scene, reflecting the desperation some hustlers faced. Moreover, since hustlers were already engaged in the illegal trade of prostitution, other criminal acts were viewed as part of living a life of crime.

Among the twenty-two profiles of hustlers, Painter included "Jack Flaherty" and "Willie O'Rourke," both of whom he had brief relationships with when he first explored the hustler world. Also included was "Theodore George Rosenbaum Avery Wade," who was Painter's roommate at the time that Painter recruited participants for the sex variants study. Wade was interested in the study and was interviewed under the name of Leonard R. The biographical sketch of "Jean Driscoll" stood out from the others because he was a homosexual prostitute. He grew up in Jacksonville and, unlike most hustlers, had a middle-class background. His parents were separated and his mother fully supported his homosexuality and cross-dressing. He came out when he was seventeen and went to work in drag shows as "Jeanne Driscoll" in Miami and New Orleans. After losing his job with the show, he became a "boy-prostitute" in various houses of female prostitution in New Orleans and then went on to hustle the streets in drag in Washington and New York. Playing both sides of the gender boundary, he also dressed and acted as a man. As a man, his clients were homosexual; as a woman, they were heterosexual, believing in most cases that they were having sex with a woman. When his feminine masquerade was exposed, his clients were usually amused. His feminine identity was further enhanced by the relationships he sought. Most of the time, he lived with a heterosexual hustler-lover "husband." These relationships typically ended when he was robbed and deserted by his lover. When Painter met him, he had been hustling for about two years and, because he enjoyed it, had no plans to quit.[98]

The fact that Painter included only one homosexual hustler among his twenty-two case studies was consistent with the ratio he reported—only one in twenty male hustlers were homosexual. In 1962, however, he acknowledged that he had underestimated the ratio because he knew so little about homosexual prostitutes. The relative rarity of such hustlers, according to Painter, was a function of the limited market and historical changes. Regarding the potential pool of clients, he believed that only a minority of homosexuals ("ki-ki queens") was attracted to other homosexuals and many of these possible clients were involved in relationships. These homosexual relationships were usually heterosexually modeled, so that the more virile partner played the role of "husband" to his partner's role as "wife." Painter observed that homosexual relationships were generally short-lived. Homosexual clients, therefore, were either "between lovers" or not attractive enough to be in a relationship. Another source of clientele for the homosexual hustler was the "wolf," mostly heterosexual men, but some homosexuals who were active pederasts seeking out sexual partners. In either case, even with Painter's overrepresentation of heterosexual hustlers, the market for male homosexual prostitutes in the 1930s became more limited. The new influx of heterosexual hustlers during the Depression opened up a clientele of homosexuals who preferred sex with virile men. In contrast to the fairies described by Lind in the 1890s, gay men in the 1930s did not have to prostitute themselves to attract heterosexual men. There were now heterosexual hustlers who could meet their sexual needs.[99]

In his conclusions, Painter discussed the social effects of male prostitution and offered suggestions about how society should deal with the issue. He appeared to equivocate about the social consequences. On the one hand, he engaged in a rather conventional diatribe, pointing out how the spread of male prostitution would lead to a lowering of moral standards. Yet, having established this argument, he ended his discussion by pointing to several positive effects. First, the spread of male prostitution would increase the awareness, and even tolerance, of homosexuality because hustlers disseminated knowledge about homosexuality to adolescent boys, thus reducing ignorance and stigma. Furthermore, there was no indication that the recent spread of male prostitution in America (beginning in the 1920s) would produce a social decline. Such prostitution had been widespread in England and Europe for at least a century without impeding social progress. Painter also noted that the greatest flowering of homosexuality had occurred during the most glorious periods of human development, such as ancient Greece, the Italian Renaissance, the Elizabethan era in England, and pre-Revolutionary France. In contrast, the most virulent purge of homosexuality was taking place in fascist Germany. And even if there were a concerted effort to eradicate male prostitution as a social institution, it would still persist since, at an informal level, it always coexisted with male homosexuality. Before the emergence of a formalized profession of male prostitution, homosexuals searched for boys in such locales as the slums, the docks, and places of amusement. With this line of argumentation, Painter really appeared to be making a case for the positive contributions male prostitution could make to society. As long as male homosexuality existed, male prostitution would be an inevitable phenomenon.[100]

Homosexuality and Society

Since male prostitution was inextricably linked with male homosexuality, the issue for society was how to deal with homosexuality. For Painter, homosexuality was a medical issue. Although he did not consider it to be an illness like a psychosis, it was a "psycho-physical" condition that produced psychological problems because male homosexuals could not find love through committed relationships and thus could not achieve the same degree of fulfillment that heterosexual men were capable of. His stated goal in writing his manuscript was to provide medical experts with first-hand knowledge about homosexuality so that they could improve upon efforts at treatment and prevention. With this objective in mind, he also hoped to reach the general public so that they could be educated and thus become sympathetic to the plight of the homosexual. Such information would also serve as a resource for homosexuals and their families seeking information and help. A complementary goal was to further the cause of homosexual rights by pointing to the futility of punitive practices by the legal system. As he argued, the widespread prevalence of homosexuality made legal persecution unenforceable. Legal toleration, on the other hand, would free the homosexual "from the fear of legal persecution and social obloquy, and . . . [make] him willing to cooperate with medical, psychological, and bio-chemical science in the effort to study homosexuality so that its cause may be understood and methods for its treatment and prevention learned."[101]

Painter believed that his book would be a first step in instituting a concerted effort to study homosexuality in America. He pointed to the need for investigating both the psychological and biochemical approaches to treatment. The sociological aspects of homosexuality also needed to be explored. Finally, a breakthrough in education was needed. He proposed the establishment of an agency that would be devoted to publishing books and pamphlets on homosexuality designed for various audiences, including scholars, parents, adolescents, legislators, and penologists. Such an agency could also arrange for the translations of the rich literature on homosexuality in German and French that could then be made available for the medical and scientific community. This would be part of an effort to create a reference library on homosexuality. Furthermore, this proposed agency would serve as a coordinating body for funding and publishing research on homosexuality.

At the very end of his manuscript, Painter pointed to the possibility that once a comprehensive program of research and education was launched and carried through, homosexuality would be found to be neither curable nor preventable. He declared, "Some writers and scholars have [already] concluded that homosexuality is unpreventable and incurable, and they have therefore decided that all anti-homosexual laws should be repealed, and that the world should prepare to have homosexuals always present, and should be taught to treat them well—allowing them to marry members of their own sex, to dress in the clothing of the opposite sex, etc."[102] What Painter was therefore really trying to achieve, despite his seeming weddedness to the medical model, was to effect social acceptance through the production and dissemination of knowledge about homosexuality. In this sense, he was furthering the work of such homophile activists as Hirschfeld and Carpenter, and anticipating the formal establishment of gay and lesbian studies in the post-Stonewall era.

Painter's ambitious proposals for the study of homosexuality and the development of a coordinating agency were remarkably consistent with the broader conception Kinsey had about studying human sexuality in general and creating an institute to oversee such a project. Shortly after completing his manuscript, Painter's foresight would be rewarded when, through the efforts of Dickinson, he would meet Kinsey and embark on a personal association that would give his life a new purpose.

Thomas Painter (*left*) with his brother, Sidney, at home in New York around 1907. Reproduced by permission of The Kinsey Institute for Research in Sex, Gender, and Reproduction, Inc.

Painter in 1911 on a family vacation in Maine. Reproduced by permission of The Kinsey Institute for Research in Sex, Gender, and Reproduction, Inc.

Painter at Yale around 1930. Reproduced by permission of The Kinsey Institute for Research in Sex, Gender, and Reproduction, Inc.

Painter (*left*) with his stepmother, father, and Sidney, on a visit to his father's home in France around 1930. Reproduced by permission of The Kinsey Institute for Research in Sex, Gender, and Reproduction, Inc.

Painter and his mother in the 1930s at Sidney's home in Connecticut. Reproduced by
permission of The Kinsey Institute for Research in Sex, Gender, and Reproduction, Inc.

Painter in 1956 at the Kinsey Institute. Reproduced by permission of The Kinsey Institute for Research in Sex, Gender, and Reproduction, Inc.

Toward Participatory Research on Homosexuality: Painter, Kinsey, and the Kinsey Institute, 1943–73

A book can end an era. An era of Hush-and-Pretend in the life of our nation may end through the Kinsey Report.

Robert Latou Dickinson, foreword to *American Sexual Behavior and the Kinsey Report*, by Morris L. Ernst and David Loth

In contrast with other gay and lesbian activist-researchers in the pre-Stonewall era, Painter was able to establish a relationship with a recognized sex researcher who fully supported his work. Earl Lind had to contend with a hesitant sponsor, physician-lawyer Alfred W. Herzog, who reluctantly agreed to publish Lind's autobiographical writings without editorial censorship. Jan Gay's association with psychiatrist George W. Henry aborted her hopes of gaining authorial voice for her project on lesbian and gay life histories. Alfred A. Gross, through his relationship with Henry, was able to carry out his mission of helping young gay men in legal trouble, but he was forced to conceal his authorship under Henry's name. Donald Webster Cory, who I discuss in the next chapter, formed a relationship with psychologist Albert Ellis but was increasingly swayed by Ellis's commitment to the medical model. Kinsey, on the other hand, acted as a source of inspiration for Painter to continue his research efforts as a participant-observer of the gay male subculture.

All of these activist-researchers shared the objective of securing homosexual rights through the production of research that revealed the experiences and struggles of an oppressed people. These activists were committed to the belief that such knowledge would demystify misconceptions, counter prejudice and stigmatization, and ultimately lead to rudimentary forms of social justice, most notably decriminalization. To further their projects, they needed the support and sponsorship of medicoscientific experts.

Even with the support of Kinsey and Kinsey's research associates, Painter, as a result of social obstacles and personal failings, was never able to convert his four-decade outpouring of ethnographic and autobiographical work into publishable form. Yet with the persistent encouragement of Kinsey and the Kinsey Institute, he was driven to keep a record of his life experiences with the goal of preserving his work and enabling future researchers to draw from it. Indeed, these materials furnish not only a fascinating look at a marginalized subculture, but also reveal the tragic circumstances and complex subjectivity of a gay man who had to struggle with oppression in his daily life. His life story therefore sheds light on what it was like to endure the social barriers that blocked his aspirations to be a published writer on male homosexuality and to freely express his concerns about social justice.

When Painter met Kinsey in 1943, Kinsey had already been at work on his study of human sexual behavior for several years. Early in his work on male sexuality, he had uncovered a higher-than-expected incidence of homosexual behavior and he went to great lengths to ensure that male homosexuals were included in his survey. Kinsey and the Kinsey Institute sought out gay men to speak about their personal experiences and social perceptions, freed from the distorted renderings of their lives imposed by the medical model. The Institute's aim was to understand homosexuality from the vantage point of those engaging in homosexual behavior. Before returning to Painter's story, I review how Kinsey became involved with research on sexuality, the nature of his thinking about homosexuality, and his relationship with the homosexual community.

KINSEY AND HOMOSEXUALITY

Kinsey was born in 1894 in Hoboken, New Jersey, where his father was an instructor at Stevens Institute of Technology. Kinsey's father was a strict disciplinarian and both of his parents were deeply religious, attributes that created a restricted home life for Kinsey in his boyhood years. Outside of this austere family atmosphere, Kinsey developed an early interest in nature and out-of-doors activities. He resisted his father's wishes for him to have a career in engineering by transferring from Stevens Institute to Bowdoin College in his junior year. At Bowdoin, acting on his interest in nature, he majored in biology. After completing his undergraduate studies in 1916, he entered Harvard's graduate program in zoology and specialized in the taxonomy of animals and plants. He completed his doctoral studies in three years and then obtained a research fellowship for a year in which he traveled to the South and to the West Coast, collecting gall wasps. In 1920 he began his academic career at Indiana University, and over the next two decades devoted himself to the study of gall wasps and earned a reputation as a well-respected researcher in entomology. In his personal life, shortly after he arrived at Indiana, he met Clara Bracken McMillen, who had completed her undergraduate studies in chemistry. This was the first woman he dated, and within a year he and Clara were married.[1]

Kinsey's career as a zoology professor took a rather abrupt turn in 1938 when he instituted a team-taught course in marriage. The noncredit course was limited to senior students. The apparent impetus for the course was a student petition from the Association of Women Students, but in reality Kinsey had instructed the students to gain approval from Indiana University president Herman B. Wells. Kinsey had a long-standing interest in the study of sex, a reaction to his own sexual frustration as a young man. This interest was first manifested in the 1920s when he encouraged his male graduate students to reveal their sex lives to him. By the 1930s he had a reputation on campus as being a sex adviser for students as well as a defender of students' rights in the face of sex-related censorship in campus publications. In his lectures in the marriage course, Kinsey railed against the social attitudes about sex. To aid his teaching, he began taking histories of students, asking them about their experience with premarital intercourse, the frequency of sex, and other related questions. At first the course seemed to be only a side interest since he was still committed to his research on gall wasps. Within a year, however, he became heavily involved with the course and in June 1939 made the first of several field trips to Chicago to obtain a wider range of sex histories. This was soon followed up with trips to the Indiana State Penal Farm to conduct interviews with the inmates and their families.[2]

While the marriage course proved to be a success with the majority of students, there was mounting criticism by the second year the course was offered. Some parents objected, but the pressure came from local clergy and other faculty. Thurman Rice, a medical school professor who had given lectures on sex in his hygiene class, led a campaign that demanded Kinsey's resignation from the university on the grounds that he talked to coeds about their sex lives. While President Wells was personally sympathetic to Kinsey's efforts, he feared the political backlash from the controversy and offered Kinsey a choice of dropping either the course or his sex history research. Kinsey resigned from the marriage course in September 1940. For the rest of his career, he was to be consumed with his ambitious project of collecting sex histories. In 1941 he received his first research grant from the Rockefeller-funded Committee for Research in Problems of

Sex. Together with his team of research collaborators, he published the results of his work on male sexual behavior in 1948 and female sexual behavior in 1953. The so-called Kinsey Reports revolutionized American society's views about sexuality by forcing open discussion and setting the stage for the sexual revolution of the 1960s. Kinsey himself reaped the benefits of acclaim for his monumental efforts but also had to endure controversy and vilification. Under political pressure, his Rockefeller funds were withdrawn shortly after his female volume appeared. Always a workaholic, he continued his commitment to sex research, but at an increasing expense to his health. He died in 1956 at age sixty-two, the result of heart complications.[3]

There has been much speculation and controversy about Kinsey's own sex life and the extent to which it drove his career as a sex researcher. Two recent biographies reveal that he had homosexual experiences. James H. Jones interprets this as evidence that Kinsey was a homosexual and, furthermore, asserts that his unconventional sexuality, which also included masochism, compromised his scientific objectivity and motivated him to promote a hidden agenda of sexual liberation. This attempt to label Kinsey as a homosexual is unconvincing, given the fact that he had a highly satisfying sex life with his wife and also had sex with other women. Jonathan Gathorne-Hardy, more accurately, points out that Kinsey was bisexual (increasingly having more sex with both sexes as he aged) and that his interest in sex research evolved as he became more aware of his own sexuality. What stands out about Kinsey's life is that as a result of overcoming his own sexual repression as well as his growing recognition of the sexual frustrations experienced by his informants, he viewed sex research as a means of producing sexual liberation. His social agenda was barely hidden. He believed that in demonstrating the diversity of sexual behavior through statistical data, American society would be liberated from its sexual ignorance and intolerance.[4]

Gathering Homosexual Sex Histories
When Kinsey made his first series of field trips to Chicago in the summer of 1939, he came in contact with a large number of homosexual men and women. A young male homosexual in Bloomington had directed him to the Rush Street area, where, with the help of a few initial contacts in a gay bar, he was able to generate a diverse sample. Kinsey was eager to collect homosexual histories because he realized that he was tapping into an aspect of sexual behavior that was, at best, only superficially understood through medical case studies. His interviews were uncovering a subculture that was barely known. Moreover, he was exploring his own sexuality through anonymous sex in public urinals ("tea rooms"). This homosexual

outlet lasted until 1948, when, with the publication of his male volume, he became a publicly recognizable figure and could not risk being detected. His homosexual exploration convinced him that all individuals were potentially bisexual.[5]

Before his visits to Chicago, he had already collected some histories from students who had had homosexual experiences. He was now able to expand his sample to include those who had a well-established pattern of homosexual behavior. His excitement over his Chicago discovery was expressed in the letters he sent to his friend and former graduate student, Ralph Voris. In his first letter to Voris about the homosexual histories he was collecting, Kinsey appended a four-page section, marked "PER-SONAL," so that he could fully reveal the "dynamite" material he had found without being concerned that Voris's wife might read what he was describing. Still guarding against the possibility that someone else might read the appended section, Kinsey refrained from using the word "homosexual," instead referring to "H——— histories." In his letter Kinsey reported:

> Am trying to get cases in all classes, from the most cultured and socially-economically [*sic*] to the poorest type of professional street solicitor. . . . Have been to Hallowe'en parties, taverns, clubs, etc., which would be unbelievable if realized by the rest of the world. Always they have been most considerate and cooperative, decent, understanding, and cordial in their reception. Why has no one cracked this before? There are at least 300,000 involved in Chicago alone. . . . I have had to do more drinking in single weekends than I thought I would ever have to do in a lifetime, and I still think it bitter. I have diaries from long years—I have whole albums of photographs of their friends, or from commercial sources—fine art to putrid. Some of the art model material is gorgeous. I want you to see it. . . . Now have a total, from all sources [including Indiana students] of 120 H——— histories.[6]

Kinsey had a very close friendship with Voris. Voris had received his doctorate under Kinsey in 1928 and then went on to teach biology at the State Teachers College in Springfield, Missouri (now Southwest Missouri State University). He died of pneumonia in 1940, at age thirty-eight. During the course of their relationship, as Wardell Pomeroy indicates, Kinsey had difficulty breaking through the conventional restraints surrounding expressions of male friendship. In his correspondence with Voris, there were instances when he could be very paternal. At other times he shared his thoughts with a confidant, as in the case of his letter about the discovery of the Chicago homosexual community. Kinsey was heartbroken at Voris's death and wrote to his widow, "Ralph will always be a major tragedy in my life." [7] He later confided to a close friend that Voris was the second great love of his life, the first being his wife. His deep feelings for Voris most likely reinforced his assumptions about his own bisexuality. [8]

After Voris's death, Kinsey turned to his work for solace. To expand his sample of homosexual histories, he was interested in including male prostitutes. He had heard about this world from the inmates at the Indiana State Penal Farm. In 1942 he made a trip to New York and focused his attention on the hustlers of Times Square. As in Chicago, he hung around bars that seemed to be homosexual hangouts. After several observational visits to bars, he noticed one patron who always seemed to be present. He approached this individual, who agreed to give his sex history. This person was a hustler by the name of Herbert Huncke. Huncke proved to be an invaluable contact, introducing Kinsey to a number of hustlers. As word got around, Kinsey became well known among the Times Square hustlers. [9]

Kinsey's Views on Homosexuality

Kinsey's first publication on homosexuality appeared in 1941 in a clinical endocrinology periodical. This article was a critical response to a series of published papers by Clifford A. Wright on the hormonal basis of homosexuality. Wright was a physician who reported his clinical findings on a sample of homosexual men. Reflecting the discovery in the 1920s that all individuals possessed both male and female hormones, Wright argued that "true" congenital homosexual men—in other words, passive male sexual inverts—had an abnormally high proportion of female hormones. He therefore advocated treatment that would reverse this hormonal imbalance. Kinsey criticized Wright's research on two grounds. First, he pointed to the inadequacy of Wright's empirical findings because of faulty sampling. He noted the small sample sizes as well as the greater variation of hormonal proportions among homosexuals than between homosexuals and heterosexuals. More significantly, however, Kinsey attacked the conceptual basis of Wright's line of research. Anticipating the conclusions he reached in his male and female volumes, Kinsey argued that homosexuality was a behavior, not an identity. There were no homosexual people and it was thus impossible to make any comparative distinctions between groups of homosexuals and heterosexuals, nor could one distinguish between passive-effeminate and active-masculine homosexuals. In support of his argument, he referred to the preliminary data he had collected from his male interviewees. He reported that 35.5 percent of his respondents had had orgasmic homosexual experience. Homosexuality was therefore simply a normal variation of human sexual behavior. Moreover, anticipating his seven-point scale of sexual orientation, he referred to cases in which men were not exclusively homosexual or heterosexual. [10]

Kinsey's article led to the establishment of his close professional relationship with Robert Latou Dickinson. Dickinson, who had championed sex research throughout his career, had read the article and wrote to Kinsey that he believed it was an important contribution to the study of homosexuality and looked forward to further analyses. Kinsey replied that it was Dickinson's sex research that had stimulated his own interest in sex research. In Dickinson's first letter to Kinsey, he also informed Kinsey about Painter's work and he continued to be helpful in seeing to it that Kinsey received Painter's manuscript. Kinsey and Dickinson met for the first time in 1943. At this occasion, on learning more about Kinsey's work, Dickinson exclaimed, with tears flowing down his cheeks, "At last! At last! This is what I have been hoping and praying for all these years."[11] Until his death in 1950, Dickinson was an avid supporter of Kinsey's work. His glowing recommendation to the National Research Council in 1943 was of immeasurable help for Kinsey receiving his first large Rockefeller research grant.

Kinsey's views about homosexuality were most fully expressed in his male and female volumes, published respectively in 1948 and 1953. With its revelations about the sexual behavior of American men, the appearance of the first volume was a publication bombshell. In the popular press, it was referred to as "the most talked about book of the twentieth century."[12] In less than two months, it sold 200,000 copies and stood in second place on the nonfiction best-seller list. The female volume generated even more controversy, and its publication in the midst of McCarthyism had serious political repercussions. Representative Louis B. Heller denounced it as "the insult of the century"[13] and called for its being barred from the mails. Concerned with the threat of a congressional investigation of Kinsey, the Rockefeller Foundation in 1954 withdrew its financial support. The unexpectedly high incidence of homosexuality was among the most controversial findings in each volume. The Kinsey team reported that since the beginning of adolescence, 37 percent of the male population had had some homosexual experience to the point of orgasm. Among women, the incidence of homosexuality was also more widespread than expected—28 percent of the female population revealed same-sex erotic responses, and 13 percent had experienced orgasm with other women.[14]

The controversy over Kinsey's reported incidence of homosexuality has been rekindled with James Jones's recent assertion that Kinsey found what he was looking for. In other words, because of his own homosexuality, he purposely inflated his sample with homosexual respondents. Kinsey, in fact, was well aware that he could be criticized for reporting a high incidence of homosexuality, but as Gathorne-Hardy points out, Kinsey as a taxonomist believed that it was essential to include extremes in any form of species variation. He was also sensitive to the unwillingness of many individuals to reveal their sexual experiences. Thus, instead of using a random sample that would have required persuading reluctant subjects to participate, he relied on volunteers. In response to the continuing criticisms that Kinsey's figures were inflated, Paul Gebhard and Alan Johnson removed such suspect data as the prison samples in the case of males and found that the percentages were only marginally less than originally reported.[15]

Kinsey's attitudes about homosexuality are best understood by placing them in the context of his scientific thinking, specifically in terms of his assumptions about sexuality, methodology, and ethics and politics. The central tenet in Kinsey's sexual worldview was the assumption that all living creatures are composed of a wide range of individual differences. Regarding human sexuality, this implied that sexual capacity could be expressed within continua ranging from celibacy to promiscuity and from exclusive heterosexuality to exclusive homosexuality. The latter continuum was expressed on a seven-point classification system, ranging from o for exclusive heterosexuality to 6 for exclusive homosexuality. Kinsey and his associates argued that abnormality was a taxonomically meaningless concept because curves of sexual variation were "not symmetrical with a particular portion of the population set off as 'normal,' 'modal,' 'typical,' or discretely different." Referring to the misuse of "abnormal" when applied to any type of sexual behavior, the Kinsey team noted, "It is not possible to insist that any departure from the sexual mores, or any participation in social taboo activities, always, or even usually, involves a neurosis or psychosis, for the case histories abundantly demonstrate that most individuals who engage in taboo activities make satisfactory social adjustments."[16]

The issue of what constitutes sexual abnormality was also addressed from another perspective. Kinsey was an essentialist who believed that culture acted as a restraint on the biologically diverse potential of sexual expression. He argued that homosexuality was a natural form of sexual expression, citing the existence of same-sex behavior in the animal world and across various cultures. Thus, if homosexuality was widely observed, it was a behavioral expression of a universal biological capacity. As the Kinsey team stated, "The homosexual has been a significant part of human sexual activity ever since the dawn of history, primarily because it is an expression of capacities that are basic in the human animal."[17] Homosexuality as an inherent part of sexual capacity was therefore not pathological; it was society that rendered it problematic.

With regard to the force of society's prohibitions, Kinsey noted that among men, upper-class professionals engaged in less same-sex behavior than their working-class peers did. His sympathies fell with working-class men because they were less socially constrained. In the case of women, however, he found that social class was generally not related to sexual behavior, therefore supporting his view that women's sexuality was more a product of biology than culture.[18]

Despite his tendency to dismiss the role of socialization for women, Kinsey was generally sensitive to the complex ways in which behavior was related to social conditions and thus had a cultural relativist view regarding the expression of sexuality. As he and his colleagues declared, "A choice of a partner in a sexual relation becomes more significant only because society demands that there be a particular choice in this matter."[19] Kinsey recognized the role that dominant sexual ideology could play in shaping scientific thought. He believed that as long as bodily harm was not involved, all forms of sexual expression were acceptable. This was a departure from the prevailing version of essentialism, represented by such pioneer sexologists as Krafft-Ebing and Freud, that appropriated heterosexuality as the mature expression of a biologically determined sexual instinct.[20]

Kinsey believed that an objective scientific approach to the study of human sexuality would produce tolerance and liberate such stigmatized forms of sexual expression as homosexuality from unnecessary social control. For Kinsey, objectivity meant that scientific inquiry could not be contaminated by prejudiced attitudes. He advocated the interview as the method for studying sexuality because it provided the means for the scientist to step outside of his or her own preconceptions and become an understanding and sympathetic listener. The interview also reflected Kinsey's commitment to the taxonomic approach he had used as a biologist. In contrast to the reliance on questionnaires by previous sex researchers, he felt that the interview represented a more in-depth approach that would achieve the taxonomic goals of measuring the wide range of human sexual variation.[21]

The interview was the most innovative feature of Kinsey's research. Although there was much skepticism by his critics about the accuracy of the data, he appears to have been especially adept at establishing rapport, as well as developing guidelines for checking on accuracy. He felt that if the interviewer showed sympathetic interest and withheld moral judgment, respondents would overcome any initial inhibitions. Moreover, he believed that people generally liked to tell their stories and were motivated more by altruism than egotism. Referring to the male sample, he and his colleagues reported, "Twelve thousand people have helped in this research primarily because they have a faith in scientific projects."[22] The interviews were directed at obtaining quantitative reports of various forms of orgasm or "sexual outlet," such as masturbation, heterosexual intercourse, and homosexual relations. Stigmatized and socially approved behaviors were thus accorded equal status. Although Kinsey was well aware of the psychological and emotional aspects of sexuality, his focus on behavioral indexes provided the basis for demonstrating the contradiction between how people were supposed to behave, according to the dictates of conventional morality, and how people actually acted.[23]

Kinsey's ethical stance was premised on his commitment to objective science as the key to social progress. A science of sexuality would contribute to a better understanding of the problems surrounding gender and sexuality. His essentialist position that sex was a "normal biologic function, acceptable in whatever form it is manifested" was aimed at liberating sexuality from its socially oppressive restraints. In the case of male homosexuality, Kinsey and his team argued, "In view of the data which we now have on the incidence and frequency of the homosexual, and in particular on its co-existence with the heterosexual in the lives of a considerable portion of the male population, it is difficult to maintain the view that psychosexual reactions between individuals of the same sex are rare and therefore abnormal or unnatural, or that they constitute within themselves evidence of neuroses or even psychoses."[24]

Kinsey's sexual tolerance provided the rationale for his political strategy. If scientific objectivity produced data that subverted the conventional morality guiding sexual behavior, then scientific discourse on sexuality could serve as a source for bringing about positive social change. In both Kinsey volumes, there were frequent critiques of the existing sex laws and the hypocrisy of trying to enforce such laws when most individuals, at some point, practiced illegal sexual activity. Kinsey realized that legal reform would not come about without changing social attitudes, but he also had faith in the power of objective scientific discourse as an agent for change. This faith reflected his liberal worldview that enlightened rationality could produce social change.[25]

Kinsey, however, was not a social revolutionary. Aside from conventional sexual mores, he did not question other social values, nor did he question the existing power structure with its inherent sexual and gender bias. As William Simon notes, his assumption of the essential naturalness of virtually all types of sexual expression encouraged a bland sexual liberalism. Thus, in the case of homosexuality, he was insensitive to the politically heuristic value that a collective homosexual identity could provide as a source of resisting oppression. In fact, he strongly argued against the need to categorize people according to sexual identity. Rather than homosexual people, there was only homosexual behavior. He advanced such a position because he was concerned that promoting the idea of a distinct homosexual identity would reify a negative homosexual stereotype.[26]

Kinsey's place in the history of sex research is seminal. The scope and depth of his work has served as a standard for all of the subsequent research on human sexuality. Moreover, his male and female volumes had a profound effect on how Americans thought about sex. The taboos about public discussion were shattered. What people did privately in their sex lives became common knowledge. The most dramatic example of this was the revelation that homosexual experience was by no means an unusual phenomenon. Among those reporting their same-sex fantasies and behaviors were individuals who identified as homosexual. These homosexual men and women were eager to tell their stories, to have their voices heard by a sympathetic scientist. The Kinsey Reports, which provided voice for an invisible minority, thus contributed to the emergence of a national homophile movement in the 1950s.[27]

Kinsey and the Homosexual Community

In preparing his male and female volumes on sexual behavior, Kinsey had established contacts with gay and lesbian circles in Chicago and New York. In 1950 he plotted out a program of research that would be undertaken once the female volume was completed. Among the nine proposed books connected with this program was one that dealt with the "heterosexual-homosexual" balance. For this project he planned to utilize all the histories he had taken, including the more than four thousand with records of homosexual experience. He therefore continually relied on his personal contacts, mostly with gay men such as Painter, to put him in touch with individuals who were willing to talk about their homosexual experiences. He believed that homosexuals were a particularly rich source of data because, given the opportunity to tell their stories, they were less inhibited than most respondents were. As Pomeroy observed, "These people poured out their lives to us with a minimum of cover-up, and because society had made them feel like such special cases, they often took a greater interest in remembering or recording their experiences."[28]

Kinsey was interested in more than histories. By the time that his male volume was published in 1948, he had amassed a large and amorphous collection of male homoerotic visual images. With the success of the book and the long-term commitment of research funding through the Rockefeller Foundation, he began a more systematic collection policy. He therefore needed a widespread network of gay men to serve as contacts for acquiring visual materials as well as oral histories and written life records in the form of diaries and scrapbooks.[29]

Among the various collaborators Kinsey worked with, he was especially close with Clarence A. Tripp. Tripp was a young photographer in his own business in New York. In 1948, when the male volume was published, he was so impressed with it that he telephoned Kinsey in Bloomington. He informed Kinsey that he was interested in sex research and wanted to write about it. Kinsey sensed that Tripp was someone worth knowing and helping and invited him for a visit to the Kinsey Institute. Tripp spent three days in Bloomington, and in exchange for the grand tour of the Institute, he gave Kinsey his sex history. When he returned to New York, he wrote Kinsey, "It is almost impossible for me to tell you how much I learned from you during my visit. . . . Little wonder you win cooperation from everyone, I feel it in myself . . . an urgency to contribute anything you could possibly use. . . . I'm with you for life and everything I can do is not enough."[30] Indeed, Tripp was helpful to Kinsey in a number of ways. He had experience in male homoerotic photography and, using paid models in his New York studio, had begun to film sexual behavior including lovemaking by same-sex couples and masturbation. Kinsey encouraged Tripp to produce a series of these films. After several were completed, the program was transferred to Bloomington when Bill Dellenback (Tripp's heterosexual business partner) joined the Kinsey Institute staff. Tripp was also useful as a contact for histories and continued to provide various photographic and film materials for the Institute's archives. He was so inspired by his association with Kinsey that he decided to return to school and eventually went on to obtain his doctorate in psychology and become a sex researcher and psychotherapist. In the 1970s he wrote *The Homosexual Matrix*, an influential theoretical treatment of homosexuality.[31]

Sam Steward was another close collaborator. He had a multifaceted career as a writer, college English instructor, and tattoo artist. He met Kinsey in Chicago in 1949 through a teaching colleague who had been Kinsey's initial homosexual contact in Chicago in 1939. He gave Kinsey his history, which lasted five hours and was very detailed because he was able to draw upon the "Stud File" (three-by-five cards) he kept on his sex partners. Steward's record keeping impressed Kinsey and the interview marked the beginning of their friendship. Steward collaborated with the Institute in various ways. He served as a contact for histories, contributed samples of his extensive homoerotic fiction and artwork, kept a journal of his customers' sexual motivations for getting tattoos, and donated his sexual-action Polaroid pictures taken in the early 1950s when these cameras first became available. Steward was also induced into taking part in one of Kinsey's films. Kinsey, knowing of his attraction to sadomasochism, invited him to Bloomington to be filmed having sex with a New York artist with a proclivity for sadism. As Steward described the event, "It was quite an experience. For two afternoons at Bloomington the camera whirred away. . . . Mike was quite a ham actor; every time he heard Bill Dellenback's camera start to turn, he renewed his vigor and youth like the green bay tree; and at the end of the second afternoon I was exhausted, marked and marred, all muscles weakened." Whenever Kinsey was in Chicago, which was often, he met with Steward. In Steward's words, Kinsey "had one of the warmest personalities I had ever met—a cordial gregarious man as approachable as an old park bench. . . . Though there was a difference of only about fifteen years in our ages . . . he became for me a sort of father-figure."[32]

Kinsey was especially interested in studying the "heterosexual-homosexual" balance in the arts, and he established close connections with many artists, musicians, and writers. Within this milieu, he was able to cultivate a network of collaborators among the gay intelligentsia. His key contact among artists was Monroe Wheeler, the director of exhibitions at New York's Museum of Modern Art. Through Wheeler, Kinsey was able to get the histories of a large group of artists. Wheeler also helped Kinsey acquire homoerotic paintings for the Institute's collection of erotic artwork. Among performing artists, Kinsey had close personal relationships with composer Ned Rorum, ballet director Lincoln Kirstein, and dancer Ted Shawn. Shawn enabled Kinsey to get histories of a number of other dancers and also contributed homoerotic photographs of dancers.[33]

Kinsey had a wide circle of contacts in the literary world. In the case of Gore Vidal, he initiated contact by writing to Vidal about his novel *The City and the Pillar*, which had been published in 1948. This was the author's first book that dealt with homosexuality and Kinsey was impressed, writing:

> I want to congratulate you on having done an excellent job with a subject which has been poorly handled in too much of the literature. . . . I am particularly impressed by your balanced understanding of the problems that are involved. There are few treatments of male homosexuality in any sort of literature which allow, as clearly as you do, that many different sorts of factors may be involved in accounting for the development of a homosexual pattern. Your understanding of the diverse social problems which arise with different sorts of cases represents an excellent comprehension of reality.[34]

Shortly after this correspondence, Kinsey arranged to take Vidal's history. Vidal recounted their meeting at the Astor Hotel:

> I can now *see* Dr. Kinsey as he walks me to the steps that connected mezzanine to lobby. He is a gray-faced man who always wears a polka-dot bow tie. He looks uncommonly tired and has not got long to live. Yet he is only fifty-four. . . . I did not believe in fixed sexual categories; and finally Kinsey appears not to have believed in them either. . . . Kinsey gave me a copy of *Sexual Behavior in the Human Male,* with an inscription, complimenting me on my "work in the field."[35]

Glenway Wescott was a writer who became a close friend of Kinsey's and collaborated on various projects. They met at a dinner party in New York given by Monroe Wheeler (Wescott's life partner) for E. M Forster, the well-known British novelist. Wescott (as well as Forster) was charmed by Kinsey's personality, and he wrote in his diary, "Kinsey has the temperament of a reformer rather than a scientist."[36] At their first meeting, Kinsey asked Wescott to collaborate with him in developing a theory about the connection between art and the sex life of artists. Wescott eagerly accepted and became a frequent visitor to Bloomington. He was appointed as a "Visiting Specialist" and worked specifically on the sex lives of contemporary authors and developed bibliographies of erotica and romance in literature. On one of these visits, he agreed to be filmed having sex with his partner Wheeler. Wescott was also instrumental in putting Kinsey in touch with other writers, thus enabling Kinsey to obtain a wide range of histories. Through Wescott's connection with Christopher Isherwood, Kinsey in 1951 first learned about the Mattachine Society, the fledgling homophile group in Los Angeles.[37]

Isherwood, Thornton Wilder, Tennessee Williams, and Allen Ginsberg were other writers Kinsey established relationships with. Before Kinsey first wrote to Williams, he had obtained the histories of most of the cast members of three separate companies playing *A Streetcar Named Desire*. From these histories, he concluded that the portrayal of such characters as Stanley and Blanche varied in relation to the sexual backgrounds of the actors, which apparently was the source of his proposal to Wescott about exploring sexual autobiography and artistic production. Williams was delighted with Kinsey's interest in *Streetcar* and wrote, "Your work, your research and its revelations to the ignorant and/or biased public, is of enormous social value. I hope that you will continue it and even extend its scope, for not the least desirable thing in this world is understanding, and sexual problems are especially in need of it."[38] Kinsey and Williams met in November 1950 and established a friendship that was carried on mostly through correspondence. Ginsberg visited the Institute and, like Wescott, agreed to be filmed having sex with his lover.[39]

Kinsey's interest in making films and acquiring a film library drew his attention to avant-garde filmmakers like Kenneth Anger. Anger worked closely with Kinsey in compiling a collection of films for the Institute, including those made by such artists as Jean Genet and Jack Smith. Anger, who spent much of his time in Europe, kept Kinsey informed about European developments in homoerotic filmmaking, photography, and books. Kinsey relied on him as a source for acquiring European materials for the Institute. In 1953, however, Kinsey was having problems with U.S. Customs, which seized a shipment of photographs and other objects. The Institute began a legal battle to retrieve these items, and the case was not successfully resolved until 1957, a year after Kinsey's death. Anger, nevertheless, was able to contribute a number of European materials during this period, including some of his own films.[40]

Kinsey's penchant for visual materials also directed his attention to the commercial filmmakers and photographers of homoerotic "beefcake" fare, an industry that was growing in the 1940s. The two major producers were Charles Renslow of Chicago's Kris Studio and Bob Mizer of Los Angeles's Athletic Model Guild. Renslow staged a sadomasochistic film for the Institute's collection. Kinsey developed a close relationship with Mizer through correspondence and frequent visits to his Los Angeles studio. At reduced cost, Mizer contributed photographic material and the physique magazines that he produced. Moreover, he gave his own history and enabled Kinsey to obtain histories from models and other photographers. In turn, Kinsey was of great help to Mizer by putting him in touch with legal advisers. Mizer continually had to fight legal battles with the post office and had to deal with harassment from the Los Angeles Police Department. At one point he came under investigation in connection with Senator Estes Kefauver's hearings on juvenile delinquency. With Kinsey's help, the American Civil Liberties Union successfully defended him. Kinsey identified with Mizer's legal problems because of his own protracted troubles with U.S. Customs. In commenting on their relationship, Mizer noted that Kinsey had "utterly changed his life."[41]

Another photographer Kinsey worked with was Otis Wade. Wade was a film hobbyist and began his career as an amateur erotic filmmaker in 1935. He kept his movies for his own use and for the enjoyment of his social circle, which included Mizer and movie producer George Cukor. Kinsey learned about Wade through artist Paul Cadmus, and beginning in 1950, Wade contributed a large collection of his films to the Institute. He also served as one of Kinsey's contacts for histories in Los Angeles. Kinsey established a personal relationship with Wade and his lover, Tommy, visiting them at their home in Los Angeles and keeping up a correspondence.[42]

Kinsey was interested in acquiring personal diaries and was instrumental in getting Painter to keep a detailed "Life Record" of his sexual life. In fact, through Painter, a male hustler contributed his life history. Another of Kinsey's homosexual correspondents contributed diaries and memoirs of his life from the 1910s though 1972. Kinsey also maintained correspondence with a wide variety of foreign informants, which provided insights for cross-cultural comparisons of homosexual behavior. An especially prodigious and detailed source of overseas observations came from Sixte Rapff, a Danish-born German businessman who lived in Palermo and traveled extensively throughout Europe and North Africa. This correspondence began in 1951, when Rapff, nearing forty at the time, wrote to Kinsey to express his gratitude for the male volume, which he had just read in its French translation. He was so impressed that he offered his services as a contributor and declared, "I want to do as much that others are not going to suffer under the misconception of this chapter of life as I had to do."[43] Kinsey welcomed Rapff's collaboration, and Rapff followed through with long letters dealing with his observations and past and present experiences in different countries, ranging from Morocco to Nazi Germany. He was also enlisted to obtain histories and contributed a variety of erotic materials. When Kinsey traveled to Europe in 1955, Rapff served as a guide by providing private "tours" in a number of cities on Kinsey's itinerary. Kinsey was very impressed with Rapff's ethnographic skills and commented that he would have made an excellent anthropologist. After Kinsey's death in 1956, Rapff maintained his contact with the Institute. Tripp assumed Kinsey's place and audiocassettes replaced the letters.[44]

Finally, Kinsey had contacts with the various homophile groups that were emerging in the early 1950s. He had learned about the Mattachine Society, which started in Los Angeles in 1951, through Isherwood and Wescott. By 1953 Mattachine had developed a national network of local chapters. Although it started out as a radical group, it became a politically moderate organization aimed at establishing an accommodative stance with the larger society, thereby hoping to create a conducive climate for changes in laws and public policy. As part of this strategy, Mattachine was interested in engaging in a dialogue with professionals, such as sex researchers, who could be influential allies if they became knowledgeable about the lives and concerns of homosexuals. Kinsey, in his communications, reinforced the desirability of such collaborative efforts, but consistent with his concerns about the social and political disadvantages of proclaiming a homosexual identity, advised the group to avoid "special pleas for a minority group."[45] As Hal Call, one of the early Mattachine leaders, recalled:

> We wanted to see changes come about by holding conferences and discussions and becoming subjects for research and telling our story. We wanted to assist people in the academic and behavioral-science world in getting the truth out to people who had influence on law and law enforcement, the courts, justice, and so on. For example, the Kinsey group in Bloomington, Indiana was soon in contact with us, and we cooperated with their work.[46]

The Daughters of Bilitis, the first lesbian organization (established in 1955), was also eager to initiate a cooperative relationship with the Institute. Like Mattachine, it encouraged its members to participate in research projects directed toward "further knowledge of the homosexual."[47] Its first contact with the Institute was in 1957, shortly after Kinsey's death. Billie Tallmij (a pseudonym), one of the pioneer members, recounted, "We thought it was very important for the women to be studied, so we banged at the door of the Kinsey Institute to try to get some kind of involvement, and we got it. They interviewed us as couples and individuals. . . . Many of the women volunteered. That took real courage."[48]

Homosexual research participants and collaborators were eager to co-operate with Kinsey. They sensed that they were interacting with a sex researcher who was willing to listen and understand their life experiences as well as to help preserve their underground subculture. Indeed, as Kinsey's biographer Jonathan Gathorne-Hardy observes, Kinsey's own sexual suffering made him identify with the suffering revealed by his respondents and informants. Moreover, his bisexuality enabled him to understand their needs and desires. Beyond this personal connection, Kinsey's homosexual associates recognized the value of scientific research as well as narrative and visual representations of their lives as significant resources in the struggle for homosexual rights. For their part, Kinsey and his research colleagues sought out an extensive network of homosexual collaborators to ensure that they would have an inclusive record of human sexual behavior. Toward this objective, they generated contributions that went far beyond the statistical treatment contained in the male and female volumes. They amassed a prodigious archival collection of narrative and visual materials reflecting the homosexual subculture of mid-twentieth-century America.[49]

Besides those people whom he personally touched, Kinsey's work had a profound effect on gay men and lesbians. His statistical revelation of how commonplace homosexual behavior was contributed to the emerging group consciousness of the postwar period. As John D'Emilio notes, "By revealing that millions of Americans exhibited a strong erotic interest in their own sex, the [Kinsey] reports implicitly encouraged those still struggling in isolation against their sexual preference to accept their homosexual inclinations and search for sexual comrades."[50] Kinsey's empirical evidence became immeasurably useful in the campaign for homosexual rights, especially in its potential to challenge the psychiatric profession. Homophile groups mourned his death as a great loss. But Kinsey's work had a double-edged effect. Its emancipatory potential in making the invisible visible also intensified hostile reaction in the form of the increased vigilance and hysteria of the McCarthy era. The federal government, for example, labeled homosexual men and women as security risks, resulting in mass firings, and gay men were increasingly targeted in police crackdowns.[51]

THE RELATIONSHIP BETWEEN PAINTER AND KINSEY
(1943-56)

Painter was among Kinsey's closest homosexual contacts and the first to establish a working relationship with the Kinsey Institute. Like his other associations with gay men, Kinsey relied on Painter to recruit participants for sex histories. While he had some reservations about Painter's manuscript on male homosexuality and male prostitution, he was generally impressed with Painter's skills as an observer and interpreter of the gay male subculture. He thus valued Painter's inside knowledge about the homosexual world and often depended on him as a sounding board for his own work. As Kinsey's research associate Wardell B. Pomeroy noted, "In a voluminous correspondence, Kinsey discussed with . . . [Painter] the subjects he talked about with others, but often it had more the sound of one insider talking to another."[52]

Painter's relationship with Kinsey was initially developed during the last two years of Painter's army service. Painter was elated when he received his first letter from Kinsey in October 1943 with the promise that "you could be of tremendous use to us."[53] In response, Painter indicated that once his army commitment was completed, he would welcome the opportunity to work with Kinsey. He also suggested that with Kinsey's sponsorship, he might be able to draw a special duty assignment that would permit him to begin his collaborative work in the army. Kinsey rather evasively replied that with a staff of seven full-time members, he had no plans to expand at the present time, nor did he hold out any hope for the chances of working out an army research assignment for Painter. Nevertheless, he looked forward to the time when Painter could visit Bloomington, which would provide the occasion to work out the specific nature of Painter's research contribution.[54]

When they met for the first time in Bloomington in August 1944, it became clearer to Painter why Kinsey was not able to offer him a staff position. Kinsey had specific qualifications for his staff members—namely, that they be happily married so as to overcome any suspicion or prejudice on the part of interviewees who might question the mores of unmarried individuals. As Painter later described his impressions of their first meeting:

> I found him interesting, his ideas sound, his work eminently valuable. In fact, he was doing what I had wanted to do (and then still wanted to do). I believe . . . that I wanted to use Kinsey for my benefit, either within the Army or after, on his staff. Kinsey didn't say "We can't possibly use an active homosexual"—he squirmed. Then when I gathered, later, what the staff qualifications were, and indeed how absolutely necessary such "Caesar's wife" behavior was, I saw it was not for me.[55]

Despite the lack of any formal association, Painter and Kinsey were able to establish a working relationship. As in the case of Kinsey's earlier visits to Chicago and New York, where he had established contacts in the homosexual community, Painter would act as a contact person. Painter indicated that he could arrange for Kinsey to get sex histories from a wide range of people in the homosexual world, including peg house madams, female impersonators, hustlers, wealthy homosexuals, and black homosexuals in Harlem. Moreover, he could also serve as a source of contacts for Kinsey's expressed interest in the theological and ministerial community. In a series of follow-up letters, Painter provided lists of names with background information. He included his many homosexual friends and acquaintances in New York, as well as people he knew at Yale and Union Theological Seminary, indicating that all of these people would, in turn, be helpful in leading Kinsey to others who could be interviewed. Painter volunteered to approach these individuals and in the case of the theology contacts, to provide them with background information about Kinsey and his work. As Painter expressed it:

> All I know is I think your work is wonderful and invaluable; that the Rockefeller Foundation backs you . . . that you are a keenly intelligent middle aged gentleman, amazingly broad-minded . . . and intensely believe in your work. Which is more than enough for me. . . . But—well, you know what they will want to know. Will you tell me so I can pass it on (including date of the Nobel Prize and degree of the Legion of Honor—posthumous, I'm afraid).[56]

Not only was Painter impressed with Kinsey, but also Kinsey, in turn, conveyed his own gratitude for the contributions that Painter could make. As he declared:

> The contacts which you propose in New York are great. I am as anxious as you that we get more material from the particular sorts of groups you have described in your last few letters. We do have a considerable amount of such material from Chicago, St. Louis, and some other places; but I think the situation is enough different in New York to make it important for us to get on the ground floor there. No one has appeared on the horizon who can help us to do that better than you. . . . [W]e will look forward to having your help to get through on the Times Square group, on your theological seminary group, on the millionaire contacts which you name, and the several others. Of course, you can be of great value to us in these contacts.[57]

In addition to providing a wide range of contacts, Painter worked with Kinsey in a variety of other ways. He maintained a correspondence with

Kinsey during his army service in which he reported his observations about homosexual behavior in the communities adjacent to the bases he was stationed at, such as Amarillo and Dayton. When Painter visited Bloomington, he gave his own sex history in an interview. Based on this, he made a number of suggestions as to additional items to be included for Kinsey's homosexual respondents, such as the ages of partners and preferences for particular types of partners. Several months before their meeting, Painter had given his library of books on homosexuality to Kinsey as well as the bibliography Legman had been working on. Painter also gave his diaries, letters, various writings, and scrapbooks filled with photographs of male hustlers and other homoerotic pictures. Painter may thus have laid the groundwork for Kinsey's continued interest in acquiring erotic visual materials. Finally, Painter shared his views about homosexuality with Kinsey. This was a particularly significant aspect of their relationship because it served as a sounding board for exchanging their ideas and dealing with their points of disagreement.[58]

One issue that they both agreed on was the question of homosexual identity. After his Bloomington visit, Painter wrote that Kinsey had confirmed his view that "There isn't any 'homosexuality'—only the homosexual aspect of sex behavior." Moreover, he concurred with Kinsey's seven-point scale, which reflected a continuum of homosexual-heterosexual behavior. Yet, unlike Kinsey, Painter in his manuscript had consistently referred to men who engaged in exclusive homosexual behavior as a sexual type, that is, "true homosexuals." With Kinsey's work, however, it now became clearer to Painter that "homosexuals" (5's and 6's) were not a distinct group. As he expressed it, "The 5 and 6 comes to think of himself as a 'homosexual,' a creature apart, distinct, separate. The term abets his attitude. But you point out he is distinctly still a part of human sexual society. . . . This has already had an effect on my mental outlook, personally, as well as my thought on the subject. I see clearly now why you don't call anyone 'homosexual'—who the hell is and who is not?"[59] Painter did acknowledge that a 5 or 6 thinks of himself as distinct, which in turn generates a particular attitude, but because he is part of a continuum of sexual behavior, this distinctiveness is illusory. What neither Painter nor Kinsey seemed to recognize was the psychological and potentially political significance that a distinct identity served for homosexuals. Homosexual men and women had to confront their sexual orientation in the face of social hostility and could thus use it as a source of resistance against heterosexist ideology.[60]

Painter's manuscript proved to be a source of contention. Painter explored how he could complement his continued work on the manuscript with Kinsey's research. He felt strongly that his manuscript, in revised form, needed to be published so that the general public could be informed about the lives, behaviors, and desires of sex "variants." In this fashion, it would serve as sociological background for Kinsey's work. He hoped to devote his energies to revising the manuscript when he was discharged from the army. He would then present his revision to Kinsey and let Kinsey decide whether it had the potential to be published. If not, Kinsey could utilize the material in his own work. In response, Kinsey indicated that he would consider how best to utilize Painter's material and how to shape it for publication.[61]

Several months later, Kinsey communicated his impressions about the manuscript, which contained some serious reservations. Kinsey was critical of Painter's medicalized view of homosexuality, which called for the treatment and prevention of a pathological form of behavior that was both a personal and social problem. What particularly upset Painter was Kinsey's statement "If you know what the world should be told and persuaded to do about the homosexual before the scientific data are collected and objectively analyzed, you cannot have much use for our project."[62] As far as Kinsey was concerned, Painter's assumption that homosexuality was pathological was a matter of moral judgment, not objective science. Moreover, Kinsey labeled Painter as a "religious romantic." Painter defended himself, declaring:

> I am primarily and unalterably motivated by a special brand of religion (of my own rational and emotional development) which leads me to believe that I must live in a certain manner. Circumstances have so grouped themselves in my life (as you know) so that homosexuality has been presented to me as my major problem. As I see it as a personal tragedy in my own life I similarly see it in society, multiplied by the number so effected. My religion impells [*sic*] me to do something about this mass tragedy. It impelled me ten years ago, and it still does.[63]

In his reply to Kinsey's criticisms, Painter was careful not to jeopardize their relationship. He attempted to convince Kinsey that in his own work he was merely collecting unbiased "fact-finding" knowledge that would hopefully lead to the goal of determining the cause and cure of homosexual behavior. He viewed his efforts as laying the groundwork for Kinsey's completed research, expressing his role as "I am to be your John the Baptist. . . . I want to till the ground so that when your work is complete the fruits of it will fall on prepared soil." In other words, he viewed his work as complementing Kinsey's. While Kinsey was still collecting his data, Painter would disseminate what he had found and thus "enlighten and familiarize . . . [the] public with the problem."[64] He believed that they could continue to work together, as long as they each kept their own "territory."

Painter had second thoughts about his reply to Kinsey's criticisms and in a follow-up letter, apologized "for words written in anger."[65] He reiterated his desire that they be mutually helpful and expressed his respect for Kinsey's commitment to scientific objectivity that was not compromised by moral judgment. He again professed his need to disseminate knowledge about the suffering associated with homosexuality, an effort aimed at rousing knowledge of the "disease" so that a "cure" could be found. In the meantime, he assumed that Kinsey's research was directed at determining the etiology of homosexuality. In response, Kinsey apologized for causing "so much disturbance." He made a point of supporting Painter by stating, "I recognize the honesty of your intention, and I deeply appreciate your interest in, and loyalty to our research." In an effort to persuade Painter to move away from his pathology mode, he noted that suffering was not unique to homosexuality. Loneliness, heartache, prostitution, and crime were found in heterosexual histories as well as homosexual ones. Sexual behavior itself, whether it was homosexual or heterosexual, was not the problem; rather, it was "the way society reacts to it."[66] Painter responded that if sexual pathology was widespread beyond homosexuality, he would want to get at the "deeper" roots, attacking them by such strategies as promoting sex education, fostering the "proper" psychological environment, and developing a broader psychiatric base for treatment.[67]

Painter, obviously, was missing what Kinsey was trying to communicate to him. He was so committed to a medical perspective on homosexuality that he was unable to recognize the nature of Kinsey's views about homosexuality. In contrast with Painter's focus on determining cause, Kinsey dismissed the question of etiology. As he was later to elaborate in his male volume, the continuum of sexual behavior from heterosexuality to homosexuality pointed to the need to understand how people develop preferences for sexual partners. As he stated:

> This problem, is after all, part of the broader problem of choices in general: the choice of the road that one takes, of the clothes that one wears, of the food that one eats, of the place in which one sleeps, and of the endless other things that one is constantly choosing. A choice of a partner in a sexual relation becomes more significant only because society demands that there be a particular choice in this matter, and does not so often dictate one's choice of food or clothing.[68]

Kinsey was committed to the objective of sexual liberation; the problematic of sexuality originated in the oppressive restraints of society, not in the individual. Painter, on the other hand, at this point in his life could not go beyond the source of suffering within the individual. His mission was to find a means of individual salvation through enlightened scientific knowledge. For Kinsey, scientific enlightenment was the road to creating social tolerance. And yet both fervently believed in the power of scientific data to produce change, and both agreed on the necessity of first-person accounts of sexual experience as the foundation for a sexual science. Their scientific worldview thus incorporated the seeds of resistance to social oppression in the form of capturing the subjective agency of individuals seeking the right to speak for themselves. Toward this end, they were able to forge a collaborative relationship.[69]

The most significant aspect of Painter's contribution was to be his diary, which he referred to as his "Life Record." In the contentious exchange over his manuscript, Kinsey had invited Painter to record his personal experiences and observations. Although he had serious reservations about the viability of Painter's manuscript for publication, it seems clear that he valued Painter's ethnographic skill at observing and recording his impressions of the homosexual subculture in which he moved. For his part, Kinsey was eager to obtain detailed individual histories. He indicated that he had extensive records on three or four other histories, although none were as detailed as what Painter had already submitted. Painter enthusiastically accepted Kinsey's invitation, and his commitment to follow through on the diary served as a means of resolving the impasse over the manuscript. When Painter was discharged from the army in September 1945, he abandoned any further work on his manuscript.[70]

Painter set the parameters for his Life Record. It was to be in the form of letters and would include correspondence with close friends as well as the correspondence with Kinsey. As it turned out, the Life Record also included Painter's earlier autobiographical essays as well as photographs, newspaper clippings, and reviews of homosexually relevant books and films. It thus took the form of journals, which were bound, in annual volumes. In addition, once the journal diaries were established, Painter periodically submitted motion pictures, family photos, nude photos (which eventually numbered close to a thousand), erotic drawings, and short stories. Painter also requested the opportunity to come to Bloomington to spend time editing his diaries and other personal documents. Kinsey cordially invited Painter to spend several weeks and this became an annual practice, which was continued after Kinsey's death in 1956.[71]

Among the materials that Kinsey was able to pick up in New York during his visit in March 1945 was an autobiographical essay Painter had written the year before. In this essay, Painter revealed the state of his feelings while in the army. His sex life had been limited to the few times when he was on leave. The imposed restrictions of army life had forced him to control his sexual behavior. As a result, he seemed to be arriving at the possibility that he might be able to continue to control his homosexual behavior after he was discharged from the service. He declared, "The Army has been making a man of me. . . . [W]hile still homosexual as ever, I am many times the person I was."[72]

He expanded on these thoughts in a letter to his best friend Bill, a gay man he had known since their student days at Yale. He believed that he could "be free of the at present unequivocal, inescapable thralldom of my sexual preference," by attacking what he viewed as the roots of his homosexuality. Painter was convinced that, in his case, the cause was psychological, not physical. Specifically, there were two factors he had to confront—a fear of women and a "psychotic admiration" of virility. He could conquer his fear of women by cultivating their "society." As he stated, "At first I must do this with an informed girl who can tutor me at no danger to my ego if and when I blunder. I must learn to escort, dance with, talk to, and make love to, women. Later on, I must make frequent trials at sexual intercourse with women, with an informed, resourceful, attractive woman." With respect to his obsession with virile, uninhibited, freedom-loving young men "of the lower classes," his therapeutic course was to

> develop my own physique as far as possible to equal those I admire. At the same time I must acquire athletic and virile skills (such as boxing, judo, wrestling, diving, ball-playing, etc.). Then I should get myself a job in which I would do what "they" do—such as in the Merchant Marine or the like. In short I must build myself to be as nearly one of them as possible. This would cut at the roots [of] this frustrated adoration of something unattainable, something godlike and remote. . . . And if I *can be* a strong, well-built, physically capable and resourceful man, then I will *be* what I remotely adore. And the absurdity of adoring a youth for being what I am will assert itself.[73]

He admitted that such a program might only achieve a "bisexuality" on his part. However, with the possible development of a heterosexual "taste and preference," he would have a chance of "eliminating" his homosexual side and thus insuring his own happiness by being able to conform to the way in which society is constructed.

Painter apparently believed that even though he was forty, it was still possible to effect change through a therapeutic strategy based on developing an alternative set of behaviors. He expressed these thoughts a few months before his visit with Kinsey. It is possible that his hopes for a change in sexual "preference" were suggested by Kinsey's view of homosexuality as a behavior rather than an identity. In fact, at the time, because of his assumption that all individuals were potentially bisexual, Kinsey believed that exclusive homosexuals could change. By 1948, however, based on the sex histories he had amassed for the male volume, he gave up this idea.[74]

Painter, after his army discharge, also gave up any illusions that he could change his sexual orientation. His narcissistic obsession with masculine virility continued unabated throughout his life and signified his internal struggle with his masculinity. Like many gay men of his generation who were sexually attracted to the heterosexual ideal of the rugged, virile male, he associated homosexuality with effeminacy. He sought out straight-appearing, physically well-endowed sex partners to compensate for his own perceived lack of masculinity.

When Painter returned to New York in 1945, an artist friend, Edward, invited him to share his six-room studio apartment. The apartment was on the fourth floor of a brownstone town house located at 1364 Sixth Avenue, an address that had double significance for Painter. Since it was on the corner of West Fifty-fifth Street, it was on the same block as his family's town house where he spent his childhood. The address also symbolized the final stage of his sexual coming out. It was while living here, between 1945 and 1952, that he felt he had fully taken on the persona of Will Finch. Looking back at this period, he reflected, "I ceased being Dr. Painter's son, a dignified, respectable, Social Register, Who's Who, serious minded, puritanical and sort of devout (in my worship of my father's image for me). And became, as far as practical, companion of the half-naked, tough, 'free' youths Will Finch dreamed of."[75]

Painter had first met Edward before the war when he lived on the floor above Matty Costello's peg house. When Painter was on furlough in New York, he stayed at Edward's new studio apartment. According to Painter, they had the same "tastes in boys." While living together, they shared "literally hundreds" of sex partners, some of whom were hustlers and others the nude models who posed for Edward. Many of the hustlers were drunks and psychopaths, which led to fights and robberies that at times resulted in the police being called. Painter became increasingly attracted to the models and took up drawing, but in 1950, with only limited artistic success, he switched to photography and learned to do his own developing and printing. Through one of Edward's models, he began to meet and photograph the young "muscle men" who posed for other homosexual photographers. His sexual interests therefore shifted to the bodybuilding "muscle boys" whom he found to be physically and personally superior to male hustlers.[76]

Painter's immediate concern, once he became a civilian, was to work out a career path. As he had confided to Kinsey and Bill during his active duty, he had no intention of pursuing the kind of routine clerical work he had performed in the army. After several months of job hunting, he informed Bill that he had not come up with anything, nor did his prospects look promising. As he declared, "I still haven't the vaguest idea as to what will turn up. I've been all the way from Macy's to Union Seminary. The general consensus is I am too old—a point of view I had foreseen, but am unable to rectify."[77] He continued his job search and managed to live off his army savings. In the fall of 1946, he went up to New Haven to consult with his Yale friend Luther Tucker, who in 1935 had given Painter a sum of $500 to support his prostitution study. Tucker was now the general secretary of Dwight Hall (the Yale Christian Association). Tucker had connections with a Negro college and suggested that Painter could obtain a teaching job there. Painter confided to Kinsey that this would be interesting work, but it would be difficult to handle the social isolation of not being close to an urban area. He therefore did not follow up on this lead, much to the dissatisfaction of Tucker. Painter continued to seek Tucker's advice, but Tucker was growing impatient with what he perceived to be Painter's unwillingness to find work.[78]

Not only was Tucker losing patience with Painter's aimless existence, but Kinsey also shared similar concerns, which he communicated to Tucker. Kinsey believed that Painter was heading for "disaster," unless he anchored his life with a steady job. Fortunately for Painter, in April 1947 he found a job that was much to his liking. He was hired as a probation officer in the New York City Children's and Family Court. The work was complex and demanding because a probation officer was largely responsible for making decisions as to whether a boy was to be sent to an institution or returned to his family. In the latter case, the officer had to diagnose the situation and counsel the parents about how to make the boy's probation a success. In order to obtain training for his work, Painter thought about getting a degree in social work, but it is not clear whether he actually applied for such a program and was turned down or simply abandoned his plans.[79]

Painter was careful not to reveal his homosexuality in his work setting. Moreover, despite some temptations, he did not allow his sexual feelings to intrude on his relationship with the boys he worked with. He believed that his homosexuality, rather than being a problem, actually made him an especially good probation officer because as an outsider, he could empathize with the boys he was responsible for. For the most part, he remained very satisfied with his work during his eight-year tenure. From time to time, however, his morale was lowered when he ran into personal conflicts with some of his supervisors. As reflected in his relationship with Kinsey, Painter stood his ground if he was challenged by a figure in authority.[80]

Once he was settled in New York, Painter conscientiously kept up his journal entries in the form of letters that were written to Kinsey as well as to friends. In addition, he set aside blocks of time, either in New York or on visits to Bloomington, to organize and edit his papers. For example, he composed a twenty-two-page chronology of the years from 1918 through 1940, which was based on diary entries he had kept for that period. He indexed and organized family photograph albums and developed an Index of Names, which was an annotated description of each person he had contact with in his life. This index was periodically updated. Other items that Painter periodically sent to Kinsey included his extensive collection of photographed sex partners, erotic drawings, short stories, and essays on various homoerotic topics, such as men's clothing styles. On several occasions, a sex partner stole his typewriter. In these instances, Kinsey came to his rescue with the purchase of a new typewriter. Painter also continued to recruit male homosexual respondents for Kinsey's sex histories, which Kinsey was gathering for a planned book on homosexuality. Most of these contacts were in New York, but Painter also had connections in Chicago.[81]

Kinsey, for his part, was delighted with the extensiveness and depth of Painter's contributions. As the collection began to take shape, Kinsey praised Painter's ability to provide a detailed record, declaring, "It is a considerable privilege to be able to see into the thinking of an individual to this degree and to know its overt expression." After several years of amassing Painter's journal entries, Kinsey appreciatively communicated:

> I think this is building into one of the most significant diaries that has ever been kept. It is a shame that it cannot be published and made a part of the world's store of data. I commend you, as I hope I have before, on the style of writing. We are certainly very much indebted to you for your honest attempt to give us a complete record. It has done a great deal for our thinking, and I hope that we will be able to pass on enough of it to the rest of the world to effect [*sic*] everybody's thinking.[82]

In October 1947 Painter agreed to legally turn over his papers to the Kinsey Institute, ensuring that his personal record would be maintained and accessible to researchers.[83]

The major purpose of Painter's journals was to provide a detailed account of his sexual life. Thus, his letters to Kinsey, which averaged about three a week, typically included a recounting of his sexual activities, ranging from masturbatory fantasies to sex acts with partners. Referring to a slow week, for example, he described his encounters with two sex partners. The first was a "big muscled" hustler he picked up on a streetcar who turned out to be on the "dull side," especially in bed. The second was a hustler he had met at Edward's studio several months before. Although "pale" and "plumper" than he had been, he still turned out to be very satisfying. During the summers, Painter often went to Coney Island, where, even if he did not meet anyone, he could indulge his voyeuristic attraction to well-built youths. At Coney Island he favored the Washington Bath, but on this slow week in July, he commented that there were not any "great professional beauties and athletes," which necessitated his searching for them on the beach. In a subsequent entry the following day, he described how he went about "cruising" the Times Square area. He "peeked" into various bars along Forty-second Street and dropped into a new bar called Perry's on Eighth Avenue, where he "saw some figures with promise." Once inside the bar, he was disappointed at what he observed, but out of the corner of his eye he caught sight of a "handsome" youth whose shirt was completely unbuttoned. He followed the youth and his companion out onto the street, where pausing to light a cigarette, he had a chance to check out the youth's torso as well as getting a closer look at the other fellow. Passing the two again on the street, this time pausing in front of a drugstore, Painter decided to let both of them go since neither held his interest. After several similar episodes that night, he went home. Generally, Painter complained about the deteriorating quality of the hustlers since the end of the war. For the most part, they were not like the well-built street hustlers he had met before the war. They were either too thin or "personally deplorable."[84]

Painter's first love affair since his army discharge took place in August 1946. He had picked up Con, a casual hustler, at the Astor Hotel bar. They were together for a week before Con, a merchant seaman, had to ship out. As in the case of his prewar love, Peter, Painter was enthralled with Con's physique and felt that he was falling in love. After Con left, Painter reported that he "wept for joy" because when Con said good-bye, he added, "But not for good. I'll be back."[85] As things turned out, Con did not return, but the brief affair stimulated Painter to try and renew one of the affairs he had had in the army. He wrote to Jim, who was twenty-one and now lived with his family in Portland, Oregon, proposing a "marriage." The marriage was to be based on a partnership in which each partner would satisfy the other's needs. In exchange for Jim's sexual favors, Painter would act as Jim's "tutor," providing the enlightenment and experience of an older man. Jim consented to Painter's proposal, if Painter would come out to Portland and try and find work there. Painter had hoped that Jim would come to New York, but with no guarantee of employment at the other end, he declined Jim's invitation.[86]

About a month after his aborted affair with Jim, Painter met Roger, who stayed with him for six months. Roger had been a drifter and petty thief who had come to New York with the hope of becoming a merchant sea-

man. Before he met Painter, he had been in the navy and had his first homosexual experience aboard ship. Back in New York, he began to look for
homosexual customers along Forty-second Street, which is where Painter
met him. About a month into their relationship, Roger protested that he
was growing "weary of homosexual life." Painter and Roger thus began an
"'experiment' . . . [of] living in a Platonic manner."[87] Painter reported, to
his surprise, that he had no desire to seek out other sex partners, nor had
he engaged in his usual homoerotic fantasy outlets of drawing or short
story writing. Moreover, he was not disturbed over the fact that Roger, despite his expressed wish to give up homosexuality, continued on occasion
to be sexually active with other partners. Reflecting about his relationship
with Roger, Painter confided to Kinsey that he had come to realize that
companionship rather than sex was what he valued. Having established a
"buddy" relationship with Roger, sex had become inconsequential.[88]

Painter's affair with Roger seemed to epitomize his search for loving relationships in which he assumed the paternal role of protector, bread-
winner, and guide for a physically desirable young man. In turn, his young
partner would provide companionship and sex, with a priority on the former. This pattern of paternalism had characterized his earlier long-term affairs with Tony and Peter, and it was also reflected in his rejected "marriage" proposal to Jim. After leaving Painter to go into the air force, Roger
continued to write. Throughout his experience as a hustler, Roger had not
thought of himself as homosexual. When he was in the service, he had had
his first sexual experience with a woman but found that he could only
achieve orgasm through a homosexual fantasy. This made him realize that
he actually was homosexual, and Painter was the first person with whom
he shared his coming out experience. In acknowledging Painter's support,
Roger declared his "love" and adoration for Painter, not in a "sexy way"
but love in a "father and son" manner. Roger was thus able to reciprocate
Painter's love.[89]

Painter's next serious affair occurred about eighteen months later, at the
beginning of 1949. At Diamond Jim's, one of the Times Square bars, he
met Porter. As in the case of Roger, Porter had come to New York with the
hope of a career in the merchant marine. With no immediate employment
openings, he turned up at the homosexual bar with the aim of hustling for
a few dollars. Painter, who had returned to live in Edward's studio after an
eighteen-month absence, took him home and offered him a room. After a
brief trip back to his home in Detroit, Porter moved in. In contrast with
Roger, Porter was receptive to Painter's sexual advances. This was a love
affair in which sex played a central role. As in his previous relationships,
Painter turned his attention to looking after Porter, especially in trying to
find a job for him. Porter, however, had complained about physical fatigue,

and so Painter arranged an examination with Harry Benjamin, the endocrinologist and sex researcher Painter had become acquainted with through his work with the sex variants committee. Benjamin reported to Painter that Porter's problems were psychosomatic. Painter also looked after Porter's dental needs and hoped to correct his remedial reading problem. Despite Painter's efforts to shape him up, Porter remained unemployed and was becoming a financial burden. Painter's friend Bill bailed Painter out by contributing $250 for expenses in exchange for Porter's sexual favors. In the past Painter had often shared his sexual partners with Bill. In the present case, jealousy was not a problem because Bill's sexual act of fellation with Porter did not conflict with Painter's preference for frictation (achieving orgasm through body rubbing). A month after declaring his love for Porter, however, Painter ended the affair because of Porter's drinking problem. Moreover, the affair, despite Bill's financial help, had put Painter into debt and it took him several months to become solvent.[90]

By 1950, as a result of his newly acquired photographic skills, Painter's preference for sex partners switched from hustlers to "muscle boy" models. Through one of Edward's art models, he met bodybuilding young men who posed professionally for homosexual photographers. The photos appeared in the homoerotic "muscle" magazines that were becoming popular in the postwar period. Painter, however, was only interested in photographing these models for his own private collection. After a posing session, he was usually successful in inducing his models to have sex, for which they would get paid. According to Painter, many of the models hustled in "private circulation," that is, to individuals to whom they were introduced. He noted that some hoped to make a career out of modeling, and in a few cases, their modeling led to successful film careers. One of Painter's sex partners, a model named Carmine, eventually went to Hollywood, where, by the late fifties, he became an established star. Thomas Waugh, in his study of the history of homoerotic photography, points out that most of the models did not identify as homosexual and they generally received very low pay for their work. Thus, Painter's observation that hustling was fairly common is not surprising.[91]

In those instances when Painter's posing sessions did not lead to sex, there were other rewards. In the case of Seymour, for example, the price for sex was beyond what Painter could afford. This nineteen-year-old model had been hustling "for years" in the Hollywood and New York photography circuits and commanding high prices (once as high as $100). Nevertheless, Painter was satisfied by having the opportunity to simply gaze at an "overpowering" physique. After the posing session was over, Painter described what followed:

He was lying on the bed, (the only place in the room to sit anyway) naked, one leg drawn up, knee bent. I maneuvered so my head (and eyes) were near that knee, looking up at him past his huge thigh, genitals, and over his massive body to his handsome smiling face. (The way we were both reclining on the big double bed and moving about for comfort made such a composition of attitudes not surprising or odd as it sounds.) Breathing in I sensed I "smelled" (inhaled, perhaps is better) a fresh, sweet, cool ozone-like air coming off him to me. I was not surprised, though pleased. It seemed quite natural and proper. . . . But it is also (and this is why it seemed so natural) illustrative of how I feel about such a body on such a healthy youth.[92]

For Painter, this kind of voyeuristic ecstasy was also embodied in the photographic act. When one of his models asked what he did with the pictures, he replied that he enjoyed "taking" them and admiring the results. As he confided to Kinsey, "Photographing a subject for me is as enjoyable, in its way, as 'having' him."[93] Painter saved all of his photographs, periodically sending them to Kinsey. Although he thought about using them for sales to muscle magazines or other homosexuals, he never followed through on this. What mattered was simply the voyeuristic act of taking pictures and saving them as a visual record. Painter's voyeuristic gratification seems to have been matched by the exhibitionism of his photographic subjects. From his descriptions, they enjoyed posing nude and watching themselves in his full-length mirror, and in some cases and without any prompting from Painter, they would have an erection while being photographed.[94]

Painter also began to cruise Times Square and the beach at Coney Island, looking for muscular youths to photograph. At Coney Island he would have his camera with him. One of his posing "pickups" on the beach was a youth named Gus, and this led to a brief affair in the summer of 1951. A longer affair of six months began two years later with Chuck, one of Edward's art models. Chuck expressed interest in having Painter photograph him and Painter enthusiastically obliged. After their first photography session, in which Chuck posed nude, he was responsive to Painter's advances. Although he preferred being fellated, Chuck gave into Painter's wish of lying on top of him and achieving orgasm through body rubbing (frictation). During their affair, Chuck continued to be romantically involved with a woman. In general, Painter felt that the "muscle boys" were "more companionable and worth knowing than hustlers."[95] They usually were better educated and came from "nice" middle-class homes.

Between the time that he returned to New York after his army discharge in 1945 and the time that he left Edward's studio, in 1952, Painter's atti-

tudes about his sexuality had changed. Looking back, this period represented the assimilation of his uninhibited alter ego, Will Finch. The gradual acceptance of his homosexuality was revealed in several journal entries
during this seven-year period. When he began his job as a probation officer in 1947, his case assignments with "neglected children" prompted him
to reflect on his own childhood experiences of neglect. Because of his parents' emotional distance and inability to provide love, combined with a pu-
ritan upbringing, Painter believed that he developed a "stuffy, puritanical
personality." He had submissively incorporated the aristocratic "snob-
bish" worldview of his parents, which resulted in his inability to experience the uninhibited sensuality of the "common people." His only rebellious outlet was to identify with his alter ego, Will Finch, the tough, "free"
youth of his daydreams. Acting on his homosexual feelings enabled him to
escape from his "mental and moral straight-jacket" and avoid being consigned to a "normal" life in which he would have been married and limited to socializing only with his own class of gentlemen and scholars. He
acknowledged that he was still inhibited in his sexuality, confiding to Kinsey, "You see, as you have frequently remarked, the remains of that [men-
tal and moral] straight-jacket in my sexual mode. In my repression of fellation and passive pedication (and of active until recently); in my hatred of
the 'fairy'; in my deploring of 'penis fetishism.'" Nevertheless, the fact that
through his homosexuality, he was able to break the bonds of his elitist and
puritanical past gave him hope for the future. In referring to his homosexual coming out, he declared, "The result was, in moral character, the props
had been knocked out from under me—and I had to build my own foundation and structure, while at the same time my sexual urges were confusing and bedeviling me. It is my fond hope and belief that now I have
worked out a modus vivendi satisfactory to the situation."[96]

These reflections indicate that Painter had moved beyond his earlier expressed yearnings to be "cured" of his homosexuality. He could now live
with his sexuality, even take pride in it as an expression of his own indi-
viduality. Moreover, he was also moving away from a self-denigrating view
of homosexuality to an understanding of the societal basis of homophobia. Sex codes were historical constructions, not natural laws. Further evidence of his growing acceptance of homosexuality was revealed in a 1951
journal entry in which he stated, "Remember I used to say 'Each and every
homosexual is an individual tragedy.' Well that statement, like most in my
manuscript I fear, was colored by the subjective. And I have changed."[97]
Painter went on to refer to the advantages that homosexual men had because of their freedom from heterosexual conventions and entanglements.
While they might be short-changed on the opportunity for long-term love
sanctioned by marriage, they more than made up for it in terms of physi-

cal gratification. Yet he still believed that if it were possible, any incipient signs of homosexuality should be "corrected" in children because of the social rejection they would face as adults. But he also was optimistic about the increasing level of social acceptance he was experiencing. He felt accepted, for example, by the muscle-boy models (whom he did not consider to be homosexual). He also observed the increasing tolerance for sexual expression, in general, among adolescents.[98]

What Painter wanted most of all was to fulfill his search for love. He viewed his early years of homosexual experience (1935–37) as a period when he was "drunk with sex." He believed that he was able to move away from his addiction through the relationships he had with Tony, Peter, and Roger, relationships that were based on love rather than being restricted to physical gratification. Painter would continue to struggle with his "long search" for love. Up to this point, the relationships that he was involved in had brought only limited satisfaction since they were one-sided on his part. At best, they were based on paternal love rather than reciprocal love. In order to attract another man, he felt confident only if he maintained a status differential in which he was favored by age and class background. As he later acknowledged, he felt a sense of "shame" in having sex with a peer. While he could not admit a sexual inferiority with a peer, it felt acceptable with a social inferior. He had also come to realize that at the time that he came out, there were no role models of committed homosexual relationships. His homosexual friends were, for the most part, as fixated on young hustlers as he was. Indeed, this suggests how common it was for gay men of this era to be enthralled with the physical prototypes of masculinity. The search for straight-appearing sex partners embodied by hustlers and models, however, held little promise for lasting relationships, and for those gay men, like Painter, who craved love, the chase for virile lovers resulted in painful and repeated rejections.[99]

In December 1952 Painter abruptly moved out of Edward's studio. The precipitating cause was a late-night visit from Jimmy F., a hustler Painter had known for about six years. Jimmy had just been released from prison on a robbery conviction. He turned up at Edward's (Painter was alone) drunk and in a violent rage, threatening Painter with a broken beer bottle. Sparing Painter as the target for his outburst, he ended up hanging Painter's cat. When they first met, Painter was sexually attracted to Jimmy because of his muscular physique. He was also sympathetic to Jimmy's struggles to survive because of Jimmy's history of childhood neglect. On several occasions he had helped Jimmy leave town to escape arrest for assault and robbery. By the time he was physically threatened, however, Painter had already become wary of Jimmy's "psychopathic" pattern of violence and crime. This episode ended their relationship, but, more significantly, Painter was now thoroughly disillusioned with hustlers and stopped going to Times Square.[100]

He also felt that the affair forced him to get out of a "rut" and that it was best that he find a place of his own. In the meantime, he moved in with Gerric, a hustler friend. Several months later he moved into the Hotel St. George in downtown Brooklyn, conveniently located near the Brooklyn Family Court that he had recently been transferred to. On New Year's Eve of 1952, with Times Square off limits, he decided to explore the homosexual bars in the Fourteenth Street district around Third Avenue. The Clock Bar, on the corner of Third and Twelfth Street, was of special interest because it was not exclusively "queer." Tough young Puerto Rican boys from the neighborhood also frequented it. The Lower East Side was one of many neighborhoods that Puerto Ricans settled in when they started to migrate in large numbers to New York after the end of World War II. Painter's first contact with Puerto Ricans had occurred the previous summer at Coney Island in connection with his search for youths to photograph. At the bar he met Bobby, one of the boys he had become acquainted with at Coney Island. Bobby expressed an interest in having his picture taken. Two nights later they again met at the bar, and Bobby and two of his friends came home with Painter. Painter was especially attracted to Bobby, a tall muscular youth of sixteen. Even though Painter did not as yet have his camera equipment with him at Gerric's place, Bobby agreed to pose in the nude and then consented to have sex with Painter, for a fee. This was Bobby's first experience with a homosexual, but he was a willing partner, allowing Painter to go through his ritual of body worship and ejaculation by means of frictation. Painter was delighted at finding someone who he felt would develop into an "excellent" bed partner. Bobby, however, did not follow through on his commitment to return the following week to be photographed and Painter lost interest in him.[101]

After his first visits, Painter became an habitué of the Clock Bar, fascinated by its young Puerto Rican clientele. Unlike Times Square, the Fourteenth Street area was not a locale for street cruising. The Clock Bar served as a neighborhood gathering place for sexual pickups and social rendezvous. What Painter especially enjoyed was the "show"; that is, "the handsome bare-armed boys, the manouvering [sic] queers, the talk, the fights, the general atmosphere of sex. It was wonderful."[102] He met a wide circle of Puerto Rican boys in the bar and through them, many others.

Painter was sexually attracted to many of the Puerto Ricans, most of whom were in their late teens, and used his photography as a means of securing bed partners. He photographed them, either at Edward's studio or in his room at the Hotel St. George. Unlike the muscle boys who were paid for having sex, the Puerto Ricans were usually paid only for posing. They felt insulted if they were propositioned for sex since this would make it appear that they were "whores." On the other hand, they were flattered to be asked to pose. They were being admired for their muscles, and because they were too poor to own cameras, they welcomed the opportunity to be photographed. Almost all of the boys agreed to pose in the nude, and this gave Painter a chance to judge them for sex. Describing the possibilities, Painter declared, "If you don't like . . . [a boy] for sex, he leaves and is paid, perhaps annoyed for not being propositioned. If you like him, you ask him. If he doesn't accept, he still gets a posing fee—no complaints. . . . You take 'no' gracefully. Often they come back for further posing sessions and then accept sex."[103] In 1955 he became involved with his first romantic relationship in the Puerto Rican community. Indio was a "highly muscled" young man of twenty-three. He had been a hustler since he was nine and was an amateur boxer. He had been married but left his wife. Within a few months their affair was interrupted for a year when Indio was imprisoned for burglary. This was the first of many affairs with young Puerto Ricans.[104]

Painter was enamored with the homoerotic flavor of Puerto Rican culture. He observed that homosexual relations were an acceptable form of sexual outlet for Puerto Rican men because, aside from female prostitutes, young women were not generally available for sex. With its Spanish heritage, Puerto Rican society valued chastity in women before marriage. Homosexuals therefore served as convenient sex partners for heterosexual "macho" youths and men. Among the Puerto Rican youths, Painter felt that he was not stigmatized. And this tolerance was more generalized because the boys would often bring him home to meet their families. As he stated, "With Puerto Ricans, I could relax. . . . I found people who accepted me as normal."[105]

In February 1956 Painter resigned from his position as a probation officer. He was in danger of facing "charges" because a "homosexual informant" revealed his sexuality. His superior suggested that he resign and he agreed. He had liked his work and felt that he was competent. Moreover, he had made a point of not allowing his sex life to intrude upon his work by being discreet in the office and avoiding any sexual involvement with the boys for whom he was responsible. He was indignant about his forced resignation and drafted a magazine article about the social injustices homosexuals faced, featuring his own case.[106]

Painter was not financially dependent on his job because just prior to his resignation, he inherited $30,000 from his best friend Bill, who, based on family wealth, was a millionaire. Bill had died the previous year and his death was not unexpected. He had been in the severe stages of alcoholism, and Painter speculated that his excessive drinking was suicidal in intent. His drinking problem was exacerbated when he was victimized by blackmail while cruising. Painter felt a deep sense of loss with Bill's death. They had known each other since their student days at Yale and had remained close. At various times Bill had helped Painter out financially. In his Index of Names, Painter's entry for Bill read "Never a finer person or a more loyal friend."[107]

With his inheritance and newly acquired free time, Painter spent much of the next two years traveling to Puerto Rico as well as Mexico and Cuba. He periodically came back to New York and made several visits to the Kinsey Institute. As he confided to Kinsey in his last letter before Kinsey's death in August 1956, his travels were directed at escaping from the emptiness of his life in New York, brought on by the loss of his work.[108]

Painter's sense of loss was heightened when he learned of Kinsey's death while he was in San Juan. He expressed his condolence in a letter to Pomeroy:

> As well as you know me there is no need for me to tell you what a blow the Doctor's death was to me. . . . You may have sensed that he took with me somewhat the place of my father, thru [*sic*] which I know no higher encomium. This was a great personal fondness in addition to respect and admiration . . . as I look around, I now feel as if my last best friend had died, of whom I surely have none to spare.
>
> As for us remaining. Sometime when you get a chance let me know if you wish this Record to continue. I certainly want it to, and feel it should. . . . I feel, as doubtless you do, that the job you are in, and to which I contribute my mite [*sic*] . . . is of very great importance, and must be carried on.[109]

Painter elaborated on his feelings about Kinsey and his accomplishments in a 1961 profile. The only valid criticism he had, which he believed was rectified in the female volume, was Kinsey's reliance on statistical facts at the expense of literary research, that is, field observations and first-person accounts of the kind Painter used in his manuscript. Painter pointed out that the main stumbling block to his knowing Kinsey was the fact that he was a "client" rather than a friend or coworker. Thus, Kinsey wore a "mask," rarely expressing what his true feelings were. In reminiscing, Painter noted that what stood out most about Kinsey was his ability to "charm" everyone, including Painter's social circle. He commented:

> For a person like me who can't tolerate most people—and can't help let them know it—this is a vast feat. Before he was known (i.e., the "Male" was published with such incredible fanfare) I introduced him to 1364 and its assorted denizens and visitants, pals and playmates. And they were as assorted a lot of toughs, criminals, thugs,

pansies, literateurs [*sic*] and plain cocksuckers as can well be imagined. And he mesmerized them all. . . . But the climatic episode was when I invited Kinsey to Indio's and my birthday party. This was in November '55 [Painter's fiftieth birthday], and his heart bothered him so that when he walked he had to pause each block to rest. I felt I was dealing with a Ming vase.

And where I took that Ming vase!—to a bull pen. About twenty boys were there, all explosively virile. And in an explosive mixture of Irish, Jew, Negro and Puerto Rican, almost all violent delinquents and fight-lovers, and racially antagonistic. Then they proceeded to consume hard liquor straight, like water. . . . That [a fight did not occur] . . . I attribute to Indio, a genius too in his way with people. Meanwhile Kinsey potted around apparently having a fine time, apparently unconscious he was sitting on a rumbling volcano. Or didn't care.

Then a wild, crazy tatooed [*sic*] Irishman, whom I had *seen* drink half an ordinary glass of whiskey at a gulp, and a few of his drunken and demented friends offered to drive Kinsey back to his hotel. In their car, probably stolen, probably licenseless, surely about to fall apart. To my horror Kinsey calmly accepted. As is typical, I gather they treated him like their dear grandmother and deposited him safe and sound at the Statler—then dashed back at 60 miles an hour wrong way on a one way avenue, roaring with glee.[110]

PAINTER AND THE KINSEY INSTITUTE (1956–73)

After Kinsey's death, Paul Gebhard was appointed as the executive director of the Institute and Wardell Pomeroy as the director of field research. Since Pomeroy dealt with field research, he took over Kinsey's role as the correspondent for Painter's journal. On his return from San Juan in September, Painter wrote to Pomeroy and poured out his feelings of despair over the loss of employment and Kinsey's death. His sense of frustration and futility persisted because as a result of being "blackballed" from city employment, he realized his job prospects were severely limited. What made the situation particularly bleak was that going back to his naive honesty of coming out at Union Seminary, he was now once again prevented from doing the kind of work he believed he was best suited for, that is, helping other people. He summed up his feelings, declaring, "I am bitter because I don't try to pass . . . like the negro [*sic*] I have nothing to hide . . . nothing to be ashamed of. I still love people and want to help them—but as far as I can see I can't. I haven't the capital to live on the income and write or research, or propagandize—and my sexuality again bars me from Foundation supported work, such as with Kinsey."[111]

Painter's despondency was not limited to his hopeless employment prospects. Referring to his personal life, he stated, "I am tired. Tired of being alone. Tired of buying companionship. Tired of putting up a cheerful front. Tired of pleasures. Tired of fighting for what I deserve . . . human rights and privileges. Tired of the race—and of the human race. Others will carry on. As I say I will not end it. But if it ends I will not fight it. Nor will I welcome it. I would accept it, in peace."[112] This outpouring suggests that Painter had contemplated suicide, and in subsequent journal entries, he often referred to the "suicide letter."

Painter did find solace in his determination to continue his Life Record. He opined, "I regard this Record as a really important contribution to my life work—probably the one objective and tangible one." With his ruminations about his own mortality, he did not want to leave his work unfinished. After learning that the Institute still had no means of remunerating him for his work, he confided to Pomeroy, "I am not working for you, but for myself. . . . As for payment, I feel *this* is *my* work."[113]

In March 1956 Painter had made his first trip to Puerto Rico. He traveled with Tony C., a New York Puerto Rican friend. Financed by his inheritance from Bill's estate, Painter was not worried about expenses and he and Tony settled into a first-class hotel in San Juan. Based on two days of observation, his first impressions of the city were not positive. Because of the recent capital investment in building construction, he found little in the way of "old world charm" or general exoticism. As for sexual interest, he noted an absence of attractive men and no evidence of a "divergence from a heterosexual norm."[114]

Based on further observation, Painter began to develop a hypothesis about why there was no public sign of homosexual activity. Commercialized prostitution was unnecessary because in Puerto Rico men were willing to engage in sex with any man who struck their fancy. Thus, all men were potentially available as sex partners. This hunch was confirmed when Tony introduced Painter to Luis, a twenty-three-year-old self-identified homosexual who acted as a community contact. According to Luis, almost everyone was agreeable "at the drop of a smile or a word."[115] This sexual accessibility was especially evident at the various small informal bars in the less conspicuous and poorer sections of the city. Luis reported that in such settings, youths were more likely to seek him out. Their primary motive was to obtain sexual release since casual sex with women, with the exception of prostitutes, was generally not available. Luis had several "pet boys" to whom he gave small gifts of money, but, for the most part, money was not expected since everyone was relatively poor. On the other hand, sex for pay was expected in the case of tourists, and sexual liaisons could be easily arranged through a homosexual contact, such as Luis.

Same-sex acts were typically limited to anal intercourse and followed a strict gender code. Homosexuals assumed the passive (feminine) role of the insertee, while their partners took the active (masculine) role of the inserter. There was no tolerance for behaviors that would have compromised the masculine role of the active partner, such as kissing another man or any other form of body contact. Moreover, in restricting their sexual behavior to the act of phallic penetration, active men did not perceive themselves to be homosexual. They were simply substituting a male sex object in the heterosexual act of intercourse. Homosexuals were defined by their role in anal intercourse, that is, as pedicants. In fact, there were only two terms used to refer to homosexuals: *maricón,* the general term, and *pato,* a pedicant. As Painter noted, the limited homosexual argot reflected the absence of a distinct homosexual subculture. Since most homosexuals were known in their own communities, there was little need for homosexual bars and other group gathering places. In San Juan there was only one small homosexual bar that catered to "flaming faggots." Like Luis, most homosexuals were "private queens"; that is, they had no need to publicly display their identity since they were known in their community. The nature of Hispanic homosexual life that Painter observed was not especially unfamiliar to him because he had become aware of it when he had immersed himself in the Puerto Rican male youth subculture in New York.[116]

Luis lived in a poor district of San Juan, known as La Perla, and this is where Painter spent his time. He frequented George's, a neighborhood bar that served as a general meeting place, especially a place where sexually accessible young men hung out. It was here that he met a number of youths with whom he had sexual affairs. Two, in particular, stood out for him—Yayito and Julio. Painter described Yayito as one of the "prettiest boys" he had ever seen, and, moreover, he caught Painter's fancy because he was a "nice boy," that is, literate, hardworking, with good parents. After a day at the beach, Painter invited him back to his hotel room. As Yayito spoke no English, Painter offered to tutor him. After a couple of hours of work, Yayito professed he was tired and stretched out on the bed. Painter took this as a sexual invitation, which it indeed was. As Painter did not engage in anal sex, he successfully negotiated other practices. As he described it, "He wanted to fuck me, of course, but after begging as prettily and sweetly as I have ever dreamed of, he took no for an answer. . . . He loved me up, kissed me, stroked me. . . . I came by frictation on his smooth, hairless thigh—and he seemed pleased and satisfied, especially with the five dollars."[117] This affair lasted for a few weeks until Yayito left for New York. During their affair Painter continued to act as a tutor and decided that when he returned to New York he would learn Spanish, which he did.

Julio was a boxer, "a youth with the body of a slender gladiator and the face of a black god (Greek, not African)."[118] He was dark-skinned (the first "Negro" Painter slept with) and racially mixed, a characteristic not uncommon in the Puerto Rican population. In fact, Painter was struck by what he found to be an absence of racism in Puerto Rican society. Painter had met Julio in a neighborhood bar and invited him to be photographed in his hotel room. As Julio spoke little English, Luis acted as an intermediary and informed Painter that Julio was willing to pose nude and have sex. As in the case of Yayito, Julio proved to be a cooperative bed partner, satisfying Painter's sexual proclivities. Based on his experience with Puerto Ricans in New York and their desire to be admired for their physical builds, Painter successfully used the promise of photography as a source for recruiting sex partners. With the exception of Yayito and Julio, however, he had a difficult time negotiating what he wanted sexually from his partners since they expected that, as a homosexual, he was a pedicant. In most cases, they reluctantly allowed him to caress and kiss them and in a few cases acceded to Painter's wishes for mutual lovemaking. Such practices were distasteful for Painter's sex partners because they perceived themselves as engaging in homosexual behavior. In contrast, when they were active pedicators, they were assuming a male heterosexual role.[119]

Over the course of his first visit to San Juan, which lasted a little over a month, Painter fell in love with La Perla, the poor district that he spent most of his time in. At first he was taken aback by the wretched housing conditions and lack of other amenities, but he was soon captivated by the carefree and exuberant spirit of the inhabitants. What was particularly significant for Painter was the fact that he felt at home in the community, commenting, "I am *still* the only outsider I have ever seen within La Perla. Even Puerto Rican outsiders are uncommon. And I still have to encounter so much as a disapproving look, tho [sic] my sexuality is as noted as myself."[120]

For most of the next two years, Painter shuttled back and forth between New York and San Juan. He had intended to travel more widely in the Caribbean and Mexico, but he only felt comfortable in Puerto Rico. In August 1956 he did take an extended trip to Mexico and Cuba, but he found little to his liking. Unlike Puerto Rico, where young men dressed in sexually provocative ways, revealing much of their upper body, Mexican men's clothing style was too physically restrictive to interest Painter. In Cuba (in the pre-Castro era), he was turned off by the commercialism of Havana and the annoyance of being pursued by female prostitutes. Increasingly in his travels, however, Painter was feeling a sense of emptiness. As he confided in what would be his last letter to Kinsey, he felt his life had no purpose. He needed work that would give him a "reason for living," and he was not very optimistic about his future chances for finding such work.[121]

By the end of 1957, Painter had used up all of the money he received from Bill's estate. Out of desperation, he approached his brother Sidney for help in finding a job. Sidney was a history professor at Johns Hopkins and had connections with booksellers. He agreed to help Painter, provided Painter became "non-overt" in his sexuality. Although he had no intention of conforming to such a demand, Painter made a promise to reform. Through Sidney, in February 1958 he obtained a job at a Doubleday's bookstore on Fifth Avenue. With the exception of a period of several months in 1959, when he was in Puerto Rico, and his two-year residency in California in the early sixties, he worked at Doubleday's until he had to quit in the mid-seventies because of poor health. With his love of books, he generally found the Doubleday job to be quite satisfying. Economically, however, with a starting salary of a little over $200 a month, he was only able to live at a level of bare subsistence.[122]

Settled once again in New York, Painter returned to the Puerto Rican bars on the Lower East Side. Over the next four years, he had a number of sexual affairs. At first he renewed his relationships with Bobby and Indio. He then became involved successively with Hector, Manuel, and Efrian. All of these men were in their early twenties. Most had a criminal record for burglary, and, as in the cases of Indio and Efrian, Painter's affairs with them were interrupted for periods when they were in jail. Some were involved in procuring female prostitutes or male hustlers. In 1959 Painter inherited some additional money from Bill's estate and returned several times to Puerto Rico. He made one of these trips with Indio and another with Hector. In each case, he met their parents and relatives. Indio and Hector had their own families in New York and each had a mistress. Indio had five sons with two women, and Hector had fathered seven children with two women. Around 1965, several years after his affair with Painter, Indio was fatally stabbed for his connection with heroin traffic. By 1968 Hector had become a "miserable heroin addict."[123]

In thinking about his Puerto Rican lovers, Painter declared that he would have preferred honest and ambitious youths, but, as in the case of Augustin with whom he had a brief affair, they rejected him when he attempted to counsel and guide them about their future. As a result, he was drawn to "low characters," criminals, and psychopaths who were attracted to him as a source for their sexual release. Unlike his earlier relationships with Peter, Tony, and Roger, in which he had taken on the role of tutor and guide, the Puerto Ricans were only willing to avail themselves of his help when they were in trouble with the law.[124]

For his part in these relationships, Painter distanced himself from the stereotypical effeminate homosexual identity. He therefore did not think of himself as "queer," a label that for him meant the antithesis of "macho."

In keeping with his aversion to a queer identity, it was especially important for him to be sure that he was not "unmanly" in the eyes of his sex partners, especially when they were macho types like Indio and Efrian. With all of his sex partners, he thus avoided anal sex, in which he would feel obliged to take the passive feminine role of the pedicant. He had mixed feelings about oral sex since over the years of his sexual experience, he had overcome his initial aversion and derived some satisfaction from being an active fellator. Nevertheless, he avoided oral sex with most of his Puerto Rican lovers for fear that he would jeopardize his masculine image. He usually got his partners to accept his preferred practice of frictation, and since his partners were usually paid for being photographed, the question of their achieving orgasm was not essential to the sexual relationship. What was particularly satisfying for Painter was that he was able to assume the active masculine role when he had sex with his virile partners. He placed his partners in the position where they had to "submit" to and accept his initiatives. As proof of his own masculinity, he preferred a sex partner "who submits to be nonsubmissive by nature, that is an aggressive male. I want to control, tame, hold, this strong, violent aggressive male—to 'have' him."[125] This was the basis for his preference for "straight" as opposed to "queer" lovers.

Painter was sexually attracted to his Puerto Rican lovers because of their youth and virility, but, as in the case of his attraction to sex partners generally, there were other sources of attraction. In a voyeuristic and aesthetic sense, he was fascinated with observing their muscular bodies. Moreover, he felt a sense of safety and protection in being held or lying next to a muscular youth, a feeling that he judged to be feminine, but since it was private it did not compromise his masculine image in the eyes of his partners. He also admired the casual, primitive, uninhibited, guileless character of these young men and of Puerto Ricans in general. These people were expressive and joyful, an idealized alternative to the Anglo-Saxon puritanism of his own upbringing. Painter's idealization of Puerto Rican primitiveness from the vantage point of his class background suggests a racist/colonial projection on his part. Yet he was able to move beyond a class/racial divide because he felt a political kinship with Puerto Ricans as an oppressed group. Without revealing his homosexual identity, he wrote a letter to the editor of the *New York Post* expressing his concerns and observations about the unfair treatment Puerto Ricans received from the police.[126]

Through his relationship with Manuel, Painter became involved with a youth gang known as the 4th Street Dragons. As leader, Manuel was the "war lord." In March 1961 this gang connection resulted in Painter's detention in the "Tombs," New York's infamous city jail. At this time Painter had begun his affair with Efrian, a member of the gang. At Efrian's urging, Painter agreed to join him for a late-night get-together with some of the other gang members at a local Puerto Rican bar. A group of eight, including Painter, Efrian, and Manuel, decided to go to a party and piled into a car, driven by one of the gang members. Returning from the party, around four in the morning, the driver was pulled over by the police for driving the wrong way on a one-way street. Raul, the driver, had no car registration, and it was later discovered that the car was stolen with stolen license plates. The group was taken to the local police station, booked for "grand larceny," and then taken to the "Tombs." Since Painter could not raise the $25 bail, he was detained. Four days later he was released when the charges were dropped because there had been no complaint lodged regarding the theft of the car. As a result of being arrested and jailed, Painter was made an honorary member of the Dragons. His brush with the law constituted the initiation rights for gang membership.[127]

When he returned to his job at Doubleday's, he explained his absence was due to being called to Baltimore to help his widowed sister-in-law (Sidney had died in 1960). His boss was peeved at not having been informed, but Painter's explanation was accepted. Missing almost a week of work, however, left Painter with no money. His old friends, Gerric and Edward, lent him the money to pay his rent.[128]

Using the excuse of helping his sister-in-law belied the fact that Painter was estranged from Sidney's widow. As adults, Painter and his brother Sidney were not close because Sidney had not accepted Painter's homosexuality. Painter therefore had relatively little contact with Sidney's wife and children. Nevertheless, the need to appropriate his family in accounting for his absence from work seems to have prompted Painter to think about his estate. A few months after the "Tombs" incident, he wrote Pomeroy requesting that Pomeroy, or the Kinsey Institute, act as the executor of his personal effects. In response, Pomeroy agreed to act as executor. With the passing of his brother, Painter was worried about what would happen to those parts of his Life Record that he might still possess at death. He also felt that if the Institute was the executor, the circumstances of his death would be known, especially if unusual as in the case of murder. Painter's reference to the possibility that his life could be taken through homicide suggests that despite his adoration of the Puerto Rican youths, he also had some concerns about his physical safety. From the time that he started to associate with hustlers, he was aware of the risk of physical attack. As he noted, the Puerto Rican "psychopaths, drug addicts, muggers, thieves, and pimps I have been having . . . were no better than the psychopaths, thieves, vagabonds etc. I had before them."[129]

Thoughts about death stimulated Painter to introspect about his life.

He confided to Pomeroy, "I get very irritated when I think of how my life has been wasted—simply because I am homosexual. And because, having no sense of guilt about it, never chose to hide it."[130] He once again referred to the cost of his coming out at Union Seminary. His public candor had dashed his hopes of becoming a teacher and having a career in which he could satisfy his need for generativity by working with young people. By being outed as a parole officer, he once again was deprived of pursuing a socially useful career. Although he enjoyed his job as a bookseller at Doubleday's (and was only able to get it by "lying" to his brother that he would no longer be overt in his homosexuality), it was a far cry from what he had expected to accomplish. Because he chose to be open and authentic about who he was, society had relegated him to what he saw as a useless job. Looking back, he wished that someone among his scholarly contacts in the medical and scientific community had guided him to think of becoming an independent professional like a lawyer or a physician. This would have allowed him to be open without the threat of bureaucratic censure or job loss.[131]

What Painter wanted to make clear was that his failure to fulfill his potential was the result of social oppression, not personal weakness. As he declared, "I did not 'fail in life,' deteriorate, degenerate, or what have you, because I was homosexual. . . . I was pushed, shoved, propelled, edged by exclusion after exclusion, systematically denied, by having doors slammed in my face, a useful, socially significant career, which I tried to achieve and ardently wanted."[132] Homosexuals, like "Negroes" and Jews, were persecuted, but unlike these stigmatized groups, homosexuals had no one to stand up for them and disturb the social conscience. Painter's social outrage was in marked contrast to the position he had taken twenty years earlier in his 1941 manuscript, in which he prioritized the inherent inferiority of homosexuality over societal oppression. The loss of his probation job in 1956 served as the catalyst for his growing radicalism. He was critical of the blatant discrimination homosexuals faced in the 1950s and early 1960s, commenting, "Society . . . lumps homosexuals with criminals, addicts and assorted 'degenerates.' . . . The State department assumes we would betray our country at the drop of a pair of pants. . . . Schools assume we would corrupt our students, Courts our clients, and so with social work etc., etc."[133]

Painter did recognize that in order to combat oppression, homosexuals had to stand up for themselves, but in alluding to homophile groups, he admitted, "I'm not the organizational, group-endeavor type." Although he expressed some interest in learning more about these groups, he viewed them as "wholly foreign to my personal interest."[134] His aversion to organized homophile activism, in part, reflected his individualistic temperament. From childhood on he tended to be a loner, and throughout his adult life he prided himself in his ability to be independent, socially and intellectually. Nevertheless, his reluctance to become involved with the emerging homophile movement of the 1950s and 1960s also reflected his ambivalence about homosexual identity. He shared Kinsey's reservations about positing a homosexual identity; that is, there were no homosexual people, only homosexual behavior. To categorize individuals as homosexual would increase their vulnerability to being stereotyped and stigmatized. Yet because he was unable to overcome his negative association of homosexuality with femininity, he projected a stereotyped view of homosexuals as a group, disparaging "queers" for being effeminate. Moreover, as a consequence of the discrimination he faced, beginning with Union Theological Seminary and exacerbated by his forced job dismissal, he frequently referred to homosexuals as a group in his various writings and viewed himself as a spokesperson for homosexuals.[135]

Painter's preferred strategy for combating homosexual oppression was the power of personal narrative as embodied in his Life Record. During the spring and summer of 1961, he devoted considerable time to updating his Index of Names, as well as working on various essays on such topics as his early sex life and his moral viewpoint. He also planned to do a comparative study involving his Puerto Rican sex partners and the hustlers he wrote about in his 1941 manuscript.[136]

This was also a period in which Painter felt especially lonely. His affair with Efrian was interrupted when Efrian was jailed in March, for five months, for having violated his parole from a previous sentence. Painter's finances were such that he was too "poor" to even afford paying for sex partners or negotiating sex by photographing them. When Efrian was released from jail in August, Painter looked forward to renewing their affair. His ensuing relationship with Efrian proved to be especially problematic, and over the course of the next ten months, Painter chronicled the increasing stress he faced.[137]

Painter was attracted to Efrian because he was virile, tough, good-looking, and bright; that is, he had all of the qualities that Painter sought in his lovers. But Painter became aware that Efrian's tough, macho demeanor appeared to mask anxieties about his own manliness. According to Painter, Efrian was uncomfortable and socially ineffectual with women, viewing them strictly as sex objects. He was proud when he managed to impregnate a woman and looked forward to having a child (preferably a son). What especially appealed to Painter in their relationship was that he believed he could help Efrian. He knew that Efrian was a psychopath, but this was the result of growing up in a family in which the children were treated like a "pack of dogs," competing with each other for meager resources with the physically strongest, which included Efrian, getting the major share. Painter was convinced that Efrian was "fond" of him, that, in fact, Efrian needed him because Painter could provide the personal caring, support, and respect that he had not gotten from his family. But Painter was also wary that his desire to help could be exploited by a "cold-blooded" psychopath like Efrian.[138]

At Efrian's urging, for the purpose of saving on rent, Painter agreed to share an apartment that was in a tenement on the Lower East Side. Efrian's sister and brother-in-law were the superintendents of the building. Painter and Efrian moved in together in January 1962. Two months later Painter temporarily returned to his former residence at a cheap West Side hotel. What Painter had not realized before they lived together was that Efrian was a compulsive gambler. Painter thought that he could "cure" Efrian and believed his promises to quit. In the meantime Efrian kept taking Painter's earnings and using it for gambling. Painter felt he had to get away, at least for a while, but within a few weeks he was back, compelled by his guilt over letting Efrian down. By June, however, Painter had reached a crisis. In order to meet Efrian's demands for money, Painter had started to steal small amounts of money at Doubleday's, which he thought he could safely accomplish. His latest attempt, however, was discovered and he feared that he might be fired. Moreover, his relationship had deteriorated to the point where Efrian was verbally abusing him with threats of physical harm. Efrian accused Painter of trying to cheat him and he would therefore have to take "measures," which Painter interpreted as "a clear implication of violence."[139] At Pomeroy's suggestion, Painter decided that he had to leave town. He believed that if he remained, Efrian would continually hound him. He compared his plight to the homosexual protagonist in Tennessee Williams's *Suddenly Last Summer* who was devoured by his boys. He had to escape to prevent being destroyed by Efrian.[140]

Painter chose San Francisco as his destination, attracted to its climate, beauty, and tolerant atmosphere. What was most important for his purposes, however, was that he had a contact there whom he felt could help him get a job and get settled. This was Harry Benjamin, the medical sex researcher who had befriended him during his association with the sex variants committee. Once settled in San Francisco, he would contact Doubleday's regarding his resignation and therefore be able to apply for unemployment insurance. Painter wrote to Gebhard, requesting that he be allowed to stop over at the Institute on his way west. With his request granted, Painter informed Doubleday's that he had to take a vacation immediately and that his vacation pay should be sent to Bloomington. He had just enough money for his bus fare to Bloomington. At the end of June, without informing Efrian, Painter left New York. He thought he could never return because of the threat that Efrian posed. He looked forward to making a new life for himself in California. Anything would be better than the last six months that he had wasted.[141]

Painter arrived in San Francisco by bus in July. On the way he spent two weeks in Bloomington working on his papers. On his first full day in San Francisco, he went to see Benjamin, whom he had not seen for ten years. He described their meeting as a "remarkable experience" because it gave him an opportunity to talk about his life to a sympathetic and interested listener whom he greatly admired. To get help in finding a job, Benjamin recommended that he contact Hal Call, one of the leaders of the Mattachine Society in San Francisco. Call suggested that he might have better opportunities in Los Angeles and directed him to get in touch with Evelyn Hooker, the psychologist who had carried out pathbreaking research in the mid-1950s that demonstrated no differences in mental health indices between samples of homosexual and heterosexual men. With no sure leads in San Francisco, Painter decided to head for Los Angeles. He was also prompted to leave San Francisco because he did not like the cool summer climate. With a loan from Benjamin to pay for his bus fare, he arrived in Los Angeles a week later.[142]

In Los Angeles Painter found affordable lodgings at the Hotel Baltimore, a "drab, no-frills" establishment with large, clean, and comfortable rooms. The hotel was in the seedy side of the downtown district, four blocks away from Pershing Square, the infamous hangout for male hustlers and homosexuals. After settling in, Painter explored the Square and nearby gay bars. Unlike New York, his cruising forays turned up little in the way of sexual interest. He was particularly interested in searching for Hispanic types, but the many Mexicans he observed did not have the kind of muscular build that had attracted him to Puerto Ricans in New York. Another turnoff was that the Mexicans were more submissive than the Puerto Ricans. As Painter noted, "Among the Spanish here I see none of the rough, tough, bare-armed, swaggering, muscular young characters one sees in New York."[143] In an attempt to establish social contacts, Painter knew that Peter was living in the Los Angeles area. He had not seen Peter in about fifteen years and was looking forward to reestablishing their friendship. Painter had a good visit with Peter and his wife, but in a subsequent phone call, Peter gave him the brush-off. Painter was disappointed and made no further effort to contact him.[144]

Within a few days of his arrival, Painter called Hooker, who was very glad to hear from him and invited him to visit her at her home. They had met in New York a few years earlier, when Pomeroy arranged for Painter to show Hooker the various gay bars in the city. At the time Hooker was beginning her ethnographic research on male homosexuality. Painter was

delighted with the opportunity to talk with Hooker. They spent an afternoon chatting about her continuing research on homosexuality and her
friends in the Los Angeles gay community, such as Christopher Isherwood.
Painter brought her up-to-date on his life and they discussed his Life
Record. Hooker expressed a keen interest in reading and studying it,
which greatly pleased Painter. Although there was no possibility of working for Hooker as a research assistant, she did offer to pay Painter for updating his bibliography on homosexuality. He wasn't sure if this was a project that she really needed or if it was simply something that she created
so that he could receive some financial help. In either case, he was very
grateful.[145]

On the recommendation of both Hooker and Benjamin, Painter looked
up Dorr Legg, the business manager of the homophile magazine *ONE*.
Painter hoped to get some leads on employment prospects as well as tips
on how to meet Hispanics. Unfortunately, Legg was unable to provide
much help with either of Painter's concerns. After a month of searching,
Painter found a full-time job at Martindale's, a bookstore in downtown
Los Angeles. He had impressed the owner by referring to his research in
"history and sociology," leaving unsaid the topic of homosexuality. Unlike
his position at Doubleday's, his job at Martindale's entailed manual work.
His annual salary was approximately $2,400—an amount slightly lower
than his New York earnings. His employment came at an opportune time
since he had practically run out of the funds provided by Benjamin and
Hooker.[146]

When Painter first arrived in Los Angeles, he was optimistic about both
his job prospects and his personal life. With respect to work, the job at
Martindale's met his immediate financial needs, but it was disappointing
in light of his hopes about finding a niche in paid research on homosexuality. He liked the climate and physical look of the city, but with his limited income, he could not take advantage of its cultural offerings. Without
a car, his mobility around the area was restricted. Unlike the convenient
subway trip to Coney Island, the beach at Santa Monica was a long bus
ride away. Especially disconcerting was the fact that his sex life was empty.
The Pershing Square hustlers and the patrons at the gay bars turned him
off, and he was having no luck in making any contacts with Mexican
youths. He missed the look and style of the New York Puerto Ricans. Even
if he were to find hustlers or youths that attracted him, his poverty would
limit any sustained activity. By the end of his first year in Los Angeles, he
was ready to return to New York. He believed that he would be safe from
Efrian if he avoided the Lower East Side. He hoped that Pomeroy would
be able to help him get his old job back at Doubleday's, a job that was
somewhat better paying and less physically strenuous.[147]

Adding to his malaise, Painter learned that Pomeroy would be leaving the Institute by the end of 1963 to go into full-time private practice as a marriage counselor in New York. Painter feared that this would jeopardize his work on the Life Record, but Pomeroy assured him that his work would continue to be supported by the Institute. Paul Gebhard would assume Pomeroy's role as correspondent and overseer. Painter also regretted losing Pomeroy as a correspondent because they had developed a close working rapport. Moreover, being less awed by Pomeroy than he was with Kinsey, Painter injected a good deal of teasing and humor in his letters to Pomeroy. With Pomeroy's encouragement, Painter renewed his commitment to keep up his Life Record and reiterated his earlier expressed belief that the Record would be "vastly instructive." As he commented, "I want a lot, not just one person to know that homosexuals aren't all a bunch of screwballs."[148]

In July 1963, just at the time that Painter was making plans to return to New York, he became entangled in a brief affair that seriously complicated his life and prevented him from leaving Los Angeles. He had met Alika, a Hawaiian who had been in Los Angeles for about a year and managed to support himself through odd jobs and hustling. One night while staying with Painter, Alika excused himself to go out for cigarettes. A half hour later when he did not return, Painter became suspicious and checked his pants pocket to see if Alika had taken his money. His money was still there, but the key for Martindale's that he kept in his pocket was missing. Alarmed, he quickly walked over to the store and found the door unlocked. He checked where the previous day's money was kept and saw that it had been taken (about $500). He then returned home and found Alika, who had come back. At first Alika denied any connection with the theft but eventually broke down and admitted his involvement. He gave the key back to Painter as well as his payment of $35 for his part in the break-in; the rest of the money had gone to the two friends who actually carried out the robbery. Painter persuaded Alika to try and retrieve the stolen money from his friends, threatening that if Alika was not back in an hour he would call the police. Painter had hoped that Alika would be back with the money by 5 A.M., which would have given him enough time to return it to the store before someone came around to collect the daily cash. At the agreed-upon time, Alika did not show up and Painter realized that he had to call the police to protect himself.[149]

After contacting the police, Painter was questioned at the store and, without revealing his sexual relationship with Alika, gave the detectives the details behind the theft. A warrant was put out for Alika's arrest, but apparently Alika and his partners in crime had fled the Los Angeles area and were not caught. This lessened the possibility for Painter that his homosexuality would be revealed to the police, but he was still not exonerated from being implicated in the theft. He was called back by the police for a polygraph test, which he failed. Indeed, his failure was not surprising since he had to hide the sexual nature of his relationship with Alika. Painter was especially wary about the Los Angeles Police Department because Chief William Parker publicly advocated jail terms for known "sexual deviates" (homosexuals). The detectives indicated that they did not think he actually committed the theft, but, on the other hand, they believed that he was an accessory to the crime and knew the whereabouts of Alika and the money. Consequently, he was arrested and subjected to further questioning. Suspecting that he might have had a sexual liaison with Alika, the detectives inquired if he had ever been married, if he knew any "girls," and if either he or Alika had any "sexual trouble." After being detained for four days without being charged, he was released from jail. At this time he learned that he had been fired from Martindale's. Fortunately he qualified for unemployment insurance since there were no conditions placed on his jail release. Nevertheless, he realized that because of the incident his job prospects would be very limited. Moreover, he had heard no word about the possibility of returning to Doubleday's, and even if there was an offer, he had no money for his trip back to New York.[150]

After about two weeks of unemployment, Painter was hired as an orderly at Pine Tree Lodge, a private sanitarium for the mentally ill and aged. It was located in La Crescenta, a Los Angeles suburb. He lived on the premises and hoped to earn enough in two months so that he could return to New York. Although he was physically isolated, he found the work tolerable. After two months had passed, however, he decided to remain at Pine Tree since he had been promoted to assistant charge attendant. This position held the promise of learning career skills in medical administration that would give him access to jobs anywhere in America. This breakthrough was dashed in January when he was infected with a skin condition from the patients and, as a result, was laid off. He was given a month's pay and placed on disability compensation. With this latest setback—another "twist of the rope"—he was once again depressed and unsure about the future.[151]

Painter moved back to the Hotel Baltimore in downtown Los Angeles. By April his situation was perilous because he was virtually broke. He called the state unemployment office, but the only job prospect was janitorial work, which he considered to be an "absurd" option. He then decided to visit the Suicide Prevention Center in the hope that they could solve his plight by finding a job for him. When he first came to Los Angeles, on Hooker's recommendation, he had unsuccessfully applied for a position at the center as a research assistant. He had to walk twenty-five city blocks from his hotel and back, but the center had no resources to enable him to find work. He was questioned about his predicament and his career history and encouraged to seek psychotherapy from the Veterans Administration Clinic. He followed up on this recommendation but found that since he did not have a service-connected disability, he did not qualify for treatment. Nevertheless, with all of these setbacks, Painter confided to Gebhard that he had no intention of committing suicide, declaring, "I find life too interesting."[152]

Compounding Painter's bureaucratic nightmare, his disability checks were delayed. He wrote that he had run out of money and consequently had not eaten for nine days. Furthermore, the hotel threatened him with eviction. In desperation, he called Hooker, who "hit the roof" when she heard that he had gone without food. She assured him that she would see to it that his disability check arrived. She called the State Public Assistance Office, and within a few days, his check came by special delivery. After being rescued from starvation, he left his hotel for the first time in several days and went to a restaurant for his first meal. Throughout this grueling experience, he kept up his journal entries. He described how he did not allow himself to think about food, relying on the reading material available in the hotel as a distraction. He forced himself to drink a lot of water and, considering the fact that he was a heavy smoker, even managed to get along after his supply of cigarettes ran out.[153]

Painter deemed it important to report his starvation experience in the Life Record, commenting to Gebhard, "This Record is of what happens to me. I didn't eat for a while, so I told you about it. I was interested in the physical phenomena accompanying it (a) because I didn't want it to go too far, so I watched carefully (b) because I found them interesting and hence worthy of report. Like anything unusual—e.g. jail, Pine Tree, how one's buttocks feel after 2,000 miles on a bus."[154] He went on to acknowledge Gebhard's expressed sympathy and concern for his predicament, but noted that it was not Gebhard's role to become personally involved. His role was to receive, process, and preserve the Record, just as Painter's role was to record and interpret his experiences and observations. Painter was voicing his commitment to the "code" of the detached scientist, embodied by his Life Record. Yet because of the nature of his project, he established very close personal bonds to the scientists who enabled him to carry out his work. Indeed Kinsey, originally, and then Pomeroy, Gebhard, and Hooker became indispensable parts of a support system that ensured that Painter's life work would survive.

After literally getting back on his feet, Painter obtained a telephone solicitation job in Santa Monica, selling subscriptions to the *Los Angeles Herald Examiner*. As it was based on commissions, he was not very optimistic about being able to stay with it. In fact, he was fired after five days. He decided that it was time to leave Los Angeles, provided he could get his job back at Doubleday's. His hopes were fulfilled with the help of Pomeroy and Gebhard. Through Pomeroy's efforts in New York, Doubleday's was prepared to accept Painter. In order to ensure Painter's protection from Efrian, Pomeroy checked to determine if Efrian was in police custody or in prison. He found no record of Efrian's incarceration but still felt that Painter could successfully avoid him in New York. Pomeroy also invited Painter to stay at his New York home until Painter found his own place. Painter's last obstacle to returning to New York was removed when Gebhard subsidized his travel fare through Institute funds.[155]

Painter arrived in New York in June 1964 in high spirits. He was delighted to be back, commenting, "Here, [I] saw more brown chests, arms, and whole torsos (bare to the waist) than two years in Los Angeles, in one afternoon."[156] He also had a new focus. He would try to be "Mr. X," that is, author his own work. Earlier, in his Los Angeles correspondence with Pomeroy, he had suggested Gore Vidal or Christopher Isherwood taking on the role of "Mr. X." Just prior to his leaving Los Angeles, he declared, "Could I be Mr. X? . . . Surely, with the freedom of printed expression we now have, there is publishable material there, in me. Perhaps I could talk it over with a N.Y. publisher, maybe use a ghost."[157] He envisioned a book that would be an updated version of his 1941 manuscript, utilizing his Life Record to include post–World War II prostitution and his experiences with Puerto Ricans. In contrast with Donald Webster Cory's *The Homosexual in America,* he would focus on poor homosexuals and male prostitutes. Moreover, unlike John Rechy's *City of Night,* which he believed overexposed the "weird queer," he would present a more sympathetic treatment of homosexuals. Painter was renewed by the prospect that his work could be published, declaring, "It will give me something to live for."[158]

After a week with the Pomeroys, Painter found a room in a Puerto Rican rooming house on West Twenty-second Street. The room, on the fifth floor of a walk-up building, had a kitchenette and a double bed. As he hoped to find a roommate, it suited his needs. He looked up one of the Puerto Ricans he met through Indio, and although they met for sex, this youth turned down his proposal for sharing living quarters. Painter found it difficult to reestablish his contacts in the Puerto Rican youth community. Heroin had taken over—Indio was dead. Hector and almost everyone else he had known were addicts. Fourteenth Street was deserted. He therefore focused his efforts on finding a roommate on Times Square. After searching for two months, no one eligible turned up. He avoided the hard-core professional hustlers who he categorized as drunken, lazy, and idle. A few youths who habituated the Square attracted him, but their look signified to him that they would be dull and boring.[159]

Then suddenly one night while walking on Forty-second Street, he was attracted to a tall, dark, and "classically" handsome youth with Hispanic features. Two friends accompanied the young man (whom he dubbed "Tony"). What especially caught Painter's eye was Tony's "magnificent musculature," revealed by the fact that all he was wearing above the waist was a windbreaker jacket that was completely unzipped. Painter followed him and his companions for about twenty minutes. At one point Tony took off his jacket while involved in a playful boxing match with one of his friends. Although tempted to act on his infatuation by making an approach, Painter stopped following the trio when he realized that they were drinking from a bottle. He did not want to get involved with anyone who was in a drunken state. He noted that Tony stopped and spoke to many of the hustlers he passed, so obviously he was "known on the Square." Painter hoped that he would be able to track him down through his own contacts among the Puerto Ricans. Tony was the ideal that he had been seeking; that is, according to Painter, "he would have been a triple A, 4 star at any time in my career, not just now."[160]

A few days later, Painter saw Tony again on Forty-second Street and followed him into the subway. As soon as Painter caught up with him, he said, "Do you want to make ten dollars?"[161] Tony consented and they went to Painter's room. After sex Painter proposed that they live together but declared that he would never pay for sex again because he did not want a "commercial" relationship. Painter learned that Tony's name was Gilbert. Gilbert was twenty-eight and revealed that he had been on heroin since he was fifteen. He "conned" Painter into giving him five dollars and an hour later returned and admitted that he had taken a heroin shot. Gilbert broke down and wept on Painter's shoulders. Painter comforted him by assuring him that the two of them could work together to overcome his habit. Gilbert declined to accept Painter's offer of moving in because of his addiction. He lived with his mother on the Upper East Side—the Puerto Rican neighborhood known as Spanish Harlem. As Painter learned, Gilbert was not Puerto Rican. His father, who abandoned the family (Gilbert had one brother), was Venezuelan; his mother was Syrian. Nevertheless, Painter considered that he was culturally a Puerto Rican since he grew up in Spanish Harlem.

After they met in August, Gilbert occasionally visited Painter but then stopped coming. In January Painter saw him in the Forty-second Street subway station and invited him home. Gilbert had been in the hospital to detoxify, and when he returned to his mother's apartment, he discovered that she had moved and thus deserted him. He had not slept or eaten in two days and gratefully accepted Painter's invitation to move in.

Gilbert never initiated sex with Painter but enjoyed it immensely. He loved to be stroked and caressed, which would lead to his getting an erection and then Painter would masturbate him. As he had been a Golden Gloves boxer with a well-developed muscular body, his virility assured him that he was heterosexual. Yet, according to Painter, he felt uncomfortable around women. He had been involved with a prostitute who was in love with him and took care of him when he was sick. However, he did not want to stay with her any longer than he had to. As he recounted, her sexual advances disgusted him. During the time that Painter knew him, he never became involved with any other woman, but when he was high on heroin, he would show interest in women passing on the street. Commenting on Gilbert's sexuality, Painter asserted:

> My relationship with him, with its minimal overt sexuality (and lacking wholly in pedication and fellation, which they [Puerto Ricans] regard as homosexual) and its deep affection, opened up his crypto-homosexuality, but to a tolerable degree, to him, because it was "*not* homosexual"—in the usual overt ways. Hence he could at once enjoy it—and deny it. I, of course never mentioned the subject—I had the substance, who cared about the label? . . . All this is why I felt I could say "He loves me in return." And for the first time in my life I had reciprocated love. And it was wonderful.[162]

For his part, Gilbert viewed Painter as a father figure. On one occasion, when Painter gave him a photograph of himself, Gilbert wrote on the back, "For the father I never had."[163] And, as Painter acknowledged, in addition to being a lover, he was a loving father.

Painter luxuriated in being in a loving relationship. Even though he lived with an addict, he never felt safer. Gilbert was huge and strong, the result of his background as a boxer and street fighter. He had a protective attitude toward Painter, which Painter perceived from the things that Gilbert said, but even more significantly, it was something that Painter felt. Although Gilbert seldom verbalized his feelings, he showed his love in other ways. He brought Painter a book, titled *The Need to Be Loved,* and another time brought a similar book. Gilbert never read the books, but it was his way of communicating love. He also told Painter that his home was where he found peace, affection, and trust. There were, however, many dark periods during their relationship. Periodically they would be separated by Gilbert's hospital stays as well as brief jail sentences, the result of being arrested for petty theft. He was unable to break his addiction and engaged in theft in order to pay for his drug supply. He stole either by shoplifting or entering parked cars and taking what he found. He would then get his money by fencing whatever he could. Often all that he ended up with from the cars he broke into were suitcases of used clothing. He gave these items to Painter, which was his way of paying Painter back for his help.

The cumulative effects of Gilbert's heroin use resulted in weight loss because he did not eat. All of his money went to heroin. He became ashamed of his body and never took off his clothes. Equally difficult for Painter were the times when Gilbert would come "down" from his drug "high." He would have a marked personality change in which he became verbally abusive and suspicious. Later, when he was in his "low" state, he would apologize and say, "Please that wasn't me talking, it was the heroin."[164] Painter found these mood swings increasingly harder to deal with.

Finally, one morning after they had been together for about three years (between hospital and jail stays), Gilbert left with Painter's paycheck. They met a week later and Gilbert said that they could no longer live together. He had initially intended to repay Painter but now realized that he would be unable to resist taking money. Gilbert thus began a period when he was homeless. Painter occasionally saw him when he needed money. Eventually Gilbert was arrested and jailed for six months. When he was released, he went to live with his mother and got hooked on heroin again. In response, Painter spent two months getting him into a methadone program. His efforts were so "desperate" for him financially that in order to save money, he moved in with Gilbert and his mother. Gilbert did well for three weeks and then disappeared. Despite being abandoned, Painter still loved him and had gladly done everything he could to help. He summed up his feelings by declaring, "I was wanted, and filled that need. I was needed, and my love filled that need. I succoured [*sic*] a lost and lonely fellow being in his most terrible years, and helped him bear them. And he responded as much as he could. Thus I was fulfilled. Thus I was useful. It is enough."[165]

After a lapse of two years, Gilbert once again entered Painter's life. In December 1971 he visited Painter, who had moved into a hotel after Gilbert left. He explained that his absence was due to the fact that he did not want to face Painter again until he was cured. He happily reported that he had been successful through a methadone program. During their second meeting, Gilbert euphemistically initiated sex by asking Painter to "scratch my back for me." At first Painter was satisfied, but as their sex continued, he began to lose interest. Gilbert had become pudgy and had lost his muscular definition, but it was much more than just the physical change. As Painter expressed it, "I am still fond of him, and find him interesting to talk to, enjoy having him around. But the great feeling is gone. . . . Two years is a long time."[166] The nature of their relationship had changed. Gilbert was independent now, and, as Painter admitted, he needed someone to "mother." Nevertheless, although their sexual relationship ended, Gilbert continued to visit and Painter realized that Gilbert needed his support. There were occasions when Gilbert lost jobs because his employers discovered that he was an ex-addict. At one point the stress resulted in Gilbert's return to heroin for a couple of weeks, but since he was still on a methadone program, he was able to break the habit. Painter now acknowledged that he and Gilbert had "a father-son relationship, of a very deep, fond and understanding nature."[167]

PAINTER'S FINAL REFLECTIONS

When Gilbert disappeared in the fall of 1969, Painter turned his attention to the Life Record. Five years earlier, when he returned from Los Angeles, he had hoped to begin working on a book based on the Life Record. His involvement with Gilbert prevented him from doing any writing, but now that their affair was over, he decided to act on his desire to write. Rather than attempt a full-scale book, Painter decided to write a series of short manuscripts summarizing his life. This retreat from his earlier ambitious plans probably reflected his realistic assessment of what he could accomplish. Five years had passed, and his emotional and physical energies had been drained by his involvement with Gilbert. His autobiographical manuscripts were labeled as "biographies," apparently a device to ensure that a potential biographer would use them as a guide in working with the Life Record. These manuscripts were written between 1970 and 1973.[168]

What underscores these final reflections is Painter's articulation of the "search" theme, that is, his lifelong search for love and companionship. Interwoven with this theme is his gradual self-identified transformation from Tom Painter to Will Finch, his liberated alter ego. As Painter noted earlier in his Life Record, his relationship with Gilbert represented the ultimate triumph of his life. He finally experienced reciprocated same-sex love, an experience he initially believed was unattainable because of society's prohibitions and the internalized homophobia of gay men. His successful search for love thus signified that he was able to defy the ideological imperative of heterosexuality by finally validating and accepting his own homosexuality—Will Finch prevailed in the end. He symbolically expressed his triumph by proclaiming:

> I am a musical bourgeois. My favorite piece is "Liebestod" from "Tristan and Isolde." I went to pieces when I heard it in Munich. The

leitmotif starting quietly then suppressed, then failing, then recurring, struggling to be heard. Her song rises, till she dies upon the corpse—ultimate tragedy is ultimate triumph. Then the music dies away in receding ways. I don't want to be sentimental but I believe there was a theme in my life, just as above, quiet and struggling at first, confused and beset by disharmonies but continuing, rising, finally winning—over a "dead" lover who smiles at me. And now I am to die—in a few years, the music fading.[169]

Throughout this period Painter continued to keep up his Life Record. As he acquired homoerotic photos, he would pass them on with commentaries. He continued his reviews of films and books that dealt with homosexuality. For example, he liked the acting in *Midnight Cowboy* but deplored the sordid depiction of the homosexual. He also commented on current events and identified with the counterculture of the late 1960s and early 1970s. Accompanying a picture of Woodstock, he wrote, "I find myself feeling more and more in tune with the 'revolutionaries'—a natural enough development being a 'hippie' as I have been for a year or so."[170] Yet he made no mention of Stonewall or the gay liberation movement. This gap in his attraction to revolutionary movements, however, was consistent with his earlier disinterest in homophile organizations. He did express skepticism that the treatment of homosexuals was improving, commenting, "Police don't like us. . . . 1972 or 1872."[171]

His Life Record still focused on his sexual experiences, except that now they rarely involved a sex partner. He was briefly involved with a hustler named Cyrus but stopped when Cyrus started to use cocaine. He often went to Forty-second Street and liked Grant's, a gay bar where he chatted with the young patrons. His sex was now restricted to masturbation, and he described how he would become stimulated through his fantasies of nude youths in provocative poses. Painter in the guise of a wealthy prince would rescue such youths from jail, work gangs, or ship galleys. These were the kind of fantasies that he used to write about in his short stories.[172]

Aside from Gilbert, he had few friends. Charlie P., a retired broadcasting executive whom he had known since the late 1930s but rarely saw in recent years, died in 1972. In the winter of 1973, he complained of health problems. He had emphysema, the result of a life history of heavy smoking. He was still working at Doubleday's and one evening almost collapsed on the way home. Another time he had a similar experience but felt safe because he was with Gilbert. He admitted, however, that he did not like to be dependent on another person. He feared the consequences of having to spend another winter in New York because of the danger of cold weather to his condition.[173]

His February 1973 entry was the last in his Life Record. By 1973 he wrote infrequently and his last set of letters was not included in the bound volumes of the Record. As his health deteriorated, Gilbert increasingly came to his aid. Eventually Gilbert's mother also helped. Painter was appreciative, and shortly before he went into a Veterans Administration hospital, he asked Gebhard, who was visiting him, for a favor. Painter would name the Institute as the beneficiary for his $1,000 life insurance policy if the Institute would give him a check for that amount, which he would then pass on to Gilbert. Gebhard agreed and Painter was able to give the money to Gilbert. Painter died on 7 July 1978, at age seventy-two. After his death, Gebhard discovered that Painter's policy was void because he had stopped paying the premiums. Was this lapse intentional? Probably not, although as in the case of Harry Benjamin, Painter had a record of not paying his debts to a researcher friend. In his state of deteriorating health, he may not have been able to mentally keep track of his financial affairs, or with his meager income, he could no longer keep up the payments. His major concern was being able to leave something for Gilbert—the person who had mattered most in his life.[174]

At the end of his essay on the "Long Search," Painter challenged his readers to evaluate his life. He acknowledged that his rhapsodic discourse of triumph and self-fulfillment could be taken as an apologetic offering by an old man for his life. He went on to comment, "I never hurt anyone nor coerced for money. I have tried to be 'good' and to do good. Some may say 'And he spent forty years paying poor boys to have homosexual relations with him, supporting a prostitution. The guy is a gigantic hypocrite.' Goodness and love! May be. That is up to . . . the reader to figure out."[175]

I do not read Painter's reflections about his life as an apologia. In his way, he did find fulfillment and validation, even though his only successful relationship came late, was relatively brief, and caused him considerable emotional pain. Despite being abandoned, he felt that he had achieved his life goal of experiencing a loving relationship. As he expressed it, "It was the journey not the arrival that mattered. For a wonderful while, I had achieved my search."[176] Gilbert's return, although anticlimatic, served to validate the significance of their relationship. It is sad, however, that Painter, throughout his life, was looking for love in all the wrong places; hoping to find it among male prostitutes and youths, like the Puerto Rican boys he met who engaged in homosexual outlets to compensate for their restricted access to having sex with women. By chance, Gilbert, who was involved with both the Puerto Rican and hustler subcultures, appears to have had homosexual leanings, which he was unable to acknowledge. So, despite Painter's earlier protestations, he was able to fall in love with another homosexual. Gilbert, of course, did not fit the homosexual stereotype because he was the epitome of the virile, aggressive male. Painter's hang-up, like many gay men of his generation, was that he loathed the association of homosexuality and effeminacy. He craved what he was not—the straight-appearing, macho male. That he and gay men, in general, did not meet the socially defined standards of masculinity was the impetus for seeking compensation by finding masculine sex partners who one could also hopefully fall in love with. What Painter lacked in idealized gender attributes could be made up by what he had to offer to poor youths—his advantages of class, education, and age. He derived deep satisfaction from being able to help the young men he was involved with. But he also felt insecure about his ability to hold on to these relationships; unless he was "needed," the bonds would break. And often, despite his power advantage of age and class, his dependency on macho youths made him vulnerable to exploitative and destructive relationships.

In his extensively detailed and rich life story, Painter has left a legacy for us about a gay man's courageous and visionary struggle for survival in the pre-Stonewall era. His story is a significant addition to the pre–gay liberation genre of coming out stories, such as Alan Helms's *Young Man from the Provinces: A Gay Life before Stonewall* and Martin Duberman's *Cures: A Gay Man's Odyssey*. And yet there is much more about his life that is significant. His ethnographic observations of the hustler, muscle boy, and Hispanic youth subcultures reveal relatively unknown facets of gay life in mid-twentieth-century America. His association with sex researchers is indicative of the common interests shared by gay and lesbian activists and sympathetic experts in promoting the cause of homosexual rights through scientific research. In this regard, his collaborative efforts with Kinsey are particularly noteworthy because Kinsey relied on Painter's expertise and contacts to ensure a meaningful and accurate representation of homosexual experience in his male study. Moreover, the support that he received, not only from Kinsey, but also from other sex researchers—including Dickinson, Benjamin, Hooker, Pomeroy, and Gebhard—attests to the high regard they had for him. They recognized the significance of his writings on male homosexuality and male prostitution as well as the uniqueness and depth of his life history.[177]

What is most tragic about Painter's life is that a highly gifted researcher and writer did not have the opportunity to publish his own work and receive the public recognition he deserved. But fortunately his work has been preserved so that scholars can make use of it. I feel a special connection with Painter because I have assumed the role of biographer—the "Mr. X" that he was hoping would come along and tell his life story. From the beginning of his efforts, he set an agenda in which his life story would serve as a vehicle for social change. He strongly believed in the need to include an insider's voice in scientific research. Through this power of subjective agency, he sought to challenge the uninformed and distorted thinking about homosexuality promulgated by the medical establishment. It is important to become aware of his efforts and recognize his contributions so that they can be appropriately incorporated in the history of the homosexual rights movement, especially in terms of what his story reveals about the struggle to obtain social justice through scientific research.

Writing in the context of the early 1970s, Painter commented on the contribution his Life Record could make by stating, "For a contemporary appeal I think the theme of the proto-hippie, the revolt from and, in my living, defiance and denial of all . . . [the] values and standards . . . of my parents."[178] His reference to his parents represented conventional values in general. He viewed his life as a prototypical struggle to resist social convention, especially heterosexist domination. His odyssey of suffering, resiliency, and resistance contributes to what Ken Plummer and Stephen Murray characterize as the major function of sexual storytelling—the building of an oppositional community.[179]

Chapter 8

Evelyn Hooker, Frank Kameny, and Depathologizing Homosexuality, 1957–73

> After the show [at Finocchio's] . . . Sammy turned to me and said,
> "We have let you see us as we are, and now it is your scientific duty to
> make a study of people like us." . . . And by "people like us" he
> meant, "We're homosexual, but we don't need psychiatrists. We don't
> need psychologists. We're not insane. We're not any of those things
> they say we are."
>
> —Evelyn Hooker[1]

In 1973, after several years of heated debate, the board of trustees of the
American Psychiatric Association (APA) made a decision to remove homosexuality as a generic category from the organization's *Diagnostic and
Statistical Manual of Mental Disorders*. The decision was double-edged,
since it also included the recommendation to add the new category of
"sexual orientation disturbance" to apply to those homosexuals who were
psychologically perturbed by their sexual orientation. Nevertheless, this
so-called "compromise" decision was challenged by a group of psychiatrists who charged the board with giving in to the political pressures of the
gay liberation movement. The board's action was subsequently upheld by
a referendum of the APA's membership. The origins of the debate over the
psychiatric status of homosexuality go back to 1957 when psychologist
Evelyn Hooker published an article reporting no differences on indices of
psychological adjustment between groups of homosexual and heterosexual men. Utilizing traditional scientific methodology, Hooker thus challenged the heretofore untested assumption that homosexuality was pathological. This was a dramatic example of emancipatory science that served

as a visible benchmark in the use of scientific research to achieve social justice. In this chapter I trace the path to normalize homosexuality, beginning with Hooker's influential role and ending with the largely successful campaign against the psychiatric establishment, led by homophile activist Frank Kameny.[2]

EVELYN HOOKER: THE MAKING OF AN ACTIVIST-RESEARCHER

In 1944, when Hooker was teaching at the University of California, Los Angeles (UCLA), she became acquainted with Sam From, a student in her introductory psychology night class. Almost immediately she realized that he was the brightest student in class. He talked with her during intermission and after class. When he learned that she commuted by streetcar because of the wartime gas rationing, he offered to drive her home. Sammy was in the junk business with his father and therefore had no problem fueling his car. Reflecting his business success, he had written million-dollar contracts with the air force and the local aircraft industry.[3]

Hooker's friendship with Sammy evolved gradually. She had a policy of not fraternizing with students, and thus Sammy's first visit to her home took place after he had finished her course. After he left, Hooker's first husband, Donn Caldwell, remarked, "Well, you told me everything else about him, why didn't you tell me he was queer?" Hooker was taken aback and asked how her husband could tell. He replied, "He did everything but fly out the window."[4] Caldwell was a Hollywood freelance screenwriter and, in contrast to Hooker, quite familiar with the homosexual subculture. Sammy was eager to develop a friendship with Hooker and Caldwell, and introduced them to his lover George A. To insure Hooker's acceptance, Sammy actually introduced George as his cousin. Over the course of the friendship, Sammy and George never directly identified themselves as gay, but they gradually became more relaxed and "let down their hair." Sammy was also eager to introduce Hooker to his friends, describing her as "another Eleanor Roosevelt."[5] Hooker was warmly welcomed into Sammy and George's circle of friends.

Hooker had known relatively little about homosexuality before she met Sammy and his friends. In fact, she had uncritically accepted the pathological textbook characterizations she used in her teaching. Her attitudes quickly changed, however, as a result of her new homosexual friendships. About a year after they met, Sammy and George invited Hooker and Caldwell to join them for a Thanksgiving holiday in San Francisco. On the first night of their visit, at Sammy's urging they went to Finocchio's, a nightclub noted for its female impersonators. It was a new experience for Hooker, but one that she thoroughly enjoyed. Apparently Sammy sensed how far Hooker had come in her willingness to learn about homosexuality. After the show he appealed to her professional responsibility by insisting that she study "people like us"; that is, nonpatient, nonprisoner homosexuals. It was only through such research that psychiatric myths could be dispelled. In response to Hooker's point that she could not do objective research if she were to study people she knew, Sammy indicated that he could easily get her a hundred homosexual men as research participants.

Hooker followed up the challenge of Sammy's research proposal by consulting Bruno Klopfer, a psychology colleague at UCLA. Klopfer was a leading authority on the Rorschach inkblot test, which was a popular psychological index of mental health. He encouraged her to carry out the research, pointing out that nothing was known about homosexuals who were not institutionalized or in clinical treatment. With Klopfer's encouragement, she decided to go ahead and generate a research study. She began by interviewing homosexual men recruited from Sammy's friendship network, but her research had to be delayed. In 1947 her six-year marriage to Caldwell had unraveled because of his problem with alcoholism. After the divorce she did not want to stay in Los Angeles. She obtained a position at Bryn Mawr College, outside Philadelphia, but after a year she was ready to return and came back to her old job at UCLA. She found lodgings in a guesthouse attached to the Brentwood home of Edward Niles Hooker, a distinguished professor of English at UCLA who had been recently divorced. After a three-year courtship, Evelyn and Edward were married in 1951. With her personal life in order, Hooker was committed to carry out her research on male homosexuality.

Before continuing the story of Hooker's work, it is important to consider her early life because it helps account for her unusual capacity to become an advocate for human rights through scientific research. Evelyn Gentry was born 2 September 1907, in her grandmother's house, next door to Buffalo Bill's home in North Platte, Nebraska. One of her favorite childhood memories was traveling west with her parents and eight siblings, perched on the front seat of a covered wagon, protected by a sunbonnet. She grew up in a succession of one-room farmhouses on the Colorado plains. In her formative years, she was painfully aware of being an outsider, stigmatized by her family's poverty and by the time she was an adolescent, socially rejected because of her nearly six-foot height. With her mother's commitment to educate her children, Hooker entered high school in Sterling, Colorado. The Sterling high school was unusually progressive, and in her senior year she was in an honors program and took a course in psychology. Although she planned to attend teacher's college, her teachers persuaded her to go to the University of Colorado, which she entered in

1924 with a tuition scholarship. At Colorado she supported herself on her earnings from housework and obtained her bachelor's degree in psychology, under the tutelage of her revered mentor, Karl Muenzinger, a comparative (animal) psychologist. In her senior year, she was offered an instructorship, which enabled her to go on for her master's degree. She could have stayed at Colorado for her Ph.D., but Muenzinger urged her to go to an eastern university. She wanted to go to Yale University and work with the comparative psychologist Robert M. Yerkes, but her department head at Colorado, a Yale Ph.D., refused to recommend a woman to his alma mater. She therefore went on to Johns Hopkins University for her doctorate in experimental psychology, which she received in 1932.[6]

Despite the worsening Depression, Hooker was able to obtain a teaching position at the Maryland College for Women, a small college near Baltimore. Her teaching career, however, was interrupted in 1934 when she contracted tuberculosis. With the help of friends, she entered a California sanitarium, where she underwent a two-year recovery. After a year of part-time teaching at Whittier College in Southern California, she won a fellowship to travel and study in Europe for the 1937–38 year. As her interests were turning to clinical psychology, she chose Berlin's Institute for Psychotherapy. In Berlin she lived with a Jewish family and through their eyes witnessed such menacing events as Kristalnacht. She learned later that all of the family members were killed in the concentration camps. During her fellowship year, she also went on a group tour to Russia, arriving just after a major purge. Her experience in two totalitarian states intensified her desire, formed in childhood, to become personally involved in the struggle to overcome social injustice.

Hooker's trip to Russia posed problems for her when she resumed her teaching position at Whittier. She and several other faculty members were "purged" as suspected subversives. As a result, in 1939 she applied for an appointment in UCLA's psychology department, chaired by Knight Dunlap, who had been her mentor at Johns Hopkins. Dunlap informed her that while he would like to appoint her, he would be unable to persuade his faculty to hire another woman when they already had three female members who were "cordially disliked." Instead, he offered her a position as a research associate in the psychology department, which she accepted in conjunction with an appointment in the extension division. With the exception of her year at Bryn Mawr, she remained at UCLA until 1970, when she went into private practice.

Hooker's compassionate attraction to the concerns of homosexuals was thus in keeping with her lifelong commitment to human rights. She had experienced social rejection as a child and adolescent, suffered the stigma of illness, witnessed the effects of racial and political persecution in her travels, and faced discrimination in her professional life. Based on her life experiences, she was predisposed to engage in research that could potentially help eradicate the injustices faced by homosexuals.[7]

HOOKER'S RESEARCH STUDIES

By the time Hooker resumed her research, she had become increasingly convinced that most of the gay men she had known appeared to be well adjusted. She did not accept the prevailing view that homosexuals were maladjusted because no one had actually studied the issue. In the psychiatric diagnostic manual, homosexuality was labeled a "sociopathic personality disorder" simply because it deviated from the heterosexual norm. She decided to use psychological tests to determine if gay men were, in fact, as well adjusted as they appeared to be on the surface. Over the course of her preliminary research, she had conducted life history interviews with seventy-four gay men. She gave each of her interviewees George Stern's *Chicago Inventory of Beliefs*, a measure designed to identify three major personality patterns. Only one of the men was categorized as an S type, a conformist, interpersonally distant, authoritarian pattern, common among heterosexuals. Most of the sample clustered around the R type, reflecting an introspective, emotionally restrained, and intellectual orientation, quite unlike most homosexuals seen in clinical settings. There were also a number of men who fell under the N category, which represented a pattern of nonconforming behavior, highly individualized and personal relationships, and a rich and spontaneous impulse life. What stood out in the results, according to Hooker, was that gay men varied widely in personality structure and thus they did not constitute a distinct clinical entity. Moreover, contrary to the conventional assumption that homosexuals were nonconformist, she reported that nonconforming sex patterns might be accompanied by complete conformity in other attitudes and behaviors.[8]

Hooker realized that her test results suffered from a lack of comparison with a heterosexual sample. Furthermore, her interviews had been relatively unplanned and she thus felt that she could not use them. In 1953 she decided to submit a grant application to the National Institute of Mental Health (NIMH). She wanted some corroborative support that her project was worth doing. John Eberhardt, the chief of the grants division, flew out to Los Angeles. It was evident to Hooker that he wanted to find out who she was. He had to be sure that she was not a lesbian. At the height of the McCarthy era, anyone with a professed interest in homosexuality was suspect. At the end of his day's visit, Eberhardt declared, "We are prepared to make you the grant, but you may not receive it. Everyone is being investigated. If you don't receive it, you won't know why and we won't know why."[9] Hooker was concerned about an investigation of her past. She and her husband had been active in the fight against the University of California loyalty oath, she had lost her position at Whittier College because of being a suspected subversive, and her first husband had been active on the side of the anti-Fascists in the Spanish civil war. To her surprise, she received the grant, but several years later she learned that McCarthy's lieutenants had, nevertheless, been monitoring her activities. She also learned from Eberhardt that federal officials in Washington derided her research, referring to it as the "Fairy Project."[10]

Hooker was excited about getting the grant because she knew that she was breaking new ground. She would be the first researcher to scientifically determine whether or not homosexuality was pathological. Her research design involved a comparison of thirty homosexual and heterosexual men who were matched for age, intelligence, and education. To test the question of whether homosexuality was pathological, she limited her sample of homosexuals to those who were not referred by a clinical agency, did not seek psychological help, and were gainfully employed. Before she could begin the research, she had to meet certain conditions set by NIMH and UCLA. NIMH's study committee felt that since she was working with "psychopathology," she would need to have a psychiatric consultant. She reluctantly approached the UCLA psychiatry chair. When she told him that she was studying "normal male homosexuals," he replied, "What do you think you are doing? There is no such person." The chair referred her to Frederic Worden, a new member of the psychiatry department. When he read her application, he said, "I have never seen such persons, but I sure would like to."[11] According to Hooker, he became a valuable consultant.

Another condition she had to deal with was the university's demand that the research be conducted on campus. She resisted this, arguing that homosexual participants would not agree to such a condition because of the personal risks attached to being openly involved in a study of homosexuality. In the context of the McCarthy era, secrecy and confidentiality had to be guaranteed for the investigation to be carried out. The university backed down on its demand. Fortunately, Hooker's home was especially conducive for protecting the identity of research participants. It was a spacious estate on an acre of ground with a garden study, separate from the house. The freestanding study served as the research site.

In order to understand each life as fully as possible, Hooker tape-recorded every testing and life history session. She assured each participant that after her secretary transcribed the tapes they would be erased. To ensure confidentiality, she turned down numerous requests by individuals who wanted to be co-investigators. Choosing to work alone in a stress-laden field entailed personal costs. As she stated, "Without a colleague with whom to share the sympathetic knowledge of human suffering, sometimes one's own vicarious suffering becomes almost unbearable."[12]

Hooker was aware that her life history and testing data would only become meaningful when she understood the cultural context of gay men's lives. She had formed many close friendships with gay men, including Sammy and his circle as well as novelist Christopher Isherwood, who lived in her guesthouse in the early 1950s. She accepted their invitations to gay parties, gay bars, and gay organizations. In this way, she became familiar with the social milieu gay men created and how this "gay world" functioned to protect its constituents and resist the oppressive and hostile pressures from the larger society.

Her public association with gay men placed her in a vulnerable position. As a result of the intense level of surveillance of gay bars by the Los Angeles Police Department in the 1950s and 1960s, the police were aware of her visits to these bars since she was the only woman present. In 1961 she was arrested and charged with conspiracy to obtain a criminal abortion. She had referred a young male friend and his girlfriend to a psychiatrist who recommended a therapeutic abortion. An obstetrician performed the abortion, but complications arose when the girl's father filed charges with the police. She was never indicted, but she believed that the police went after her because of her research on homosexuality.[13]

Hooker's experiences as a participant observer in the Los Angeles gay male community served as a point of departure for her research. In 1956, in her first published paper on homosexuality, she analyzed the relationship between the individual personality dynamics of her sample of gay men and the group dynamics of their subculture. In contrast to the prevailing view that homosexuality was rooted in early unresolved inner conflicts and identification patterns, she argued that homosexuality had to be understood from the perspective of a minority group. According to Hooker, homosexual communities, with their own norms of behavior, exerted strong conformity pressures on their members. As a result of such group dynamics, she stated, "Many homosexuals are beginning to think of themselves as constituting a minority group, sharing many of the problems of other minority groups, having to struggle for their 'rights' against the prejudices of a dominant heterosexual majority."[14]

Like other minority groups, homosexuals as out-group members reacted to the cultural pressures of the dominant majority. She noted a striking parallel between the traits of victimization that social psychologist Gordon W. Allport attributed to members of minority groups and the traits characterizing homosexuals. Based on her life history interviews, for example, she reported that many of her gay male subjects had an "obsessive concern" with homosexuality as a target of possible attack. Interpreting obsessiveness as a defense against victimization deviated from the conventional psychiatric practice of labeling homosexuality as an obsessive-compulsive personality disorder. Similarly, the withdrawal and passivity that characterized many of her homosexual participants represented defensive strategies rather than deep-seated personality traits. As these examples suggest, Hooker emphasized the need to consider the situational factors homosexuals faced before any conclusions could be drawn about long-standing pathological personality patterns.[15]

Most of Hooker's gay male subjects had participated extensively in the Los Angeles homosexual community. She therefore drew upon her life history data as well as her firsthand impressions as a participant observer to depict the nature of the homosexual world. As Hooker pointed out, the homosexual world functioned to support and reward the cultural, social, and sexual needs of its participants. It enabled individuals to "come out"; that is, to define and validate their self-concept as a homosexual. The path to self-definition occurred under such varied conditions as the gay bar, the "queer" tank in a city jail, or a park bench. In such settings and circumstances, individuals struggling with their sexuality came to the realization that they were not alone, that there was a world out there that they could become a part of and receive the social support for who they were.

The homosexual world was made up of many homosexual groups, including cliques in gay bars, street-corner groups, and informal social networks. Such groups provided the specific social support within the homosexual community. While Hooker concluded that the homosexual world contributed to the mental health of its constituents, she pointed out that there was a negative side, manifested in various forms of group pathology. In some homosexual groups, for example, all relationships tended to be sexualized, leading to group tension and, in some instances, excessive exhibitionism. Moreover, conformity pressures, especially in terms of such prototypes as the effeminate male, discouraged a diversity of roles and personal growth. Finally, the tendency among gay men to view women as threatening was reinforced because few heterosexual women were part of the male homosexual community. Her tendency to reduce the promiscuity, exhibitionism, and sexism of gay culture to group pathology suggests some elements of antigay thinking on her part, at least at the time she wrote her first article on homosexuality.

In later publications Hooker provided more in-depth and nuanced ethnographic analyses of the homosexual world. Her purpose in her first published paper was to offer a sociological foundation for understanding the personality dynamics of gay men. As she noted, aside from impressionistic accounts by homosexuals, such as Donald Webster Cory's *The*

Homosexual in America, there were no sociological treatments of homosexuality. At the time she was unaware of Thomas Painter's work. Indeed, she was among the first American trained social scientists to undertake ethnographic research on male homosexuality that incorporated the input of homosexuals. The same year her article appeared, sociologists Maurice Leznoff and William A. Westley published a paper about the Montreal male homosexual community. Hooker understood gay men from their point of view. This was the strength of her research strategy—to share the perceptions of her research participants. Kinsey had done some of this in his visits to homosexual centers, but it was as a means of obtaining subjects for his sex histories, which focused on sexual behavior. Hooker framed her study of personality dynamics in the context of the gay male subculture and its relation to a hostile society.[16]

Comparing Homosexual and Heterosexual Men
Hooker had no difficulty in recruiting gay men for her study. With the help of the Mattachine Society, she found many more than the thirty she needed. The problem was in recruiting heterosexual men. She first approached the personnel director of a labor union, but reflecting the conservative climate of the 1950s, he refused. Even though Hooker assured him that she was not doing a "Kinsey study," he still resisted, claiming, "Any study that involves sexuality . . . might boomerang, and I would lose my job." She resorted to enticing men who showed up at her home for inspections or repairs. Her husband commented, "No man is safe on Saltair Avenue."[17] In exchange for paying for the expense of hiring a baby-sitter, for example, she lined up a fire inspector who introduced her to a policeman who agreed, in exchange for some personal counseling. She also made successful contacts at UCLA. After two years she had her matched sample of thirty homosexual and heterosexual men.[18]

Each of the participants was given three projective personality tests—the Rorschach test (composed of inkblots), the Thematic Apperception Test (TAT), and the Make-a-Picture-Story test (MAPS). These were widely used measures of personality dynamics, aimed at identifying patterns of psychological maladjustment. The underlying assumption of such ambiguous test materials was that they would prompt respondents to reveal their innermost anxieties, fears, and wishes, in essence, tapping into unconscious processes. Hooker scored the sixty test protocols and then submitted them to three judges who were internationally renowned psychological experts on projective tests. Bruno Klopfer and Mortimer Meyer analyzed the Rorschach protocols; Edwin Shneidman handled the TAT and the MAPS (a test he had constructed).

The judges received the test materials in random order and, with the exception of age, all of the identifying information was removed. The judges were assigned two tasks: to arrive at an overall adjustment rating on a five-point scale and for each matched pair of Rorschach protocols, to distinguish between the homosexual and the heterosexual respondent. The judging was labor intensive and took several months to complete. The results revealed that on all three tests, two-thirds of both the homosexual and heterosexual participants were assigned a rating of average or better than average adjustment. As Hooker concluded, there was no association between maladjustment and homosexuality. Underscoring this conclusion, she noted that as in the case of heterosexuals, adjustment among homosexuals varied widely. She went on to comment:

> It comes as no surprise that some homosexuals are severely disturbed. . . . But what is difficult to accept (for most clinicians) is that some homosexuals *may* be very ordinary individuals, indistinguishable, except in sexual patterns, from ordinary individuals who are heterosexual. Or . . . that some *may* be quite superior individuals, not only devoid of pathology . . . but also functioning at a superior level [of adjustment].[19]

Indeed, the notion that some homosexuals might be functioning at a superior level of mental health was inconceivable for most clinicians, as exemplified by George W. Henry's conclusions in *Sex Variants* and *All the Sexes.*[20]

With respect to the second task, the Rorschach judges did no better than chance in distinguishing between the homosexual and heterosexual respondents. Hooker reported the judges commenting, "There are no clues. . . . I just have to guess."[21] After the judging was completed, the judges indicated that the records they thought to be homosexual were not like the disturbed records of homosexuals they were familiar with in their clinical practice. Recalling the dramatic impact of such unexpected findings, Hooker declared, "At that time, the 1950s, every clinical psychologist worth his soul would tell you that if he gave projective tests he could tell whether a person was gay or not. I showed that they couldn't do it."[22]

Hooker reported the results of her study in 1956 at the annual meeting of the American Psychological Association in Chicago. Her presentation was held before a packed audience in a large ballroom of one of the convention hotels. The atmosphere was charged with excitement. After completing her presentation, she was bombarded with questions, her listeners shocked by the disconfirmation of their beliefs about homosexuality. She acknowledged the tentativeness of her results, limited by a small sample and open to challenge because of the highly subjective nature of projective tests. But she had dramatically opened the debate about the previously untested assumptions that homosexuality was linked to psychological maladjustment. She was prepared to take on the challenge of pursuing her investigation of homosexuality as a means of overcoming prejudice and injustice.[23]

When she returned from Chicago, she met with her gay participants at a Hollywood restaurant. They were ecstatic to learn about what she had reported, shouting, "We knew it all the time!"[24] Bertram R. Forer, executive editor of the *Journal of Projective Techniques,* was eager to publish her study. She was reluctant, believing her results were too premature for publication. But Forer persevered and her study was published in 1957, providing for the wide dissemination of her results throughout the mental health community. Regrettably, two years before the publication, Sam From, who had inspired the study, was killed in a head-on car collision. Compounding this personal loss, in 1957 Hooker's husband Edward died of a sudden heart attack in front of her eyes.[25]

Ethnographic Research

After recovering from her husband's death, Hooker returned to work. Her new project was to follow up the preliminary ethnographic research she had reported in her first published paper on homosexuality. She intended to demonstrate, in greater depth, the cultural context that framed the personality dynamics of gay men. In 1961, at the meeting of the International Congress of Applied Psychology in Copenhagen, she presented her ethnographic observations and interpretations, based on her extensive experience as a participant observer in the Los Angeles gay male community. This paper, in an expanded form, reached a wide audience when it was published in 1965 in psychoanalyst Judd Marmor's influential interdisciplinary edited book on homosexuality.[26]

Hooker's in-depth ethnographic portrayal of the homosexual community in American society was the first published work of its kind in the scientific literature. While there had been earlier publications by homophile authors, such as Edward Prime-Stevenson, Earl Lind, and Donald Webster Cory, they were highly personalized and generally inaccessible because of limited publication. What is especially significant about Hooker's ethnographic reports is that because they were authored by a social scientist, they legitimized the study of the homosexual subculture as a bona fide scientific enterprise.[27]

Hooker defined her research role as a nonevaluative one in which she strove to see the homosexual world through the eyes of her research subjects—in her words, "to look with the subject at his world as he knows it."[28] Her desire to capture the experiences and outlooks of homosexual subjects was consistent with the objectives that Jan Gay and Thomas

Painter had sought in their research projects. She stressed that it was necessary to adopt a nonjudgmental attitude in order to gain the trust of the
gay men she interacted with. As a representative of the dominant culture,
she had to overcome the expectation by her subjects that she would judge
their behaviors and experiences with moral disapproval. To enlist their full
cooperation, they had to be convinced of her genuine interest in understanding their world. Only then would they shed their protective masks.
Beyond gaining the cooperation of her subjects, she defined their role as an
interactive one in which they not only helped her, but also sought to
broaden their own knowledge and insight about their community.

Hooker noted that her observations and various interviews were based
on a wide cross section of the Los Angeles male homosexual community,
including male prostitutes, bisexuals, bartenders, and bar owners, as well
as adolescents and the aged. The Los Angeles community was not unique;
it reflected the patterns common to homosexual collectives in every large
American city. Unlike a traditional community, defined by geographical
limits with institutions serving a residential population, homosexuals constituted a loosely organized society or world with a unified character. It
was thus a community in the sense of a collective of persons engaging in
common activities and having a sense of psychological cohesion. Homosexuals tended to reside in various areas spread throughout the metropol-
itan region. The concentrated character of these neighborhoods was generally not known except in the homosexual community and, in many
instances, by the police.

The homosexual world, according to Hooker, was made up of visible
or public institutions, such as bars and baths, and the invisible private activities engaged in by friendship cliques. As social institutions, gay bars
were especially significant because they served functions that were central
to the homosexual community. As a social meeting place, they provided
the means for gay men to become socialized to the homosexual community as well as to gain a sense of self-definition and communal bonding.
Once established into friendship cliques, many gay men no longer had to
rely on the bar scene for their social needs. Bars also served as sexual meeting places frequented by a wide representation of types, socioeconomic
levels, and social strata within the homosexual world.

Hooker conceptualized gay bars as "free markets" because they functioned as business enterprises and served as sources for the negotiation
and exchange of sexual services. She provided an extensive description of
the "cruising" strategies used by the bar clientele in their sexual negotia-
tions and went on to observe that these exchanges reflected an expectation
that sex could be had without obligation or commitment. Hooker rejected
the standard reductive psychodynamic explanation of homosexual prom-

iscuity as simply a manifestation of the homosexual's "primary narcissism." Nor did she rely on her earlier explanation of "group pathology." Instead, she interpreted promiscuity within the systemic context of the sexual market. Gay men, pressured toward secrecy and the risks of revealing one's sexual identity, preferred to promote their "cosmetic" self rather than their genuine self on the market. Moreover, the negative sanctions of society against homosexual relationships, the lack of a strong norm of monogamy because of the relative absence of women in the male homosexual world, and the market character of the bar setting all combined to produce the kind of promiscuous sexual exchange noted as such a stable feature of the gay world.

More significantly, and in contrast with her earlier work, she moved beyond analyzing gay culture primarily in terms of its promiscuity. Based on interviews and her own observations, Hooker concluded that the public institutions, such as bars, constituted only a small part of the total community. To understand the whole, one had to be familiar with the secret and private activities of the world of social friendship cliques. In this milieu there were gay men living in long term relationships who rarely frequented bars or other public establishments because of their sexually competitive character. There were also men, especially those of high socioeconomic status, who avoided the bar scene because of the fear of exposure or arrest. Friendship networks tended to cut across occupational and social class levels, but rarely included heterosexuals because such contacts forced homosexuals to put on their protective masks. She did not specifically consider race in her work but may have implied interracial friendship patterns in her remarks about social class.

Hooker indicated that she found many gay men involved in long-term relationships but could not provide accurate estimates since she was not engaged in a survey. She noted the difficulties encountered in these relationships because of the strains of a hostile heterosexual society as well as those of the homosexual community. Contrary to conventional belief, she pointed out that most couples were not dichotomized into clear-cut masculine and feminine roles, either sexually or socially.[29]

She concluded her ethnographic paper with a report of how homosexuals perceived their sexual identity. Based on interviews, most of her respondents believed that they had no choice in their sexual preference because they were either born as homosexuals or early familial influences determined the outcome. They therefore believed that homosexuality was as "natural" for them as heterosexuality was for others.

Although Hooker had only published about twelve papers on homosexuality, beginning in 1956 and ending in 1969, the novelty of her approach produced considerable controversy in the medical and mental health community. She thus became the target of detractors as well as an inspiration to mainstream dissenters.

The Impact of Hooker's Research

Beyond demonstrating that clinicians could not distinguish between homosexual and heterosexual men, Hooker's research findings challenged conventional psychoanalytic and psychiatric thinking about homosexuality. Citing her own testing and life history data, she noted that there were wide individual variations in homosexual patterns and lifestyles. Homosexuals differed from one another to the same extent that heterosexuals did. Indeed, this accounted for the difficulties experienced by her three judges in differentiating between the two groups of subjects. It was therefore problematic to claim, as most clinicians did, that it was possible to characterize male "homosexual personality" in terms of such "signs" as femininity, fear of women, narcissism, sexual compulsiveness, and paranoid disposition.[30]

If the assumption that homosexuality was a distinct clinical entity could be dispelled, then there were questions about the related belief that pathogenic parent-child relations could account for the development of homosexuality. A unitary model of psychologically unhealthy parental patterns, such as an overprotective, possessive mother and a distant, detached father, could not explain the variability among homosexuals. In reviewing the empirical literature, she observed that the evidence in support of pathological family origins was contradictory. She concluded, "From the limited evidence currently available, it is clear that the diverse forms of adult homosexuality are produced by many combinations of variables, including biological, cultural, psychodynamic, structural, and situational. No single class of determinants, whether psychodynamic, cultural, or biological, accounts for all or even one of these diverse forms."[31]

Included in Hooker's review was the 1962 monograph by psychoanalyst Irving Bieber and his associates. This was a significant and much cited study because, unlike previous clinical reports involving a small number of cases, it was based on a large sample of psychoanalytic patients. Questionnaire data were obtained from 77 psychoanalysts on 106 male homosexual patients (30 of whom identified themselves as bisexual) and a comparison group of 100 male heterosexual patients. The assumption that homosexuality was pathological was never questioned. The study's purpose was to examine the etiological factors contributing to the pathology. The major finding supported the psychoanalytic thesis of pathogenic parent-child relations. In comparison with the heterosexual patients, homosexual patients had a significantly greater incidence of a "close-binding-intimate" mother who favored her son over her husband, and a father who was detached or hostile. This "triangular system" in which the son was dominated by his mother and alienated from his father thwarted the development of the normal heterosexual drive. Nevertheless, Bieber and his associates were optimistic that homosexuality could be reversed through psychotherapy, provided that homosexual patients were motivated to change. Indeed, they reported modest success rates in which 27 percent of the homosexual sample became exclusively heterosexual by the end of treatment, but this result was based on combining those who began treatment as exclusively homosexual with those who began treatment as bisexual.[32]

For those professionals committed to the medical model of homosexuality, the Bieber study was interpreted as a clear-cut validation of the etiological thesis of family pathology as well as support for the positive prognosis in treating homosexuality. Critics, including Hooker, however, pointed to numerous shortcomings in the study. Most blatant was the conventional willingness by psychoanalysts to generalize their findings from a limited clinical sample. As Hooker had pointed out, it was impossible to determine if the reported parent-child pathogenic findings were specifically associated with homosexuality or with a general pattern of maladjustment among homosexuals who sought treatment. Other critics noted that the higher incidence of a disturbed family background among the homosexual patients could be interpreted as a reaction to, rather than a cause of, homosexuality since homosexuals were more likely to face parental rejection when their sexuality was revealed in late childhood or adolescence. The report of therapeutic success was also questioned because self-identified bisexuals were categorized into the homosexual group. Only 19 percent of the patients who were exclusively homosexual at the start of therapy were exclusively heterosexual when the treatment was terminated. Also problematic was the lack of systematic follow-up data after treatment was terminated. Without such evidence, shifts to a "heterosexual adjustment" could have been short-lived and induced by pressures to conform to therapeutic expectations.[33]

With the buttressing of the psychoanalytic theory of family pathology by the Bieber study, Hooker's research received only passing notice in the mainstream psychiatric literature on homosexuality. Bieber summarily dismissed her comparative study of homosexual and heterosexual men. He opined, "Since . . . the implication of the [Hooker] findings and conclusions are at marked variance with those of our own and other studies, we suspect that the tests themselves or the current methods of interpretation and evaluation are inadequate to the task of discriminating between homosexuals and heterosexuals."[34]

By 1973, however, Hooker's research received extensive scrutiny by the defenders of the medical model in the throes of the bitter debate to remove homosexuality from the American Psychiatric Association's diagnostic manual. Led by psychoanalyst Charles Socarides, a psychiatric study group appointed two psychoanalytically oriented psychologists, Reuben Fine and Toby B. Bieber (Irving Bieber's wife and one of his coauthors), to evaluate Hooker's research. Hooker was taken to task for engaging in biased sampling. According to Fine, her "adjusted" sample of male homosexuals was composed of men who simply "denied" the need for therapy. Moreover, this sample consisted of an "aggressive group of homosexuals" determined to prove that they were well adjusted. Other aspects of the critique were similarly couched in the orthodox psychiatric assumption that homosexuality constituted psychopathology, and, consequently, any empirical evidence that was not consistent with this presumption was the result of faulty theorizing or methodology. Adhering to the medical model, Bieber was willing to accept Hooker's claim that there were "well-adjusted" homosexuals in her sample. But she added, "One can be well adjusted according to criteria such as an ability for effective work, positive relationships with others, apparent contentment, and so forth, and still be severely neurotic."[35]

Hooker's research, on the other hand, served as a catalyst for an emerging network of dissenting medical and mental health professionals, who, in turn, reinforced her efforts. Her work, for example, attracted the attention and support of Wardell Pomeroy and his colleagues at the Kinsey Institute. On Pomeroy's invitation, she made her first visit to the Institute in 1958 and received "in-service training." She had considered her own research as a validation of Kinsey's position. Phillip Sapir and Harold Hildreth of NIMH took a personal interest in her work and were instrumental in sustaining her endeavors. Sapir, who succeeded John Eberhardt as the chief of the grants division, was responsible for the series of grants she received after her initial one. At various times he also invited her to give seminars at NIMH to research scientists interested in her work. These contacts were of immense help in guiding her research as well as validating the worthiness of her work. Hildreth was influential in NIMH's decision in 1961 to give her a Research Career Award, which she held until 1970 when she left UCLA.[36]

Hooker's research also caught the attention of a small group of dissident psychiatrists who would become important allies to homophile activists in the campaign to remove homosexuality from the psychiatric nomenclature. Hendrik M. Ruitenbeek invited her to include her 1957 journal article comparing the adjustment of homosexual and heterosexual men in his 1963 edited book, *The Problem of Homosexuality in Modern*

Society. This edited volume constituted a cross section of sentiment, ranging from support for the medical model by psychoanalyst Sandor Rado and psychologist Albert Ellis to critiques by psychoanalysts Ruitenbeek and Ernest van den Haag.[37]

Judd Marmor, a psychoanalyst who spearheaded the dissident psychiatrists' campaign in the early 1970s to declassify homosexuality, included Hooker's work on the homosexual community in his edited volume in the mid-1960s. When he first became familiar with her study on the adjustment of gay men, he was sympathetic to her position but still believed homosexuality was a "developmental deviation." Marmor envisioned his book as a corrective to the stereotyped generalizations in the psychiatric literature on homosexuality. Like Ruitenbeek, he included a cross section of viewpoints, ranging from the orthodox position of Bieber and Rado to the dissenting views of Hooker and Thomas Szasz. In other publications Szasz had produced scathing criticisms about psychiatric practices in general. Marmor, in his introductory chapter, supported Hooker's conclusion that sexual deviance, in itself, did not necessarily constitute social maladjustment but still clung to his belief that exclusive homosexual behavior represented a "functional limitation in the capacity for heterosexuality."[38] Nevertheless, he also acknowledged that the attitudes toward homosexuality were culturally determined. By the early 1970s he had arrived at the position that psychiatry had to recognize the cultural shift in attitudes and support homosexuals in their struggle for social acceptance.[39]

Hooker's work had opened the debate about homosexuality as mental illness. As such, it forced critics to defend their orthodox positions as well as inspiring doubters and dissidents to produce their own reevaluations and tests of her original research. One of Hooker's greatest satisfactions was to witness the validation of her own findings by other researchers. Psychologist Marvin Siegelman, in a 1972 published study, mounted the most striking confirmation of her work. Using large numbers of homosexual and heterosexual men and objective measures of neuroticism, his results corroborated Hooker's finding of no differences in adjustment between the two samples. As Hooker recalled in learning of his study, "What Dr. Siegelman had demonstrated was that the results of my research were not dependent on projective tests. The results were not artifacts: They were *true*."[40]

Most significantly, Hooker's work led to a government appointment. In September 1967 she was invited by Stanley F. Yolles, the director of NIMH, to head the Task Force on Homosexuality, which would be aimed at making recommendations on research and social policy issues.

THE NIMH TASK FORCE ON HOMOSEXUALITY

The initiative taken by the NIMH in 1967 to establish a Task Force on Homosexuality reflected the rising tide of the community mental health movement, which had begun in the early 1960s. Within the liberal zeitgeist of the Kennedy and Johnson administrations, federal programs were instituted to promote deinstitutionalization of the mentally ill, community mental health centers, public education, and the special concerns and needs of the poor and oppressed sectors of American society. Not only was treatment extended in the form of community outreach, but also prevention strategies that involved grassroots community organizations were fostered.[41]

Hooker was invited by NIMH director Stanley F. Yolles to come to Washington and "tell him what we ought to be doing about homosexuality." He added, "We want to sweep it out from beneath the rug."[42] In response, Hooker suggested that what was needed was an interdisciplinary group of experts who could pool their knowledge to deal with the issues surrounding homosexuality. Yolles asked for a list and promised to make the appointments for a "blue ribbon task force."

Hooker as chair selected fourteen experts to comprise the task force. The membership included psychiatrists Judd Marmor and Jerome D. Frank, sexologists Paul H. Gebhard and John Money, anthropologist Clelland Ford, legal scholar Morris Ploscowe, and David C. Bazelon, chief judge of the U.S. Court of Appeals. Most of the members were known for their dissenting views toward psychiatric orthodoxy. Homophile leaders were thus optimistic that the task force was "stacked" in their favor. Hooker made a point of not selecting anyone who might appear to be biased. She therefore avoided appointing such a potential candidate as psychiatrist Martin Hoffman, who was privately gay.[43]

Hooker proposed an agenda for the task force that included a comprehensive outline of needed research and a possible endorsement of a model penal code and an NIMH center for the study of sexuality. As it turned out, not all of the task force members supported her positive views on homosexuality and, consequently, could not endorse a penal code in which homosexuality was no longer seen as a crime. Three members (Clelland Ford, Henry W. Riecken, and Anthony F. C. Wallace) wrote dissenting opinions, arguing that NIMH as a research institution could not recommend social policy, and there were not enough data to justify the position that homosexuality was "normal."[44]

In its final report, issued in October 1969, the task force made recommendations that, for the most part, reflected Hooker's agenda. The introduction to the report set the tone with the statement that "homosexuality presents a major problem for our society largely because of the amount of injustice and suffering entailed in it not only for the homosexual but also for those concerned about him."[45] The establishment of an NIMH Center for the Study of Sexual Behavior was recommended, which would have a mandate to coordinate research, training, and treatment services, as well as to insure that the study of homosexuality was placed within the context of the broad range of sexuality.

Other recommendations delineated future research directions, training needs, prevention, treatment, and social policy. The inclusion of prevention and treatment indicated that the medical model was, to some extent, still adhered to, even by the majority who endorsed the report. Prevention was conceived in terms of the need to determine how to prevent "the development of a homosexual orientation in an individual child or adolescent." Treatment was specifically endorsed for homosexuals who had "some heterosexual orientation" and were motivated to change.[46]

The political impact of the report was reflected in the social policy recommendations. The report called for the repeal of laws that criminalized homosexual acts between consenting adults. Precedents to this recommendation, notably the British Wolfenden Report of 1957, were cited in support. The report also opposed employment discrimination against homosexuals.[47]

Overall, the task force report was a liberal call for tolerance toward homosexual men and women. While incorporating some aspects of the medical model (prevention and selective treatment), the report challenged the psychiatric orthodoxy of labeling all homosexuals as pathological. Reflecting this dissenting view, the report stated, "Homosexual individuals vary widely in terms of their emotional and social adjustments. Some persons who engage in homosexual behavior function well in everyday life."[48]

The tolerant and liberal tone of the 1969 report proved to be too controversial for the Nixon administration. As a result, the report was buried and its publication delayed until 1972. The NIMH director, Yolles, was fired and the federal government refrained from sponsoring any of the research recommended by the task force. The gay community, nevertheless, became aware of the final report when it was published in 1970 in *Homophile Studies*, a quarterly sponsored by the homophile group ONE, Incorporated. Dorr Legg, the quarterly's editor, pointed to the need to disseminate the report's "clearcut [sic] calls for action" in the face of the government's inaction regarding publication and implementation. While there were reservations about the recommendations on prevention and treatment, homophile leaders applauded the report's overall challenge to the medical model as well as its social policy recommendations.[49]

THE HOMOPHILE CHALLENGE TO THE MEDICAL MODEL

The publication of the NIMH Task Force report in *Homophile Studies* added ammunition for the campaign to remove homosexuality from the American Psychiatric Association's (APA) *Diagnostic and Statistical Manual of Mental Disorders.* Homophile activists and their sympathetic supporters within the APA led this effort. The successful outcome of the campaign in 1973 was the result of forces both within the mental health community and the homophile movement. By the early 1970s a vocal minority of dissidents had emerged within the APA that was willing to challenge the entrenched defenders of the medical model of homosexuality. While the APA rebels began to push for change, it was the rising political pressure from the homophile activists that forced the psychiatric profession to confront its hostility to gay men and lesbians. To account for the final breakthrough in the movement to depathologize homosexuality, it is necessary to examine the changing dynamics within the homophile movement that produced the militant protest against the psychiatric establishment.

Beginning in the early 1960s, the homophile movement underwent a metamorphosis from a cautious, accommodative stance to one marked by the militant liberatory politics of emerging social movements, such as the civil rights struggle and the student and antiwar protests. The shift reflected the revolutionary changes affecting American society, which moved from the politically oppressive and socially conservative climate of the fifties to the confrontational politics and socially liberating milieu of the sixties.

By the early 1950s the term "homophile" became the preferred label among homosexual activists. Unlike "homosexual," with its negative, lustful connotation, homophile implied same-sex friendship and love and was thus perceived to be more socially acceptable. The first homophile organizations had to proceed cautiously in the wake of McCarthy-driven persecutions. According to John D'Emilio, for example, between 1950 and 1953, forty to sixty homosexual men and women per month were dismissed from federal government jobs. The labeling of homosexuals as national security risks gave free rein to local police departments in harassing gay men and lesbians. Throughout the 1950s there were relentless crackdowns, often leading to substantial arrests in many cities.[50]

The Mattachine Society, created in 1951 in Los Angeles, actually began as a left-wing, radical organization under the leadership of Harry Hay. The society sought to mobilize a large homosexual constituency toward collective political action. Within two years, however, Hay was displaced. The new leadership adopted an accommodative strategy aimed at achieving social acceptance. Members were encouraged to conform to normative standards of proper behavior and dress, thereby projecting an image that minimized the differences between homosexuals and heterosexuals. It was assumed that once social hostility was reduced, it would be possible to effect changes in laws and social policy. Along similar lines, the Daughters of Bilitis (DOB), founded in 1955 in San Francisco, promoted public education and social change within the confines of acceptable modes of behavior by its members.[51]

Not all homophile activists, however, promoted accommodation. ONE, Incorporated, the third group to emerge in the 1950s, was an offshoot of the Mattachine Society. In contrast to Mattachine and DOB, which focused on developing a national network of local chapters, ONE devoted its efforts to publishing a monthly magazine, which began in 1953. Rather than directing its readers to socially conform, *ONE Magazine* inspired a sense of defiant pride in a deviant identity. ONE also fostered educational objectives and in 1956 established the ONE Institute of Homophile Studies. The institute offered courses and beginning in 1958 published a periodical, the *ONE Institute Quarterly of Homophile Studies*. These efforts anticipated the emergence of institutionalized curricula and periodicals in gay and lesbian studies in the post-Stonewall era.[52]

ONE believed that homosexuals should possess the authority to make judgments about homosexuality and speak on their own behalf. In sharp contrast, Mattachine and DOB deferred to professionals as sources of expertise who could best speak about homosexuality. Accordingly, beginning in 1953 the Mattachine leadership pursued a strategy of offering the organization's services to researchers as well as enlisting the help of professionals, including law enforcement workers, attorneys, and mental health specialists, to project accurate public information regarding homosexuals and homosexuality. As Hal Call, one of the Mattachine leaders, phrased it, the objective was "to ride the coattails"[53] of recognized authorities to bring about social change. Research, in particular, was recognized as a significant means of changing public attitudes, and Mattachine, as well as the DOB, maintained close contact with the Kinsey Institute. When Kinsey died in 1956, *ONE Magazine* published a tribute. The trust in research also accounted for Mattachine's interest and cooperation in Hooker's work.[54]

To encourage contact and establish dialogue, professionals were invited to Mattachine and DOB meetings and encouraged to publish articles in the *Mattachine Review* and the DOB's *Ladder*. Both of these magazines were founded in 1955. Mattachine and DOB maintained neutrality and promoted a diversity of opinion in their publications. By avoiding the stance of impassioned partisans, they strove to gain the support of a broad base of professionals who would be influential allies in the struggle to achieve social acceptance. Moreover, in professing neutrality, they reflected the wide diversity of opinion among the readership. In letters and articles written by members, viewpoints ranged from expressions of gay pride to assertions that homosexuality was a great tragedy.[55]

The views of professionals who opposed the medical model appeared in the homophile press. Hooker, for example, spoke about her research at discussion groups, and a summary of her preliminary findings appeared in the first issue of the *Mattachine Review* in 1955. Two years later her published article on the comparison between homosexual and heterosexual men was reprinted in the *Review*. Another homophile supporter, psychiatrist Blanche M. Baker, in an article in the *Ladder*, was quoted on the need for homosexuals to accept themselves and inform their family and friends of their sexual preference.[56]

In contrast to these dissident voices, there were expressions of orthodox psychiatric thought. Albert Ellis, a clinical psychologist who had considerable experience working with homosexuals, was a frequent lecturer at Mattachine meetings and a contributor to the *Review* and *ONE*. He asserted that homosexuality was a neurosis that reflected a phobia of the opposite sex and a compulsive fixation on members of the same sex. Furthermore, he argued that through psychotherapy, homosexuals could achieve satisfactory heterosexual relations. Ellis's articles attracted critical letters rejecting his views. Nevertheless, the editorial response in the *Review* adhered to a neutral stance, proclaiming in such declarations as "We hesitate to comment that either Ellis or his critics is to be regarded as wrong or right. . . . We shall not evade an issue simply because it may be controversial and Albert Ellis dared to face it."[57]

Homosexual contributors also voiced support for the medical model. Ken Burns, for example, one of the leaders of Mattachine, stressed the need for prevention in terms of controlling the social and familial determinants of homosexuality. There were limits, however, in the extent to which the disease model was accepted. Edmund Bergler, a psychoanalyst, presented a scathing portrait of homosexuals in his 1956 book, *Homosexuality: Disease or Way of Life?* He characterized homosexuals as "miserable souls" and "unreliable troublemakers." His book was widely denounced in both the *Review* and the *Ladder*.[58]

The negative reaction to Bergler in the late 1950s signaled the beginning of a mounting challenge to the medical model. This challenge was part of the dramatic shift toward confrontational politics that marked the homophile movement in the 1960s. As D'Emilio points out, the liberalizing climate of the new decade lifted the veil of secrecy surrounding homosexuality and produced a new openness to explore an unknown, exotic side of American society. A proliferation of material on gay life thus appeared in pornography, literature, and the mass media. This new social awareness led to changes in how gay men and lesbians were perceived. In place of the stereotype of isolated, deviant individuals, a significant minority of opinion viewed homosexuals as members of a group. This new image also enabled homophile activists to attract a growing constituency of gay men and lesbians as well as needed support from significant professional allies in law and mental health.[59]

Until the 1950s the Victorian code of law and custom dominated the sexual content of literature and the mass media. While there were some breakthroughs in the 1930s, the grip of censorship finally began to erode by the late 1950s under the weight of a series of Supreme Court rulings that supported challenges to the obscenity statutes. In 1959 William S. Burroughs's *Naked Lunch* and in 1963 John Rechy's *City of Night* presented graphic depictions of gay sex and the homosexual underworld of sexual predators and hustlers. The production and consumption of sexual material became widespread in the 1960s. This change was especially evident in the proliferation of content about male and female homosexuality, ranging from gay male pornography to lesbian pulp fiction. Positive gay characters and subplots appeared in such best-selling novels as James Baldwin's *Another Country* and Mary McCarthy's *The Group*. In 1961 Hollywood reversed the three-decade ban on portrayals of homosexuality on the screen. In order to gain the approval of the Motion Picture Production Code, however, the depictions conformed to the stereotyped views of homosexuals as psychologically tortured or morally corrupt. Increasing social recognition was also achieved through the introduction of journalistic accounts of the gay and lesbian subculture in newspapers, such as the *New York Times* and the *Washington Post,* and weekly magazines, including *Life* and *Look*. Moreover, the new media interest in homosexuality paved the way for pulp homophobic books, such as Jess Stearn's *The Sixth Man* on gay male life and his companion piece, *The Grapevine,* on lesbian life. Setting the tone for the male homosexual as a sexually promiscuous and hence dangerous figure, *The Sixth Man*'s dust jacket included the quote, "One out of every six men in America is a homosexual. This is the report of one of the most frightening surveys conducted since the Kinsey books."[60]

The rising familiarity with gay life led to increasing debate over the legal status of homosexuality. In England the influential Wolfenden Report was released in 1957. This report by a government-appointed commission argued that homosexuality by consenting adults in private should be decriminalized. In 1962 the American Law Institute concurred by advocating the elimination of sodomy statutes. Little progress, however, was made in the 1960s in changing the American legal codes.[61]

The homophile challenge to the medical model was waged against this backdrop of a rising public awareness of gay men and lesbians as a group. Such recognition also played into the perception of a minority group struggling for its civil rights, and this was a strategy adopted by the proponents of eradicating the psychiatric status of homosexuality. While the sentiment to confront the psychiatric establishment was building, there was still a strong current of support within homophile circles for maintaining the view that homosexuality was a form of psychopathology. It was not until 1965 that this internal conflict was resolved in favor of those who supported confrontation with the psychiatrists. The conflict centered on two homophile leaders—Frank Kameny, who opposed the medical model, and Edward Sagarin, who supported it.

Frank Kameny and the Attack on the Medical Model

Franklin E. Kameny was born in New York City in 1925 to a Jewish middle-class family. He was a precocious child and at fifteen entered Queens College in New York. In 1943 he joined the army and was involved in combat in Holland and Germany. After the war he continued his education and in 1956 received his doctorate in astronomy from Harvard. Although he was aware of his homosexual feelings as a teenager, it was not until he was twenty-nine that he had his first sexual experience with another man. After completing his doctorate, he taught at Georgetown University in Washington, D.C., for a year and then began working for the U.S. Army Map Service. In December 1957, five months into his employment, he was fired. Investigators had discovered a 1956 arrest on charges of "lewd conduct." To make matters worse, a month after his dismissal, the Civil Service Commission barred him from further employment by the federal government. He filed one of the first lawsuits contesting job discrimination against homosexuals, but by 1961 all his legal efforts had failed.[62]

His firing created extreme hardship. He was unable to find another job and lived on handouts from the Salvation Army. After exhausting legal redress, he came to the realization that the time had arrived to fight collectively. Vaguely aware of the homophile movement during the mid-1950s, he had been in contact with Mattachine and ONE while pursuing his legal case. In 1961 he decided to organize a Mattachine chapter in Washington.

In launching the Washington Mattachine, Kameny worked closely with Jack Nichols. When they first met in 1960, Nichols was twenty-two. He had acknowledged his gayness to himself and his FBI agent father while he was in high school. At fifteen, reading Cory's *The Homosexual in America* had radicalized him. In November 1961 about a dozen men and women gathered to form the Mattachine Society of Washington and elected Kameny as president. As it turned out, the group was an independent organization since the national society had dissolved itself the previous spring. Various local chapters, however, continued to use the name.

With Kameny's leadership, the Washington chapter moved to the vanguard of homosexual rights activity. Through his legal battle, he had gained useful experience about how government bureaucracy functioned and how it worked as an impediment to the civil rights objectives of homosexuals. Kameny's academic training also contributed to his ability to create and articulate a philosophy and strategy with respect to the movement's goals. In contrast with the neutrality that characterized the homophile movement of the 1950s, he advocated a militant political stance. Moreover, he was supremely self-confident and a charismatic speaker who conveyed the persona of a crusader. His presence and oratory attracted attention. In addressing the Washington Mattachine members, he declared, "We cannot stand upon an ivory-tower concept of aloof, detached dignity. . . . This is a movement, in many respects, of down-to-earth, grassroots, sometimes tooth-and-nail politics."[63]

Kameny turned to the civil rights movement as a guiding force for homophile activism. In following through on this approach, he propelled the Washington Mattachine to engage in a series of challenges to the discriminatory policies of the federal government. The breakthrough in forcing policy change came about with the help of the American Civil Liberties Union (ACLU). The ACLU took the case of Bruce Scott, who had been denied federal employment on grounds of "convincing evidence" of homosexual conduct. In July 1965 the United States Court of Appeals ruled that the charges against Scott were too vague to bar him from federal employment. With the support of the ACLU, the Washington Mattachine also forced the District of Columbia police to be held accountable for the mistreatment of homosexuals.

The militancy of Kameny and the Washington Mattachine was not an isolated case. Under the leadership of Randy Wicker, the old guard of the New York Mattachine was being challenged. While an undergraduate at the University of Texas in the late 1950s, Wicker had been active in the civil rights movement. When he settled in New York in 1961, he transferred his political enthusiasm to the cause of homosexual rights. He focused on media coverage and challenged the New York Mattachine's policy of deferring to the opinion of professionals. He advocated that homosexuals should be allowed to speak for themselves on radio broadcasts and supply material for press coverage.[64]

Kameny's and Wicker's collectivist strategy attracted attention among an emerging network of aggressive homophile activists. Barbara Gittings, who founded the New York chapter of the DOB in 1958, became the leader of the militant wing of the organization. Her thinking had been profoundly changed by Kameny's views. She recalled, "He was a big influence on me because he had such a clear and compelling vision of what the movement should be doing and what was just. He believed that we should be standing up on our hind legs and demanding our full equality and full rights."[65]

At Kameny's suggestion, the homophile groups in the East agreed to form a loosely structured coalition. The East Coast Homophile Organization (ECHO) was organized in January 1963. Over the next two years, ECHO served as a source for solidifying a militant wing of the homophile movement. In 1965 the conflict between the old guard and the radicals was brought to a head over the issue of the medical model.

For Kameny and his supporters, the sickness theory stood in the way of the struggle for equality. As Kameny observed in an article on psychiatry and homosexual rights, homosexuals were denied federal employment not because they were security risks by virtue of being vulnerable to blackmail, but rather "on the grounds that because psychiatrists term homosexuality a sickness, all homosexuals are unstable." He went on to point out that the sickness model "is recognized as not only destructive to the self-respect, self-esteem, self-confidence, and self-image of the homosexual . . . but as perhaps the major supportive factor currently behind . . . the negative attitude of society at large."[66]

In various articles he critically reviewed the psychiatric research on homosexuality, noting its methodological weaknesses, faulty definitions of terms, such as sickness and neurosis, and its poor logic and unclear thinking. He concluded that without valid scientific evidence, homosexuality could not be considered an illness or pathology. On the contrary, he boldly advocated that it had to be considered as a preference or orientation not different from heterosexuality and fully on a par with it.[67]

Following from his critique of the medical model, Kameny exhorted homophile activists to reject their long-standing commitment to research, arguing, "Those who allege sickness have created *their* need for *their* research. Let *them* do it." According to Kameny, the so-called experts were factually and morally wrong. Like Gay and Painter, he believed that homosexuals had to speak in their own voice, noting, "We are the true authorities on homosexuality whether we are accepted or not."[68] He felt so strongly about the irrelevance of research that he even questioned the need for Hooker's work. While acknowledging that her research on psychological adjustment played a significant role in the attack against psychiatric "propaganda," he opined that logically her work was not of fundamental importance because it was based on the question of whether homosexuality was pathological.[69]

It was in his speeches that Kameny was especially influential in directing the homophile movement to challenge the psychiatric establishment and generally to become more aggressive in its political tactics. In a speech to the New York Mattachine in July 1964, he declared, "The entire homophile movement . . . is going to stand or fall upon the question of whether homosexuality is a sickness, and upon our taking a firm stand on it." He challenged his audience to adopt his position that "until and unless valid positive evidence shows otherwise, homosexuality *per se* is neither a sickness, a defect, a disturbance, a neurosis, a psychosis, nor a malfunction of any sort."[70]

Kameny's speech electrified the audience and served as a catalyst for increased activism among the memberships of both the New York and Washington Mattachine groups. In February 1965 the Washington society adopted an antisickness resolution. In the spring and summer of 1965, demonstrations with picket lines were carried out in front of the United Nations in New York, the White House and government offices in Washington, and Independence Hall in Philadelphia. The marchers targeted the federal government with signs such as "Fifteen Million U.S. Homosexuals Protest Federal Treatment."[71]

While these demonstrations were very small when compared with the civil rights marches of the early 1960s, they signaled the radicalization of the movement. As Kameny later reflected, the sight of people publicly identifying themselves as homosexuals "created the necessary mindset for gays demonstrating in public."[72] Without them, he believed that Stonewall in 1969 might never have taken place. Moreover, some of the first homophile demonstrations produced immediate effects. The day after picketing the State Department, for example, Secretary of State Dean Rusk had to answer a reporter's question about the department's policy on hiring homosexuals. These demonstrations also brought media coverage on television and in the press.[73]

By early 1965 the militant wing of the homophile movement was in ascendance and eventually would lead the attack on the medical model. The old guard, however, was still not ready to relinquish its hold. The final confrontation between the two camps came in the New York Mattachine's May 1965 elections. The issue of the sickness theory played a major role in the election. Julian Hodges led the militant slate of offices. He was originally with the old guard, but Kameny's 1964 speech profoundly redirected his views to the militant side. Kameny and Ruitenbeek, the psychoanalyst who supported the homophile rejection of the medical model, ran on the

Hodges slate, seeking positions on the board of directors. Among those on the opposing side was Edward Sagarin, who had earlier vowed to quit the New York chapter if it adopted an antipathology position.[74]

Edward Sagarin and the Defense of the Medical Model
It was ironic that Sagarin championed the medical model against the challenge by the militants. Under the pseudonym of Donald Webster Cory, he had written the highly influential book *The Homosexual in America*, first published in 1951. The book was both an introduction to the main currents of gay male life (he subsequently wrote a book on lesbianism) and a call to arms for collective action. Striking a revolutionary tone, he targeted heterosexual society as the problem and anticipated the militants' appeal for protest. In his words:

> There are no minority problems. There are only majority problems. There is no Negro problem except that created by whites; no Jewish problem except that created by Gentiles. To which I add: and no homosexual problem except that created by the heterosexual society. . . . If [the homosexual] . . . does not rise up and demand his rights, he will never get them, but until he gets those rights, he cannot be expected to expose himself to the martyrdom that would come if he should rise up and demand them.[75]

Underscoring the dilemma homosexuals were caught in, he added, "If only all the inverts, the millions in all lands, could simultaneously rise up in our full strength! For the fact is that we homosexuals are defeated by the self-perpetuation of the folkways which inflict severe punishment on those who protest against the folkways. Again the circle is vicious."[76]

For Sagarin the resolution of the dilemma was to be found through the freedom of expression. Homosexuals had to fight for the right to freely speak for themselves as well as to promote the realistic representation of homosexuality in various media outlets, including newspapers, novels, the radio, and the theater. He also exhorted homosexuals to fight for sexual freedom by promoting legal reform. Above all, he asserted the value of homosexuality as a distinct cultural force that was an inseparable part of a diverse, democratic society:

> It is the inherent lack of assimilability that is the greatest historic value of homosexuality. Any minority which does not commit antisocial acts, which is not destructive of the life, property, or culture of the majority or of other minority groups, is a pillar of democratic strength. So long as there are such minorities in our culture, whether of a sexual or religious or ethnic character, there will be many broths in the melting pot, many and variegated waves in the seas. No force

will be able to weave these groups into a single totalitarian unity which is the unanimity of the graveyard.[77]

These sentiments stood in marked contrast to the gathering wave of oppression during the McCarthy era. They inspired many gay men and lesbians to become involved in the homophile movement. Jack Nichols, for example, had been radicalized when he read the book as a teenager; Barbara Gittings first became involved as an activist when she read the book. William Wynkoop, who became a supporter of the militants, was overwhelmed when he read it. He recalled that he thought it was a historical breakthrough because nothing like it had been published before. He, like other gay men and lesbians of his generation, would not have been aware of earlier books authored by self-identified homosexuals, such as Edward Prime-Stevenson and Earl Lind, which were generally unknown because of their limited publication.[78]

The Homosexual in America sold well in large cities but was ignored by the general press. As a mark of its success, the book went through seven printings from 1951 through 1957. That it was published at all was surprising, given the censorship restrictions of the 1950s. In fact, the publisher, Jae Greenberg, who had published a few gay novels, had been charged with sending obscene materials through the mail. The case was eventually settled for a fine of $3,500 and a guarantee to keep the three novels in question out of print.[79]

Sagarin was an unlikely figure to act as a prophet for the emergence of the homophile movement of the 1950s and 1960s. At the time he wrote his book, he was a married man in his late thirties with a son. While his wife knew about the nature of his writing, she was not aware of the extent to which his own personal experiences contributed to the project. Physically, he suffered from congenital scoliosis, a lateral curvature of the spine, which produced a noticeable hump on the right side of his back as well as a limp when he walked. Professionally, he worked in the perfume industry, specializing in sales and management. This was not his true calling, however, since he was forced to drop out of college during the Depression. Nevertheless, a born scholar, he taught an adjunct course on the chemistry of cosmetics at Columbia University and published two books on the science and technology of the cosmetics industry. The opportunity to publish his book on homosexuality came about through a friend who was a printer for Greenberg. The printer introduced Sagarin to Brandt Aymar, a Greenberg editor.[80]

In the preface to the book, Sagarin recounted his tortured journey in coming to terms with his homosexuality. He was first aware of his sexual feelings in early adolescence. By his early twenties, he had avidly read all of the available literature on homosexuality. He fought against his sexual inclinations, but his struggles proved fruitless. Recognizing that he could not change who he was, he immersed himself in gay life. Yet he still felt "trapped by a human tragedy to which I could not adjust."[81] He hoped to resolve his conflict and openly proclaim his gayness by finding love with another man. But after a series of brief relationships, he was convinced he would never find permanent homosexual love. Consequently, at the age of twenty-five, he married a woman he had known from childhood. Still struggling with his homosexuality, he began psychoanalytic treatment. Once in treatment, he realized that he could not overcome his homosexual impulses. He then entered into a closeted homosexual life while maintaining, in his words, a "successful marriage."[82]

Sagarin's internal struggle and his compartmentalized life seemingly compromised the extent to which he was able to project a radical call to arms. In contrast to Kameny, who viewed the medical model as the major impediment to homosexual rights, Sagarin in his book incorporated aspects of the sickness theory. In subsequent writings, he became more forceful in his support of the medical model.

In *The Homosexual in America,* Sagarin accepted the standard psychiatric theory of family pathology as the cause of homosexuality. He referred to such examples as an excessively close mother-son bond and a distant father-son relationship. Based on his own experience, however, he did not concur with the view that homosexuality could be "cured." Therapy could only be useful as a means of achieving self-acceptance and thus becoming a "well-integrated and happy" homosexual. To support his argument, he cited therapists, such as psychiatrist George Henry and psychoanalyst Clara Thompson, who promoted such adjustment goals with homosexual patients.[83]

Thus, while advocating the objective for gay man and lesbians to gain self-acceptance, he clung to the medicalized notion that homosexuality was the result of some combination of unhealthy conditions early in life that arrested psychosexual development. Consequently, it was not on a par with heterosexuality. Also reflecting his own adjustment of living a double life as a married man and a closeted gay man, Sagarin supported the need for some homosexuals to enter into marriage. Since his book focused on male homosexuality, his comments were with respect to gay men. Among the reasons he cited for seeking marriage were the "inability to create [a] permanent relationship with [a] male companion or lover."[84] On the other hand, marriage was not needed if one had success in the hope of finding a "male life-mate." In his own case, at the time he wrote his book, he had found a gay companion but nevertheless chose to maintain his marriage.[85]

The multiple printings of Sagarin's book in the 1950s indicated to publishers that there was a market for books aimed at a homosexual book-buying public. In 1956 Sagarin published an edited book, *Homosexuality: A Cross Cultural Approach*. This was a collection of previously published essays by homophile authors, including John Addington Symonds, Edward Carpenter, and Richard Burton. The book also included scientific articles by such authors as Kinsey, Henry, and Albert Ellis, and two of Sagarin's own essays.[86]

In 1960 a second edition of *The Homosexual in America* was published. In the preface to the new edition, Sagarin acknowledged limitations to the book. While he would not retreat from his earlier support of legal rights and civil liberties for homosexuals, he felt that he had not placed enough emphasis on the psychological maladjustment of homosexuals and the "limitations of homosexuality as a way of life."[87] Moreover, he suggested that it was possible, at least for some homosexuals including him, to change. He proclaimed:

> Once it is recognized that one can accept the homosexual as a human being, can demand the rights that belong to him, without denying that his behavior (or desire for such behavior) is a symptom of an emotional maladjustment, then the need for reorientation is complemented by the psychological foundations that may make it possible. Change toward acceptance of the heterosexual life, rather than suppression of the homosexual one, is aided by a freedom from guilt and fear, and hence becomes far less difficult than I had anticipated in the original text. In as much as this is a subjective study, I am happy to say that I found such change not only possible, but personally rewarding.[88]

In the interim between the two editions, Sagarin had apparently become more comfortable with his life choice of maintaining both his marriage and his love affair with a black boyfriend. But it was more than personal experience that redirected his thinking. He acknowledged the influence of psychologist "Dr. Albert Ellis, who has aided immeasurably to shape my thinking . . . and has given help and encouragement in my own subjective reorientation."[89]

Sagarin first came in contact with Ellis in 1951 when he was searching for a professional to provide an introduction to the original edition of his book. Most likely at the suggestion of the publisher, it was assumed that an endorsement by a recognized expert would act as a protection against the threat of censorship. Sagarin first approached Kinsey but was unsuccessful. To maintain his image of scientific objectivity, Kinsey avoided any public support of activities or materials pertaining to homosexual rights.

Nevertheless, Kinsey enthusiastically approved of Sagarin's book and recommended Ellis, who had been a strong supporter of Kinsey's work. Ellis agreed to write the introduction in which he heartily endorsed Sagarin's effort as "by far the best non-fictional picture of the American homosexual and his problems that has yet been published." Yet he also took issue with the author's "pessimism concerning the possibility of adjusting homosexuals to more heterosexual modes of living."[90] As expressed in the preface to the second edition, a decade later Sagarin had moved closer to Ellis's view.

Ellis had most clearly enunciated his position on homosexuality in an article entitled "Are Homosexuals Necessarily Neurotic?" which appeared in *ONE Magazine* in 1955 and was reprinted in Sagarin's book *Homosexuality: A Cross Cultural Approach.* For Ellis, individuals who engaged in homosexual behavior were not necessarily neurotic as long as at some point in their lives, they also engaged in equally satisfying heterosexual expression. Thus, it was only homosexuals who exclusively desired same-sex experience who were neurotic. Such individuals were marked by a compulsive need to engage in homosexual acts and an accompanying underlying or conscious fear of heterosexual behavior. Ellis referred to Sagarin (using his pseudonym of Cory) as an example of a homosexual who was not neurotic because of his capacity to engage in heterosexual behavior. Reaching out to his homosexual readers, Ellis declared, "Let you homosexuals face it . . . every mother's son of you who is exclusively desirous of homosexual relations, is indubitably neurotic. Those of you, like Cory himself, incidentally, who are capable of being happily married and having heterosexual satisfactions right along with your homosexual affairs, may not necessarily be emotionally disturbed."[91]

After the second edition of *The Homosexual in America* was published, Sagarin elaborated on his support of the medical model in various writings. In *The Homosexual and His Society,* coauthored with John P. LeRoy, who was a homophile activist with some background in psychology, the authors characterized all homosexuals as suffering from emotional difficulties. Acknowledging that societal hostility contributed to the emotional problems, the authors, nevertheless, noted that homosexuality was a path chosen because of "unresolved feelings of inadequacy, misapprehensions about and fears of the other sex, family disorganization, inability to make sex-role identification as required by society, or for a variety of other reasons." Yet the authors also argued that some homosexuals were reasonably well adjusted. According to Sagarin and LeRoy, despite the fact that individuals become homosexual because of "unhealthy circumstances in early life," many, including those who were exclusively homosexual, were able to lead productive and emotionally and sexually fulfilling lives.[92]

In 1975, twenty-five years after the first edition, *The Homosexual in America* was reprinted. In the foreword Sagarin declared that, for the most part, the book no longer expressed the views of its author. He came out even more strongly than he had in the 1960s in endorsing the medical model. He believed that homosexuality was a mental illness marked by "distress, loneliness, promiscuity, search for affection with little success, depression, [and] superficial gaiety."[93] In contrast to what the gay liberation movement was advocating in the 1970s, he stressed that homosexuality was not equal to heterosexuality. Moreover, he eschewed his earlier doubts about the possibilities for change and asserted that homosexuals could profit from therapy.

The Emergence of Radical Protest and Gay Liberation

The battle lines for the New York Mattachine's May 1965 elections were clearly drawn. Sagarin reiterated his published stand in various speeches to homophile groups. At the 1964 DOB convention in New York, for example, he chastised the movement for "alienating itself from scientific thinking . . . by the constant, defensive, neurotic, disturbed denial" that homosexuality was a sickness.[94]

The militants stressed their sharp differences with the old guard. Julian Hodges, who headed the militant slate, sent a letter to the membership urging them to avoid electing the opposing board of directors because it was "split down the middle on such vital issues as whether or not homosexuality is an illness, whether or not the Society should be primarily a 'civil rights' organization, and whether the Society should aim its program to the homosexual community in general or to the individual homosexual."[95]

In private correspondence, Kameny wrote to Sagarin:

> You have left the mainstream for the backwaters . . . you have fallen by the wayside, lost most of your effectiveness . . . you have become no longer the vigorous Father of the Homophile Movement, to be revered, respected and listened to, but the senile Grandfather of the Homophile Movement, to be humored and tolerated at best; to be ignored and disregarded usually; and to be ridiculed, at worst.[96]

In the elections the militants thrashed the old guard, gaining two-thirds of the vote. The victory, however, came about with some tampering of the ballots. To make sure that Hodges would be the winner, he and his ally Dick Leitsch had steamed open the envelopes the night before the election was held and changed some of the ballots. The old guard was not aware of the tampering, and many, including Sagarin, left the organization, some forming an alternative West Side Discussion Group.[97]

After 1965 Sagarin dropped his pseudonym of Cory and in 1966 completed his doctorate in sociology at New York University. His dissertation was a study of the New York Mattachine Society. He put his career as a homophile activist behind him and became a university professor, teaching and writing on social deviance and criminology. He kept his "Cory" authorship hidden. In 1973 he wrote a scathing essay review of a series of recently published gay liberationist books. The following year at the annual meeting of the American Sociological Association, he appeared as a panelist at a session on homosexuality. He attacked "pro-gay" sexologists, such as Hooker and John Gagnon. In response, Laud Humphreys, author of the infamous 1970 book *Tearoom Trade: Impersonal Sex in Public Places,* challenged him. Humphreys, enraged by Sagarin's views, purposely intermixed "Dr. Sagarin" and "Mr. Cory" in addressing his questions. Finally, in response to Humphreys's question "And where did you get *your* data?" Sagarin responded, "I am my data," and left the platform in tears.[98] Sagarin died of a heart attack in 1986 at age seventy-three.

The militants' victory had pervasive effects in boosting the homophile movement. Membership increased significantly, not only in the New York Mattachine, but also in several other groups, including the Society of Janus of Philadelphia and the Washington Mattachine. The spring and summer of 1965 were marked by protests, such as a sit-in in a Philadelphia restaurant that refused to serve men and women suspected of being gay, and campaigns that were waged against police harassment in Chicago and San Francisco.[99]

The shift from accommodation to visible protest brought the homophile movement increasingly closer to the civil rights movement. At the 1966 Kansas City meeting of the newly created North American Conference of Homophile Organizations (NACHO), Kameny asserted that the problems homosexuals faced were issues of "prejudice and discrimination." In the same year Dick Leitsch, president of the New York Mattachine, challenged a nationwide gathering of activists to "demand" homosexual rights, including the right to cruise, the right to work, and the right to public accommodations.[100]

The infusion of civil rights thinking to the homophile movement was most clearly reflected in 1968 when NACHO adopted a resolution introduced by Kameny. Assimilating the nationalist turn of the civil rights movement in the late 1960s to black power and black pride, Kameny's resolution proclaimed:

> BECAUSE many individual homosexuals, like many of the members of many other minority groups[,] suffer from diminished self-esteem, doubts and uncertainties as to their personal worth . . . *and*

> BECAUSE, therefore, many individual homosexuals, like many

members of other minority groups, are in need of psychological sustenance to bolster and to support a positive and affirmative attitude toward themselves and their homosexuality ... *and* ...

BECAUSE the Negro community has approached similar problems and goals with some success by the adoption of the motto or slogan: *Black is Beautiful*

RESOLVED: that it be hereby adopted as a slogan or motto ... that

GAY IS GOOD[101]

This was a striking statement and a sharp break from the accommodationist stance of adjusting or fitting into the larger society. Paralleling the demand by the militant wing of the civil rights movement for black nationalism as opposed to integration, homophile leaders asserted the principle that homosexuals take pride in themselves and their community. To achieve equality, gay men and lesbians had to go beyond simply attacking the assumption that they were inferior because of illness; they had to assert their strength and worth based on what made them different and unique as a community. The slogan "Gay is Good," according to Kameny, strategically served as a rallying point and a consciousness-raising device to create the sense of group solidarity and community that was needed for effective social action.[102]

The 1968 NACHO resolution represented the growing militancy of the homophile movement, but it would still take a highly visible event to ignite a mass movement of gay and lesbian protest. Stonewall and gay liberation were still a year away. By the mid-1960s the pace of demonstrations, legal challenges, and, especially in San Francisco and New York, political influence was on the rise. Moreover, in San Francisco in 1965, there was a melding of the gay subculture with the gay rights movement. In general, homophile activists, of both accommodationist and militant persuasions, had remained aloof from direct contact with the gay subculture. They tended to view bar patrons as stereotypically frivolous or decadent. In response to the escalating level of police harassment in San Francisco's gay bars, a coalition of gay activists and liberal ministers successfully challenged police practices. For the first time, a gay community began to collectively identify with the cause of gay rights.[103]

The first signs of a direct physical confrontation with the medical and mental health professionals began in 1968. In April a gay student group at Columbia University picketed a panel discussion on homosexuality sponsored by the medical school. The authorities had refused the students' request to include a homosexual on the program. Student representatives interrupted the meeting and demanded that in the future any discussion of

homosexuality be placed "in its proper setting as a sociological problem of deeply entrenched prejudice and discrimination against a minority
group."[104] In the same year, when the American Medical Association met
in San Francisco, activists held a well-received press conference to protest
psychoanalyst Charles Socarides's extremist portrayal of homosexuality as
"a dread dysfunction, malignant in character, which has risen to epidemic
proportions." When he proposed a government-financed center for the
cure and rehabilitation of the "sexually deviant," the homophile activists
compared his proposal to a "final solution."[105]

The activism of the homophile movement in the late 1960s still essentially adhered to peaceful, nonconfrontational tactics. In contrast, other
liberation movements increasingly turned to radical forms of protest. By
1965 the optimistic hopes of the civil rights movement for integration
goals gave way to militant calls for black power that challenged the inherent racism of American society. In 1967 and 1968, a wave of riots broke
out in urban black ghettos. The New Left activism of the student protests
against the Vietnam War moved from peaceful demonstrations to active
resistance. In April 1968, the evening after the student homophiles at Columbia picketed the medical school, student radicals occupied buildings
on the main campus to protest the increased military involvement in Vietnam and the university's treatment of blacks in its surrounding neighborhoods. The following September, at the Democratic Party convention in
Chicago, police battled student protesters in the streets.[106]

Most younger gay men and lesbians were more attracted to the New
Left's objectives of ending inequality at home and interventions abroad
than to the homophile movement's civil rights goals of redressing griev-
ances. Many joined such New Left groups as the Students for a Democratic Society rather than any of the homophile groups within NACHO.
As Martin Duberman notes, while NACHO was centrist in its approach
to most issues, it had adopted a radical stance with respect to confronting
the psychiatric establishment. Yet most younger gays and lesbians had not
as yet overcome their own presumptions that homosexuality was abnormal.[107]

The impact of radical liberatory politics, however, began to affect homophile organizations. The homophile student group at Columbia became radicalized when it joined the student occupation of the campus. It
brought its New Left agenda to the 1968 Chicago meeting of NACHO.
Rejected at the conference, the student group devoted its attention to organizing student homophile societies on other campuses. In the same year,
radical forces finally overtook the DOB, which had maintained its conservative, accommodative perspective despite internal challenges going back
to the mid-1960s. Rita Laporte, a radical feminist, became president and,

with Barbara Grier as editor, transformed the *Ladder* into a lesbian-feminist publication. After a two-year struggle by the old guard to reclaim the magazine, the organization folded when Laporte and Grier published the magazine independently. In San Francisco the Society for Individual Rights (SIR), which was founded in 1964, purged its magazine editor, Leo Laurence, when he adopted a New Left perspective.[108]

On the night of Friday, 27 June 1969, New York City police conducted a routine raid of the Stonewall Inn, a gay bar in the heart of Greenwich Village. The bar was an especially likely candidate for a raid since it was reputed to be Mafia owned and catered to drag queens and teenage hustlers. Unexpectedly, the patrons resisted, leading to rioting that lasted well into the night and public demonstrations and gatherings by gay men and lesbians that continued throughout the weekend. This first event of collective resistance sparked the modern gay and lesbian political movement. It has come to signify, as Duberman points out in his book *Stonewall*, "that moment in time when gays and lesbians recognized all at once their mistreatment and their solidarity."[109]

The Stonewall riot produced a nationwide grassroots movement. Adopting the perspective and tactics of the New Left, the Gay Liberation Front (GLF) was founded in New York a few weeks after the riot. Over the next several months, local GLF groups emerged in several cities, including San Francisco, Berkeley, Los Angeles, and Minneapolis. Many of the GLF leaders had been active in New Left student organizations as well as radical civil rights and radical feminist groups. The GLF defined itself as a "revolutionary group of men and women formed with the realization that complete sexual liberation for all people cannot come about unless existing social institutions are abolished."[110]

As a revolutionary movement, gay liberation groups sought to ally themselves with other radical youth groups. They participated in antiwar marches and demonstrations, joined in protests against imprisoned Black Panther leaders, and attended various meetings of feminist and student groups. Moreover, utilizing confrontational tactics, they organized marches and demonstrations protesting bar raids and street arrests as well as sit-ins in the offices of publishers who wrote negative articles about gays. To commemorate the first anniversary of Stonewall, two to three thousand people marched in Central Park in New York and there were other marches across the country.[111]

Within a few years of its founding, the Gay Liberation Front and its encompassing radical agenda would be superceded by organizations devoted specifically to gay and lesbian issues. Internal schisms began as early as the fall of 1969 when the Gay Activists Alliance (GAA) was established. Dissidents attacked the GLF for being too anarchic and preoccupied with revolutionary rhetoric to plan effective action. Nevertheless, these breakaway groups continued to employ the GLF's confrontational tactics.[112]

In 1970 medical and mental health professionals became the targets of these confrontational tactics. Activists disrupted or "zapped" sessions on homosexuality at meetings of the American Medical Association, the Behavior Modification Conference, and the American Psychiatric Association (APA). The confrontation with the APA was especially significant because it marked the opening of a four-year campaign to remove homosexuality from the organization's official nomenclature of mental illness, the *Diagnostic and Statistical Manual of Mental Disorders (DSM)*. The final struggle in the early 1970s to wrest homosexuality from the grip of the psychiatric establishment was sparked by the radical politics of the nascent gay and lesbian liberation movement. Kameny and his supporters had initiated the struggle in the mid-1960s, but they were liberal reformers committed to peaceful protests. Nevertheless, because of the disruptive confrontations mounted by the younger generation of radical liberationists, sympathetic psychiatrists would call upon Kameny and his cohorts to establish a presence in the APA.[113]

CONFRONTING THE AMERICAN PSYCHIATRIC ASSOCIATION

The immediate objective of the early protests against the organizations of mental health professionals had been to establish a dialogue in which the voices of homosexuals were represented. At the 1970 APA meeting, during sessions dealing with homosexuality, demonstrators shouted, "Stop talking *about* us and start talking *with* us! We're the people whose behavior you're trying to change. Start talking with us!"[114] In the session in which a paper on aversive conditioning was presented, the heckling from gay and feminist protesters resulted in the chairperson adjourning the meeting. The veneer of professional decorum broke down as one enraged psychiatrist shouted, "They should be killed," and another, "Give back our air fare." At another session protesters engaged Bieber in a dialogue, in which he defended his position by declaring, "I never said homosexuals were sick, what I said was that they have displaced sexual adjustment." In response, a protester retorted, "That's the same thing, motherfucker."[115]

Kent Robinson, a psychiatrist sympathetic to the demand by the gay protesters to have their voices heard, was concerned about the possibility that the entire 1971 meeting might be disrupted. He approached Larry Littlejohn, one of the organizers of the protest, and learned that homosexuals wanted to present a panel at the next year's convention. Robinson was able to get the program chair to accept such a panel and agreed to chair the session. At Littlejohn's suggestion, Robinson contacted Kameny, who organized a panel of six gay people, including himself, Littlejohn, DOB founder Del Martin, and Jack Baker, the gay president-elect of the University of Minnesota student body. For the first time, gay men and lesbians achieved their long-sought objective of being able to speak for themselves at a meeting of mental health professionals. The session was called "Lifestyles of Non-Patient Homosexuals," which the gay activists informally labeled "Lifestyles of Im-Patient Homosexuals." Reflecting the confrontational tone of the panel, Kameny proclaimed, "We're rejecting you all as our owners. We possess ourselves and we speak for ourselves and we will take care of our destinies."[116]

At the convention Kameny and Gittings also organized an exhibit called "Gay, Proud, and Healthy: The Homosexual Community Speaks." The exhibit contained photos of loving gay and lesbian couples, as well as literature on the gay liberation movement. The gay and lesbian presence at the meeting encouraged a handful of gay psychiatrists to initiate contact with the gay activists. The activists learned that for several years there was a closeted Gay-PA that met during the annual conventions. This group was planning to become more open and political within the APA.[117]

While Kameny and his fellow activists had achieved official recognition in the program and exhibit hall, they realized that demonstrations were also necessary to maintain political pressure. The convention, which was in Washington, D.C., had been targeted by the local Gay Activists Alliance, and Kameny worked with the GAA leaders in planning the demonstrations. At the widely attended Convocation of Fellows, gay and antiwar protesters stormed the proceedings. In the midst of the uproar, Kameny grabbed the microphone and, borrowing from the antiwar rhetoric, proclaimed, "Psychiatry is the enemy incarnate. Psychiatry has waged a relentless war of extermination against us. You may take this as a declaration of war against you."[118] Indeed, the political pressure from the previous year was sustained, even intensified, as the fist-shaking psychiatrists accused the demonstrators of using Nazi-like tactics.[119]

Toward the end of the 1971 convention, Kameny and Littlejohn approached Robinson and indicated that they wanted to formally initiate their demand for the deletion of homosexuality from the APA's official nosology, the *DSM-II*. Robinson submitted their request to the association's Committee on Nomenclature. While nothing came of this first initiative, it marked the beginning of the tactical move to effect change within the APA organization apparatus that controlled diagnostic policy.[120]

In contrast to the disruptions that marked the two previous meetings, the 1972 APA convention was relatively free of any public confrontation surrounding the issue of homosexuality. Robinson played a central role in insuring a gay presence on the program and organized a panel that included both gay activists and psychiatrists who were sympathetic to the diagnostic deletion of homosexuality. Psychiatrists Judd Marmor and Robert Seidenberg joined Kameny and Gittings. Rounding out the panel was a gay psychiatrist who dramatically appeared as "Dr. Henry Anonymous." Lesbian activist Kay Lahusen had suggested the need for a gay psychiatrist and successfully recruited one who was willing to participate anonymously and disguised with a wig, mask, and extra-large tuxedo, as well as a microphone that distorted his voice.[121]

In their presentations Kameny and Gittings moved away from characterizing all psychiatrists as enemies of the gay and lesbian movement. Gittings, in particular, pointed to the gay psychiatrists and appealed to the need for a dialogue within the profession with this group. Dr. Anonymous informed the audience that there were more than two hundred homosexual psychiatrists attending the convention. Underscoring his disguised appearance, he poignantly depicted the stress experienced by gay psychiatrists who had to be closeted in order to survive professionally. He declared, "As psychiatrists who are homosexual, we must know our place and what we must do to be successful. . . . Much like a black man with white skin who chooses to live as a white man, we can't be seen with our real friends, our real homosexual family, lest our secret be known and our doom sealed." At the close of the session, Dr. Anonymous left the room still guarding his secret. John Fryer did not formally reveal his identity until the annual APA meeting in 1994.[122]

Seidenberg and Marmor each criticized the profession for its hostility to homosexuals. Marmor traced his own history of combating psychiatric orthodoxy, beginning with his 1965 introduction to *Sexual Inversion*. In that paper he had concluded that exclusive homosexuality was not inherently pathological, but it nevertheless represented a limitation to mature heterosexual development. By 1972, initially prompted by Hooker's work, he had reached the conclusion that there was no more justification for labeling exclusive homosexuality as a mental illness than there would be for exclusive heterosexuality. He also noted that while there was strong resistance to change within the APA, there were a growing number of members who shared his views. Marmor became an important ally to gay and lesbian activists when he ran for the APA presidency in 1974 on a platform that included the removal of homosexuality from the *DSM*.[123]

The 1972 panel on homosexuality marked a turning point. For the first time at an APA convention, members publicly supported the gay cause to depathologize homosexuality. The dissident movement within the profession was gaining momentum. Kameny and Gittings were delighted with the success of the panel. While change was emerging within the profession, Gittings noted that such a movement would have taken decades. It was the political pressure from the disruption of the previous years that served as the catalyst for rapid reform.[124]

Reflecting the emergence of internal professional debate, a series of position papers was published in the 1972 volume of the *International Journal of Psychiatry*. In response to a set of questions raised by Richard Green about the orthodox medical model, Marmor and Martin Hoffman voiced opposition to the traditional perspective while Charles Socarides and Lawrence Hatterer defended it. A year earlier members of two APA committees, the Task Force on Social Issues and the Committee on Nomenclature, had recommended that the classification of homosexuality be reconsidered. In reaction to the rising debate, the defenders of the medical model, led by Socarides, stiffened their opposition. In 1972 a study group chaired by Socarides reiterated the standard psychoanalytic position that homosexuality was a "disorder of sexual development . . . determined . . . [by] a faulty family constellation."[125]

In the fall of 1972, Robert Spitzer, a member of the APA's Committee on Nomenclature, came in contact with Gay Activists Alliance demonstrators at the New York meeting of the Association for Advancement of Behavior Therapy. Impressed by their arguments demanding the removal of homosexuality from the *DSM*, he agreed to present their views to the nomenclature committee. He also agreed to sponsor a debate at APA's 1973 convention on the question of whether homosexuality should be in the APA nomenclature.[126]

The GAA appointed Charles Silverstein, a gay psychologist who directed a homosexual and bisexual counseling center, to prepare a written argument for the deletion of homosexuality from the psychiatric nosology. To support the case for deletion, Silverstein also included supportive statements from several sympathetic mental health professionals, including psychiatrist Seymour Halleck and psychologists Wardell Pomeroy and Alan Bell. In his presentation to the nomenclature committee in February 1973, Silverstein cited the pioneering work of Hooker, Kinsey, and Ford and Beach, refuting the thesis that homosexuals were psychologically maladjusted. He also referred to the more recent research by psychologists and psychiatrists, such as Marvin Siegelman and the team of Marcel Saghir and Eli Robins. The written presentation ended with an appeal for immediate action. The nomenclature committee was favorably impressed and agreed to recommend that the issue about the diagnostic status of homosexuality be resolved at the 1973 APA meeting in May.[127]

Spitzer played a central role in following through on the nomenclature committee's decision to settle the diagnostic controversy. When the issue first came to his attention the previous fall, he was open to the need for discussion, but he did not personally support the idea of declassifying homosexuality. He was, however, subsequently influenced by Silverstein's arguments. He finally became convinced of the need for revision when he reviewed the primary sources, especially Saghir and Robins's large-scale study based on psychiatric interviews, which supported Hooker's research demonstrating no differences in mental health between homosexual and heterosexual samples.[128]

At the 1973 convention, Spitzer organized and chaired a panel, titled "Should Homosexuality Be in the APA Nomenclature?" that was attended by almost one thousand psychiatrists. Among the panelists, Marmor, Green, and Robert Stoller, as well as GAA activist Ronald Gold, strongly endorsed declassification, while Bieber and Socarides reiterated their emphatic defense of the medical model. The most significant consequence of the panel was the follow-up report by Spitzer, in which he outlined his proposal for deleting homosexuality from the psychiatric nomenclature. He argued that "a significant proportion of homosexuals" were satisfied with their homosexuality, showed no significant sign of pathology, and were able to function quite effectively. While homosexuality was an "irregular form of sexual behavior," it failed to meet either of the two criteria that defined all of the other mental disorders in the psychiatric nosology; that is, it did not cause subjective distress or impair social effectiveness.[129] Thus, Spitzer's argument for deleting homosexuality was not that it was within the "normal" range of sexual behavior, but rather that it did not meet the definition of mental illness. Logically following from this line of reasoning, he argued that the *DSM* should not only delete homosexuality, but also add a new category, "sexual orientation disturbance," to apply to those homosexuals who were troubled by their sexual orientation.[130]

As Ronald Bayer observes in his detailed analysis of the declassification of homosexuality, Spitzer's position served as a compromise. It satisfied the gay activists' demands for deletion and, at the same time, by adding a new category, appealed to those psychiatrists who held to the assumption that homosexuality was a suboptimal form of functioning. Yet there was still a sizable portion of psychiatrists who vehemently opposed any revision to psychiatric orthodoxy. Moreover, the gay activists did not accept the new category of sexual orientation disturbance and urged that a decision on this be delayed until after the deletion issue was resolved. The political showdown of diagnostic politics began with the presentation of Spitzer's proposal to the nomenclature committee. The committee's response was divided, and the proposal was passed on to higher echelons of the APA. In December 1973 the proposal, having successfully passed through a series of committees, was presented to the APA's board of trustees, the final arbiter.[131]

The board, with a vote of thirteen to zero and two abstentions, approved of the deletion of homosexuality and the addition of sexual orientation disturbance. A civil rights proposal opposing discrimination against homosexual men and women was also approved. In a press release, APA president Alfred Freedman noted the tremendous social significance of the board's action but emphasized that the declassification of homosexuality did not imply that it was "normal" or as desirable as heterosexuality. Robert Spitzer was more candid. When asked by a reporter for the *Advocate* whether the board's decision signified that times had changed or simply meant that the APA had been wrong all along, he responded, "I would have to say we were wrong."[132]

Gay leaders pointed to the limitations of the APA decision but nevertheless hailed it as a historic step. Ronald Gold announced, "We have won the ball game. . . . No longer can gay people grow up thinking they're sick."[133] In front pages across the country, headlines read "Doctors Rule Homosexuals Not Abnormal" and "Victory for Homosexuals."[134] Howard Brown, a noted gay physician, ironically declared, "The board's vote made millions of Americans who had been officially ill that morning officially well that afternoon. Never before in history had so many people been cured in so little time."[135]

The "ball game," however, had an extra inning to go. Led by Socarides and Bieber, the infuriated opposition demanded a referendum of the APA membership. In preparation for the vote, the newly created National Gay Task Force (NGTF) orchestrated a campaign to insure a favorable outcome. A statement urging a vote to retain the nomenclature change was sent to the members. The statement was drafted jointly by Spitzer and Gold. The three APA presidential candidates, one of whom was Marmor, agreed to sign the statement. The NGTF underwrote the full cost of the mailing. Nevertheless, to protect against negative reactions to gay political pressure, no mention was made about NGTF's involvement in writing and funding. Somewhat over ten thousand psychiatrists participated in the April 1974 referendum. The results were, in Bayer's words, "a clear, though not overwhelming" endorsement of the board's decision for nomenclature change—58 percent in favor, 37 percent opposed.[136]

Frank Kameny and Bruce Voeller, the executive director of the NGTF, were present at the APA headquarters in Washington when the vote was announced. When they heard the news, they were ecstatic. Shortly after, Voeller wrote in the *Advocate,* "All gays . . . can now view themselves with pride. . . . We're a day nearer the time when young gays will look at us with incomprehension and some embarrassment when we reminisce about such things as being in the closet and being told we're sick."[137]

Not all mental health professionals accepted the official removal of homosexuality from the psychiatric roster of mental illnesses. Socarides, in his writings, continued to carry on his disease model of homosexuality and in 1992, with psychologist Joseph Nicolosi, established the National Association for Research and Therapy of Homosexuality (NARTH), an organization committed to defending the rights of therapists to treat "dissatisfied" homosexuals. Claims of successful "reparative" or "conversion" therapy by advocates such as Socarides and Nicolosi have been refuted. In a review of the relevant research, Douglas C. Haldeman concluded, "Conversion therapy . . . reinforces the social stigma associated with homosexuality, and there is no evidence . . . to suggest that sexual orientation can be changed."[138] Continued lobbying efforts by gay and lesbian activists led to the removal in 1986 of "ego-dystonic homosexuality" (sexual orientation disturbance) from the psychiatric nosology. Thus, the last official vestige of a sanctioned medical model disappeared from American psychiatry.[139]

SANITY AND EMPOWERMENT

Thrusting off the straitjacket of sickness empowered gay men and lesbians in two ways. First, it accorded them a sense of personal pride and group solidarity, resources necessary to resist the power of heterosexist ideology. Frank Kameny had coined the motto "Gay is Good" as a rallying cry for the struggle for homosexual rights. Looking back in 1995, shortly before his seventieth birthday, he declared, "If I had to choose one particular thing I've done and put it at the pinnacle of all of which I'm proud, it would be 'Gay is Good.' It encapsulates, in a way that has been taken up by others, everything that I stand for and have worked for."[140]

Second, removing the official stamp of illness enabled gay people and their supporters to establish a legitimate foundation for communication. By the mid-1970s a fledgling interdisciplinary field of gay and lesbian studies had emerged. No longer relegated to the margins of private printings, personal journals, pulp fiction, nonmainstream publishers, and pseudonymed authorship, gay people and, more generally, supporters of homosexual rights were free to speak in their own voice. An invisible gay and lesbian minority could become visible by communicating their experiences and concerns to the larger society. An oppressed community could challenge and interrogate the intellectual, cultural, and institutionalized forces of domination. Lesbian and gay studies has implications beyond merely rendering the lives, experiences, concerns, and cultural patterns of gay and bisexual people. It subverts heterosexuality and patriarchy. The emergence of lesbian and gay studies has not been a simple linear story of progress. Stripping away the tag of pathology has not necessarily led to an embrace of lesbian and gay scholars in the academy. There have also been internal struggles for voice, most notably lesbians against gay male dominance, gay people of color against white dominance, and bisexuals and transgenderists against gay and lesbian dominance.

The removal of homosexuality from the psychiatric nosology was a turning point in the century-long struggle for lesbian and gay voice. It came about by a two-pronged attack. First, psychiatric orthodoxy had to be challenged on rational grounds; that is, the medicoscientific underpinning of homosexuality as pathology had to be revealed as myth and ideology. Kinsey's revelations about the higher-than-expected incidence of homosexual behavior set the stage for the ensuing challenge. Hooker's pathbreaking empirical comparison of the psychological adjustment of homosexual and heterosexual men opened the debate among mental health professionals.

Once armed with the scientific ammunition that could undermine the psychiatric establishment, homophile activists, led by Kameny's doggedness and oratorical talent, as well as dissident psychiatrists and psychologists were successfully able to mount their campaign of confrontation. And the political pressure of confrontation was a necessary ingredient. Through disruptive tactics, the psychiatrists were forced to listen and in the end the majority could not refute the evidence first generated by a compassionate, brave, and lone voice—Evelyn Hooker.

And what became of the two heroes in this saga? Kameny continued to be active in gay and lesbian political organizations and in 1971 became the first openly gay candidate for political office. He lost his race to be the congressional representative for the District of Columbia. Hooker ended her association with UCLA in 1970, shortly after her work on the NIMH Task Force on Homosexuality was completed. She went into private practice as a clinical psychologist and most of her patients were gay men and lesbians. She became a revered mentor for lesbian and gay psychologists and received professional awards and honors, including a mental health center at the University of Chicago that bears her name. She died in 1996 at age eighty-nine.

The impact of Hooker's work touched the lives of many. In a particularly dramatic instance of this, she cited the case of a young woman who "when her parents discovered she was a lesbian . . . put her in a psychiatric hospital. The standard procedure for treating homosexuals in that hospital was electroshock therapy. Her psychiatrist was familiar with my work, and he was able to keep them from giving it to her."[141]

Yet outside the circle of mental health specialists and those people she personally touched, her work, until recently, has not been well known. Belatedly, in 1991 the American Psychological Association gave her one of its awards for "Distinguished Contribution to Psychology in the Public Interest." The 1992 film documentary *Changing Our Minds: The Story of Dr. Evelyn Hooker* has provided some popular recognition of her accomplishments. This film was the result of the devotion she had received from the gay and lesbian psychologists she worked with. Aside from the fact that she championed a cause outside of mainstream scientific interest, her relative professional obscurity reflects the fact that her corpus of published work included only about a dozen scientific papers. Connected with her NIMH Research Career Award, she had planned to write two books—one on the life histories of the gay men she interviewed, the other on the gay male subculture. Both would have been groundbreaking contributions. Edwin Shneidman, her close friend and colleague, observes that Hooker suffered from a deep sense of inferiority. The roots of this may go back to her childhood as a poor, gangling girl who excelled academically—attributes that set her apart from her peers. And regardless of possible childhood origins, she suffered from being relegated to marginal status at UCLA because of her gender. Moreover, as Shneidman notes, she was overwhelmed by a sense of responsibility to represent and speak for the gay men she studied, men who could not speak freely about their lives. These internal struggles worked against her ability to complete and communicate her pioneering work in written form.[142]

But Hooker's own fragility and pain contributed to her gift for identifying and connecting with others who suffered. Although she was not religious, she had an evangelical quality that compelled her to act as a champion for human rights. Her friend Sam From was undoubtedly attracted to her because of these empathic attributes. And so he mobilized her to lead a crusade to emancipate gay people through her research. From's part in impelling a sympathetic and perceptive scientist to become involved in the cause of homosexual rights reflected the active role that gay people played in shaping the science that affected their lives. Whether embarking on their own scientific projects, as in the case of Magnus Hirschfeld, Jan Gay, and Thomas Painter, and/or collaborating with sex researchers (Alfred Gross with George Henry, Painter with Kinsey), gay people have historically recognized that science can be a powerful site for combating oppression and effecting social justice.

Epilogue:
Beyond 1973

> Cultural imperialism . . . [is] the decision made by one group of
> people that another shall be cut off from their past, shall be kept from
> the power of memory, context, continuity. This is why lesbians, meet-
> ing, need to tell and retell stories. . . . These stories, which bring us to-
> gether and which also confirm for each of us the path and meaning of
> her individual journey, are like the oldest tribal legends: tales of birth
> and rebirth, of death and rebirth; sometimes—too often—of death
> without rebirth.
>
> —Adrienne Rich[1]

The official eradication of homosexuality as an illness, coupled with the
political impact of Stonewall, presented new opportunities to utilize the
resources of scientific inquiry in the interests of social justice for gay
people. Over the past three decades, there has been an explosion of scientific research on gay, lesbian, and bisexual issues. I can only attempt to
highlight some of the significant trends that have taken place. In order to
contextualize this corpus of work, I briefly sketch out the path that the
American gay and lesbian movement has taken as well as the institutional
infrastructures that emerged to support, and in some cases resist, these
projects. After looking at some examples of gay and lesbian emancipatory
research, I close by revisiting the pre-Stonewall activist-researchers.

In the aftermath of Stonewall, the coming out story embodied the explosion of gay and lesbian visibility on the national landscape. Sharing the
painful journey and the epiphany of accepting and revealing one's sexual
identity served to cement the new group consciousness of lesbians and gay
men. Moreover, coming out represented an annunciation of gay and les-

bian pride to straight society. Sickness was replaced by a celebration of gay and lesbian identity. Coming out no longer signified the pre-Stonewall introduction to gay society. It now symbolized the challenge to be accepted into the straight world.[2]

By the mid-1970s, however, the gay and lesbian movement faced growing tensions from within its ranks as well as rising social hostility in the wake of the conservative turn of the country. The male-dominated gay rights movement of the early 1970s alienated lesbians, who, in turn, felt increasing affinity with the women's movement. Lesbian feminism was concerned not only with homophobia, but also with sexism. The definition of lesbianism reached beyond its sexual connotation to include "political lesbians," that is, women who felt an emotional solidarity with, though not sexual attraction to, other women. Lesbian separatism consolidated a new sense of lesbian identity infused with the precepts of feminist nationalism. Nevertheless, as Barry Adam notes, the removal of sexuality from lesbian identity also produced tensions within the lesbian movement regarding the distinct nature of lesbianism.[3]

By the late 1970s a reactionary trend against the gains of the civil rights and women's movements took hold. The conservative backlash in the form of the New Right became especially virulent against the gay and lesbian movement. In fact, as John D'Emilio points out, gays and lesbians became the scapegoats of the New Right's agenda to preserve "family values." Gays and lesbians posed a threat to the traditional view of the nuclear family with its inscribed gender roles and patriarchal hierarchy. Indeed, by the 1970s the stability of the nuclear family was besieged by the growing divorce rate. Gender roles within intact families were also being redefined as growing numbers of women joined the workforce. Moreover, gays and lesbians built their lives outside of the heterosexual nuclear family and thus for the New Right signified a threat to conventional domestic relations.[4]

The New Right's antigay attack was sparked in 1977 by the Dade County, Florida, "Save Our Children" campaign, launched by Anita Bryant. The campaign, led by a coalition of conservative religious leaders and politicians, was successful in repealing a six-month civil rights ordinance prohibiting sexual orientation discrimination. In response, gay and lesbian political organization was successful the following year in turning back an antigay initiative in California. Nevertheless, as D'Emilio observes, by the early 1980s the New Right, not the gay and lesbian movement, was setting the terms of the debate. Throughout the 1980s and 1990s, the gay and lesbian movement was involved in fighting against various antigay initiatives with mixed success.

Lesbian and gay politics was also reshaped by the impact of the AIDS epidemic, starting in the early 1980s. Adding ammunition to the New

Right's pro-family agenda, gay men were targeted as public menaces. Evangelical religious leaders and conservative politicians led the attack. Under the guise of public health, as Stephen Murray points out, homosexuality was remedicalized. Gay men were blamed for being struck with and spreading AIDS.[5]

In response, gay and lesbian activists mounted an effective campaign to deal with the epidemic and the attack by the New Right. AIDS brought about a rapprochement between gay and lesbian organizations as well as establishing coalitions with mainstream institutions, such as the public health system. It also produced a return to the confrontational radical protests of the gay liberation era in the form of "queer politics." By the early 1990s militant action groups appeared, such as Queer Nation and ACT UP. The term "queer" in the pre-Stonewall era had been used as a self-identification by gay men and pejoratively by straight society. In the 1990s it signified a radical identity of proclaiming difference from heterosexist society and thus became an umbrella term uniting gays, lesbians, bisexuals, transsexuals, transgenderists, and any others, including heterosexuals, who challenged heterosexism. Moreover, queer nationalism became a force in countries where gay civil rights had met with little success. "Queer" as a label, however, also turned away many gays and lesbians because of its pejorative association and its signification of separatism, which goes against coalition politics.[6]

In the 1990s and into the twenty-first century, the struggle for gay and lesbian rights has become more visible. Heterosexist institutions, such as the military, child adoption, and marriage, have been challenged. Gays and lesbians who want to have the same rights as heterosexuals have in joining the military, adopting children, and entering into legalized relationships threaten the very core of heterosexist ideology. Especially with respect to marriage, gay and lesbian unions undermine the heterosexist assumptions that sex, not love, defines what it means to be homosexual. Beyond the challenges to the military, the family, and legalized relationships, by the 1990s gays and lesbians became increasingly visible in various institutions, including politics, the media, and the university. It is thus not surprising that there has been a backlash in the form of increasing antigay violence. The 1998 brutal killing of Matthew Shepard, a gay college student, raised the national consciousness about a basic issue of gay and lesbian rights—hate crimes, specifically, and the need to combat homophobia, generally.

Gay and lesbian studies emerged within the wake of the gay and lesbian movement of the 1970s. The Gay Academic Union was organized in 1973 and brought together academicians from diverse fields who were connected by their desire to confront homophobia and create a place for gay and lesbian studies in their universities. This relatively short-lived organization, however, was unable to resolve the tensions generated by the dominance of gay men, which resulted in the alienation and departure of most lesbian members by 1975. A more successful approach to the nurturing of gay and lesbian studies was the establishment by the mid-1970s of lesbian and gay caucuses within various professional organizations, including psychiatry, psychology, sociology, anthropology, history, and modern languages. These organizations provided academic networks that supported research and theorizing on gay and lesbian issues. The interdisciplinary *Journal of Homosexuality* was founded in 1974 and has since served as a significant vehicle for disseminating research. By the late 1980s gay and lesbian studies achieved formal status within academic settings, encompassing such subfields as literary criticism, film studies, gender studies, philosophy, history, anthropology, sociology, psychology, and biology. The model had already been pioneered in Dutch universities as early as 1978. The first American department of gay and lesbian studies was established at the City College of San Francisco in 1988. Research centers were established at Yale in 1987 and the City University of New York in 1990. These beginnings led to the establishment of gay and lesbian curricula and programs in many colleges and universities in the 1990s.[7]

With the rise of the New Right in the 1980s, however, a research infrastructure appeared that was antithetical to the interests of gay and lesbian rights. Paul Cameron, a psychologist associated with the Family Research Council, a pro-family organization founded in the early 1980s, conducted a series of survey research studies in the 1980s and 1990s. This research program was aimed at demonstrating that homosexuals were a threat to public health, the social order, and the well-being of children. While his work appeared in quasi-scientific periodicals and was thus rarely cited in the mainstream scientific literature, it had an impact on public policy. He was a paid consultant in the 1992 Colorado political campaign to support discrimination against gay men, lesbians, and bisexuals. His work was also cited by the Pentagon's Military Working Group, which recommended against President Clinton's plan in the early 1990s to allow openly gay personnel to serve in the military. Moreover, *The Gay Agenda,* a widely distributed, church-produced video, featuring sensationalistic footage of lewd behavior at a gay pride parade, contained statistics on homosexual promiscuity based on Cameron's research.[8]

Psychologist Gregory M. Herek critically reviewed Cameron's work and concluded that it was so seriously flawed on methodological grounds that it was scientifically meaningless. Purportedly based on a national survey of sexual attitudes and behavior, the research suffered from inadequate sampling, an unacceptably low response rate, a poorly constructed questionnaire, and poorly trained interviewers who may have been biased. In addition, Cameron's biases were publicized to potential respondents while data were being collected.[9]

Beginning in the 1990s, the Family Research Council has worked closely with various organizations aimed at converting gay men and lesbians to a heterosexual adjustment. These include the National Association for Research and Therapy of Homosexuality (NARTH), an association of mental health professionals who claim therapeutic success, and Exodus International, a religious network committed to eradicating homosexual behavior through Christian inspiration. There is no scientific evidence that sexual orientation can be changed and, as psychologist Douglas C. Haldeman points out, it is ethically irresponsible to promote such programs that reinforce the stigma of homosexuality.[10]

Gay and lesbian research in the post-Stonewall era developed within the supportive context of the gay and lesbian movement and in response to the antigay attack, led by the New Right. It thus serves as a vehicle for representing and understanding the experiences and concerns of gay people as well as providing accurate data to challenge social hostility and heterosexist institutions. Reflecting the climate of gay and lesbian liberation in the 1970s, the experience of forming a gay or lesbian identity became an early focus of research. Summarizing this work in the late 1980s, Richard Troiden delineated a normative model in which an individual journeys from the first signs of sexual difference, through phases of identity confusion, identity acceptance (coming out), and finally a commitment to adopting homosexuality as a way of life. Central to the capacity to accept oneself as gay or lesbian was the sense of belonging to a community of others who shared the pain of alienation and became empowered by self-validation. The political impact of gay and lesbian liberation plus the removal of the aura of institutionalized pathology had made a difference. Compared with the pre-Stonewall era, a much more visible and diverse gay and lesbian community was available as a resource for self-acceptance. Most significant was the fact that gay men and lesbians were accorded the opportunity to tell their stories to social scientists who were sensitive to their own reflexive position as a partner in a dialogue with their research participants. They were thus concerned with conveying the feelings and experiences of the people they studied.[11]

The research on identity, however, tended to accentuate a fixed, monolithic gay and lesbian identity. More recent research has been expanded to include the racial and ethnic diversity of the gay and lesbian community. This work reveals the complex nature of multiple sources of oppression and discrimination. Lesbians of color, for example, must deal not only with homophobia, but also racism and sexism and thus face a confusing maze of loyalties and estrangements. Generational differences in identity have also been examined. Research demonstrated that by the 1990s, as gays and lesbians became more visible, gay and lesbian youths became more victimized as targets of antigay attacks. Moreover, reflecting the general trends of adolescent sexuality, gay and lesbian youths came out at earlier ages. The net result of these historical changes is that gay and lesbian youths, as a group, suffer higher-than-average rates of suicide and other mental health problems as well as other risk factors, including familial rejection and exposure to HIV/AIDS.[12]

The research on gay and lesbian relationships provides an excellent example of how research results can refute stereotypes and thus present an accurate and realistic depiction of gay and lesbian life. This had been the objective of such pioneer activist-researchers as Jan Gay and Thomas Painter. The stereotypes about relationships that have been refuted include the belief that homosexuals do not want enduring relationships and cannot achieve them, and the assumption that gay relationships are unhappy, dysfunctional, and deviant. Research on gay and lesbian parenting is another example of countering stereotyped beliefs. Research consistently demonstrates that the children of gay and lesbian parents do not differ from children of heterosexual parents in overall social or psychological adjustment. This refutes the general assumption that gays and lesbians have adverse effects on their children and thus has significant implications in the campaign for the legal protection of gays' and lesbians' parental rights. In general, research on gay relationships and parenting challenges the heterosexist definitions and meanings of marriage and family.[13]

The examination of antigay attitudes and behavior provides insight into the motivations that drive prejudice toward gays and lesbians. Individuals committed to traditional norms and values believe that their interests and status will be lost by social change. They have a stake in upholding the social order and thus possess a general willingness to submit to legitimate authority. Lesbians and gays are viewed as threats to conventional values and hence are perceived to hold dissimilar values. This profile of prejudiced individuals suggests strategies for producing attitude change. A study by Geoffrey Haddock and Mark P. Zanna found that antigay attitudes were reduced when research subjects were given information that gay men, in fact, believed in such traditional values as individual freedom and the importance of the nuclear family. Other research indicates that antigay attitudes and antigay violence serve as vehicles for maintaining gender norms and as compensations for feelings of alienation and social powerlessness. In general, as Herek points out, research on antigay sentiments holds the promise of combating prejudice and enriching intergroup relations.[14]

Research on gay and lesbian issues as well as bisexuality and transgenderism is an intrinsic part of the continuing struggle by sexual and gender minorities for social justice. It provides gays, lesbians, bisexuals, and transgendered people the opportunity to express their concerns and portray their lives and cultural milieu, in essence, to articulate, to make visible, to demystify the gay and transgender experience, and thereby influence public policy. In the twenty-first century, emancipatory research will continue to be generated and utilized as it was in the past, when it was successfully used to challenge the assumption that homosexuality was pathological. Over the last three decades, emancipatory research has shed light on a number of issues, including identity, diversity within the lesbian and gay community, and the nature of committed relationships and gay families. It has also served as a means of challenging the organized oppression of the New Right. Most significantly, research on gay and transgender issues has emancipatory potential not only for sexual and gender dissenters, but also for the larger society. It is part of the larger framework of gaining knowledge about our cultural diversity and, as such, breaks down rigid boundaries of gender, sexuality, family relations, and class and racial hierarchies. It is likely that as we move thorough the twenty-first century, the emancipatory science of sexuality and gender will be actively engaged in both assessing and driving the changing definitions of marriage, family, and gender.[15]

But the liberatory spirit of emancipatory research aimed at rights for sexual and gender minorities has a long history that predates the 1970s. Magnus Hirschfeld captured that spirit with his aphorism *Per scientiam ad justitiam*—"Through Science to Justice." In America in the early twentieth century, there were several isolated attempts by homosexual activist-researchers to mount a defense of homosexuality, most notably Edward Prime-Stevenson and Earl Lind. Prime-Stevenson, drawing in part on Hirschfeld's work, provided a comprehensive history and ethnography of the gay world, but his work remained obscure because of its limited publication. Lind wrote about his own personal experience of alienation and oppression and provided a moving and enriched documentation of life in the urban gay subculture of the late nineteenth and early twentieth centuries. His work was also consigned to obscurity because of limited accessibility.

The two most remarkable figures in this long history are Jan Gay and Thomas Painter. Gay, influenced by the work of Hirschfeld, launched an ambitious case history study of lesbians and attempted to bring it to publication with the sponsorship of recognized medical and scientific experts. With sexologist Robert Latou Dickinson's support, she expanded her study to include gay men. Unfortunately, her project was taken over by psychiatrist George W. Henry and she lost her input and authorship. Her daring and creative legacy, however, has survived in the published case histories in Henry's *Sex Variants,* which contain the voices of the gay and lesbian research participants. Thus, through her efforts, we have a window on the gay and lesbian urban subculture of the 1930s.

Thomas Painter undertook a pioneering ethnographic project about the lives and experiences of gay men and male hustlers in the 1930s. His work was never published, in part because of his own lack of discipline, but also because he had no institutionalized support. As an openly gay man, he was blocked from any official research or academic affiliation. Fortunately, he was inspired by Alfred Kinsey to keep a journal of his life experiences and consequently provided a detailed and enriched account of his life over a thirty-year period. With the support of Kinsey and his colleagues at the Kinsey Institute, Painter's work has been preserved. It provides a unique and valuable look at male prostitution in early-twentieth-century America. The great tragedy of both Gay's and Painter's lives is that because of who they were, openly homosexual, their contributions were consigned to obscurity and their potential as researchers was robbed.

Alfred A. Gross, as a result of his own shrewdness and cunning, was more successful in managing his career as a gay activist-researcher. Using his association with Henry, he was able to carve out a career as a researcher and a social worker. Although beset by his own homophobia, he was able to create and manage a community organization that delivered spiritual, psychological, legal, and vocational help to young gay men in legal trouble. And remarkably, he carried this out in the 1950s and early 1960s, when there were no established models for such an enterprise. By the mid-1960s, with the rise of a militant homophile movement, his paternalistic approach became outdated and he grudgingly acknowledged this when he retired in the early 1970s.

This early history would not be complete without including the contributions and efforts by two compassionate professional sex researchers, Alfred Kinsey and Evelyn Hooker. Kinsey's studies on the sexual behavior of American men and women had profound effects in liberalizing sexual attitudes. In particular, his demonstration of the commonplace of homosexuality became a source of support for the fledgling homophile movement of the 1950s. Moreover, he established a wide variety of close, personal relationships with gay men, including Painter, and as such, was an inspiring figure. Evelyn Hooker's friendship with a group of young gay men instilled a deep commitment to carry out research that would challenge the untested assumption that homosexuals were psychologically maladjusted. Indeed, her research sent shock waves through the mental health community and served, along with Kinsey's work, as the rationale for challenging the American Psychiatric Association's designation of homosexuality as a mental illness. Research results alone would not be enough to produce institutional change, but with the political leverage of the homophile movement, led by activist Frank Kameny, the official medical model was erased. With the legitimacy of "sanity" and the impact of gay liberation, gay and lesbian research came of age. This emancipatory research is the legacy of the courageous efforts by a group of pioneering activist-researchers and the dogged determination by two caring professional scientists.

Notes

Chapter 1

1. On critical or emancipatory social science, see Brian Fay, *Critical Social Science* (Ithaca, N.Y.: Cornell University Press, 1987); Patti Lather, *Getting Smart: Feminist Research and Pedagogy With/In the Postmodern* (New York: Routledge, 1991), chaps. 1, 2.

2. On situated knowledges, see Donna Haraway, *Simians, Cyborgs, and Women: The Reinvention of Nature* (New York: Routledge, 1991).

3. Donna Haraway, "Primatology Is Politics by Other Means," in *Feminist Approaches to Science,* ed. Ruth Bleier (New York: Pergamon, 1986), 77–118.

4. James D. Steakley, "*Per scientiam ad justitiam:* Magnus Hirschfeld and the Sexual Politics of Innate Homosexuality," in *Science and Homosexualities,* ed. Vernon A. Rosario (New York: Routledge, 1997), 133–54.

5. George Chauncey Jr., Martin Duberman, and Martha Vicinus, introduction to *Hidden from History: Reclaiming the Gay and Lesbian Past,* ed. Martin Duberman, Martha Vicinus, and George Chauncey Jr. (New York: New American Library, 1989), 1–13.

6. George W. Henry, *Sex Variants: A Study of Homosexual Patterns,* 2 vols. (New York: Hoeber, 1941).

Chapter 2

1. Havelock Ellis, *Sexual Inversion,* 2nd ed. (Philadelphia: F. A. Davis, 1901). On Jeb Alexander, see Paul Robinson, *Gay Lives: Homosexual Autobiography from John Addington Symonds to Paul Monette* (Chicago: University of Chicago Press, 1999), 269–82. Jeb Alexander, *Jeb and Dash: A Diary of Gay Life, 1918–1945,* ed. Ina Russell (Boston: Faber and Faber, 1993).

2. Jeffrey Weeks, *Coming Out: Homosexual Politics in Britain, from the Nineteenth Century to the Present,* rev. ed. (London: Quartet Books, 1990), chap. 3; Randolph Trumbach, "Sodomitical Assaults, Gender Roles, and Sexual Development in Eighteenth-Century London," *Journal of Homosexuality* 16, nos. 1/2 (1988): 407–49. Also see David Higgs, ed., *Queer Sites: Gay Urban Histories since 1600* (New York: Routledge, 1999).

3. Quoted in Jonathan Ned Katz, ed., *Gay/Lesbian Almanac: A New Documentary* (New York: Harper & Row, 1983), 157.

4. Ibid., 258.

5. For histories of the late-nineteenth- and early-twentieth-century gay communities, see George Chauncey, *Gay New York: Gender, Urban Culture, and the Making of the Gay Male World, 1890–1940* (New York: Basic Books, 1994); David K. Johnson, "The Kids of Fairytown: Gay Male Culture on Chicago's Near North Side in the 1930s," in *Creating a Place for Ourselves: Lesbian, Gay,*

and Bisexual Community Histories, ed. Brett Beemyn (New York: Routledge, 1997), 97–118; Nan Alamilla Boyd, "'Homos Invade S.F.!'" in Creating a Place for Ourselves, ed. Beemyn, 73–95.

6. On the Newport community, see George Chauncey Jr., "Christian Brotherhood or Sexual Perversion? Homosexual Identities and the Construction of Sexual Boundaries in the World War I Era," in Hidden from History: Reclaiming the Gay and Lesbian Past, ed. Martin Duberman, Martha Vicinus, and George Chauncey Jr. (New York: New American Library, 1989), 294–317. On the New York gay community, see Chauncey, Gay New York. Some labels had different meanings in different locations. In Newport during the World War I era, "queer" was used to refer to effeminate gay men. In New York beginning around the turn of the twentieth century, "queer" was associated with masculine-identified gay men.

7. Lillian Faderman, Odd Girls and Twilight Lovers: A History of Lesbian Life in Twentieth-Century America (New York: Columbia University Press, 1991), chap. 1; Joanne Meyerowitz, "Sexual Geography and Gender Economy: The Furnished Room Districts of Chicago, 1890–1930," in Gender and American History since 1890, ed. Barbara Melosh (New York: Routledge, 1993), 43–71.

8. Leila J. Rupp, "'Imagine My Surprise': Women's Relationships in Mid-Twentieth Century America," in Hidden from History, ed. Duberman, Vicinus, and Chauncey, 395–410. On the changes in American views about sexuality between the 1880s and the 1920s, see John D'Emilio and Estelle B. Freedman, Intimate Matters: A History of Sexuality in America, 2nd ed. (Chicago: University of Chicago Press, 1997), chaps. 8–10.

9. On lesbian communities in America in the 1920s, see Faderman, Odd Girls, chap. 3. On lesbian Harlem, see Faderman, Odd Girls, 72–79; Eric Garber, "A Spectacle of Color: The Lesbian and Gay Subculture of Jazz Age Harlem," in Hidden from History, ed. Duberman, Vicinus, and Chauncey, 318–31.

10. On Salt Lake City's Bohemian Club and gay and lesbian community, see D. Michael Quinn, Same-Sex Dynamics among Nineteenth-Century Americans: A Mormon Example (Urbana: University of Illinois Press, 1996), chap. 6.

11. Erwin J. Haeberle, "Sexology: Conception, Birth, and Growth of a Science," in Emerging Dimensions of Sexology: Selected Papers from the Proceedings of the Sixth World Congress of Sexology, ed. R. Taylor Segraves and Erwin J. Haeberle (New York: Prager, 1984), 9–28.

12. For a discussion of the history and legacy of sexology, see Jeffrey Weeks, Sexuality and Its Discontents: Meanings, Myths and Modern Sexualities (London: Routledge & Kegan Paul, 1985), chap. 4.

13. On Ulrichs, see Hubert Kennedy, Ulrichs: The Life and Works of Karl Heinrich Ulrichs, Pioneer of the Modern Gay Movement (Boston: Alyson, 1988); idem, "Karl Heinrich Ulrichs, First Theorist of Homosexuality," in Science and Homosexualities, ed. Vernon A. Rosario (New York: Routledge, 1997), 26–45. Ulrichs's work has been translated; see Karl Heinrich Ulrichs, The Riddle of Man-Manly Love, 2 vols., trans. Michael A. Lombardi-Nash, introduction by Vern L. Bullough (1864–80; reprint, Amherst, N.Y.: Prometheus Books, 1994).

14. Quoted in Katz, Gay/Lesbian Almanac, 273, excerpt reprinted from Havelock Ellis, "Sexual Inversion in Women," Alienist and Neurologist 16

(1895): 141–58. Karl Friedrich Otto Westphal, "Die conträre Sexualempfindung: Symptom eines neuropathischen (psychopathischen) Zustandes," *Archiv für Psychiatrie und Nervenkrankheiten* 2 (1869): 73–108; Richard von Krafft-Ebing, *Psychopathia sexualis, with Especial Reference to Contrary Sexual Instinct: A Medico-Legal Study,* trans. Gilbert Chaddock (1886; reprint, Philadelphia: F. A. Davis, 1893). On Hirschfeld, see James D. Steakley, *"Per scientiam ad justitiam:* Magnus Hirschfeld and the Sexual Politics of Innate Homosexuality," in *Science and Homosexualities,* ed. Rosario, 133–54.

15. Sigmund Freud, *Three Contributions to the Theory of Sex* (1905; reprint, New York: Dutton, 1965); George Chauncey Jr., "From Sexual Inversion to Homosexuality: Medicine and the Changing Conceptualization of Female Deviance," in *Passion and Power: Sexuality in History,* ed. Kathy Piess and Christina Simmons (Philadelphia: Temple University Press, 1989), 87–117.

16. Symonds wrote two privately published pamphlets on homosexuality, in 1883 and 1891, one dealing with ancient Greece and the other with ethics in modern society. On Carpenter and Westermarck, see Edward Carpenter, *Intermediate Types among Primitive Folk: A Study of Social Evolution,* 2nd ed. (London: Allen & Unwin, 1919; reprint, New York: Arno Press, 1975); Edward Westermarck, *The Origin and Development of Moral Ideas,* 2nd ed., 2 vols. (London: Macmillan, 1917), vol. 2, chap. 43, "Homosexual Love."

17. Lisa Duggan, "The Trials of Alice Mitchell: Sensationalism, Sexology, and the Lesbian Subject in Turn-of-the-Century America," *Signs: Journal of Women in Culture and Society* 18 (1993): 791–814; Ellis, *Sexual Inversion,* 121. Mitchell was convicted of murder and sent to the Tennessee State Insane Asylum, where she died in 1898, apparently a suicidal death.

18. Radclyffe Hall, *The Well of Loneliness, with a Commentary by Havelock Ellis* (New York: Covici-Friede, 1928); Duggan, "Alice Mitchell," 810. On the connection between medical discourse and lesbian self-representations in the early twentieth century, see Esther Newton, "The Mythic Mannish Lesbian: Radclyffe Hall and the New Woman," in *Hidden from History,* ed. Duberman, Vicinus, and Chauncey, 281–93. On the connection between Hall's own sexual identity and her novel *The Well of Loneliness,* see Judith Halberstam, *Female Masculinity* (Durham, N.C.: Duke University Press, 1998), chap. 3.

19. Quoted in Katz, *Gay/Lesbian Almanac,* 196.

20. Ibid., 187, 191. For an overview of early American medical case reports, see Bert Hansen, "American Physicians' Earliest Writings about Homosexuals, 1880–1900," *Millbank Quarterly* 67 (1989): 92–108.

21. Quoted in Katz, *Gay/Lesbian Almanac,* 319.

22. Quoted in Harry Oosterhuis, "Richard von Krafft-Ebing's 'Step-Children of Nature': Psychiatry and the Making of Homosexual Identity," in *Science and Homosexualities,* ed. Rosario, 67, 69, 80.

23. Ibid., 76, 75.

24. Katharine Bement Davis, *Factors in the Sex Life of Twenty-two Hundred Women* (New York: Harper & Brothers, 1929; reprint, New York: Arno Press, 1972). On Davis's life and career, see Ellen Fitzpatrick, *Endless Crusade: Women Social Scientists and Progressive Reform* (New York: Oxford University Press, 1990). On American sex surveys, see Vern L. Bullough, *Science in the Bedroom: A History of Sex Research* (New York: Basic Books, 1994), 107–19.

25. Quoted in Davis, *Sex Life,* 282, 283. In some of the case studies, homo-

sexual experiences were problematic. One single woman confided that she was "ashamed" and believed that her one homosexual experience had been "mentally injurious." The married women expressed a variety of feelings. Some believed that their premarital homosexual experiences helped their marriage, others that it worked against their ability to have a successful marriage.

26. Samuel Kahn, *Mentality and Homosexuality* (Boston: Meador, 1937), 14, 25.

27. Alexander Berkman, *Prison Memoirs of an Anarchist,* introduction by Hutchins Hapsgood, new introduction by Paul Goodman (1912; reprint, New York: Schocken, 1970). Excerpts dealing with homosexuality are reproduced in Jonathan Ned Katz, ed., *Gay American History: Lesbians and Gay Men in the U.S.A.* (New York: Crowell, 1976), 537, 538. Katz notes that, according to Emma Goldman, one commercial publisher approached about printing Berkman's work wanted the homosexual material to be removed.

28. On Terman's career, see Henry L. Minton, *Lewis M. Terman: Pioneer in Psychological Testing* (New York: New York University Press, 1988). On the development of the M-F test, see Lewis M. Terman and Catharine Cox Miles, *Sex and Personality: Studies in Masculinity and Femininity* (New York: McGraw-Hill, 1936). All of the gay men in the volunteer sample were effeminate and played the passive role sexually (as judged by the researchers) and, as Terman expected, they scored in the femininity end of the M-F test. Eighteen gay male case studies were included in *Sex and Personality.* In the 1920s and 1930s, there were also a series of studies carried out by sociology students at the University of Chicago in which gay men were recruited to take part in investigations of urban life in Chicago. As in the case of Terman's volunteers, these unpublished investigations convey the same quality of eagerness among the recruited subjects to participate in research about homosexuality. On the Chicago studies, see Johnson, "The Kids of Fairytown."

29. Quoted in Oosterhuis, "Richard von Krafft-Ebing's," 77.

30. Ibid., 72–79.

31. Quoted in Katz, *Gay/Lesbian Almanac,* 338, 458.

32. Xavier Mayne [Edward I. Prime-Stevenson], *The Intersexes: A History of Similisexualism as a Problem in Social Life* (Naples: privately printed, 1908; reprint, New York: Arno Press, 1975); Earl Lind [pseud.], *Autobiography of an Androgyne* (New York: Medico-Legal Journal, 1918; reprint, New York: Arno Press, 1975); Ralph Werther [alternative pseudonym for Earl Lind], "A Fairie's Reply to Dr. Lichtenstein," *Medical Review of Reviews* 27 (1921): 539–42. On American medical views about homosexuality, see Jennifer Terry, *An American Obsession: Science, Medicine, and Homosexuality in Modern American Society* (Chicago: University of Chicago Press, 1999), chap. 3; Erin G. Carlston, "'A Finer Differentiation': Female Homosexuality and the American Medical Community, 1926–1940," in *Science and Homosexualities,* ed. Rosario, 177–96.

33. Quoted in Katz, *Gay/Lesbian Almanac,* 424.

34. See, for example, Magnus Hirschfeld, *Die Homosexualität des Mannes und des Weibes* (Berlin: Louis Marcus, 1914); Edward Carpenter, *The Intermediate Sex* (London: Allen & Unwin, 1908).

35. Edward I. Prime-Stevenson, *The White Cockades: An Incident of the "Forty-five"* (New York: Scribner, 1887); idem, *Left to Themselves: Being the Ordeal of Philip and Gerald* (New York: Hunt and Eaton, 1891); Xavier Mayne [Ed-

ward I. Prime-Stevenson], *Imre: A Memorandum* (Naples: R. Respoli, 1906; reprint, New York: Arno Press, 1975); idem, *The Intersexes*; Carpenter, *The Intermediate Sex;* Hirschfeld, *Die Homosexualität.* There is a question about where and when *The Intersexes* was printed. Katz, in his *Gay American History,* 631, believes that Prime-Stevenson's Naples publisher, R. Respoli, published his book. Prime-Stevenson (*The Intersexes,* xii) indicated that the book had been essentially written by 1901, but there was a publication delay. The published version appears to have actually been printed after 1908 as there is a reference to an April 1909 item (521). Only 125 copies were printed (v). There is only limited information of Prime-Stevenson's life. For a pioneering article, see Noel L. Garde [pseud.], "The Mysterious Father of American Homophile Literature; A Historical Study," *ONE Institute Quarterly of Homophile Studies* 1, no. 3 (fall 1958): 94–98.

36. Mayne [Prime-Stevenson], *The Intersexes,* ix–x. Prime-Stevenson used a variety of terms for homosexuality that were popular in the discourse of the late nineteenth century. These included similisexualism, homosexualism, Uranianism (for men), and Uraniadism (for women). The latter two were derived from Plato's *Symposium.*

37. Mayne [Prime-Stevenson], *The Intersexes,* 515.

38. Ibid., 129, chaps. 5, 6.

39. Ibid., 121.

40. Ibid., 119–22; the case studies appear on 88–110.

41. Ibid., 280, chaps. 8, 9.

42. Ibid., 640.

43. Ibid., 638–41, 426–38, 221–22.

44. Lind, *Autobiography,* 1–3, 26.

45. Earl Lind [pseud.], *The Female-Impersonators* (New York: Medico-Legal Journal, 1922; reprint, New York: Arno Press, 1975), 67; emphasis in original.

46. Lind, *Autobiography,* 82–83.

47. Ibid., 24–25.

48. Ibid., xii.

49. Sales for *The Female-Impersonators* were targeted to clergymen, teachers, and writers as well as the same readership for *Autobiography* (physicians, lawyers, legislators, psychologists, and sociologists). A planned third book by Lind, *Riddle of the Underworld,* to be published by the *Medico-Legal Journal,* was advertised at the end of *The Female-Impersonators,* but it is not clear if this was eventually published and, if so, whether any copies survived. This third book was to deal at greater length with the fairy subculture.

50. Lind, *Female-Impersonators,* 48, 39. Crisp described his political use of effeminacy in Quentin Crisp, *The Naked Civil Servant* (New York: Holt, Rinehart & Winston, 1977). On Crisp, also see Robinson, *Gay Lives,* 149–67.

51. Byrne R. S. Fone, *A Road to Stonewall: Male Homosexuality and Homophobia in English and American Literature, 1750–1969* (New York: Twayne, 1995), 207. On the prevalence of homosexual relations engaged in by working-class youths, see Chauncey, *Gay New York,* chap. 3.

52. Lind, *Female-Impersonators,* 151.

53. Fone, *Road to Stonewall,* 207. On the cultural role of the fairy, see Chauncey, *Gay New York,* chap. 2.

54. Claude Hartland, *The Story of a Life* (St. Louis: privately printed, 1901; reprint, San Francisco: Grey Fox Press, 1985), v.

55. Julie Abraham, "Introduction to the New Edition," in Diana Frederics [pseud.], *Diana: A Strange Autobiography* (New York: Dial Press, 1939; reprint, New York: New York University Press, 1995), xvii–xxxv; Mary Casal [pseud.], *The Stone Wall; An Autobiography* (Chicago: Enycourt Press, 1930; reprint, New York: Arno Press, 1975). On Casal, also see Katz, *Gay American History,* 548–50.

56. Victor Robinson, introduction to Frederics, *Diana,* xxxvii. On Frederics's use of autobiography, see Abraham, "Introduction to the New Edition."

57. Elisabeth Craigin [pseud.], *Either Is Love* (New York: Harcourt Brace, 1937; reprint, New York: Arno Press, 1975), 147–48.

58. Ibid., 69.

59. Frederics, *Diana,* 72–73.

60. Mildred J. Berryman, "The Psychological Phenomena of the Homosexual," unpublished manuscript, 13 November 1938, June Mazer Lesbian Collection, Gay and Lesbian Archives, West Hollywood, Calif. A brief summary of the study appears in Vern Bullough and Bonnie Bullough, "Lesbianism in the 1920s and 1930s: A Newfound Study," *Signs: Journal of Women in Culture and Society* 2 (1977): 895–904. A more extensive treatment is provided in Quinn, *Same-Sex Dynamics,* chap. 7.

61. Quoted in Quinn, *Same-Sex Dynamics,* 218, 219.

62. Ibid., 203.

63. Quoted in Bullough and Bullough, "Lesbianism in the 1920s and 1930s," 903, 902. It is not clear why Berryman's gay male sample was primarily made up of effeminate men. According to Quinn (*Same-Sex Dynamics,* 206), her study included less than one-fifth of the gay men she knew. In contrast, about half of the lesbians she knew were included in her sample. It is thus possible that her masculine bias may have influenced the representativeness of her male sample. In Terman's study of masculinity-femininity, all of the gay men in his San Francisco sample were effeminate. In that case, friendship networks may have been the major influencing factor because the sample was recruited by the first gay man interviewed, who was himself effeminate. In the case of the much larger gay male sample included in the New York sex variants study (see chapter 3), there was a cross section of effeminate and masculine volunteers.

64. Quoted in Quinn, *Same-Sex Dynamics,* 219.

65. Mayne [Prime-Stevenson], *The Intersexes,* 515. On other cities, see Chauncey, *Gay New York;* Terman and Miles, *Sex and Personality* (San Francisco); Johnson, "Kids of Fairytown" (Chicago).

66. Quinn, *Same-Sex Dynamics,* 196; Bullough and Bullough, "Lesbianism in the 1920s and 1930s," 896–98.

67. On the history of American gay male fiction, see Fone, *Road to Stonewall.* On lesbian novels as well as plays in the 1930s, see Faderman, *Odd Girls,* 99–105.

Chapter 3

1. Jan Gay, "Qualifications for the Proposed 'Evaluation of the Group Therapy Techniques and Dynamics of Alcoholics Anonymous'" (typescript, 3 pp.), 1, attached to Gay to Alfred C. Kinsey, 25 October 1950, Kinsey Institute Archives, Indiana University. Quote reprinted by permission of The Kinsey Institute for Research in Sex, Gender, and Reproduction, Inc.

2. George W. Henry, "Psychogenic Factors in Overt Homosexuality," *American Journal of Psychiatry* 93 (1937): 898. A more extended version of this case study was included in George W. Henry, *Sex Variants: A Study of Homosexual Patterns*, 2 vols. (New York: Hoeber, 1941), 2:563–70. In the latter publication, the pseudonym was changed to Pearl M. and instead of being identified as an actress, she was listed as a singer. In actuality this woman was Edna Thomas, an African American actress who was prominent in Harlem homosexual circles. Thomas's lesbian partner was also included in Henry, *Sex Variants*, 2:672–81, as Pamela D. For a discussion of Harlem's homosexual subculture, see Eric Garber, "A Spectacle in Color: The Lesbian and Gay Subculture of Jazz Age Harlem," in *Hidden from History: Reclaiming the Gay and Lesbian Past*, ed. Martin Duberman, Martha Vicinus, and George Chauncey Jr. (New York: New American Library, 1989), 318–31.

3. On Dickinson, see David M. Kennedy, *Birth Control in America: The Career of Margaret Sanger* (New Haven: Yale University Press, 1970), chap. 7; James Reed, *From Private Vice to Public Virtue: The Birth Control Movement and American Society since 1830* (New York: Basic Books, 1978), 143–93.

4. Louise Stevens Bryant to Elizabeth Campbell, 18 April 1935, Louise Stevens Bryant Papers, Sophia Smith Collection, Smith College.

5. On Reitman's life and career, see the introduction in Ben L. Reitman, *The Second Oldest Profession: A Study of the Prostitute's "Business Manager"* (New York: Vanguard Press, 1931), xiii–xx; Candace Falk, *Love, Anarchy, and Emma Goldman* (New Brunswick, N.J.: Rutgers University Press, 1990), 46–66. Attesting to the fact that Reitman had no contact with his first child (Jan Gay), he expressed his regret at deserting his daughter in a letter he wrote to Emma Goldman, 12 January 1911, cited in Falk, *Love,* 93. Had Reitman been a part of Gay's life, he would have undoubtedly supported her work as a lesbian activist. He was sympathetic to homosexuality and was interested in documenting the lives of social outcasts. His work *Second Oldest Profession* deals with the world of pimps and prostitutes. He also documented the life of a female hobo in Ben L. Reitman, *Sister of the Road: The Autobiography of Box-Car Bertha* (New York: Sheridan House, 1937). On the radical beginnings of the birth control movement before World War I, see Linda Gordon, *Women's Body, Women's Right: A Social History of Birth Control in America* (New York: Viking, 1976), chap. 10.

6. Jan Gay, *On Going Naked* (New York: Holburn Press, 1932); *This Naked World* (independent film, 1935, story by Jan Gay, UCLA Film Archive). I would like to thank Jennifer Terry for calling my attention to this film and for her description of it. Gay wrote several children's books, which include *Pancho and His Burro* (New York: Morrow, 1930), *The Shire Colt* (New York: Doubleday, Doran, 1931), *The Mutt Book* (New York: Harper, 1932), and *Tom Cats* (New York: Knopf, 1932). Biographical information on Gay is based on the following sources: Obituaries of Jan Gay, *San Francisco Chronicle,* 12 September 1960, 39; *Independent Journal* (Marin County), 12 September 1960, 10; *New York Times,* 13 September 1960, 37; Thomas Painter, "Gay, Jan," in Index of Names, annotated index file, first compiled in the late 1940s and updated in 1961, Thomas Painter Papers, Kinsey Institute Archives; research proposal (untitled) attached to Robert Latou Dickinson to Lewis M. Terman, 28 January 1935, Lewis M. Terman Papers, box 12, folder 26, Stanford University Archives; Jan Gay, "An Evaluation of the Group Therapy Techniques and Dynamics of Alcoholics Anony-

mous," research proposal attached to Gay to Kinsey, 25 October 1950, Kinsey
Institute Archives. For a discussion of the lexicon of male homosexuals before
1940, see George Chauncey, *Gay New York: Gender, Urban Culture, and the
Making of the Gay Male World, 1890–1940* (New York: Basic Books, 1994),
12–23. I would like to thank Brian Freeman for drawing my attention to the *San
Francisco Chronicle* and *Independent Journal* obituaries of Jan Gay, which identified Ben L. Reitman as her father.

7. In her research proposal (Gay, "Evaluation," typescript, 2), Gay stated: "A
manuscript based on these notes was tentatively accepted by a London publisher
when I asked leave to verify medically some of the statements based on assumption, observation, literature" (quote reprinted by permission of The Kinsey Institute for Research in Sex, Gender, and Reproduction, Inc.). This was written at
least fifteen years after such an incident took place, and in the context of her application for a research fellowship, Gay may have chosen to describe the incident
in a more proactive way. It seems more likely, however, that her "leave" to obtain
medical verification would have been initiated by the publisher rather than on
her own. In either case, it seems evident that in order for her to publish the manuscript, she would have had to have sponsorship and/or collaborative authorship
with medical or scientific experts. Background information on Gay's research is
also provided in Jennifer Terry, "The Seductive Power of Science in the Making
of Deviant Subjectivity," in *Science and Homosexualities,* ed. Vernon A. Rosario
(New York: Routledge, 1997), 271–95. Terry interviewed Richard Plant, who
knew Gay (personal communication with the author, 15 February 1994). On
Hirschfeld's research, see Magnus Hirschfeld, *Die Homosexualität des Mannes
und des Weibes* (Berlin: Louis Marcus, 1914); James D. Steakley, *"Per scientiam
ad justitiam:* Magnus Hirschfeld and the Sexual Politics of Innate Homosexuality," in *Science and Homosexualities,* ed. Rosario, 133–54. Copies of Hirschfeld's
Psychobiological Questionnaire are available in the Hirschfeld Scrapbook, Kinsey Institute Archives, Indiana University.

8. Robert Latou Dickinson and Lura Beam, *A Thousand Marriages: A Medical Study of Sex Adjustment* (Baltimore: Williams & Wilkins, 1931); idem, *The
Single Woman: A Medical Study in Sex Education* (Baltimore: Williams & Wilkins, 1934). In these books, Beam adopted a feminist perspective by focusing on
the changing historical context that affected women's lives between 1895 and
1930, as well as by analyzing the dominant-submissive relationship between the
male physician (Dickinson) and his female patients. Regarding Beam's role in
both books, see Louise Stevens Bryant, preface to *Single Woman,* vi. On Beam's
background and career, see "Lura Beam," in *Who Was Who in America* (Chicago: Marquis, 1982–85), 8:27. On Dickinson's views about marriage and the
family, see Reed, *Private Vice,* 147–48.

9. Dickinson and Beam, *Single Woman,* 204, 432.

10. For the homosexual cases, see ibid., chap. 9. The example of Dickinson's
advice giving is in on p. 222. The twenty-eight female cases were out of a total
number of 350 cases containing details of sexual experience. The male cases included three husbands of patients and one case of a man who proposed marriage
to a patient. Fifteen of the women and three of the men subsequently married.
On Davis's study, see chapter 2.

11. Beam wrote a privately published biography of Bryant—Lura Beam, *Bequest from a Life: A Biography of Louise Stevens Bryant* (Baltimore: Waverly

Press, 1963). Beam's hagiographic biography and the few surviving letters from Bryant to Beam attest to the nature of their relationship. Bryant's letters are contained in the Bryant Papers in the Sophia Smith Collection. In connection with his research on the American birth control movement, James Reed interviewed and corresponded with Beam in the early 1970s. He reports that in a postcard to him, Beam insisted that she and Bryant were not lovers (personal communication with the author, 21 September 1995). According to Reed, this denial reflected her concerns that the nature of her relationship with Bryant not be a part of the public record.

12. Dickinson's views about homosexuality were spelled out in his unpublished manuscript, "Section on Homosexuality for 'The Doctor as Marriage Counselor,'" undated but most likely written in 1940 or 1941, Robert Latou Dickinson Papers, box 11, folder 28, Countway Library of Medicine, Boston. This manuscript was part of his planned book *The Doctor as Marriage Counselor*, which he never completed.

13. Eugen Kahn, foreword to Henry, *Sex Variants*, 1:viii.

14. Gay's recollection of Dickinson's reaction to her manuscript is contained in Gay, "An Evaluation." Gay also noted that Josephine H. Kenyon, a pediatrician with a special interest in women's health and a member of the National Committee on Maternal Health, was very supportive of her work. On Kenyon, see Obituary of Josephine H. Kenyon, *New York Times*, 11 January 1965, 45. For a biography of Clarence Gamble, see Doone Williams and Greer Williams, *Every Child a Wanted Child: Clarence James Gamble, M.D. and His Work in the Birth Control Movement* (Boston: Countway Library of Medicine, 1978). On Clarence Gamble's relationship with Dickinson, see Reed, *Private Vice*, 225–26. Sidney Gamble's contribution of $1,000 is recorded in the Minutes of the 28 December 1934 meeting of the National Committee on Maternal Health, distributed 11 February 1935, Dickinson Papers, box 2, folder 12.

15. Thomas Painter, "Chronology"; idem, "Dickinson, Robert L. Dr.," in Index of Names, Painter papers; Gay, "Qualifications." Reference to the preliminary interviews is contained in a memorandum from Bryant to Haven Emerson, chairman, National Committee on Maternal Health, 12 December 1934, Bryant papers, box 12, folder 122.

16. Bryant to Campbell, 18 April 1935. Although the maternal health committee backed Bryant, the episode proved to be a wrenching experience for her. A minority of the committee members backed Dickinson and resigned in protest. Bryant, herself, resigned shortly after this mass resignation and appears to have suffered a nervous breakdown (see Beam, *Bequest*, 94–95). As James Reed suggests, Bryant's reaction reflected her sense of defeat at the hands of Dickinson (personal communication to the author, 21 September 1995). He refused to bow to her executive authority and was able to get his way by his ability to secure funds through his connections with Clarence and Sidney Gamble. In her career as a social scientist, Bryant had had previous struggles with men in positions of power (see Beam, *Bequest*). She did not want to appear as a strident feminist and thus avoided confrontation. The reference to the National Research Council's Committee for Research in Problems of Sex is contained in Carney Landis to Eugen Kahn, 25 March 1935, Adolf Meyer Papers, ser. 2, unit 179, the Alan Chesney Medical Archives of the Johns Hopkins Medical Institutions. Landis pointed out that the National Research Council's executive committee opposed sponsor-

ing research on homosexuality, reflecting the unwillingness of social scientists, in general, from being connected with such a controversial topic.

17. Gay, "Qualifications"; Dickinson to Terman, 28 January 1935, Terman Papers; Dickinson and Landis to Terman, 11 February 1935. The psychiatrists included Clarence O. Cheney, George W. Henry, Eugen Kahn, Marion Kenworthy, Robert W. Laidlaw, Adolf Meyer, and Edward A. Strecker. Rounding out the committee were endocrinologist Harold D. Palmer, gynecologist Robert L. Dickinson, pediatrician Josephine H. Kenyon, anatomists Earl T. Engle and Philip Smith (included to provide expertise on the reproductive systems of homosexual women), physical anthropologist Earnest A. Hooten, sociologists Maurice R. Davie and Dorothy Swaine Thomas, and psychologists Carney Landis, Karl S. Lashley, Catharine Cox Miles, and Lewis M. Terman. In 1938 Cheney, Kenworthy, and Hooten left the committee and were replaced with Karl M. Bowman, a psychiatrist, and Austin H. MacCormick, New York City's correction commissioner.

18. For reviews of Meyer's writings and influence, see Alfred Lief, ed. *The Commonsense Psychiatry of Adolf Meyer* (New York: McGraw-Hill, 1948); Gerald N. Grob, *Mental Illness and American Society, 1875–1940* (Princeton: Princeton University Press, 1983), 112–18, 149–57. Also see Theodore Lidz, "Adolf Meyer and the Development of American Psychiatry," *American Journal of Psychiatry* 123 (1966): 320–32. On Henry, see George W. Henry, "Psychiatric and Constitutional Factors in Homosexuality: Their Relation to Personality Disorders," *Psychiatric Quarterly* 8 (1934): 243–64; George W. Henry and Hugh M. Galbraith, "Constitutional Factors in Homosexuality," *American Journal of Psychiatry* 90 (1934): 1249–70; George W. Henry to Oskar Dietheim, 15 November 1938, Medical Biography File of George W. Henry, Medical Archives, New York Hospital–Cornell University Medical Center. According to Gay, Henry was not the first choice to direct her project (Gay, "Qualifications"). He was brought in after the sudden death of another psychiatrist (unnamed). On Kahn's views on homosexuality, see Eugen Kahn, *Psychopathic Personality*, trans. H. Flanders Dunbar (New Haven: Yale University Press, 1931). Reference to Kahn's election as committee chairman is in the Minutes of the meeting of the Committee for the Study of Sex Variants, 29 March 1935, Meyer Papers. On Terman and Miles's masculinity-femininity scale, see Lewis M. Terman and Catharine Cox Miles, *Sex and Personality: Studies in Masculinity and Femininity* (New York: McGraw-Hill, 1936).

19. Minutes of the meeting of the Committee for the Study of Sex Variants, 29 March 1935. Appeals for funding were made to ten foundations (Laidlaw to Adolf Meyer, 12 December 1935). The controversial nature of homosexuality as an area of research was undoubtedly a problem. The Josiah Macy Jr. Foundation, for example, feared that it would lose support from conservative and wealthy donors. The total figure of $7,500 from Gamble is the sum of several installments that were made available from 1934 to 1938, as recorded in Kahn and Laidlaw to Terman, 6 June 1938, Terman Papers.

20. Thomas Painter, "Male Homosexuals and Their Prostitutes in Contemporary America," 2 vols. (unpublished manuscript, 1941), Painter Papers; George W. Henry and Alfred A. Gross, "Social Factors in the Case Histories of One Hundred Underprivileged Homosexuals," *Mental Hygiene* 22 (1938): 591–

611; idem, "The Homosexual Delinquent," *Mental Hygiene* 25 (1941): 420–42; Kahn to Terman, 1 February 1940, Terman Papers.

21. Henry, *Sex Variants,* 1:vi, ix. On the ideology of the mental hygiene movement, see Fred Matthews, "In Defense of Common Sense: Mental Hygiene as Ideology and Mentality in Twentieth-Century America," *Prospects* 4 (1979): 459–516.

22. Henry, *Sex Variants,* 1:x; Gay, "Qualifications." Henry did not specify what these personal and family histories consisted of. In his proposal for the study, submitted to the Committee for the Study of Sex Variants, he indicated that the fieldworker (Gay) was to obtain such information as she could from her social contacts with the subjects—George W. Henry, "Proposal for Study of Homosexuality," undated, Meyer Papers, ser. 2, unit 179, no. 2 (includes Committee for the Study of Sex Variants correspondence, 2 May 1935 to 18 September 1935). The committee, however, was familiar with Gay's experience in collecting lesbian case histories, and Henry thus seems to have relied on this experience in outlining her role in the sex variants study. On Gay's protocol, see Terry, "Seductive Power," 275–76. Regarding the pseudonyms, first names were originally used, as in the case of "Mary Jones" (see note 2). The participants, at least in some cases, appear to have selected the pseudonyms. This is suggested in the case of Will G., who was Thomas Painter. Painter had previously made use of the pseudonym "Will Finch," as indicated in Painter, "Chronology," Painter Papers. Henry's procedure for the interviews is outlined in George W. Henry to Members of the Committee for the Study of Sex Variants, "Psychiatric Guide for Study of Homosexuals," undated, attached to Laidlaw to Terman, 17 November 1936, Terman Papers. Henry was assisted in the interviews by another psychiatrist, August E. Witzel of Brooklyn State Hospital. It is not clear whether Witzel conducted some of the interviews himself, acted as a co-interviewer in some cases, or was involved in the follow-up phase. All of the procedures for the study are described in Henry, *Sex Variants,* 1:ix–xvii.

23. Henry refers to the approximate size of the original sample in a later publication. See George W. Henry, *All the Sexes: A Study of Masculinity and Femininity* (New York: Rinehart, 1955), xii.

24. Jennifer Terry, "Lesbians under the Medical Gaze: Scientists Search for Remarkable Differences," *Journal of Sex Research* 27 (1990): 317–39. Terry provides an expanded analysis of the sex variants study, which is especially comprehensive in dealing with the physical measures and their significance, in idem, *An American Obsession: Science, Medicine, and Homosexuality in Modern Society* (Chicago: University of Chicago Press, 1999), chap. 6. The results of the psychological and medical assessments appear in Henry, *Sex Variants,* as "Appendix II: Masculinity-Femininity Tests," 2:1030–34; "Appendix III: Physical Characteristics Suggesting Masculinity or Femininity," 2:1037–56; "Appendix IV: Anthropological Data," 2:1058–63; George W. Henry, Robert P. Ball, and John R. Carty, "Appendix V: Internal Pelvic Measurements of Sex Variants," 2:1065–82; Robert Latou Dickinson, "Appendix VI: The Gynecology of Homosexuality," 2:1085–146.

25. Henry, *Sex Variants,* 1:xi, xiv. Each autobiography contained two sections, one on family background, the other on personal history. The background information provided by Gay contributed to Henry's introductory impressions in

each case. Henry acknowledged that he included observations Gay made based on her interactions with the participants (xi).

26. Ibid., 2:864; 1:144; 2:795. For an extensive analysis of the participants' narratives, see chapter 4.

27. Dickinson, "Gynecology," 1096–97; emphasis in original.

28. Henry's overall conclusions are contained in "Appendix I: Impressions," in *Sex Variants*, 2:1023–28. For comments on body build, see *Sex Variants*, 2:1061–62. On Dickinson's analysis, see Dickinson, "Gynecology." To underscore his argument for distinct lesbian physical characteristics, Dickinson provided a set of his own drawings based on the sex variants sample. See Dickinson, "Drawings Illustrating Gynecological Variations," in *Sex Variants*, 2:1116–46. For an analysis of the medical examinations, also see Terry, *American Obsession*, 198–212.

29. Henry, *Sex Variants*, 2:1024. In addition to the family charts, Henry also made use of the results of the Terman-Miles masculinity-femininity test, which he reported demonstrated that sex variants generally did not conform to the test norms for males and females. See Henry, *Sex Variants*, 2:1034.

30. By the 1930s, reflecting the influence of psychoanalytic views, pathogenic family dynamics was assumed to be a primary determinant of homosexuality. While Henry did not adopt an orthodox Freudian perspective with its focus on arrested psychosexual development and oedipal conflict, his emphasis on mother attachment was consistent with psychoanalytic thinking. On historical trends in the medical literature, see Peter Conrad and Joseph W. Schneider, *Deviance and Medicalization: From Badness to Sickness* (St. Louis: Mosby, 1980), 172–214; David F. Greenberg, *The Construction of Homosexuality* (Chicago: University of Chicago Press, 1988), 397–433; George Chauncey Jr., "From Sexual Inversion to Homosexuality: Medicine and the Changing Conceptualization of Female Deviance," in *Passion and Power: Sexuality in History*, ed. Kathy Piess and Christina Simmons (Philadelphia: Temple University Press, 1989), 87–117.

31. Henry, *Sex Variants*, 1:xiv–xix. In this introductory section of the *Sex Variants* monograph, Henry cited the case of T., a homosexual man who was the victim of a community vice crusade.

32. Ibid., 2:1028. For Henry's views on treatment, also see Henry and Gross, "Homosexual Delinquent," 420–42. See chapter 5 for Henry's views on treatment in the 1940s and 1950s.

33. Henry, *Sex Variants*, 1:440, 450, 486–87.

34. A reference to Gay's manuscript is cited in Gay, "An Evaluation," 2. For Henry's acknowledgment, see "Introduction," in Henry, *Sex Variants*, 1:xi–xix. Some suggestion of Gay's original contribution is contained in an outline, apparently produced by Dickinson, entitled "Research in Homosexuality" (typescript, 8 January 1935), Dickinson Papers, box 6, folder 235. Included in the outline is a section on "Literature," which was to be made up of a bibliography and abstracts, as well as a study of the work of Hirschfeld's Institute for Sexual Science.

35. Henrika Kuklick and Robert E. Kohler, "Introduction," *Osiris* 11 (1996): 1–14. On Gay's life after the sex variants project, see chapter 4.

36. Henry and Gross, "Social Factors"; idem, "Homosexual Delinquent."

37. Henry and Gross, "Social Factors," 602, 609. For the legal crackdown and a characterization of male prostitution in New York City during the 1930s, see Chauncey, *Gay New York*, chap. 12, 191–93.

38. Henry, *Sex Variants,* 1:x.

39. Ibid., 1:370, 787–89, 745, 772. Painter revealed his identity as "Will G." in Painter, "Male Homosexuals."

40. Henry, *Sex Variants,* 1:161, 167; 2:826, 820; 1:180; 2:608.

41. "Brief for Petitioner," *Gloria Record on Review* (1940), 11, New York State Liquor Authority Papers, New York State Library, Albany. The Liquor Authority targeted Gloria's because it had hired Jackie Mason, a well-known gay man, as manager and thus a draw for homosexual patrons. For more details on the case, see Chauncey, *Gay New York,* 337–39.

42. Henry, *Sex Variants,* 2:1026. On Painter's familiarity with the Gloria bar, see Thomas Painter, "Homosexual Resorts in New York, as of May, 1939," manuscript notes, Painter Papers.

43. For background on the medicalization of homosexuality, see chapter 2.

44. Kahn, foreword to Henry, *Sex Variants,* 1:vii. The sex crime panic focused on male homosexuals who were depicted as sexual predators committing violent sex attacks and recruiting victims to their lifestyle. As a consequence, several states passed "sexual psychopath laws." See Estelle B. Freedman, "'Uncontrolled Desires': The Response to the Sexual Psychopath, 1920–1960," *Journal of American History* 74 (June 1987): 83–106.

45. Dickinson, "Gynecology," 1085; emphasis in original. For the Davis survey, which is discussed in chapter 2, see Katharine Bement Davis, *Factors in Twenty-two Hundred Women* (New York: Harper & Brothers, 1929; reprint, New York: Arno Press, 1972).

46. Henry, "Psychogenic Factors," 904–5.

47. Henry, *Sex Variants,* 2:1025; E. E. Mayer, "Discussion," in Henry, "Psychogenic Factors," 906.

48. Henry, *Sex Variants,* 2:1025.

49. Dickinson spelled out his views about homosexuality and marriage in Dickinson, "Section on Homosexuality." On Dickinson's beliefs about marriage and sexual adjustment, see Reed, *Private Vice,* 147–48. Also see Jennifer Terry, "Anxious Slippages between 'Us' and 'Them': A Brief History of the Scientific Search for Homosexual Bodies," in *Deviant Bodies: Critical Perspectives on Difference in Science and Popular Culture,* ed. Jennifer Terry and Jacqueline Urla (Bloomington: Indiana University Press, 1995), 129–69, where she points out that Dickinson's fostering of sexual adjustment in marriage was an outgrowth of his larger eugenic interests in promoting marriage and reproduction among the "fit." Henry briefly referred to treatment in *Sex Variants,* 2:1028. He elaborated on the goals of therapy and other intervention strategies in *All the Sexes.*

50. Henry, "Psychogenic Factors," 903.

51. Henry, *Sex Variants,* 2:1026–27; idem, "Psychogenic Factors," 902.

52. Henry, "Psychogenic Factors," 905.

53. Dickinson, "Gynecology," 1089.

54. Henry, "Psychogenic Factors," 901. On the discourse on family during the interwar period, see Christopher Lasch, *Haven in a Heartless World: The Family Besieged* (New York: Basic Books, 1977), 22–43; Paula Fass, *The Damned and the Beautiful: American Youth in the 1920s* (New York: Oxford University Press, 1979). Several members of the Committee for the Study of Sex Variants were interested in marriage counseling and marital adjustment, namely, Dickinson, Kenyon, Laidlaw, and Terman. Of these, Terman published exten-

sively, most notably, Lewis M. Terman et al., *Psychological Factors in Marital Happiness* (New York: McGraw-Hill, 1938). On the discourse about sexual roles in marriage, see Christina Simmons, "Modern Sexuality and the Myth of Victorian Repression," in *Gender and American History since 1890,* ed. Barbara Melosh (New York: Routledge, 1993), 17–42.

55. Henry, *Sex Variants,* 2:1027.

56. On the shift from sexual inversion to sexual object-choice, see Chauncey, "From Sexual Inversion to Homosexuality." On the emergence of a heterosexual identity, see Jonathan Ned Katz, *The Invention of Heterosexuality* (New York: Dutton, 1995).

57. Henry, *Sex Variants,* 2:1024, 1026.

58. Henry's questions about sex practices were included in his interview protocol, "Psychiatric Guide for Study of Homosexuals." His conclusion about the active/passive distinction appeared in *Sex Variants,* 2:1034.

59. On the changes in psychiatry, see Walter Bromberg, *Psychiatry between the Wars, 1918–1945* (Westport, Conn.: Greenwood Press, 1982); Grob, *Mental Illness;* Elizabeth Lunbeck, *The Psychiatric Persuasion: Knowledge, Gender, and Power in Modern America* (Princeton: Princeton University Press, 1994). In the 1930s American psychoanalysts were also becoming increasingly interested in the treatment of homosexuality. See Kenneth Lewes, *The Psychoanalytic Theory of Male Homosexuality* (New York: Simon & Schuster, 1988), 95–121.

60. Henry, *Sex Variants,* 1:xii–xiii.

61. Henry gave an example of how the family of an arrested male homosexual was stigmatized by the community in which they lived (ibid., xii–xiii).

62. The M-F test proved to be influential in the development of multidimensional psychological measures of personality and psychopathology. The most widely used instrument was the Minnesota Multiphasic Personality Inventory (MMPI), which was constructed in 1943 to assess various psychiatric syndromes, such as depression, hysteria, and schizophrenia. This test battery also included a measure of masculinity-femininity (Mf), which incorporated some of the Terman-Miles test items. The MMPI Mf scale was developed to measure "inversion." On the MMPI Mf scale and other measures of masculinity-femininity, see Miriam Lewin, "Psychology Measures Femininity and Masculinity, 2: From '13 Gay Men' to the Instrumental-Expressive Distinction," in *In the Shadows of the Past: Psychology Portrays the Sexes,* ed. Miriam Lewin (New York: Columbia University Press, 1984), 179–204.

63. William Alanson White, "The Meaning of the Mental Hygiene Movement," address delivered at a 1915 conference in Boston; quote cited in Matthews, "In Defense of Common Sense," 484.

64. Henry, *All the Sexes.*

65. See chapter 8 for an overview of the American homophile movement in the postwar era.

Chapter 4

1. On life histories, see Mark Freeman, *Rewriting the Self: History, Memory, Narrative* (New York: Routledge, 1993).

2. George W. Henry, *Sex Variants: A Study of Homosexual Patterns,* 2 vols. (New York: Hoeber, 1941), 1:xi.

3. For Painter's case presentation (Will G.), see ibid., 370–83. Painter's review

of *Sex Variants* is in Painter, "Male Homosexuals," appendix (untitled, no page numbers). In Painter's papers, the identity of another *Sex Variants* case is revealed—Victor R., a well-known proprietor of various New York City male brothels in the 1930s and 1940s.

4. Henry, *Sex Variants*, 2:563.

5. Simon Callow, *Orson Welles: The Road to Xanadu* (New York: Viking, 1995), 224.

6. Biographical information on Edna Thomas is available in the Clippings File on Edna Thomas, New York Public Library for the Performing Arts, Lincoln Center, New York. Henry initially used the pseudonym "Mary Jones" for Thomas in his preliminary publication of the case in "Psychogenic Factors." Henry identified her occupation in ibid., 896, and then in *Sex Variants*, 2:563. On Orson Welles's connection with Thomas, see Callow, *Orson Welles*, 216–45. The accuracy of the Harlem cases was indicated by Eric Garber, personal communication with the author, 16 May 1994. Also see Eric Garber, "A Spectacle in Color: The Lesbian and Gay Subculture in Jazz Age Harlem," in *Hidden from History: Reclaiming the Gay and Lesbian Past,* ed. Martin Duberman, Martha Vicinus, and George Chauncey Jr. (New York: New American Library, 1989), 318–31. In addition to the three Harlem-connected cases cited, there were three others, all of whom were African American lesbians.

7. On the changing meanings of "coming out," see George Chauncey, *Gay New York: Gender, Urban Culture, and the Making of the Gay World, 1880–1940* (New York: Basic Books, 1994), 6–8; John Loughery, *The Other Side of Silence: Men's Lives and Gay Identities: A Twentieth-Century History* (New York: Holt, 1998), 69–70. Rudolph von H. was the transvestite who explored homosexual relations. His case appears in Henry, *Sex Variants*, 1:487–98.

8. Quoted in Chauncey, *Gay New York*, 101.

9. On the distinction between fairies and queers, see ibid., chaps. 2, 4.

10. Henry, *Sex Variants*, 1:429–30, 307–8, 529. Those I categorized as fairies in the Henry sample were Malcolm E., Theodore S., Walter R., Dennis C., Gabriel T., Antonio L., Daniel O'L., Victor R., and Julius E.

11. Ibid., 1:167, 326, 446. Victor R. was a friend of Thomas Painter. For more about Victor R., see chapter 6.

12. Ibid., 1:288. Walter R. was Caska Bonds, who was associated with Harlem heiress A'Lelia Walker and known for parties he hosted in his Harlem home. On Bonds, see Garber, "A Spectacle of Color."

13. Henry, *Sex Variants*, 2:1034.

14. Ibid., 1:414.

15. Ibid., 1:431–32. Daniel O'L.'s reference to "Greeks around the corner" suggests that his clients were heterosexual-identified men. In the homosexual subculture, such men were commonly referred to as "trade."

16. Ibid., 1:432–35. On trade and "husbands" of fairies, see Chauncey, *Gay New York*, chap. 3.

17. Henry, *Sex Variants*, 1:447, 435. Among the fairies, those who also had a transvestite identity were Malcolm E., Antonio L., Daniel O'L., Victor R., and Julius E.

18. Ibid., 1:497, 494, 494–95. See Magnus Hirschfeld, *The Transvestites: An Investigation of the Erotic Drive to Cross Dress,* trans. M. Lombardi-Nash (1910; reprint, Amherst, N.Y.: Prometheus Books, 1991). For discussions of

Hirschfeld's work, see Vern L. Bullough, *Science in the Bedroom: A History of Sex Research* (New York: Basic Books, 1994), 219; Vernon A. Rosario II, "Trans (Homo) Sexuality? Double Inversion, Psychiatric Confusion, and Hetero-Hegemony," in *Queer Studies: A Lesbian, Gay, and Transgender Anthology,* ed. Brett Beemyn and Micky Eliason (New York: New York University Press, 1996), 35–63. Krafft-Ebing and Ellis also identified transvestitism, and Ellis made the distinction between those who simply dressed as the opposite sex and those who wished to live as the opposite sex. See Richard von Krafft-Ebing, *Psychophilia sexualis with Especial Reference to the Antipathetic Sexual Instinct,* trans. F. J. Rebman (Brooklyn: Physicians and Surgeons Book Co., 1908); Havelock Ellis, *Sexual Inversion,* Vol. 2 of *Studies in the Psychology of Sex* (Philadelphia: F. A. Davis, 1901).

19. The cases of Howard N. and Moses I. appear in Henry, *Sex Variants,* 1:499–522, 534–46. On transgenderism and transsexualism, see Vern L. Bullough and Bonnie Bullough, *Cross Dressing, Sex, and Gender* (Philadelphia: University of Pennsylvania Press, 1993); Kate Bornstein, *Gender Outlaws: Beyond Sexual Dimorphism in Culture and History* (New York: Zone Books, 1994).

20. Henry, *Sex Variants,* 1:542.

21. Ibid., 1:422.

22. On the emergence of homosexual communities and Earl Lind, see chapter 2. On the distinction between fairies and queers, see Chauncey, *Gay New York,* chaps. 2, 4. The reference to love for men as more masculine than love for women, which was inspired by Walt Whitman's *Calamus* poems, is cited in ibid., 104–5.

23. Henry, *Sex Variants,* 1:133, 122, 123. Those categorized as queers in the Henry sample were Tracy O., Jacob L., Norman T., Thomas B., Nathan T., Rodney S., Michael D., Eric D., Salvatore N., Louis E., Robert T., Paul A., Gene S., James D., Noel W., Archibald T., Irving T., José R., Leo S., Will G., Reginald M., Max N., and Percival G.

24. Ibid., 1:151–52.

25. Jeb Alexander, *Jeb and Dash: A Diary of a Gay Life, 1918–1945,* ed. Ina Russell (Boston: Faber and Faber, 1993), 90–91 (entry for 4 February 1927). On Alexander, see chapter 2.

26. Henry, *Sex Variants,* 1:255. Gene S.'s revulsion toward effeminate homosexuals was so extreme that he commented, "I don't think it's too good a plan to have homosexuality too much accepted because it gives pansies too much chance. I think the police should stamp it out. That is what Hitler is doing" (255).

27. Ibid., 1:247, 226.

28. Ibid., 1:95, 105, 379. Will G. was Thomas Painter, who recruited some of the male participants for the sex variants study.

29. Ibid., 1:338–39.

30. David K. Johnson, "The Kids of Fairytown: Gay Male Culture on Chicago's Near North Side in the 1930s," in *Creating a Place for Ourselves: Lesbian, Gay, and Bisexual Community Histories,* ed. Brett Beemyn (New York: Routledge, 1997), 97–118. Chauncey, in his analysis of the New York gay world, also points to a pattern among many homosexual men who as young men appropriated a fairy identity to satisfy their need to "come out flaming." See Chauncey, *Gay New York,* 102.

31. Henry, *Sex Variants,* 1:300; Chauncey, *Gay New York,* 105.

32. Henry, *Sex Variants,* 1:36. The other bisexual man was Sydney H.

33. Ibid., 1:460, 472. In the homosexual subculture of the interwar period, there were several types of male prostitutes. Some fairies engaged in prostitution, as exemplified in the Henry sample by Daniel O'L. and Victor R. In fact, fairy prostitutes were around since the emergence of homosexual communities in American cities in the late nineteenth century. There were also well-dressed, gay-identified hustlers serving a middle-class clientele. Finally, there were nongay "rough" hustlers who appealed to a broad cross section of gay men. By the 1930s the straight-identified hustler became the dominant type of male prostitute. For a discussion of male prostitution in the 1930s, see chapter 6 and Chauncey, *Gay New York,* 191–93.

34. Henry, *Sex Variants,* 1:67, 151. On sexual preference and its connection to Alfred Kinsey's measures of "homosexual outlet," see Vivienne Cass, "The Implications of Homosexual Identity Formation for the Kinsey Model and Scale of Sexual Preference," in *Homosexuality/Heterosexuality: Concepts of Sexual Orientation,* ed. David P. McWhirter, Stephanie A. Sanders, and June Machover Reinisch (New York: Oxford University Press, 1990), 239–66.

35. Henry, *Sex Variants,* 1:297, 375.

36. Ibid., 1:152.

37. Ibid., 1:378.

38. Ibid., 1:431, 136–37.

39. Ibid., 1:93, 135, 113. Several of the homosexual man and lesbians referred to medical sources. This is not surprising because many of the participants were college educated. In contrast, David Johnson, in his analysis of the Chicago male homosexuals, who as a group had less education, reported that most had never read a medical text. See Johnson, "Kids of Fairytown," 111.

40. Henry, *Sex Variants,* 1:113, 135, 114.

41. Ibid., 1:431, 531.

42. Ibid., 1:389, 346, 105.

43. Ibid., 1:156, 143, 254.

44. Ibid., 2:1023.

45. Ibid., 1:146.

46. Ibid., 1:143. All of the respondents returned for a follow-up interview after the two-year interval.

47. Ibid., 1:280, 279.

48. Ibid., 1:282.

49. Ibid., 1:370, 383, 393, 402, 411, 414. It was not uncommon in the medical literature to dismiss any expressions of pride in being homosexual or of social protest about the treatment of homosexuals as signs of pathology. For an example, see "Dr. John F. W. Meagher: Some Homosexuals 'Have a . . . Psychopathic Pride in Their Condition,'" in *Gay/Lesbian Almanac,* ed. Jonathan Ned Katz (New York: Harper & Row, 1983), 455–58.

50. Henry, *Sex Variants,* 1:98, 242, 99.

51. Ibid., 1:141, 146.

52. On lesbian gender roles before World War II, see Elizabeth Lapovsky Kennedy and Madeline D. Davis, *Boots of Leather, Slippers of Gold: The History of a Lesbian Community* (New York: Routledge, 1993), 29–38; Lillian Faderman, *Odd Girls and Twilight Lovers: A History of Lesbian Life in Twentieth-*

Century America (New York: Columbia University Press, 1991), 105–12. On Alice Mitchell, see Lisa Duggan, "Trials of Alice Mitchell: Sensationalism, Sexology, and the Lesbian Subject in Turn-of-the-Century America," *Signs: Journal of Women in Culture and Society* 18 (1993): 791–814. On Radclyffe Hall's inspiration for gender reversal, see Esther Newton, "The Mythic Mannish Lesbian: Radclyffe Hall and the New Woman," in *Hidden from History,* ed. Duberman, Vicinus, and Chauncey, 281–93.

53. The nineteen mannish women were Pamela D., Julia I., Rowena K., Mildred B., Irene K., Virginia K., Myrtle K., Eloise B., Ursula W., Sadie S., Kathleen M., Nora M., Alberta I., Patricia D., Marvel W., Regina C., Betty E., Yetta T., and Gladys H.

54. Henry, *Sex Variants,* 2:813, 745, 813, 814.

55. Ibid., 2:783, 863.

56. Ibid., 2:838, 678. On the stone butch, see Judith Halberstam, *Female Masculinity* (Durham, N.C.: Duke University Press, 1988), chap. 4.

57. Henry, *Sex Variants,* 2:805, 814, 880. Marvel's partner Ellen T. corroborated this by stating, "In my present relationship, I feel protected" (2:794).

58. The ten feminine women were Pearl M., Mae C., Charlotte N., Angelina T., Aimee C., Sara B., Frieda S., Ellen T., Birdie K., and Susan N.

59. Henry, *Sex Variants,* 2:705, 707, 633, 567. Pearl M.'s real identity was Edna Thomas, a black actress, best known for her role as Lady Macbeth in Orson Welles's 1936 Harlem production of *Macbeth.* See Callow, *Orson Welles,* 216–45. Thomas's partner, Olivia Windham, was Pamela D. (Eric Garber, personal communication to the author, 16 May 1994).

60. Henry, *Sex Variants,* 2:913, 914, 705.

61. The eleven bisexual women were Caroline E., Molly N., Roberta H., Fannie E., Blanche T., Marian J., Rose S., Rebecca R., Olga R., Martha D., and Maria S. While there is some overlap, my categorization does not agree with Henry's. Henry placed several of the bisexual women in the "narcissistic" category. See ibid., 2:549–60.

62. Ibid., 2:978, 969, 692–93, 645, 648.

63. Ibid., 2:659, 669.

64. Ibid., 2:929, 932, 1005, 1006.

65. Ibid., 2:873, 780, 954, 942, 754, 873.

66. Ibid., 2:617, 911, 912, 594.

67. Ibid., 2:715, 576. Having crushes on older girls and teachers, as well as being an object of adoration by younger girls, was a common pattern among school-age girls in the era of the late nineteenth century and early twentieth century. See Martha Vicinus, "Distance and Desire: English Boarding School Friendships, 1870–1920," in *Hidden from History,* ed. Duberman, Vicinus, and Chauncey, 212–29; Blanche Wiesen Cook, *Eleanor Roosevelt, Volume One, 1884–1933* (New York: Viking, 1992), 102–24.

68. Henry, *Sex Variants,* 2:848, 823, 631, 976, 1004.

69. Ibid., 2:782, 887, 861–62.

70. Ibid., 2:566, 706, 912, 968.

71. Ibid., 2:873, 804, 850, 955.

72. Ibid., 2:677, 632.

73. Ibid., 2:669, 634, 795.

74. Ibid., 2:864, 815, 785, 567, 815.

75. On lesbian culture during the 1930s and class differences in the 1950s, see Faderman, *Odd Girls,* 105–12, 175–87. On Kennedy and Davis's Buffalo study, see Kennedy and Davis, *Boots of Leather,* 29–38, 323–71. On the Cherry Grove study, see Esther Newton, "The 'Fun Gay Ladies': Lesbians in Cherry Grove, 1936–1960," in *Creating a Place for Ourselves,* ed. Beemyn, 145–64.

76. Henry, *Sex Variants,* 2:839, 841, 818, 681.

77. Ibid., 2:895–96, 797.

78. Ibid., 2:651, 960, 728, 797. With respect to Ellen and Marvel, Marvel did acknowledge that she felt that Ellen was too inhibited about sex. Nevertheless, she had no doubts about their mutual love. In her words, "Nobody's future looks very good to me. Mine is as good as anybody's. I fear war and fascism. . . . Otherwise the future is all right. I have the only thing we can get—love" (2:892).

79. Ibid., 2:600, 982, 867, 864. Elizabeth Kennedy and Madeline Davis noted the pattern of serial monogamous relationships among lesbians in their study of the Buffalo community from the 1930s to the 1950s—see Kennedy and Davis, *Boots of Leather,* chap. 7. Among the factors they accounted for in the persistence of the system of serial monogamy were the lack of legalized marriage, neither partner being economically dominant, and the focus on finding romance and sexual pleasure.

80. George W. Henry, "Psychiatric Guide for Study of Homosexuals," attached to Robert W. Laidlaw to Lewis M. Terman, 17 November 1936, Lewis M. Terman Papers, box 12, folder 26, Stanford University Archives.

81. Henry, *Sex Variants,* 1:199; 2:957; 1:180; 2:669.

82. Ibid., 2:699; 1:239; 2:852.

83. Ibid., 1:365, 366; 2:608, 609; 1:518. Caroline was twenty-one when she first saw Henry. He attributed her homosexuality to "an adolescent groping for affection which [her] family had failed to provide" (2:611). It was thus a passing phase. Henry was optimistic about "heterosexual adjustment" in cases in which there was not a long history of homosexual experience.

84. Ibid., 1:326; 2:839, 864.

85. Ibid., 1:127, 143–44, 255, 404. Other expressions of commitment are cited in chapter 3.

86. Ibid., 1:524, 393; 2:892. Jennifer Terry provides an extensive analysis on the subjectivity of the sex variants participants in terms of the tensions in their relationship with Henry. She utilizes Foucault's conceptualization of relational power and applies it to exchanges between Henry and the sex variants participants. See Jennifer Terry, *An American Obsession: Science, Medicine, and Homosexuality in Modern Society* (Chicago: University of Chicago Press, 1999), chap. 7.

87. Henry, *Sex Variants,* 2:772, 707; 1:280.

88. Ibid., 1:255, 531; 2:987.

89. Ibid., 2:795; 1:370, 380.

90. Ibid., 2:700, 705, 758, 891, 772. On lesbians' appropriation of masculinity and gender subversion, see chapter 2; Halberstam, *Female Masculinity,* chap. 3.

91. Henry, *Sex Variants,* 1:300.

92. bell hooks, *Talking Back: Thinking Feminist, Thinking Black* (Boston: South End Press, 1989), 43.

93. M. F. Ashley Montagu, Review of *Sex Variants: A Study of Homosexual Patterns,* by George W. Henry. *Psychiatry* 4 (1941): 631–33.

94. Kum-Kum Bhavani, "What's Power Got to Do with It? Empowerment and Social Research," in *Deconstructing Social Psychology,* ed. Ian Parker and John Shotter (New York: Routledge, 1990), 141–52. On issues of empowerment in social science research, also see hooks, *Talking Back,* chap. 7; Jill G. Morawski and Robert Steele, "The One or the Other? Textual Analysis of Masculine Power and Feminist Empowerment," *Theory & Psychology* 1 (1991): 107–31.

95. Gershon Legman to Alfred C. Kinsey, 3 November 1942, Kinsey Institute Archives, Indiana University. Thomas Painter (Will G.) also critiqued Henry for distorting parts of the narrative. On Painter's critique, see chapter 3. On the glossary, see Gershon Legman, "The Language of Homosexuality: An American Glossary," in Henry, *Sex Variants,* appendix VII, 2:1149–79.

96. Kinsey to Gay, 22 January 1943, Kinsey Institute Archives. Biographical information on Gay is contained in Thomas Painter, "Gay, Jan," in Index of Names, Thomas Painter Papers, Kinsey Institute Archives; Gay to Kinsey, 19 August 1946 and 25 October 1950; Obituaries of Jan Gay, *San Francisco Chronicle,* 12 September 1960, 39; *Independent Journal* (Marin County), 12 September 1960, 10; *New York Times,* 13 September 1960, 37; Certificate of Death, Jan Gay, Office of the Marin County (California) Assessor-Recorder, 11 September 1960. At the suggestion of Dickinson in 1943, Kinsey sought out Gay as a consultant for his research on male sexual behavior. Since she was out of the country, they did not meet until 1946, at which time they had one brief meeting. In 1950, when she applied for a Guggenheim Fellowship for research on Alcoholics Anonymous, Kinsey turned down her request for a letter of recommendation on the basis that he was not familiar enough with her training or experience in scientific research.

97. On the functions of coming out stories, see Ken Plummer, *Telling Sexual Stories: Power, Change and Social Worlds* (New York: Routledge, 1995), chap. 6. On the publication and distribution of the 1948 edition of *Sex Variants,* see Terry, *American Obsession,* 458. The 1948 edition did not include the nude photographs and Gershon Legman's glossary of homosexual slang. In 1955 Henry published a popularized version of the *Sex Variants* monograph—George W. Henry, *All the Sexes: A Study of Masculinity and Femininity* (New York: Rinehart, 1955). This had wide readership, but Henry did not reprint the *Sex Variants* autobiographies, preferring instead to quote various short excerpts interspersed with his commentary. He also included references to many other cases from his clinical practice. On *All the Sexes,* see chapter 5.

Chapter 5

1. Biographical information on Gross comes from the following sources: "Alfred Artyn Gross," in program for Church of the Holy Communion service, 14 June 1970, George W. Henry Collection, Elihu Burritt Library, Central Connecticut State University; Alfred A. Gross, "Looking Backward—and Forward," address appended to Ruth P. Berkeley and Alfred A. Gross, "The Twenty-third Report of the George W. Henry Foundation, Inc.," 1 April 1971, Henry Collection; phone interview with Clarence A. Tripp, 1 August 1996; Tripp to Alfred C. Kinsey, 11 February 1948, Kinsey Institute Archives, Indiana University; Thomas Painter, "Gross," in Index of Names, annotated index file, Thomas Painter Papers, Kinsey Institute Archives. There is no surviving paper trail of Gross's cleri-

cal position or the circumstances of his defrocking. Two of his contemporaries, Tripp and Painter, each independently corroborate his dismissal. Because of his close connection with the Episcopal Church and Episcopal clerics, I am assuming he was an Episcopal priest.

2. On New York's campaign against sex crimes and the policing of homosexuality in the 1930s, see Jennifer Terry, *An American Obsession: Science, Medicine, and Homosexuality in Modern Society* (Chicago: University of Chicago Press, 1999), chap. 8. Also see, George Chauncey, *Gay New York: Gender, Urban Culture, and the Making of the Gay World, 1890–1940* (New York: Basic Books, 1994), chap. 12; Estelle B. Freedman, "'Uncontrolled Desires': The Response to the Sexual Psychopath, 1920–1960," *Journal of American History* 74 (June 1987): 83–106.

3. Terry, *American Obsession,* 277.

4. George W. Henry and Alfred A. Gross, "Social Factors in the Case Histories of One Hundred Underprivileged Homosexuals," *Mental Hygiene* 22 (1938): 600. In reviewing the practices of the courts in homosexual cases, the authors noted that there was considerable variability in judicial practices, which in some instances resulted in rulings of injustice.

5. Ibid., 610, 611.

6. "The Study of the Sex Offender Sponsored by the Committee for the Study of Sex Variants," unpublished manuscript attached to Eugen Kahn to Lewis M. Terman, 1 February 1940, Lewis M. Terman Papers, box 12, folder 26, Stanford University Archives. The need for a study of sex offenders was first brought to the sex variants committee by Henry in June 1938—see Kahn and Robert Laidlaw to Adolf Meyer, 6 June 1938, Adolf Meyer Papers, series II, unit 179, Alan Mason Chesney Medical Archives of the Johns Hopkins Medical Institutions. The impetus for the study was connected with Mayor La Guardia's formation of the Committee for the Study of Sex Offenses and the implementation of psychiatric assessments at Bellevue Hospital. Henry and Gross's research proposal was thus based on this policy, although it provided for a more comprehensive assessment of sex offenders as well as a follow-up program.

7. On the trend toward community care in social welfare and correction, see James Leiby, *A History of Social Welfare in the United States* (New York: Columbia University Press, 1978), chap. 14. On New Deal social welfare policy, see Walter I. Trattner, *From Poor Law to Welfare State: A History of Social Welfare in America,* 6th ed. (New York: Free Press, 1999), chap. 13.

8. George W. Henry and Alfred A. Gross, "Social Factors in Delinquency," *Mental Hygiene* 24 (1940): 59–78.

9. George W. Henry and Alfred A. Gross, "The Homosexual Delinquent," *Mental Hygiene* 25 (1941): 420–442. For prison practices on homosexual segregation, see Chauncey, *Gay New York,* 91–92. For the expansion of psychiatry into the community, see Walter Bromberg, *Psychiatry between the Wars, 1918–1945* (Westport, Conn.: Greenwood Press, 1982); Gerald N. Grob, *Mental Illness and American Society, 1873–1940* (Princeton: Princeton University Press, 1983).

10. Paul Blanshard to Henry, 1 April 1941; Alfred A. Gross to Blanshard, 17 April and 2 October 1941, Society for the Prevention of Crime Papers, box 61, Rare Book and Manuscript Library, Columbia University. The Society for the Prevention of Crime was one of several organizations founded in the late nine-

teenth century to deal with the problems of vice and crime. See Timothy J. Gilfoyle, "The Moral Origins of Political Surveillance: The Preventive Society in New York City, 1867–1918," *American Quarterly* 18 (1986): 637–52; John D'Emilio and Estelle B. Freedman, *Intimate Matters: A History of Sexuality in America,* 2nd ed. (Chicago: University of Chicago Press, 1997), chaps. 7, 9.

11. For the World War II policy of excluding homosexuals, see Allan Bérubé, *Coming Out under Fire: The History of Gay Men and Women in World War Two* (New York: Penguin, 1990), chap. 1. Harry Stack Sullivan initiated the plan for psychiatric screening and did not believe that homosexuality should be included among the categories of mental disorder. He clashed with the selective service director, Major General Lewis B. Hershey, over Hershey's downgrading of psychiatric screening and resigned in November 1941. For the role that Sullivan's own homosexuality played in his career, see Michael S. Allen, "Sullivan's Closet: A Reappraisal of Harry Stack Sullivan's Life and His Pioneering Role in American Psychiatry," *Journal of Homosexuality* 29, no. 1 (1995): 1–18. For Henry's views on homosexuality in the military, see George W. Henry, *All the Sexes: A Study of Masculinity and Femininity* (New York: Rinehart, 1955), 375–76.

12. The fact that Gross did all of the interviewing regarding the psychiatric screening for the selective service was revealed by Clarence A. Tripp (phone interview, 1 August 1996), who worked with Henry as a photographer during the war. Tripp also indicated that Gross was greatly resented by the men he screened because of his penchant for groping and lewdness. Further corroboration of Gross's role in screening is indicated by Thomas Painter, who knew Gross during the war. See Painter, "Autobiography," unpublished manuscript, December 1941, 13–14, Painter Papers.

13. The controversy over Henry and Gross's work at the Payne Whitney Clinic is reflected in the correspondence in Henry's medical biography file, Medical Archives, New York Hospital–Cornell University Medical Center. The relevant correspondence is between 28 July 1942 and 5 January 1944. The Stork Club incident was referred to in Thomas Rennie to Oskar Dietheim, 23 July 1943.

14. George W. Henry, *Sex Variants: A Study of Homosexual Patterns,* one-volume edition (New York: Hoeber, 1948), vii; idem, *All the Sexes,* 576; Painter, "Autobiography," 13–14.

15. George W. Henry to Judge Edgar Bromberger, 31 December 1947, Society for the Prevention of Crime Papers.

16. George W. Henry, *Sex Variants: A Study of Homosexual Patterns,* 2 vols. (New York: Hoeber, 1941), 2:1028; idem, *All the Sexes,* 587.

17. Henry to Bromberger, 31 December 1947, 8–9.

18. Henry did refer to some cases in which his patients eventually married and had children, but even in these instances he voiced his reservations, as exemplified by his statement that "homosexuals marry and have children, but a successful marriage is something else again"; cited in Jess Stearn, *The Sixth Man* (New York: Macfadden Books, 1962), 22. Regarding Gross's authorship: phone interview with Tripp, 1 August 1996; Tripp to Kinsey, 11 February 1948, Kinsey Institute Archives. Gross's ghostwritten article was George W. Henry, "Pastoral Counseling for Homosexuals," *Pastoral Psychology* 2, no. 11 (1951): 33–39. Gross revealed his authorship of this article in his correspondence with Clinton R. Jones, 30 April 1969, Henry Collection. Henry's views about the difficulty of

achieving heterosexual adjustment contrasted with the conventional psychiatric thinking of the 1950s. For a review of the psychiatric views on homosexuality in the postwar period, see chapter 8.

19. Tripp to Kinsey, 11 February 1948, Kinsey Institute Archives; Austin H. MacCormick to Alfred A. Gross, 23 April 1948, Society for the Prevention of Crime Papers; Vern L. Bullough, *Science in the Bedroom: A History of Sex Research* (New York: Basic Books, 1994), 167; Wardell B. Pomeroy, *Dr. Kinsey and the Institute for Sex Research* (1972; reprint, New Haven: Yale University Press, 1982), 255. Also see Howard Whitman, "The Biggest Taboo," *Collier's* (15 February 1947): 24, 38–40. Tripp, who worked closely with Kinsey and knew Henry and Gross, provided details about this episode because Kinsey wanted to avoid having his work distorted by such popularized outlets. For the relationship between Tripp and Kinsey, see chapter 7. The Quaker committee under Wertham became known as the Quaker Readjustment Center and continued to function, at least through the mid-1960s, as a social agency primarily concerned with homosexual men in trouble with the law. A brief history of the Quaker committee and the Henry Foundation appears in Edward Sagarin, "Structure and Ideology in an Association of Deviates" (Ph.D. diss., New York University, 1966; reprint, New York: Arno Press, 1975), 59–63. Sagarin indicates that Wertham developed a supportive attitude toward organized groups of homosexual activists. Thus, he believed that homophile groups as well as social agencies, like the Quaker Readjustment Center, would be helpful to the cause of homosexual rights. In this respect, he differed from Henry, who distrusted homophile organizations.

20. Gross's role as founder of the Henry Foundation is referred to in Clinton R. Jones, introduction to "The Church and the Homosexual," by Alfred A. Gross, unpublished manuscript, October 1978, Henry Collection.

21. George W. Henry, "Report of the Psychiatrist-in-Chief," 1 April 1949; Gross to Charles Cook, 13 October 1948 and 15 April 1949, Society for the Prevention of Crime Papers. On the participation of religious organizations in the homophile movement, see John D'Emilio, *Sexual Politics, Sexual Communities: The Making of a Homosexual Minority in the United States, 1940–1970*, 2nd ed. (Chicago: University of Chicago Press, 1998), 193–95. In 1955, after about seven years of operation, Henry reported that the Henry Foundation processed about sixteen hundred cases of arrested men referred to the foundation and about five hundred cases who were voluntary self-referrals—see Henry, *All the Sexes*, 576.

22. "The George W. Henry Foundation, Statement of Purposes and Functions as Prepared by Dr. Henry," quotes from one-page typescript, undated but most likely prepared in 1948, in the Tripp folder of correspondence, Kinsey Institute Archives.

23. Henry, "Pastoral Counseling," 38. Since the article dealt with counseling, Henry's authorship was necessary for credibility. Gross had no professional credentials, so that even coauthorship would probably have compromised credibility.

24. Gross to Cook, 15 December 1948, Society for the Prevention of Crime Papers, permission to quote granted by Rare Book and Manuscript Library, Columbia University.

25. Gross to Cook, 1 October 1949, permission to quote granted by Rare Book and Manuscript Library, Columbia University.

26. George W. Henry, "Fifth Annual Report of the George W. Henry Foundation," excerpt quoted in Sagarin, "Structure and Ideology," 60. It is likely that these were actually Gross's words.

27. The critique appeared in W. L., "The Case of the Well-Meaning Lyncher," *ONE Magazine,* (November 1953): 10–11. The author (W. L.) was Bill Lambert, one of the magazine's founders and one of its writers during 1953, the first year of publication. On the early homophile press, see Jim Kepner, *Rough News, Daring Views: 1950s' Pioneer Gay Press Journalism* (New York: Harrington Park Press, 1998).

28. Henry, "Report of the Psychiatrist-in-Chief" (1949), 8–9. Henry had pointed to the problem of antihomosexual prejudice and the consequent danger of community "witch-hunting" in the *Sex Variants* monograph—Henry, *Sex Variants* (1941), 1:xv. On the postwar community-oriented programs for ex-prisoners, see Leiby, *Social Welfare,* 290–96.

29. Alfred A. Gross, "The Homosexual in Society," typescript of an address given before the seminar of the Brooklyn Division of the Protestant Council, 20 June 1947, 3, Society for the Prevention of Crime Papers. Henry's "Pastoral Counseling" article (written by Gross) also contains a reference to homosexuals as a minority group.

30. Gross to Cook, 1 March 1950, permission to quote granted by Rare Book and Manuscript Library, Columbia University.

31. Painter's reference to Gross appears in Painter, "Gross."

32. On the origins of the homophile movement in the 1950s, see D'Emilio, *Sexual Politics,* chaps. 4, 5. On Hay, see Harry Hay, *Radically Gay: Gay Liberation in the Words of Its Founder,* ed. Will Roscoe (Boston: Beacon Press, 1996). On the reorganization of the Mattachine Society, see Hal Call, "Gay Sexualist," in *Making History: The Struggle for Gay and Lesbian Equal Rights, 1945–1990: An Oral History,* ed. Eric Marcus (New York: HarperCollins, 1992), 59–69. See chapter 8 for a more extensive discussion of the postwar homophile movement.

33. Sagarin, "Structure and Ideology," 61. On Sagarin, see chapter 8; on Kinsey, chapter 7; on Hooker, chapter 8.

34. Sagarin, "Structure and Ideology," 61; Ruth P. Berkeley and Alfred A. Gross, "The Seventeenth Annual Report of the George W. Henry Foundation, Inc.," 1 April 1965, Henry Collection; Clinton R. Jones, "A Report of the Hartford Chapter of the George W. Henry Foundation," appended to Ruth P. Berkeley and Alfred A. Gross, "The Twenty-first Annual Report of the George W. Henry Foundation, Inc.," 1 April 1969. Henry apparently continued to be involved with clients at the foundation, at least through the early 1960s. In an interview conducted around 1961, he referred to a physical attack by one of his patients, which resulted in the loss of sight in his right eye—see Stearn, *Sixth Man,* 24. I would like to thank Jennifer Terry for calling my attention to the George W. Henry Collection, housed in the Elihu Burritt Library, Central Connecticut State University. This collection on the Hartford chapter of the Henry Foundation provides a rich source of material on the liaison between homophile activists and liberal church groups in the 1960s and 1970s.

35. Information on the dissolution of the Henry Foundation comes from my phone interview with Clinton R. Jones, 17 January 2000. Jones, who was the canon of Christ Church Cathedral in Hartford, organized the Hartford chapter of the Henry Foundation and served on the New York foundation's board of di-

rectors. On the Wolfenden Report, see D'Emilio, *Sexual Politics,* 144–45. The report was first issued in Britain in 1957 but did not become influential in America until the mid-1960s. The cited views of the foundation appeared in the annual reports of 1965, 1971, and 1972, coauthored by Berkeley and Gross, Henry Collection. On Gross's death, see Obituary of Alfred A. Gross, *New York Times,* 2 June 1987, sec. IV, p. 23.

36. Henry, *All the Sexes,* 567–80.

37. Ibid., 581–88 ("General Impressions" chapter). While Henry acknowledged that there was considerable variability among homosexuals, he spelled out a set of defining characteristics for male and female homosexuals as empirical support for his gender inversion model (286–87). These distinctive signs of gender inversion included body form, facial characteristics, style of talk, clothing, jewelry, cosmetics, posture, and gait. Lesbians were thus portrayed as possessing short hair, a deep voice, businesslike talk, tailored clothing, a conservative use of cosmetics, and a swaggering gait. He indicated that such a composite of defining traits was supported by observations made on the sample of forty men and forty women in his 1941 sex variants study. Hedging on the generalizability of such distinguishing characteristics, he cautioned that they only had value as general impressions.

38. For the change in psychiatric and psychoanalytic thinking about homosexuality, see Ronald Bayer, *Homosexuality and American Psychiatry: The Politics of Diagnosis,* rev. ed. (Princeton: Princeton University Press, 1987), chap. 1; Kenneth Lewes, *The Psychoanalytic Theory of Male Homosexuality* (New York: Simon & Schuster, 1988), 95–121. For the report of the Bieber study, see Irving Bieber et al., *Homosexuality: A Psychoanalytic Study of Male Homosexuals* (New York: Basic Books, 1962).

39. Henry also included a section on male prostitution, which was largely based on Painter's 1941 unpublished manuscript. Henry, however, provided no acknowledgment of Painter's work nor any mention of the fact that what he was describing was the pre–World War II subculture of male prostitution. See Henry, *All the Sexes,* 395–400. For a discussion of Painter's work and his concerns about Henry's plagiarism, see chapter 6.

40. Ibid., 289.

41. Ibid.

42. Donald Webster Cory [Edward Sagarin], *The Homosexual in America: A Subjective Approach* (New York: Greenberg, 1951). On Sagarin, see chapter 8. Rinehart, the publisher of *All the Sexes,* was an established trade publisher. The book appears to have had a wide readership and was reprinted in two popular paperback editions in the 1960s. See George W. Henry, *Masculinity and Femininity* (New York: Collier Books, 1964); idem, *Society and the Sex Variant* (New York: Collier Books, 1965).

43. Quoted in Henry, *All the Sexes,* 293.

44. Quoted in ibid.

45. For discussion of schoolgirl crushes, see Martha Vicinus, "Distance and Desire: English Boarding School Friendships, 1870–1920," in *Hidden from History: Reclaiming the Gay and Lesbian Past,* ed. Martin Duberman, Martha Vicinus, and George Chauncey Jr. (New York: New American Library, 1989), 212–29; Lillian Faderman, *Odd Girls and Twilight Lovers: A History of Lesbian Life in Twentieth-Century America* (New York: Columbia University Press, 1991),

18–22. For discussion of the butch/femme roles, see Faderman, *Odd Girls,* chap. 7; Elizabeth Lapovsky Kennedy and Madeline D. Davis, *Boots of Leather, Slippers of Gold: A History of a Lesbian Community* (New York: Routledge, 1993), chap. 6.

46. Quoted in Henry, *All the Sexes,* 299.

47. Quoted in ibid., 301–2.

48. See Faderman, *Odd Girls,* 175–87.

49. Henry, *All the Sexes,* 302.

50. Ibid., 303.

51. Ibid., 315.

52. Ibid., 427. Henry's general comments on the failure of law enforcement appear on 423–26.

53. Ibid., 587. On residential centers for juvenile offenders, see Leiby, *Social Welfare,* 293.

54. Henry, *All the Sexes,* 587–88.

55. For discussion and examples of psychiatric hostility toward homosexuals, see Lewes, *Male Homosexuality,* 95–121; Bayer, *Homosexuality and American Psychiatry,* 28–38, 78–80. The most virulent example of intemperate discourse is contained in the writings of psychoanalyst Edmund Bergler. See Edmund Bergler, *Homosexuality: Disease or Way of Life?* (New York: Hill & Wang, 1956). There is no record of Henry trying to implement his program of rural resettlement in connection with his work at the Henry Foundation. Through the foundation, he and Gross did, in some instances, work with community agencies. This occurred in the case of the Long Island gay resort of Fire Island in which the foundation worked with the courts to obtain a reduced sentence for two homosexual defendants charged with public indecency. Another case involved relocating a young homosexual (caught in a sexual act) from the small town where he was arrested to New York City, where he could be better protected from the public disgrace he faced in his own community. These cases were reported in Henry, "Report of the Psychiatrist-in-Chief," (1949), 9–10, Society for the Prevention of Crime Papers.

56. Henry, *All the Sexes,* 528–29.

57. For an analysis of the trends in psychiatry in the 1950s and 1960s, see Gerald N. Grob, *From Asylum to Community: Mental Health Policy in Modern America* (Princeton: Princeton University Press, 1991), chap. 11. Grob points out that there was an overall trend to liberalism among the younger generation of psychiatrists that began after World War II. However, the development of a stance of social activism did not emerge until the 1960s. Also see Lewes, *Male Homosexuality,* 140–72, for a discussion of the conservatism of American psychoanalysis during the 1950s.

58. Thompson was a psychoanalyst closely connected with Harry Stack Sullivan. In contrast to Henry, she pointed to the advantages for homosexuals of belonging to a culturally denigrated group. In Clara Thompson, "Changing Concepts of Homosexuality in Psychoanalysis," *Psychiatry* 10 (1947): 183–89, she asserted, "One can feel defiant, brave, strong, and as a member of a band united against the world, lessen the feeling of ostracism" (189). Laidlaw's introduction was made at the 1951 meeting of the American Association of Marriage Counselors. See "When Is an 'H' Not an 'H'?" *About Time: Exploring the Gay Past,* ed. Martin Duberman, rev. ed. (New York: Meridian, 1991), 190.

59. Phone interview with Tripp, 1 August 1996. Henry refers to his connection with the sanitarium, Brooklea Farm, in Henry to Blanshard, 17 March 1941, Society for the Prevention of Crime Papers.

60. Tripp (phone interview), who worked for Henry as a photographer during World War II, characterized Henry as intellectually shallow.

61. Alfred C. Kinsey, Wardell B. Pomeroy, and Clyde E. Martin, *Sexual Behavior in the Human Male* (Philadelphia: Saunders, 1948); Henry, *Sex Variants* (1948). Tripp (phone interview) recalls that when he brought Henry a copy of Kinsey's book, Henry felt threatened by it because Kinsey was stealing his thunder.

62. Gross to Jones, 30 April 1960, Henry Collection, permission to quote granted by Elihu Burritt Library. Regarding the reference to Esau in the Old Testament, Esau sold his birthright to Jacob. Gross's suggestion that it was an open secret that he ghosted Henry's article probably reflected the fact that Canon Jones only came to know Gross in 1965, after Henry had died. Apparently, Gross's clerical history and his homosexuality was not an open secret, as surmised from my phone interview with Jones, 17 January 2000.

63. Alfred A. Gross, *Strangers in Our Midst* (Washington, D.C.: Public Affairs Press, 1962); idem, "The Church's Mission to the Sexually Deviated," typescript of an address delivered before the Missionary Society of the Berkeley Divinity School, New Haven, 23 November 1964, Henry Collection; idem, "A Minority Becomes Articulate," typescript of a lecture delivered before the Clinical Training (Divinity) Students at St. Lukes Hospital, New York, 13 April 1972, 5.

Chapter 6

1. Wardell B. Pomeroy, *Dr. Kinsey and the Institute for Sex Research* (1972; reprint, New Haven: Yale University Press, 1982), 169.

2. Thomas Painter, "Male Homosexuals and Their Prostitutes in Contemporary America," 2 vols., unpublished manuscript, 1941, Thomas Painter Papers, Kinsey Institute Archives, Indiana University, appendix, 1:7. All quotes in this chapter from the Kinsey Institute Archives are reprinted by permission of the Kinsey Institute for Research in Sex, Gender, and Reproduction, Inc.

3. On Foucault's views about subjective agency, see David M. Halperin, *Saint Foucault: Towards a Gay Hagiography* (New York: Oxford University Press, 1995).

4. Thomas Painter, "Long Search," unpublished autobiographical essay, 1973, Painter Papers, 1.

5. Eve Kosofsky Sedgwick, *Tendencies* (Durham, N.C.: Duke University Press, 1993); Judith Butler, *Bodies that Matter: On the Discursive Limits of "Sex"* (New York: Routledge, 1993). Also see Halperin, *Saint Foucault.*

6. My portrayal of Painter's life is based on his various unpublished autobiographical essays, written between 1970 and 1973, which are contained in the biographical file in the Painter Papers. These papers also contain an extensive collection of personal diary-journals, as well as other personal memorabilia. In addition, Painter's published autobiographical account of his life through his early thirties as well as his family background appears in George W. Henry, *Sex Variants: A Study of Homosexual Patterns,* 2 vols. (New York: Hoeber, 1941), 1:370–83, under the pseudonym of Will G.

7. Thomas Painter, "Biography V," unpublished autobiographical essay, undated but written around 1970, 1.

8. Henry, *Sex Variants,* 1:375.

9. Thomas Painter, "Will Finch," unpublished autobiographical essay, 1970, 1.

10. For an analysis of the transformations in idealized masculinity, see E. Anthony Rotundo, *American Manhood: Transformations from the Revolution to the Modern Era* (New York: Basic Books, 1993). On Painter's characterization of Theodore Roosevelt, see "Roosevelt, Theodore," in Index of Names, annotated index file, first entries undated but most likely compiled in the late 1940s when Painter first worked on his papers at the Kinsey Institute, revised in 1961, Painter Papers.

11. Painter, "Will Finch," 4–5.

12. On E. M. Forster and *Maurice,* see Byrne Fone, *A Road to Stonewall: Male Homosexuality and Homophobia in English and American Literature, 1750–1969* (New York: Twayne, 1995), chap. 10; Christopher Lane, "Betrayal and Its Consolations in *Maurice,* 'Arthur Snatchfold,' and 'What Does It Matter? A Morality'" in *Queer Forster,* ed. Robert K. Martin and George Piggford (Chicago: University of Chicago Press, 1997), 167–91.

13. The episodes of wrestling are referred to in Thomas Painter, unpublished, untitled autobiographical essay, 1 February 1944, 49; idem, "Biography VII," unpublished autobiographical essay, 1970, 1.

14. Painter, "Biography VII," 3.

15. Will G., in Henry, *Sex Variants,* 1:378. In referring to his orgasm, Painter described his preferred mode of sexual practice, known as frictation (body rubbing). In a related statement, Painter declared, "In my habitual relations I lie on the body and go off on the stomach. The hair acts as a stimulus on my testicles" (378).

16. Ibid.

17. Painter, "Biography VIII," unpublished autobiographical essay, undated but written around 1970, 5. Adler generally ascribed psychopathology and social deviancy to faulty family dynamics. He theorized homosexuality as a compensation for inferiority feelings and a revolt against the demands of social life. The revolt originates in the child's belligerent, inimical position in the family. On Adler's views about homosexuality, see Alfred Adler, *The Practice and Theory of Individual Psychology* (1924; reprint, New York: Harcourt, Brace, 1927), 184–96.

18. Painter, "Biography VII," 2–3.

19. "Jack Flaherty" was the pseudonym that Painter used. Biographical sketches of Flaherty appear in the Index of Names, and in Painter, "Male Homosexuals," 2:103–4. To protect the anonymity of Painter's sex partners and homosexual friends, I use only first names or the pseudonyms that Painter used.

20. Painter, "Biography V," 3.

21. Thomas Painter, "Biography VI," unpublished autobiographical essay, 1970, 6.

22. Painter, "Biography V," 4.

23. Painter, "Biography VIII," 9. "Willie O'Rourke" was the pseudonym that Painter used. His biographical sketch appears in idem, "Male Homosexuals," 2:104–5.

24. Painter, "Biography VIII," 7; "Tucker, Luther," Index of Names. Dickinson's favorable impression of Painter was most likely helped because Dickinson, a gynecologist, had known Painter's father. Moreover, he checked with Union Theological Seminary and, at least for a recommendation regarding research on homosexuality, Painter received a favorable endorsement. See Minutes of the meeting of the Executive Committee of the National Committee on Maternal Health, 5 December 1934, Robert Latou Dickinson Papers, box 6, folder 225, Countway Library of Medicine, Boston. Painter's contribution to recruiting the male sample appears to have been limited to a small subsample of the hustlers he knew. Henry, who cross-referenced friendship networks in each of his case studies, listed Peter R., Leonard R., and Victor R. under Will G. (Painter's pseudonym), in Henry, *Sex Variants,* 1:370. Peter R. and Leonard R. were hustlers—the latter was Painter's nonsexual roommate for several months. Victor R. was a hustler who ran a male brothel.

25. Henry, *Sex Variants,* 1:379.

26. Ibid.; emphasis in original.

27. Ibid., 380. For the case of Will G., see ibid., 370–83. Unlike the other participants in the sex variants study, it appears that Henry knew Painter's real identity since Painter was employed by the sex variants committee. In the introduction to the case of Victor R. (ibid., 438), Henry indicated that because of Victor R.'s reluctance to participate, a "field worker" had to accompany him to the interview. Painter, who was a friend of Victor R. and had recruited him for the study, would have been the field-worker referred to. Painter had an aversion to any personality characteristic or sexual practice that had a feminine connotation. For example, in his essay on his ideal sexual object, included in Henry's case study of Will G. (ibid., 379–80), Painter indicated that he generally eschewed kissing or being kissed. He appeared to think of the label of "homosexual" as an embodiment of the fairy stereotype, which was the exact opposite of his virile, rugged image of Will Finch. In his manuscript on male homosexuality and male prostitution, he spelled out his rejection of effeminate homosexuals—see Painter, "Male Homosexuals," 1:155–56.

28. Painter's description of voyeuristic arousal appears in Thomas Painter to Alfred C. Kinsey, 9 September 1953, Journal (1953), Painter Papers.

29. Robert W. Laidlaw, "Resumé of the [sex variants] Committee's Activities since the Last Meeting Held on March 29th, 1935," attached to Laidlaw to Lewis M. Terman, 18 September 1935, Lewis M. Terman Papers, box 12, folder 26, Stanford University Archives, 2.

30. Legman's work with the maternal health committee is referred to in the correspondence between Robert Latou Dickinson and Gershon Legman, 22 August 1937 to 4 February 1943, box 1, folder 83, Dickinson Papers.

31. Painter, "Biography VIII," 7.

32. Thomas Painter, unpublished, untitled autobiographical essay, March 1939, 12.

33. Ibid., 16. Painter distinguished the casual hustler from the professional hustler, who relied exclusively on prostitution for his livelihood over an extended period of time. See Painter, "Male Homosexuals," 2:3–7.

34. Thomas Painter, "Chronology III," unpublished memorandum, 1969, 1.

35. Painter maintained friendships with Tony and Peter for several years after his sexual relationship with them ended, and he financially helped Tony start a

coal business. Regarding "kept boys," see Painter, "Male Homosexuals," 2:3–7, for his classification of male prostitutes. In addition to the professional and casual prostitute, there was also the "private prostitute." A "kept boy" came under this category. This was a person involved in an extended relationship with a homosexual who, in return for sexual favors, provided financial support. Painter reported that Tony had some conflict about being thought of as a "kept boy," as evidenced by his brief breakup of their relationship at the time Painter was to receive his father's inheritance (Painter, "Biography VII," 12).

36. Painter, "Male Homosexuals," 1:42.

37. Legman's claims to authorship are referred to in Legman to Alfred C. Kinsey, 3 November 1942, 21 March 1943, and 13 April 1943, Kinsey Institute Archives. The glossary, under Legman's name, appeared in Henry, *Sex Variants*, 2:1149–79. Legman wrote a hundred-page section on annotated toilet epigraphs, which did not appear in Painter's manuscript. According to Painter (autobiographical manuscript, September 1944, Painter Papers), these epigraphs were actually collected by a hustler-friend who Painter hired to make the collection. Legman succeeded in getting Painter to pay him for his bibliographic work, which amounted to about $2,000 (Legman to Kinsey, 5 April 1945, Kinsey Institute Archives). When Painter went into the army in 1942, Legman continued to work on the bibliography under Kinsey's supervision, but Kinsey severed his connection when he found errors in Legman's work (Kinsey to Legman, 26 March 1945). The bibliography project did provide Painter with a library of books on homosexuality, which he donated to Kinsey ("Legman, Gershon," Index of Names). Dickinson became acquainted with Legman in 1937, shortly after Legman came to New York from his home in Scranton, Pennsylvania. At the time Legman, who was about nineteen, was interested in a career as a scientific writer-researcher. He did not have the money for a college education. Initially Dickinson considered him to be a very good library researcher and bibliographer (Dickinson to Smith Ely Jelliffe, 8 June 1937, Dickinson Papers). When Kinsey, in 1945, began to have trouble in his dealings with Legman's bibliographic work, Dickinson changed his opinion (see chapter 7). Legman eventually became a well-respected independent scholar of erotic humor. See Janny Scott, "Gershon Legman, Anthologist of Erotic Humor Dies at 81," *New York Times*, 14 March 1999, 29.

38. Painter, "Biography V," 5.

39. "Schwartz, Leonard (Sgt.)," Index of Names.

40. Dickinson sent a letter on Painter's behalf to several senior army and navy officers (Dickinson to Whom It May Concern, 25 February 1944, Painter Papers). Even before Painter enlisted in the army in March 1942, Dickinson attempted to secure a special position for Painter (Dickinson to Admiral Edward R. Stitt, 12 December 1941). Attached to these letters was a one-page résumé of Painter's background and personal qualifications as well as Dickinson's personal impressions.

41. Robert Latou Dickinson, notes on Painter's manuscript, 21 November 1941, box 11, folder 49, Dickinson Papers. In these notes, Dickinson indicated that in order to make the manuscript a medical book, "Dr." had to appear on the title page. It is not clear what Dickinson had in mind; that is, a medical coauthor or a foreword or introduction by a physician. It may have been the latter since Dickinson indicated to Painter that the book should be his work (Dickinson to

Thomas Painter, 16 February 1942, Painter Papers). References to Painter's work appear in Dickinson to Kinsey, 18 June 1941, and Kinsey to Dickinson, 23 June 1941, Kinsey Institute Archives. Regarding Kinsey's publication, see Alfred C. Kinsey, "Criteria for a Hormonal Explanation of the Homosexual," *Journal of Clinical Endocrinology and Metabolism* 1 (1941): 424–28.

42. Kinsey to Dickinson, 16 February 1943.

43. Painter to Dickinson, quote referred to in "Henry, Dr. George," Index of Names.

44. Kinsey to Legman, 18 May 1943.

45. Kinsey to Painter, 27 October 1943.

46. Painter to Kinsey, 14 November 1943.

47. Kinsey to Painter, 18 November 1943.

48. Painter donated his library at Legman's suggestion and viewed it as an essential part of Kinsey's plans for a research center on sexuality. He referred to the model of Magnus Hirschfeld's Institute for Sexual Science (Painter to Kinsey, 11 February 1944, Painter Papers). Painter was paid $450 for his library (Dickinson to Painter, 19 December 1945). When he went into the army, Painter had loaned his manuscript to Alfred A. Gross, Henry's research associate. Painter claimed that Gross refused to return the manuscript ("Gross," Index of Names). Painter's manuscript included a critique of Henry's *Sex Variants* monograph (Painter, "Male Homosexuals," vol. 1, section of eight pages, unnumbered). Painter criticized Henry for his lack of bibliographical citations of the literature on homosexuality as well as his inaccuracies regarding the cases of Will G. (Painter) and Leonard R. (a friend of Painter's). Painter's personal animosity toward Henry stemmed from his dislike of Gross. He felt that Gross was Henry's "stooge" and that they were involved, during the war, in running a "racket" of diagnosing homosexuality for the selective service ("Gross," Index of Names). On Henry and Gross's wartime work, see chapter 5.

49. Painter, "Biography V," 5.

50. Kinsey to Legman, 9 August 1943, Kinsey Institute Archives.

51. When Kinsey acquired the typescript, he had it bound in two volumes. On Edward Prime-Stevenson and Earl Lind, see chapter 2; on Donald Webster Cory, see chapter 8.

52. Thomas Painter, "De Profundis," essay in appendix in Painter, "Male Homosexuals," 1:1.

53. Ibid., 1–2; emphasis in original. Oscar Wilde wrote a well-known essay using the same title, but Painter does not refer to Wilde. With his interest in religion, Painter appears to have drawn his "confession" from the New Testament, Psalm 130. Later in his essay, most likely referring to his failed relationships with Tony and Peter, Painter stated, "Having tasted love, how can I live without it?" (3).

54. Painter, "Male Homosexuals," 1:16.

55. Kinsey to Painter, 27 October 1943. Painter suggested that a sex research committee ("Male Homosexuals," 1:12–16) should be broadly constituted to include medicoscientific experts as well as clergy, penologists, and representatives from the homosexual community. Dickinson in his notes on Painter's manuscript listed a number of individuals, including himself and Robert Laidlaw, the secretary of the sex variants committee. Painter envisioned his committee as primarily involved in promoting research rather than, as in the case of the Kinsey Institute, conducting its own research.

56. Painter, "Male Homosexuals," 2:241. On the paradox of "coming out," see Eve Kosofsky Sedgwick, *Epistemology of the Closet* (Berkeley: University of California Press, 1990), 67–90. The pervasiveness of self-blame ascribed to inner pathology is evident in the Henry case studies (see chapter 4) as well as sources that touch on self-characterization and coming out in the 1950s and 1960s. See Donald Webster Cory [Edward Sagarin], "A Preface to the Second Edition: One Decade Later," in *The Homosexual in America*, 2nd ed. (New York: Castle Books, 1960), xix–xxv; Peter M. Nardi, David Sanders, and Judd Marmor, *Growing Up before Stonewall: Life Stories of Some Gay Men* (New York: Routledge, 1994); Martin Duberman, *Cures: A Gay Man's Odyssey* (New York: Dutton, 1991).

57. Painter's commentary on lesbianism appears in Painter, "Male Homosexuals," 1:40.

58. While Painter was generally critical of the American literature on homosexuality, he did note that there were some valuable contributions. Among these he included the works of Earl Lind and Edward Prime-Stevenson (see chapter 2), as well as Clarence Joseph Bulliet, *Venus Castina: Famous Female Impersonators, Celestial and Human* (New York: Covici-Friede, 1928); and George Devereaux, "Institutionalized Homosexuality of the Mohave Indians," *Human Biology* 9 (1937): 498–527. He was especially positive about Devereaux's work because it did not contain a negative view about homosexuality and was based on interviews that described homosexual practices.

59. Painter, "Male Homosexuals," 1:101. Painter's citation of the New York homosexual subculture included an 1879 thirty-six-page pamphlet, titled *Sodom in Union Square; or Revelations of the Doings in 14th St. by an Ex-Police Captain.*

60. Painter, "Male Homosexuals," 1:106. Consistent with Henry and Gross's observation (see chapter 5), Painter pointed out that blackmail and victimization were more of a threat to homosexuals who were not socially well connected. On the police and legal crackdowns in the 1930s, see Estelle B. Freedman, "Uncontrolled Desires: The Response to the Sexual Psychopath, 1920–1960," *Journal of American History* 74 (June 1987): 83–106; George Chauncey, *Gay New York: Gender, Urban Culture, and the Making of the Gay Male World, 1890–1940* (New York: Basic Books, 1994), 331–54; Jennifer Terry, *An American Obsession: Science, Medicine, and Homosexuality in Modern Society* (Chicago: University of Chicago Press, 1999), chap. 8.

61. In Painter's analysis of sexual orientation categories, he was critical of such researchers as Henry who erroneously classified male hustlers as homosexuals. On Kinsey's classification scheme, see Alfred C. Kinsey, Wardell B. Pomeroy, and Clyde E. Martin, *Sexual Behavior in the Human Male* (Philadelphia: Saunders, 1948), 638. On Ulrichs, see Hubert Kennedy, *Ulrichs: The Life and Works of Karl Heinrich Ulrichs, Pioneer of the Modern Gay Movement* (Boston: Alyson, 1988); idem, "Karl Heinrich Ulrichs: First Theorist of Homosexuality," in *Science and Homosexualities*, ed. Vernon A. Rosario (New York: Routledge, 1997), 26–43. Ulrichs was the first to argue that some individuals were bisexual.

62. Painter, "Male Homosexuals," 1:132, 134. In noting that male homosexuals were sexually aggressive, Painter was also critical of the common tendency among sex researchers to classify homosexuals as active and passive. He argued

that sexual practices among homosexual men involved each person assuming a variety of roles.

63. Painter's observation of working-class tolerance for homosexuality is consistent with what Chauncey reports in his treatment of gay male history from 1890 to 1940—see Chauncey, *Gay New York,* 47–63.

64. Painter, "Male Homosexuals," 1:154.

65. Painter did acknowledge that among the "minority" of male homosexuals who were attracted to other homosexuals, relationships did, at times, develop. He believed, however, that these relationships did not generally last for a long period of time (ibid., 2:180–81). On friendships in the gay male subculture of pre–World War II, see Chauncey, *Gay New York,* chap. 6. In Paul Robinson, *Gay Lives: Homosexual Autobiographies from John Addington Symonds to Paul Monette* (Chicago: University of Chicago Press, 1999), chap. 5, Robinson contrasts the lives of Jeb Alexander with Donald Vining. Alexander, in his diary (1918–45), depicted a life filled with loneliness, while Vining, in his diaries (1933–46, 1946–54), wrote about the significance of friendships and long-term relationships in his life.

66. Painter, "Male Homosexuals," 1:159–60.

67. Ibid., 1:160.

68. Ibid., 1:170; emphasis in original.

69. Ibid., 1:178–79.

70. Ibid., 1:180. On Cory's characterization of bars, see Donald Webster Cory [Edward Sagarin], *The Homosexual in America: A Subjective Approach* (New York: Greenberg, 1951), chap. 11; on Hooker's portrayal, see Evelyn Hooker, "Male Homosexuals and Their 'Worlds,'" in *Sexual Inversion: The Multiple Roots of Homosexuality,* ed. Judd Marmor (New York: Basic Books, 1965), 83–107. On Cory and Hooker, also see chapter 8.

71. Painter, "Male Homosexuals," 1:180; emphasis in original.

72. Ibid., 1:180–81.

73. Ibid., 1:183. The "commercial cocktail hour" was by invitation only and required an entrance fee, which covered the cost of liquor. According to Painter, these events became less popular by the late 1930s because of police crackdowns, based on the fact that the hosts did not have liquor licenses.

74. Ibid., 1:186.

75. Ibid., 1:190–92.

76. On drag balls, see Chauncey, *Gay New York,* 332. Chauncey describes the drag balls in New York, many of which were held in Harlem. Painter also referred to Harlem as a popular site for drag balls. Related to his discussion of drag balls, he also briefly described the Philadelphia Mummer's Parade on New Year's Day and the Mardi Gras in New Orleans.

77. Ibid., 24, 22.

78. Painter's critique of his own work on male prostitution appears on a page attached to the cover page of Painter, "Male Homosexuals," vol. 2, dated 2 September 1962. Painter became familiar with the muscle-boy and Hispanic subcultures after World War II and wrote extensively about them in his journals. This will be covered in chapter 7. In his volume, Painter also noted another form of male prostitution—men who prostitute themselves to women ("gigolos")—but considered this to be rare and beyond the scope of his work. Regarding the het-

erosexual male prostitutes during the Depression era, see Chauncey, *Gay New York*, 191–93, who, in addition to citing Painter's manuscript, refers to other sources, including Tennessee Williams, *Memoirs* (New York: Bantam, 1976). Overall, male prostitution has not been a well-researched area. Outside of the work by Lind and Painter, nothing appeared in the American scientific literature until 1946. For this early literature, see William Marlin Butts, "Boy Prostitutes of the Metropolis," *Journal of Clinical Psychopathology* 8 (1946–47): 673–81; H. Laurence Ross, "The Hustler in Chicago," *The Journal of Student Research* 1 (September 1959): 13–19; Albert J. Reiss Jr., "The Social Integration of Queers and Peers," *Social Problems* 9 (1961): 102–20. Also see the novel by John Rechy, *City of Night* (New York: Grove Press, 1963), and his autobiographical treatment, *The Sexual Outlaw: A Documentary* (New York: Grove Press, 1977). For recent work, see Samuel M. Steward, *Understanding the Male Hustler* (New York: Harrington Park Press, 1991); Donald J. West in association with Buz de Villiers, *Male Prostitution* (New York: Harrington Park Press, 1993).

79. Painter, "Male Homosexuals," 2:1.

80. Painter noted that women, unlike men, could not conduct their business independently; that is, they had to work out of whorehouses and were often dependent on a pimp. Furthermore, female prostitutes were stigmatized and had little chance of getting married.

81. On the Forty-second Street scene, see Chauncey, *Gay New York,* 192–93.

82. Painter, "Male Homosexuals," 2:41, 44, 45, 46. Black hustlers, however, in both Harlem and Times Square had no problem in attracting white customers. Painter commented that some gay white men had an exclusive passion for blacks.

83. With the repeal of Prohibition, restrictive legislation was passed in state legislatures throughout the country that governed the conduct of taverns and limited the clientele they could serve. See Chauncey, *Gay New York,* 335–54.

84. Painter, "Male Homosexuals," 2:64.

85. Ibid., 2:12. Painter cited an unpublished glossary of prostitution slang compiled by David W. Maurer but does not indicate how the term originated. Maurer had also compiled a glossary of homosexual terms, which Legman made use of in his glossary that appeared in Henry, *Sex Variants*.

86. Painter ("Male Homosexuals," 2:72) did not refer to the work of Richard Burton, the nineteenth-century ethnographer who first described the peg house. On Burton, see Richard Burton, ed. and trans., *A Plain and Literal Translation of the Arabian Nights' Entertainments, Now Entitled The Book of the Thousand Nights and A Night, with Introduction, Explanatory Notes on the Manners and Customs of Moslem Men and a Terminal Essay upon the History of the Nights,* 10 vols. (London: Kama Shastra Society, 1885). For analyses of the Walsh scandal, see C. A. Tripp, *The Homosexual Matrix* (New York: McGraw-Hill, 1975), 224–27; Lawrence R. Murphy, "The House on Pacific Street: Homosexuality, Intrigue, and Politics during World War II," *Journal of Homosexuality* 12, no. 1 (1985): 27–49. For a description of Beekman's house, see Martin Duberman, *About Time: Exploring the Gay Past,* rev. ed. (New York: Meridian, 1991), 72–73. Because of its location near the Brooklyn Navy Yard, Beekman's house catered to servicemen who were paid for having sex with homosexual clients. Through political pressure, Senator Walsh was exonerated of any connection with prostitution, even though the evidence pointed to his having been a

frequent visitor to the house. There was, however, no evidence that he had any contact with the two German aliens who were also house clients. As for the Germans, although there was no evidence that they had spied, they were imprisoned for the duration of the war. Beekman, the peg house proprietor, was arrested for sodomy and imprisoned for twenty-two years, even though he had cooperated by identifying the German aliens.

87. "Husband" was a term that also had a more general usage. It referred to straight-appearing men who became involved in homosexual relationships but did not identify themselves as homosexual. See Chauncey, *Gay New York,* 86–96.

88. See "Costello, Matty"; "Rogers, Danny," Index of Names, Painter Papers. On Costello, also see "Victor R.," in Henry, *Sex Variants,* 1:438–50.

89. Painter, "Male Homosexuals," 2:74.

90. As a protection against blackmail or other forms of victimization, it was a general practice among gay men to use only first names for introductions. The use of a pseudonym was a common practice at Gustave Beekman's house—see Murphy, "The House on Pacific Street," 29–30.

91. Painter to Paul H. Gebhard, 24 April 1962, Journal (1962), Painter Papers, 1.

92. Painter, "Male Homosexuals," 2:82.

93. The closing down of peg houses is referred to in Murphy, "The House on Pacific Street." The post–World War II changes in male prostitution are referred to in "Costello, Matty," and "Rogers, Danny," Index of Names.

94. Painter, "Male Homosexuals," 2:88.

95. Painter (ibid., 2:83–86) also described how homosexuals in small cities and towns explored locales where young boys worked or gathered, such as gas stations, town squares, or general stores, and the conversational strategies they used to seduce desired sex partners. Even though most of these boys were not hustlers, some would be "seduced" by the offer of paid sex. Regarding suede shoes, Painter indicated that 90 percent of the buyers were homosexuals.

96. Of the sixty-seven hustlers, Painter (ibid., 2:176–77) indicated that forty-five were professionals; the remainder were either casual hustlers or "kept boys."

97. Ibid., 2:165.

98. On Leonard R., see Henry, *Sex Variants,* 1:451–65. Painter's profile was consistent with the autobiographical text in the Henry monograph. The biographical sketch of "Jean Driscoll" appears in Painter, "Male Homosexuals," 2:117–18.

99. Painter, "Male Homosexuals," vol. 2, 1962 critique. As in the case of Jean Driscoll, homosexual hustlers were often involved in a series of relationships with heterosexual hustlers who took the role of "husband." To cater to the "wolf" clientele, a "colony" of homosexual hustlers functioned on West Seventy-second Street in Manhattan because this location was close to the point of disembarkation for sailors.

100. Painter, however, also pointed to the social and economic hardships male prostitutes endured and argued that improving the opportunities for poor youths would reduce their attraction to prostitution.

101. Ibid., 2:206.

102. Ibid., 2:241.

Chapter 7

1. For biographies of Kinsey, see Cornelia V. Christenson, *Kinsey: A Biography* (Bloomington: Indiana University Press, 1971); Wardell B. Pomeroy, *Dr. Kinsey and the Institute for Sex Research* (1972; reprint, New Haven: Yale University Press, 1982); James H. Jones, *Alfred C. Kinsey: A Public/Private Life* (New York: Norton, 1997); Jonathan Gathorne-Hardy, *Alfred C. Kinsey: Sex the Measure of All Things* (London: Chatto & Windus, 1988).

2. Jones, *Kinsey,* chap. 14; Gathorne-Hardy, *Kinsey,* 91–98, 124–30.

3. Jones, *Kinsey,* chaps. 17, 18. The "Kinsey Reports" were Alfred C. Kinsey, Wardell B. Pomeroy, and Clyde E. Martin, *Sexual Behavior in the Human Male* (Philadelphia: Saunders, 1948); Alfred C. Kinsey, Wardell B. Pomeroy, Clyde E. Martin, and Paul H. Gebhard, *Sexual Behavior in the Human Female* (Philadelphia: Saunders, 1953).

4. Jones, *Kinsey;* Gathorne-Hardy, *Kinsey.* Kinsey's penchant for sexual liberation was practiced, at his insistence, by the staff of male sex researchers, who engaged in wife swapping—see Gathorne-Hardy, *Kinsey,* 168.

5. Gathorne-Hardy, *Kinsey,* 137–38.

6. Alfred C. Kinsey to Ralph Voris, quote cited in Pomeroy, *Dr. Kinsey,* 63–64.

7. Kinsey to Geraldine Voris, 9 October 1940, Kinsey Institute Archives, Indiana University. All quotes in this chapter from the Kinsey Institute Archives are reprinted by permission of the Kinsey Institute for Research in Sex, Gender, and Reproduction, Inc.

8. Pomeroy, *Dr. Kinsey,* 47, 50; Jones, *Kinsey,* 271–72; Gathorne-Hardy, *Kinsey,* 149–50.

9. Pomeroy, *Dr. Kinsey,* 132–34; interview with Herbert Huncke, *Alfred Kinsey: Pioneer of the Sexual Revolution,* film produced by the BBC, 1996. Huncke became a writer who was closely associated with the Beat group of writers, including William S. Burroughs, Jack Kerouac, and Allen Ginsberg. He introduced Kinsey to Burroughs, who in turn recruited a number of volunteers for Kinsey to interview. Huncke died in 1996 at the age of eighty-one—see "Transaction," *The Advocate,* 17 September 1996, 23. On Huncke, also see Herbert Huncke, *Guilty of Everything* (New York: Hanuman Books, 1990).

10. Alfred C. Kinsey, "Criteria for a Hormonal Explanation of the Homosexual," *Journal of Clinical Endocrinology and Metabolism* 1 (1941): 424–28; Clifford A. Wright, "Endocrine Aspects of Homosexuality: A Preliminary Report," *Medical Record* 142 (1935): 407–10; idem, "Further Studies of Endocrine Aspects of Homosexuality," *Medical Record* 147 (1938): 449–52; idem, "The Sex Offender's Endocrines," *Medical Record* 149 (1939): 399–402; Samuel J. Glass, H. J. Deuel, and Clifford A. Wright, "Sex Hormone Studies in Male Homosexuality," *Endocrinology* 26 (1940): 590–94. For an analysis of the Kinsey and Wright articles, see Stephanie H. Kenen, "Who Counts When You're Counting Homosexuals? Hormones and Homosexuality in Mid–Twentieth Century America," in *Science and Homosexualities,* ed. Vernon A. Rosario (New York: Routledge, 1997), 197–218. On the history of endocrinology, see Nelly Oudshoorn, "Endocrinologists and the Conceptualization of Sex, 1920–1940," *Journal of the History of Biology* 23 (1990): 163–86. Wright made a distinction between the congenital (passive) male homosexual and the acquired (active) male homosexual. His hormonal explanation only referred to the congenital homosexual. His

classification was quite common in the early twentieth century, stemming from Freud's and Ellis's consideration of innate versus acquired homosexuality. See Sigmund Freud, *Three Essays on the Theory of Sexuality* (1905; reprint, New York: Basic Books, 1953), 2–7; Havelock Ellis, *Studies in the Psychology of Sex. Volume II. Sexual Inversion,* 3rd ed., revised and enlarged (Philadelphia: Davis, 1928), 75–89.

11. Dickinson's remarks on meeting Kinsey, cited in Pomeroy, *Dr. Kinsey,* 157; Robert Latou Dickinson to Kinsey, 18 June 1941; Kinsey to Dickinson, 23 June 1941.

12. Regina Markell Morantz, "The Scientist as Sex Crusader: Alfred C. Kinsey and American Culture," *American Quarterly* 29 (1977): 563.

13. Pomeroy, *Dr. Kinsey,* 341.

14. The reported incidence of male homosexuality was reported in Kinsey, Pomeroy, and Martin, *Male,* 650; the incidence of female homosexuality, in Kinsey, Pomeroy, Martin, and Gebhard, *Female,* 474–75.

15. Jones, *Kinsey,* 349, 376, 382, 533; Gathorne-Hardy, *Kinsey,* 282–86, 362–63; Paul H. Gebhard and Alan B. Johnson, *The Kinsey Data: Marginal Tabulations of the 1938–1963 Interviews Conducted by the Institute for Sex Research* (Philadelphia: Saunders, 1979). In 1953 a team of statisticians evaluated Kinsey's male volume and concluded that his sampling procedures were appropriate and that overall his work was "outstanding." See William G. Cochran, Frederick Mosteller, and John W. Tukey, *Statistical Problems of the Kinsey Report on Sexual Behavior in the Human Male* (Washington, D.C.: American Statistical Association, 1954), 2.

16. Kinsey, Pomeroy, and Martin, *Male,* 199.

17. Ibid., 666. On Kinsey's essentialism, see Janice M. Irvine, *Disorders of Desire: Sex and Gender in Modern American Society* (Philadelphia: Temple University Press, 1990), 31–66.

18. On Kinsey's views about the differences between men and women on social conditioning, see Kinsey, Pomeroy, Martin, and Gebhard, *Female,* 685–89.

19. Kinsey, Pomeroy, and Martin, *Male,* 661.

20. On Kinsey's biological perspective, see James D. Weinrich, "The Kinsey Scale in Biology, with a Note on Kinsey as a Biologist," in *Homosexuality/Heterosexuality: Concepts of Sexual Orientation,* ed. David P. McWhirter, Stephanie A. Sanders, and June Machover Reinisch (New York: Oxford University Press, 1990), 115–37.

21. Kinsey's rationale for the interview is discussed in Kinsey, Pomeroy, and Martin, *Male,* 35–62.

22. Ibid., 41.

23. Pomeroy, *Dr. Kinsey,* 139. On Kinsey's skill as an interviewer, see Morantz, "Scientist as Sex Crusader," 569; Pomeroy, *Dr. Kinsey,* 5; Samuel M. Steward, *Chapters from an Autobiography* (San Francisco: Grey Fox Press, 1981), 98. According to Steward, Kinsey took up smoking and drinking (to a limited extent) to put his respondents at ease.

24. Kinsey, Pomeroy, and Martin, *Male,* 263, 659.

25. On homosexual offenses, see ibid., 664–66; Kinsey, Pomeroy, Martin, and Gebhard, *Female,* 483–86.

26. William Simon, "Kinsey: An Immodest Appreciation," *Sexualities* 1 (1998): 94–96. See Morantz, "Scientist as Sex Crusader," 584, who notes that al-

though Kinsey was accepting of homosexuality, he remained bound to the Victorian ideal of happy, stable marriages. Also see Paul Robinson, *The Modernization of Sex* (New York: Harper & Row, 1976), 69, who points out that Kinsey was critical of the high incidence of male homosexual promiscuity. On Kinsey's views about homosexual identity, see Kinsey, Pomeroy, and Martin, *Male,* 614–17, 636–38.

27. On an assessment of Kinsey's legacy as a sex researcher, see "Kinsey: A 50th Anniversary Symposium," ed. Peter M. Nardi and Beth E. Schneider, *Sexualities* 1 (1998): 83–106.

28. Pomeroy, *Dr. Kinsey,* 139. On Kinsey's plans to study the "heterosexual-homosexual" balance, see ibid., 445–47.

29. Thomas Waugh, *Hard to Imagine: Gay Male Eroticism in Photography and Film from Their Beginnings to Stonewall* (New York: Columbia University Press, 1996), 391. Another source for acquiring visual materials was provided by law enforcement agencies, which, with the arrangements initiated by Kinsey, sent confiscated homoerotic photography to the Kinsey Institute Archives.

30. Cited in Pomeroy, *Dr. Kinsey,* 6.

31. Clarence A. Tripp to Kinsey, 3 November 1948 and 31 July 1951, Kinsey Institute Archives; interview with Bill Dellenback, 26 June 1996. On Tripp's association with Kinsey, also see Pomeroy, *Dr. Kinsey,* 5, 173–75, 308–9; Jones, *Kinsey,* 605–6; Gathorne-Hardy, *Kinsey,* 294–96; Waugh, *Hard to Imagine,* 394–95, 398–99. Also see, C. A. Tripp, *The Homosexual Matrix* (New York: McGraw-Hill, 1975). The films were made in the attic of Kinsey's home in order to avoid the ethical issues that would have ensued if they were made on the Indiana University campus. Gay men were especially eager to volunteer, and the films were therefore disproportionately homoerotic in content. For an analysis of the Kinsey films, see Waugh, *Hard to Imagine,* 398–400.

32. Steward, *Chapters,* 102, 98–99. For other recent writings of Steward, see idem, *Bad Boys and Tough Tattoos: A Social History of the Tattoo with Gangs, Sailors, and Street-Corner Punks, 1950–1965* (Binghamton, N.Y.: Harrington Park Press, 1990); idem, *Understanding the Male Hustler* (New York: Harrington Park Press, 1991). Steward also wrote several homoerotic novels under the pseudonym of Phil Andros.

33. Pomeroy, *Dr. Kinsey,* 190–93; Jones, *Kinsey,* 611–12; Waugh, *Hard to Imagine,* 395; Ned Rorum, *Knowing When to Stop: A Memoir* (New York: Simon & Schuster, 1994), 345–47; Ted Shawn to Kinsey, 22 March 1946. Rorum kept up a correspondence with Kinsey, in which he reported his observations of homosexuality during his frequent visits to Europe and North Africa.

34. Kinsey to Gore Vidal, 4 April 1949.

35. Gore Vidal, *Palimpsest: A Memoir* (New York: Random House, 1995), 102–3; emphasis in original.

36. Glenway Wescott, *Continual Lessons: The Journal of Glenway Wescott, 1937–1955,* ed. Robert Phelps with Jerry Rosco (New York: Farrar, Straus and Giroux, 1990), 245–46.

37. On Wescott's work in Bloomington, see Pomeroy, *Dr. Kinsey,* 194–96; Jones, *Kinsey,* 611–12; Gathorne-Hardy, *Kinsey,* 351–54. Wescott informed Kinsey about the Mattachine Society in Glenway Wescott to Kinsey, 6 November 1951. Kinsey and Wescott had a sexual relationship (see Gathorne-Hardy, *Kinsey,* 354–56). On Wescott's relationship with Wheeler, see Gathorne-Hardy, *Kin-*

sey, 322–24. Wescott and Wheeler were also closely associated with photographer George Platt Lynes—see Anatole Pohorilenko and James Crump, *When We Were Three: The Travel Albums of George Platt Lynes, Monroe Wheeler, and Glenway Wescott, 1925–1935* (Santa Fe: Arena Editions, 1998).

38. Cited in Pomeroy, *Dr. Kinsey*, 191.

39. On Ginsberg's visit to the Institute, see Barry Miles, *Ginsberg: A Biography* (New York: Simon & Schuster, 1989), 386.

40. Waugh, *Hard to Imagine*, 392, 395–96; Kinsey to Kenneth Anger, 11 June 1954, 26 January, 14 May, and 4 August 1956.

41. Quote from Thomas Waugh's interview with Bob Mizer, June 1991, cited in Waugh, *Hard to Imagine*, 394; correspondence between Kinsey and Bob Mizer, 5 May 1948 through 18 July 1955.

42. Waugh, *Hard to Imagine*, 352–56, 392–93; Kinsey to Otis Wade, 10 May 1955.

43. Sixte Rapff to Kinsey, 27 July 1951, as cited in "Dr. Kinsey and Mr. 'X,'" in Martin Duberman, *About Time: Exploring the Gay Past*, rev. ed. (New York: Meridian, 1991), 196. Duberman used the pseudonym of Mr. X.

44. For Rapff, also see Pomeroy, *Dr. Kinsey*, 402–5, 424, 429, 440 (Pomeroy used the pseudonym RJ); Waugh, *Hard to Imagine*, 393–94. For Painter's contact, see "Thomas_____, Life Story of a Hustler," in Painter's 1947 bound Journal, Painter Papers. For the life story covering 1909 through 1972, see "My Gay Life," in Duberman, *About Time*, 68–79.

45. Kinsey quote, cited in John D'Emilio, *Sexual Politics, Sexual Communities: The Making of a Homosexual Minority in the United States, 1940–1970*, 2nd ed. (Chicago: University of Chicago Press, 1998), 83–84.

46. Hal Call, "Gay Sexualist," in *Making History: The Struggle for Gay and Lesbian Equal Rights, 1945–1990: An Oral History*, ed. Eric Marcus (New York: HarperCollins, 1992), 63. In addition to the Mattachine Society, Kinsey maintained contact with ONE, Inc., an offshoot of Mattachine that published the homophile magazine *ONE*. He was also in touch with Edward Sagarin, an activist who was one of the leaders of the Veterans Benevolent Association, a discussion group based in New York. For a discussion of the rise of the homophile organizations, see chapter 8.

47. Memorandum by Del Martin (president) to the membership of the San Francisco chapter, Daughters of Bilitis, undated, but distributed in advance of the meeting of 5 June 1959, Kinsey Institute Archives.

48. Billie Tallmij, "The Teacher—Billie Tallmij," in *Making History*, ed. Marcus, 76.

49. Gathorne-Hardy, *Kinsey*, 33, 363. As Gathorne-Hardy concludes, Kinsey was a very complex man whose personal relationships included both supportive and empathic associations with students and research collaborators and, at times, controlling and possessive interactions with students and Institute staff members.

50. D'Emilio, *Sexual Politics*, 37.

51. For the impact of Kinsey's work on the homophile movement, see Salvatore J. Licata, "The Homosexual Rights Movement in the United States: A Traditionally Overlooked Area of American History," *Journal of Homosexuality* 6, nos. 1/2 (1980–81): 161–89; D'Emilio, *Sexual Politics*, 33–37; Irvine, *Disorders of Desire*, 54; Waugh, *Hard to Imagine*, 401; Ronald Bayer, *Homosexuality and*

American Psychiatry: The Politics of Diagnosis, rev. ed., (Princeton: Princeton University Press, 1987), 45–46; Stephen O. Murray, *American Gay* (Chicago: University of Chicago Press, 1996), 47–48. Murray, in contrast with the other commentators, expressed reservations about how influential Kinsey's published volumes were to the homophile movement, but he acknowledged their role in raising group consciousness. For an example of Kinsey's revered standing in the homophile movement, see Lyn Pedersen [Jim Kepner], "A Tribute to Dr. Kinsey," in Jim Kepner, *Rough News, Daring News: 1950s' Pioneer Gay Press Journalism* (New York: Harrington Park Press, 1998), 127–31. On the McCarthy era persecution of homosexuals, see D'Emilio, *Sexual Politics,* 40–53.

52. Pomeroy, *Dr. Kinsey,* 169.

53. Kinsey to Thomas Painter, 27 October 1943, Kinsey Institute Archives.

54. Painter to Kinsey, 14 November 1943, Journal (1943–44), Thomas Painter Papers, Kinsey Institute Archives; Kinsey to Painter, 18 November 1943, Kinsey Institute Archives.

55. "Kinsey," 1, in Index of Names, annotated index file, Painter Papers. On the qualifications for being on Kinsey's staff, see Pomeroy, *Dr. Kinsey,* 101–3.

56. Quote in Painter to Kinsey, 25 November 1944, Journal (1944–45), Painter Papers; correspondence between Kinsey and Painter from 11 August 1944 to 25 November 1944, Kinsey Institute Archives and Painter Papers.

57. Kinsey to Painter, 24 August 1944, Kinsey Institute Archives.

58. On Painter's army observations—Kinsey to Painter, 21 August 1945. On Painter's suggested interview items for homosexuals—Painter to Kinsey, 23 September 1944, Journal (1944–45). On Painter's library—Kinsey to Painter, 8 February 1944, Kinsey Institute Archives; Painter to Kinsey, 11 February 1944, Journal (1943–44); Dickinson to Painter, 19 December 1945, Painter Papers. Painter's library consisted of many books on homosexuality that were not easily accessible from booksellers. He was paid $450 for his library. On Painter's personal collection—Painter to Kinsey, 11 February 1944, Journal (1943–44) and March 1945 (day not indicated), Journal (1944–45). Because of the pornographic nature of some of Painter's personal materials, he enlisted the help of Harry Benjamin, an endocrinologist who pioneered in the study of transsexualism. Painter had met Benjamin through Dickinson. On several occasions, Benjamin collected Painter's materials in suitcases, which Kinsey picked up during his visits to New York. For Benjamin's work on transsexualism, see Harry Benjamin, *The Transsexual Phenomenon* (New York: Julian Press, 1966).

59. Painter to Kinsey, 17 August 1944, Journal (1944–45).

60. Painter and Kinsey each independently arrived at the conception of a homosexual/heterosexual continuum in their writings in 1941. See Kinsey, "Criteria," 425; Thomas Painter, "Male Homosexuals and Their Male Prostitutes in Contemporary America," 2 vols., unpublished manuscript, 1941, 1:131, Painter Papers. Kinsey, himself, could not avoid the occasional reference to sexual type, as in the case of "homosexual individuals" and "homosexual males"—see Kinsey, Pomeroy, and Martin, *Male,* 632. Furthermore, as Paul Robinson points out, Kinsey believed that individuals who were involved in homosexual behavior displayed distinct characteristics, such as promiscuity and unstable sexual relationships—see Robinson, *Modernization,* 69–71.

61. Painter to Kinsey, 17 August 1944, Journal (1944–45); Kinsey to Painter, 24 August 1944, Kinsey Institute Archives.

62. Painter to Kinsey, 30 December 1944, Journal (1944–45).

63. Ibid. Kinsey's letter has not survived in the file of the Kinsey-Painter correspondence in the Kinsey Institute Archives, but portions of the letter are referred to in Painter's reply of 30 December 1944.

64. Ibid.

65. Painter to Kinsey, 14 January 1945, Journal (1944–45).

66. Kinsey to Painter, 19 January 1945, Kinsey Institute Archives.

67. Painter to Kinsey, 24 January 1945, Journal (1944–45).

68. Kinsey, Pomeroy, and Martin, *Male,* 661.

69. Although Painter targeted the search for etiology as the key to releasing homosexuals from their suffering, he also expressed the belief that if after a concerted research effort, the cause of homosexuality could not be determined and thus treatment would not be possible, then homosexuals must be given the opportunity to live freely. He did not share this point with Kinsey in his correspondence but expressed it in his manuscript ("Male Homosexuals," 2:241) and in an autobiographical essay, dated 1 February 1944, which is in his 1943–44 Journal. In this essay he declared, "I have a work . . . a contribution to make. That others must not bear what I bear, that the homosexual must not occur, or if he must that he must be freed to take his proper place in society. . . . Either there must be no more of us or we must be free. . . . Do away with the whole twisted, sordid, sad, horrid thing, if possible; if not give . . . [homosexuals] a chance—a chance for the 'dignity, honor and peace' which all men have, and also a fairer chance for the joy of life, which all men have" (54).

70. Painter to Kinsey, 30 December 1944, Journal (1944–45); Kinsey to Painter, 31 March 1945, Kinsey Institute Archives.

71. Painter to Kinsey, 30 December 1944, Journal (1944–45).

72. Thomas Painter, autobiographical essay, 1 February 1944, Journal (1943–44), 55. Painter later revealed that he did have sexual relationships with six fellow servicemen while he was stationed at Amarillo Airfield Base (Painter to Kinsey, 25 September 1946, Journal [1946]). Since he provided the dates of his sexual abstinence, these experiences occurred after he had written his autobiographical essay. Thus, after about two years of self-imposed sexual abstinence, Painter did seek out sexual encounters while he was living on base.

73. Quotes in Painter to Bill_____, 26 June 1944, Journal (1944–45); emphasis in original. It is not clear whether this letter was written before Painter became sexually active at the Amarillo base. To ensure confidentiality, only first names or pseudonyms are used for Painter's homosexual friends and sex partners.

74. On Kinsey's views about exclusive homosexuals changing their sexual preference, see Gathorne-Hardy, *Kinsey,* 140.

75. Thomas Painter, "Biography VI," unpublished autobiographical essay, 1970, 4. Painter moved out of Edward's apartment in 1946 because Edward needed the space for a new lover—Painter to Cher Mon Lieutenant (Bill), 7 April 1946, Journal (1946). Painter returned about eighteen months later. During the interim, he rented a room on Second Avenue near Forty-second Street.

76. Thomas Painter, "Biography VIII," 15; idem, "Biography V," unpublished autobiographical essays, written around 1970, 5, 8. Painter had begun to photograph his sex partners in the late 1930s, using the facilities and help of a photographic studio. His collection of photos (totaling around two thousand) from both the pre- and postwar periods is included in his papers at the Kinsey Institute.

77. Painter to Cher Mon Lieutenant (Bill), 7 April 1946, Journal (1946).

78. Painter to Kinsey, 22 September 1945, Journal (1944–45), 25 September 1946, Journal (1946); Painter to Bill, 11 April 1945 (date erroneously changed to 1946), Journal (1946); Luther Tucker to Painter, 20 and 25 March 1947, Journal (1947). As part of the Journal collection, Kinsey received copies of Tucker's letters to Painter.

79. Painter to Kinsey, 22 September 1945, Journal (1944–45), 27 March 1947, 2 April 1947, and 13 May 1947, Journal (1947). According to Paul Gebhard, Kinsey was generally "exasperated" with Painter's lifestyle because he continually overspent whatever finances he had (interview with Paul H. Gebhard, 22 March 1996). Painter's plans about a social work degree are indicated in Painter to Robert W. Laidlaw, 15 May 1947, Dickinson folder, Painter Papers. The letter is addressed to "Doctor," which is the salutation he used in his letters to Kinsey and Dickinson, but it seems clear that this letter was written to Laidlaw. In the letter, Painter indicated that he hoped to apply to the Columbia University School of Social Work. He expressed his concern that he might not be accepted because Marion Kenworthy, who was on the social work faculty and had been a member of the sex variants committee, knew he was homosexual. At his job, Painter was discreet about his sexual identity.

80. Painter to Kinsey, 27 February 1949, Journal (1949), and 26 January 1953, Journal (1953).

81. Painter to Kinsey, 11 July 1946, Journal (1946), and 21 May 1947, Journal (1947); Thomas Painter, "Male American Costumes, 1850–1950," Journal (1950), twenty pages. In this essay, Painter noted the trend toward more physically revealing dress.

82. Kinsey to Painter, 13 August 1946 and 27 June 1949, Kinsey Institute Archives.

83. "Agreement between Thomas Painter and Alfred C. Kinsey," 24 October 1947, Painter correspondence folder.

84. Painter to Kinsey, 29 and 30 July 1946, and 1 November 1946, Journal (1946), Painter Papers.

85. Painter to Kinsey, 8 August 1946, Journal (1946).

86. Painter to Kinsey, 28 August 1946 and 22 September 1946, Journal (1946). The correspondence between Painter and Jim took place before Painter obtained his position as a probation officer.

87. Painter to Kinsey, 1 January 1947, Journal (1947).

88. Painter to Kinsey, 11 December 1946, Journal (1946), and 4 March 1947, Journal (1947).

89. Roger_____ to Painter, 7 and 23 September 1947, Journal (1947).

90. Painter to Kinsey, 14 January, 5 March, 2 and 23 April, and 29 August 1949, Journal (1949).

91. Painter, "Biography V," 5; idem, "Biography VII," 17. On the postwar muscle magazines, see Waugh, *Hard to Imagine*, 215–53; F. Valentine Hooven III, *Beefcake: The Muscle Magazines of America, 1950–1970* (Cologne: Taschen, 1995). On the models, see Waugh, *Hard to Imagine*, 232–37. In the film *Beefcake*, about photographer Bob Mizer's Athletic Model Guild, there is the suggestion that hustling was fairly common among the models (*Beefcake*, 1999, film directed and produced by Thom Fitzgerald).

92. Painter to Kinsey, 7 May 1953, Journal (1953).

93. Painter to Kinsey, 9 September 1953, Journal (1953).

94. Painter to Kinsey, 19 April 1949, Journal (1949), 7 May 1953 and 19 September 1953, Journal (1953). After Kinsey's death in 1956, Painter continued the practice of sending all of his photographs to the Kinsey Institute. These are part of the Painter Papers at the Institute.

95. Thomas Painter, "Long Search," unpublished autobiographical essay, written around 1973, 3; Painter to Kinsey, 1 September 1951, Journal (1951), and 14 and 16 September 1953, Journal (1953).

96. Painter to Kinsey, 16 August 1947, Journal (1947).

97. Painter to Kinsey, 16 April 1951, Journal (1951).

98. Painter discussed the relativism of sex codes in connection with his descriptions of his fantasized homophile society, "Jedma," in Painter to Kinsey, 23 February 1949, Journal (1949). His increasing optimism was expressed in Painter to Kinsey, 12 July 1953, Journal (1953).

99. Painter to Kinsey, 29 January 1953, Journal (1953). In this letter, he was reporting his reactions to the film *Come Back Little Sheba,* which was about an alcoholic man in a loveless marriage. He identified his earlier sexual compulsion to hustlers with the drunken husband's attachment to a woman he did not love. Painter's later reflections appeared in Thomas Painter, "Biography VII," unpublished autobiographical essay, 1970, 2.

100. Painter described his association with Jimmy F. in various Journal entries, including Painter to Kinsey, 25 June, 31 July, and 29 August 1949, Journal (1949), as well as in an untitled short story, dated September 1953, Journal (1953).

101. Painter to Kinsey, 3 and 29 January 1953, Journal (1953); "The Clock Bar," 7 January 1961, Journal (1961). On the history of the Puerto Rican migration to the United States, see History Task Force, Centro de Estudios Puertorriqueños, *Labor Migration under Capitalism: The Puerto Rican Experience* (New York: Monthly Review Press, 1979). With the muscle-boy models and Puerto Ricans, Painter adapted his frictation method so that he ejaculated in a side position, rather than on top of his partners. This made his sex partners more comfortable since they were not in the female position when Painter reached orgasm.

102. Painter, "The Clock Bar," 2.

103. Painter, "Biography V," 8–9.

104. Ibid., 22–24. Indio eventually remarried in Puerto Rico and had five sons by his two wives.

105. Painter, "Biography VIII," 19. Painter's observations on the influence of Spanish culture on the sexual mores of Puerto Rican society in the 1950s is consistent with Ian Lumsden's analysis of sex and gender codes in Cuba during the same period. See Ian Lumsden, *Machos, Maricones, and Gays: Cuba and Homosexuality* (Philadelphia: Temple University Press, 1996), chap. 2.

106. Painter. "Biography V," 6; idem, untitled typescript (twelve single-spaced pages), February 1956. According to a penciled note, Painter was thinking of submitting the article to the *Reader's Digest,* but there is no indication that he followed through on this. In the article, he pointed out the common misconceptions about homosexuals, such as the belief that they were sexual predators and incapable of being in loving relationships. He argued for the need for public education and research and denounced the criminalizaton of homosexuality.

107. "_____, Bill," Index of Names. On Bill's death—Painter to Kinsey, 25 February 1953, Journal (1953), and 24 August 1956, Journal (1956).

108. Painter to Kinsey, 24 August 1956, Journal (1956).

109. Painter to Wardell B. Pomeroy, 29 August 1956, Kinsey Institute Archives. According to Paul Gebhard (interview, 22 March 1996), Kinsey sensed that Painter "worshiped" him. It is evident from Kinsey's correspondence that he thought highly of Painter as a scholar. Gebhard indicates, however, that Kinsey was exasperated with Painter's lifestyle of reckless spending, in which he would often end up in debt.

110. "Kinsey," Index of Names, 2–3; emphasis in original.

111. Painter to Pomeroy, 12 September 1956, Journal (1956). On the post-Kinsey directorship, see Pomeroy, *Dr. Kinsey,* 448. Pomeroy and Gebhard had proposed that they be appointed as codirectors, but the Indiana University administration divided their responsibilities. Pomeroy had a reputation as a sexual Don Juan. His compulsive sexuality included both sexes, but with a decided preference for women. On Pomeroy, see Jones, *Kinsey,* 481–82; Gathorne-Hardy, *Kinsey,* 205. Gebhard had liberal sexual attitudes and was attracted to Kinsey's promotion of extramarital relationships among the Institute staff. On Gebhard, see Jones, *Kinsey,* 499–500; Gathorne-Hardy, *Kinsey,* 246.

112. Painter to Pomeroy, 12 September 1956, Journal (1956). In this letter, Painter also revealed that he had been worried about physical symptoms that might have suggested cancer of the abdomen. The medical tests proved to be negative. A later reference to the "suicide letter" appeared in Painter to Pomeroy, 5 June 1961, Journal (1961).

113. Painter to Pomeroy, 22 October 1956, Journal (1956); emphasis in original.

114. Painter to Neddie, 10 March 1956, Journal (1956). Neddie was a friend of Painter's deceased friend Bill. Most of Painter's Journal entries during his travels in 1956 and 1957 were in the form of letters to Neddie, who in turn passed them on to the Kinsey Institute.

115. Painter to Neddie, 15 March 1956, Journal (1956).

116. Painter to Neddie, 24 March and 19 April 1956, Journal (1956). This gendered pattern of sexual acts has been noted in subsequent analyses of male homosexuality in Latin America. See Barry D. Adam, "In Nicaragua: Homosexuality without a Gay World," *Journal of Homosexuality* 24, nos. 3/4 (1993): 171–81; Joseph Carrier, *De Los Otres: Intimacy and Homosexuality among Mexican Men* (New York: Columbia University Press, 1995); Stephen O. Murray, *Latin American Male Homosexualities* (Albuquerque: University of New Mexico Press, 1995); Lumsden, *Machos, Maricones, and Gays;* Annick Prieur, *Mema's House, Mexico City: On Transvestites, Queens, and Machos* (Chicago: University of Chicago Press, 1998). Chauncey also noted a similar pattern of gendered homosexual relations in his analysis of the working-class male subculture of New York in the early twentieth century. See George Chauncey, *Gay New York: Gender, Urban Culture, and the Making of the Gay Male World, 1890–1940* (New York: Basic Books, 1994), 65–97. Also see chapter 4 for a discussion of the cross-gendered male homosexual identity of the "fairy." Luis was very willing to cooperate with Painter as a homosexual informant. Referring to Luis's contribution, Painter wrote to Neddie, 10 April 1956, Journal (1956), "I myself and this Record are vastly obligated to his infinitely patient cooperation with

little return. Maybe he gets benefit from his constant association with me and the glamour of that association."

117. Painter to Neddie, 18 March 1956, Journal (1956).

118. Painter to Neddie, 12 April 1956, Journal (1956).

119. Painter to Neddie, 16 April 1956, Journal (1956).

120. Painter to Neddie, 10 April 1956, Journal (1956); emphasis in original.

121. Painter to Kinsey, 24 August 1956, Journal (1956).

122. Painter to Pomeroy, 25 February 1958, Journal (1958).

123. Painter, "Biography VIII," 25.

124. Painter to Pomeroy, 12 July 1961, Journal (1961).

125. Painter to Paul H. Gebhard, 15 March 1964, Journal (1964). In the post–World War II period, in contrast to the 1930s, the use of the label "fairy" to distinguish effeminate homosexuals appears to have declined. "Queer" thus tended to be used in a more generic sense to refer to all male homosexuals. See chapter 4 for a discussion of the fairy-queer distinction in the 1930s.

126. Painter to Pomeroy, 13, 27, and 29 July 1961, Journal (1961); Painter to "Editor of the *Post*," undated, Journal (1961). It is not clear that this letter was actually sent, and if so, whether it was published.

127. Painter to Pomeroy, 30 March 1961, Journal (1961). Efrian and Manuel, being under twenty-one, were sent to the Brooklyn jail. Efrian was detained for five months for violating parole. Painter gave a vivid account of his experience in jail. The inmates that he met were petty criminals. Their plight helped him adjust because he felt that they faced more serious consequences. He reported that he was treated "politely" by the guards. Painter's willingness to take his "medicine" without complaint appeared to convince the gang members that he was not a "detective" spying on them. This suggests that, at least, some of the Puerto Rican youths had suspicions that Painter's interest in them was more than sexual. Painter was amused by his new status in the gang, commenting, "I am not certain of the virtues of this status, but perhaps it has some."

128. Painter to Pomeroy, 1 April 1961, Journal (1961).

129. Painter to Pomeroy, 10 July 1961, Journal (1961). Painter's request for Pomeroy to be his executor was made in Painter to Pomeroy, 5 June 1961, Journal (1961). When Pomeroy left the Institute in 1963, the Institute took over the function of acting as Painter's executor. In this letter, Painter left instructions to be cremated. Painter's concerns about the fate of his papers were compounded by the fact that he had no close friends who could look after his estate. After Bill's death in 1955, Painter had no friends of long standing. Although he saw Edward from time to time, they had drifted apart. He also periodically saw Charlie P., whom he first met in 1937, but this was not a close friendship.

130. Painter to Pomeroy, 11 July 1961, Journal (1961).

131. By being publicly out as a homosexual, however, it seems doubtful that the researchers Painter worked with, such as Dickinson, Henry, and Laidlaw, would have recommended him for medical or law school.

132. Painter to Pomeroy, 12 July 1961, Journal (1961).

133. Painter to Pomeroy, 11 July 1961, Journal (1961).

134. Painter to Pomeroy, 12 July 1961, Journal (1961), and 5 May 1962, Journal (1962).

135. In his writings, Painter frequently referred to an idealized society that promoted sexual freedom. In such a society, he argued, homosexual practice

would be common, but there would be little need for individuals to take on a homosexual identity.

136. Painter to Pomeroy, 26 April and 10 July 1961, Journal (1961).

137. Painter to Pomeroy, 10 July and 26 August, 1961, Journal (1961). When Efrian got out of jail, Painter made arrangements for Pomeroy to interview Efrian on one of Pomeroy's visits to New York (the interview took place in May 1962). This was part of Painter's continuing relationship with the Kinsey Institute, in which he served as a contact in New York for sex histories.

138. Painter to Pomeroy, 6 and 30 November 1961, Journal (1961), and 11 March and 5 May 1962, Journal (1962).

139. Painter to Pomeroy, 20 June 1962, Journal (1962).

140. Painter to Pomeroy, 19 June 1962, Journal (1962).

141. Painter to Pomeroy, 20 June 1962, Journal (1962). Benjamin divided his time between New York and San Francisco.

142. Painter to Pomeroy, 20 and 21 July 1962, Journal (1962). On Call, see Hal Call, "Gay Sexualist," in *Making History,* ed. Marcus, 59–69. Hooker's career is discussed in chapter 8. While still in San Francisco, Benjamin helped Painter secure a six-month bank loan. Benjamin was forced to repay the loan when he found out that Painter had never signed for it. As endorsee, Benjamin was the only signatory for the loan. Benjamin did not hear from Painter until February 1963. In his reply, Benjamin expressed his displeasure with Painter over the circumstances of the bank loan, but on learning of Painter's low income in Los Angeles, Benjamin released him from any obligation of repayment—Harry Benjamin to Painter, 19 February 1963, Journal (1963).

143. Painter to Pomeroy, 27 July 1962, Journal (1962).

144. Painter to Pomeroy, 30 August 1962, Journal (1962).

145. Hooker did not hire any assistants for her research because she did not want to jeopardize the confidentiality of her research subjects. Painter was very impressed with Hooker's knowledge about homosexuality as well as her dedication to the cause of homosexual rights. He did, however, have some reservations about her writings, believing that their comprehension was limited by academic jargon. His comments were noted in "Dr. Hooker," Index of Names, entries March and June 1966. In Painter's discussion with Hooker, she inquired about how she could gain access to his Life Record since she would not have the time to spend at the Kinsey Institute. This prompted Painter to ask Pomeroy if single volumes could be loaned out (there is no indication that Pomeroy or the Institute was willing to endorse such a policy). Because of the problem of access, Painter also expressed concern about how a future biographer would be able to work with the Life Record—Painter to Pomeroy, 31 July 1962, Journal (1962).

146. Painter to Pomeroy, 16 and 31 August 1962, Journal (1962).

147. Painter to Pomeroy, 6 February, 12 April, and 4 July 1963, Journal (1963).

148. Painter to Pomeroy, 27 May 1963, Journal (1963). Pomeroy was a psychologist by training.

149. Painter to Pomeroy, 10 July 1963, Journal (1963).

150. Painter to Pomeroy, 16 and 17 July 1963, Journal (1963). Painter expressed his concerns about Chief Parker in Painter to Pomeroy, 6 February and 4 July 1963, Journal (1963).

151. Painter to Pomeroy, 24 July and 20 October 1963, Journal (1963);

Painter to Gebhard, 29 January and 25 March 1964, Journal (1964). With
Pomeroy's departure from the Kinsey Institute at the end of 1963, Painter now
wrote to Gebhard.

152. Painter to Gebhard, 25 March, 8 and 9 April 1964, Journal (1964).

153. Painter to Gebhard, 7, 10, 16, and 19 April 1964, Journal (1964).

154. Painter to Gebhard, 29 April 1964, Journal (1964).

155. Painter to Gebhard, 2, 6, 9, and 20 May 1964, Journal (1964); Painter,
"Biography VIII," 26.

156. Painter to Gebhard, 22 June 1964, Journal (1964).

157. Painter to Gebhard, 6 May 1964, Journal (1964).

158. Painter to Gebhard, 13 May 1964, Journal (1964). In correspondence
with Pomeroy (Painter to Pomeroy, 8 December 1962, Journal [1962]), Painter
considered the possibilities of Gore Vidal and Christopher Isherwood as "Mr.
X." On Cory, see Donald Webster Cory [Edward Sagarin], *The Homosexual in
America: A Subjective Approach* (New York: Greenberg, 1951). Cory's work is
discussed in chapter 8. On Rechy, see John Rechy, *City of Night* (New York:
Grove Press, 1963); "Rechy, John (Francisco)," in *Gay and Lesbian Literature,*
ed. Sharon Malinowski (Detroit: St. James Press, 1994), 318–21. In a review
(Painter to Pomeroy, 8 May 1963, Journal [1963]), Painter thought that *City of
Night* was significant because it was the first extensive treatment of the heterosexual male prostitute. However, he felt that it was a poor novel, reflecting "card-
board" images of hustlers and unsympathetic renderings of homosexuals.

159. Painter to Gebhard, 26 August 1964, Journal (1964); Painter, "Biography V," 7; idem, "5 Years," unpublished manuscript, undated, but most likely
written toward the end of 1969, bound in the 1969–70 Journal.

160. Painter to Gebhard, 31 August 1964, Journal (1964).

161. Painter, "5 Years," 2. Painter later learned that "Tony" was on his way
to a sexual rendezvous with a man who had offered him five dollars, but Painter's
offer won out.

162. Ibid., 13; emphasis in original.

163. Ibid., 14.

164. Ibid., 9.

165. Ibid., 17. Gilbert introduced Painter to his mother late in their relationship. She was grateful for the help that Painter gave to her son. She appeared to
Painter to be very neurotic. When he lived with her, he felt that she wanted to
have sex with him, but he was convinced that if he made any advances, she
would have vehemently protested and then evicted him.

166. Painter to Gebhard, 24 January 1972, Journal (1972–73).

167. Painter to Gebhard, 15 February 1973, Journal (1972–73). Painter became quite absorbed about the plight of drug addicts and wrote a letter to Max
Lerner, the liberal *New York Post* columnist, about their hardships and the difficulties of getting admitted to methadone programs. From reading his columns,
Painter judged that Lerner would be sympathetic and might be an influential
voice in reform attempts—Painter to Max Lerner, undated, bound in the 1969–
70 Journal.

168. Indeed, I have found these manuscripts to be very useful and have frequently cited them in this chapter and chapter 6. They are not bound in the annual Journals but are collected in a folder in the Painter Papers. The "Biographies" are numbered V through IX, and there are two manuscripts, titled

"Development of Muscle Fetish" and "Long Search." The numbering system suggests that there were earlier manuscripts in the biography series, but they may have been earlier drafts that Painter did not send to the Kinsey Institute. In a letter (Painter to Gebhard, 15 February 1972, Journal [1972–73]), Painter expressed his concerns about maintaining confidentiality in any published version of his life. He thought that a pseudonym should be used for his own identity, and he was especially concerned about ensuring the confidentiality of the men whom he was sexually involved with. For about fifteen years after his death in 1978, his papers (although not his 1941 manuscript on male homosexuality and prostitution) were labeled under the pseudonym of Will Finch.

169. Painter, "Long Search," 4. In his 1941 manuscript on male homosexuality and prostitution, Painter advanced the view that homosexual men were consigned to a loveless existence —see chapter 6.

170. Painter to Gebhard, 6 April 1970, Journal (1969–70).

171. Painter to Gebhard, 15 February 1972, Journal (1972–73). The review of *Midnight Cowboy* was in Painter to Gebhard, 23 February 1970, Journal (1969–70).

172. Painter to Gebhard, 24 January and 15 April 1972, and 14 and 19 February 1973, Journal (1972–73).

173. Painter to Gebhard, 25 January and 19 February 1973, Journal (1972–73).

174. Interview with Gebhard, 22 March 1996; letter from Gebhard to the author, 14 July 1996. Painter's last set of letters remains in the uncatalogued correspondence files of Paul Gebhard at the Kinsey Institute.

175. Painter, "Long Search, " 5–6.

176. Ibid., 4.

177. Alan Helms, *Young Man from the Provinces: A Gay Life before Stonewall* (Boston: Faber and Faber, 1995); Martin Duberman, *Cures: A Gay Man's Odyssey* (New York: Dutton, 1991). Also see Paul Robinson, *Gay Lives: Homosexual Autobiographies from John Addington Symonds to Paul Monette* (Chicago: University of Chicago Press, 1999), chaps. 5, 6; Peter M. Nardi, David Sanders, and Judd Marmor, eds., *Growing Up before Stonewall: Life Stories of Some Gay Men* (New York: Routledge, 1994).

178. Painter, "Biography V," 10.

179. Ken Plummer, *Telling Sexual Stories: Power, Change and Social Worlds* (New York: Routledge, 1995), 43–45, 118–19; Stephen O. Murray, "Subjectivities of Some Dark(-Haired) Objects of Desire," *Journal of Homosexuality* 35, no. 1 (1998): 114–33.

Chapter 8

1. Evelyn Hooker, "The Psychologist—Dr. Evelyn Hooker," in *Making History: The Struggle for Gay and Lesbian Equal Rights, 1945–1990: An Oral History,* ed. Eric Marcus (New York: HarperCollins, 1992), 18.

2. Ronald Bayer, *Homosexuality and American Psychiatry: The Politics of Diagnosis,* rev. ed. (Princeton: Princeton University Press, 1987), 3; Evelyn Hooker, "The Adjustment of the Male Overt Homosexual," *Journal of Projective Techniques* 21 (1957): 18–31.

3. Hooker, "The Psychologist"; "Awards for Distinguished Contribution to Psychology in the Public Interest: Evelyn Hooker," *American Psychologist* 47

(1992): 501–3; Jim Kepner, "A Memory of Dr. Evelyn Hooker," *ONE/IGLA Bulletin,* no. 3 (1997): 10–11; Andrew M. Boxer and Joseph M. Carrier, "Evelyn Hooker: A Life Remembered," *Journal of Homosexuality* 36, no. 1 (1998): 1–17; *Changing Our Minds: The Story of Dr. Evelyn Hooker,* film, Frameline Distribution, San Francisco, 1992.

　　4. Hooker, "The Psychologist," 17.

　　5. *Changing Our Minds.*

　　6. Edwin S. Shneidman, "Evelyn Hooker (1907–1996)," *American Psychologist* 53 (1998): 480–81; "Awards"; Kepner, "A Memory"; Boxer and Carrier, "Evelyn Hooker"; *Changing Our Minds.*

　　7. Hooker's husband Edward remained puzzled by her interest in homosexuality, never fully realizing the compassion that drove her research interest—see Shneidman, "Evelyn Hooker."

　　8. *Changing Our Minds;* Kepner, "A Memory"; Evelyn Hooker, "Inverts Are Not a Distinct Personality Type," paper presented at the annual meeting of the Western Psychological Association, Los Angeles, May 1954.

　　9. Evelyn Hooker, "Reflections of a 40-Year Exploration: A Scientific View on Homosexuality," *American Psychologist* 48 (1993): 450.

　　10. Boxer and Carrier, "Evelyn Hooker"; *Changing Our Minds;* Hooker, "The Psychologist." The National Institute of Mental Health (NIMH) had been created in 1946 and was a relatively new part of the U.S. Public Health Service. Hooker received a series of NIMH research grants until 1961, when she received an NIMH Research Career Award.

　　11. Hooker, "The Psychologist"; idem, "Reflections," 450.

　　12. Hooker, "Reflections," 451.

　　13. Ibid., 451–52.

　　14. Evelyn Hooker, "A Preliminary Analysis of Group Behavior of Homosexuals," *Journal of Psychology* 42 (1956): 217. When Hooker began her research in 1953, she had not yet adopted a minority group perspective. At that time she worked closely with the homophile group the Mattachine Society, which was instrumental in recruiting her sample of gay men. Dismissing the notion of gay consciousness or identity, she advised Mattachine to avoid any reference in their policy statement to homosexuals as a minority group, pointing out that "only the mode of sexual behavior would differentiate and distinguish a homosexual"—cited in John D'Emilio, *Sexual Politics, Sexual Communities: The Making of a Homosexual Minority in the United States, 1940–1970,* 2nd ed. (Chicago: University of Chicago Press, 1998), 84.

　　15. Gordon W. Allport, *The Nature of Prejudice* (Cambridge, MA: Addison-Wesley, 1954).

　　16. Evelyn Hooker, "Male Homosexuals and Their 'Worlds,'" in *Sexual Inversion: The Multiple Roots of Homosexuality,* ed. Judd Marmor (New York: Basic Books, 1965), 83–107; idem, "The Homosexual Community," in *Perspectives in Psychopathology: Readings in Abnormal Psychology,* ed. Joseph O. Palmer and Michael J. Goldstein (New York: Oxford University Press, 1966), 354–64; Donald Webster Cory [Edward Sagarin], *The Homosexual in America: A Subjective Approach* (New York: Greenberg, 1951); Maurice Leznoff and William A. Westley, "The Homosexual Community," *Social Problems* 3 (1956): 257–63. When Hooker began her analysis of the homosexual subculture, she asked a sociologist colleague to help her locate sociological material on homo-

sexuality. According to Hooker, "His reply was that there was none and that any sociologist who dared to try to obtain it would be suspect," (Hooker, "A Preliminary Analysis," 220).

17. Hooker, "The Psychologist," 22, 23.

18. In the preliminary screening for her sample, Hooker eliminated several men, some because of marked signs of pathological disturbance, others because of their history of mixed homosexual and heterosexual experience. To dispel the concern about participating in a "sex study," all of the participants were informed that the project involved a comparison of homosexual and heterosexual men. A few of the heterosexual men were eliminated when they appeared to be disturbed by a follow-up question regarding whether they had had any homosexual inclinations or experience. For details of the sampling procedure, see Hooker, "The Adjustment."

19. Hooker, "The Adjustment," 29; emphasis in original. Only the Rorschach was used in the task of distinguishing matched pairs of subjects because the picture story tests (TAT and MAPS), by their content, could elicit sexual themes.

20. For Henry's views, see chapters 3 and 5.

21. Hooker, "The Adjustment," 23.

22. Hooker, "The Psychologist," 24. In a follow-up study, Hooker analyzed her test data (for the thirty matched pairs of subjects) according to the scoring categories or "signs" on the Rorschach commonly used by clinical psychologists to diagnose male homosexuality, such as feminine identification in men, body narcissism, and anal preoccupation. She reported that, with the exception of a few cases, the homosexual and heterosexual records could not be distinguished according to the Rorschach signs. See Evelyn Hooker, "Male Homosexuality in the Rorschach," *Journal of Projective Techniques* 22 (1958): 33–54.

23. Hooker, "The Psychologist," 24; Boxer and Carrier, "Evelyn Hooker"; *Changing Our Minds.* Hooker kept the protocols and personal documents from her study in three locked file cabinets in her home. She had promised the research participants that she would maintain strict confidentiality. Shortly before her death in 1996, she shredded all of these materials.

24. Hooker, "The Psychologist," 25.

25. Hooker, "The Adjustment," Editorial Note, 18; Shneidman, "Evelyn Hooker"; Evelyn Hooker to Isadore From, undated but postmarked, 30 December 1955, Evelyn Hooker Papers (Collection 523), Department of Special Collections, University Research Library, University of California, Los Angeles. In her letter of condolence to Sam From's father (cited in Boxer and Carrier, "Evelyn Hooker"), Hooker wrote, "I doubt that he knew how profoundly he altered my life."

26. Evelyn Hooker, "The Homosexual Community," in *Proceedings of the XIVth International Conference of Applied Psychology,* vol. 2, *Personality Research* (Copenhagen: Munksgaard, 1962), 40–59; Hooker, "Male Homosexuals." The paper was also published as Hooker, "The Homosexual Community," in *Perspectives,* ed. Palmer and Goldstein. According to Boxer and Carrier ("Evelyn Hooker"), Hooker was encouraged to undertake her ethnographic research by sociologist colleague Harold Garfinkel, who provided guidance for her fieldwork. For an example of Garfinkel's work, see Harold Garfinkel, "Studies of the Routine Grounds of Everyday Activities," *Social Problems* 2 (1964): 225–50.

27. Xavier Mayne [Edward I. Prime-Stevenson], *The Intersexes: A History of Similisexualism as a Problem of Social Life* (Naples: privately printed, 1908;

reprint, New York: Arno Press, 1975); Earl Lind [pseud.], *Autobiography of an Androgyne* (New York: Medico-Legal Journal, 1918; reprint, New York: Arno Press, 1975); Cory [Sagarin], *Homosexual in America*. On Prime-Stevenson and Lind, see chapter 2. There were some precedents in the scientific literature, but they were not as focused as Hooker's ethnographic work. In 1951 Clelland S. Ford and Frank A. Beach, in their cross-cultural survey of studies of sexual behavior, referred to existing ethnographic accounts of homosexual activities in non-Western societies. Their work was significant because it pointed to the cross-cultural variation in the acceptance of homosexuality. See Clelland S. Ford and Frank A. Beach, *Patterns of Sexual Behavior* (New York: Harper & Brothers, 1951). In 1956 Maurice Leznoff and William A. Westley published a brief study of the Montreal male homosexual subculture, based on interviews with sixty respondents—see Leznoff and Westley, "The Homosexual Community." British sociologist Michael Schofield, using the pseudonym of Gordon Westwood, published a series of studies of male homosexuality in Great Britain, which included some ethnographic analysis. See Gordon Westwood [Michael Schofield], *Society and the Homosexual* (London: Gollancz, 1952); idem, *A Minority: Life of the Male Homosexual in Great Britain* (London: Longmans, 1960).

28. Hooker, "Male Homosexuals," 91.

29. Hooker also carried out a study of the relationship between sexual practices and gender identity, reported in Evelyn Hooker, "An Empirical Study of Some Relations between Sexual Patterns and Gender Identity in Male Homosexuals," in *Sex Research: New Developments*, ed. John Money (New York: Holt, Rinehart and Winston, 1965), 24–52. This research was based on an eight-year series of interview follow-ups of her original sample of thirty gay men, whose psychological test profiles had been compared with a matched group of thirty heterosexual men and reported in Hooker, "The Adjustment." Hooker found that for the majority of her homosexual subjects, there was no consistent relationship between the sexual practices engaged in and psychological gender identity.

30. Evelyn Hooker, "What Is a Criterion?" *Journal of Projective Techniques* 21 (1959): 278–81; Hooker, "Male Homosexuality in the Rorschach," 52–53. The psychoanalyst Clara Thompson, who Hooker cited in many of her publications, had earlier challenged the assumption that homosexuality was a clinical entity. See Clara Thompson, "Changing Concepts of Homosexuality in Psychoanalysis," *Psychiatry* 10 (1947): 183–89.

31. Evelyn Hooker, "Homosexuality," in *The International Encyclopedia of the Social Sciences* (New York: Macmillan, 1968), 225. Also see, idem, "Parental Relations and Male Homosexuality in Patient and Nonpatient Samples," *Journal of Consulting and Clinical Psychology* 33 (1969): 140–42.

32. Irving Bieber et al., *Homosexuality: A Psychoanalytic Study of Male Homosexuals* (New York: Basic Books, 1962). The publication was sponsored by the Society of Medical Psychoanalysts.

33. Hooker, "Male Homosexuality in the Rorschach"; idem, "Homosexuality." For reviews of other critics of the Bieber study, see Bayer, *Homosexuality and American Psychiatry*, 28–34; Kenneth Lewes, *The Psychoanalytic Theory of Male Homosexuality* (New York: Simon & Schuster, 1988), 206–12. The criticism that Bieber's conclusions were biased because they were based on a clinical sample produced a series of research studies that extended the comparison of

family backgrounds to nonclinical samples of male homosexuals and heterosexuals. The results did not generally support Bieber's findings. The most definitive study was carried out by Marvin Siegelman, who controlled for the general level of adjustment among nonclinical homosexual and heterosexual subjects. For the results of this study and a review of other studies, see Marvin Siegelman, "Parental Background of Male Homosexuals and Heterosexuals," *Archives of Sexual Behavior* 3 (1974): 3–18.

34. Bieber et al., *Homosexuality,* 305–6.

35. By the mid-1960s, Socarides became the leading defender of the medical model of homosexuality. By theorizing that the etiology stemmed back to the pre-oedipal, rather than the oedipal, phase of development, he characterized homosexuality as more severely pathological than it was generally considered to be. See Charles W. Socarides, *The Overt Homosexual* (New York: Grune and Stratton, 1968). For the report of the psychiatric study group, see "Homosexuality in the Male: A Report of a Psychiatric Study Group," *International Journal of Psychiatry* 11 (1973): 460–79. Fine and Bieber's evaluations appear in appendices to the report, "Homosexuality in the Male," 472–76.

36. Hooker's first visit to the Kinsey Institute is referred to in Evelyn Hooker to Wardell B. Pomeroy, 24 September 1958, Kinsey Institute Archives, Indiana University. Pomeroy also introduced Hooker to Thomas Painter, who served as a guide for Hooker's visits to gay bars in New York. On Painter, see chapter 7. On Hooker's debt to Kinsey, see Evelyn Hooker and Mary Ziemba-Davis, "Epilogue," in *Homosexuality/Heterosexuality: Concepts of Sexual Orientation,* ed. David P. McWhirter, Stephanie A. Sanders, and June Machover Reinisch (New York: Oxford University Press, 1990), 399–401. Hooker's support from NIMH is referred to in Hooker, "Reflections"; phone interview with Edwin S. Shneidman, 23 June 1998.

37. Hendrick M. Ruitenbeek, ed., *The Problem of Homosexuality in Modern Society* (New York: Dutton, 1963). Ten years later, reflecting the impact of the campaign to remove homosexuality as a diagnostic category, Ruitenbeek published another edited volume—see idem, *Homosexuality: A Changing Picture* (London: Souvenir Press, 1973).

38. Judd Marmor, "Introduction," in *Sexual Inversion,* ed. Marmor, 16.

39. Judd Marmor, "The Good Doctor—Judd Marmor," in *Making History,* ed. Marcus, 250–55; idem, "Homosexuality—Mental Illness or Moral Dilemma?" *International Journal of Psychiatry* 10 (1972): 114–117; Bayer, *Homosexuality and American Psychiatry,* 60–64. On Szasz, see Thomas Szasz, *The Myth of Mental Illness,* rev. ed. (New York: Harper and Row, 1974).

40. Hooker, "Reflections," 452, emphasis in original; Marvin Siegelman, "Adjustment of Male Homosexuals and Heterosexuals," *Archives of Sexual Behavior* 2 (1972): 9–25. Siegelman's article included a review of previous studies that had compared homosexual and heterosexual samples (some clinical, some nonclinical) in indices of adjustment.

41. On the rise of the community mental movement, see Gerald N. Grob, *From Asylum to Community: Mental Health Policy in Modern America* (Princeton: Princeton University Press, 1991). On the role of social science experts in community mental health programs, see Ellen Herman, *The Romance of American Psychology: Political Culture in the Age of Experts* (Berkeley: University of California Press, 1995), chaps. 8, 9.

42. Hooker, "Reflections," 452.

43. Kepner, "A Memory"; D'Emilio, *Sexual Politics,* 217. One of the members, Judge Bazelon, resigned a few months before the final report was issued in October 1969. Hooker's avoidance of appointing any homosexuals was consistent with her policy of not appearing to compromise her objectivity in the eyes of her colleagues by joining any homophile groups. In 1952 she turned down an invitation from the Los Angeles Mattachine Society to join their board of directors—see D'Emilio, *Sexual Politics,* 73.

44. Hooker, "Reflections," 452.

45. National Institute of Mental Health Task Force on Homosexuality, *Final Report and Background Papers* (Washington, D.C.: Department of Health, Education, and Welfare, 1972). The *Final Report* was also reprinted as "Final Report of the Task Force on Homosexuality," in *The Homosexual Dialectic,* ed. Joseph M. McCaffrey (Englewood Cliffs, N.J.: Prentice-Hall, 1972), 146.

46. "Final Report," 151, 152.

47. Ibid., 152–55. On the Wolfenden Report and the events leading up to it, see Jeffrey Weeks, *Coming Out: Homosexual Politics in Britain* (London: Quartet, 1972), chaps. 14, 15.

48. D'Emilio, *Sexual Politics,* 217; "Final Report," 146.

49. "Final Report of the Task Force on Homosexuality," *Homophile Studies: ONE Institute Quarterly* 22 (1970): 5–12; Dorr Legg, "Editorial," ibid.; Kepner, "A Memory," 11; Boxer and Carrier, "Evelyn Hooker," 4; David P. McWhirter, "Prologue," in *Homosexuality/Heterosexuality,* ed. McWhirter, Sanders, and Reinisch, xvii–xviii.

50. On the origins of "homophile," see Dorr Legg, *Homophile Studies in Theory and Practice* (San Francisco: ONE Institute Press and GLB Publishers, 1994), 25–27. On the McCarthy purges and the oppression of gay life in the 1950s, see D'Emilio, *Sexual Politics,* 40–53; idem, "The Homosexual Menace: The Politics of Sexuality in Cold War America," in *Passion and Power: Sexuality in History,* ed. Kathy Piess and Christina Simmons (Philadelphia: Temple University Press, 1989), 226–40; Barry D. Adam, *The Rise of a Gay and Lesbian Movement,* rev. ed. (New York: Twayne, 1995), 60–65; Jennifer Terry, *An American Obsession: Science, Medicine, and Homosexuality in Modern Society* (Chicago: University of Chicago Press, 1999), chap. 11.

51. On Hay, see Stuart Timmons, *The Trouble with Harry Hay, Founder of the Modern Gay Movement* (Boston: Alyson, 1990); Harry Hay, *Radically Gay: Gay Liberation in the Words of Its Founder* (Boston: Beacon Press, 1996). On the Mattachine Society and the Daughters of Bilitis in the 1950s, see D'Emilio, *Sexual Politics,* 57–125. On the Daughters of Bilitis, also see Phyllis Lyon and Del Martin, "Reminiscences of Two Female Homophiles," in *Our Right to Love: A Lesbian Resource Book,* ed. Ginny Vida (Englewood Cliffs, N.J.: Prentice-Hall, 1978), 124–28; Manuela Soares, "The Purloined *Ladder:* Its Place in Lesbian History," *Journal of Homosexuality* 34, nos. 3/4 (1998): 27–49.

52. On ONE, Incorporated, see Legg, *Homophile Studies,* 3–5; D'Emilio, *Sexual Politics,* 108–9; Jim Kepner, *Rough News, Daring News: 1950s' Pioneer Gay Press Journalism* (New York: Harrington Park Press, 1998), 1–12. On the ONE Institute, see Legg, *Homophile Studies,* part I.

53. Hal Call, quoted in D'Emilio, *Sexual Politics,* 83.

54. Ibid., 83–84, 108–9; Lyn Pedersen [Jim Kepner], *"ONE Magazine,*

August–September 1956 'A Tribute to Dr. Kinsey,'" reprinted in Kepner, *Rough News,* 127–31. Pedersen was a pseudonym for Jim Kepner, one of the major writers for *ONE Magazine.*

55. Bayer, *Homosexuality and American Psychiatry,* 73–81.

56. Evelyn Hooker, "Inverts Are Not a Distinct Personality Type," *Mattachine Review* (January 1955): 20–22; idem, "The Adjustment of the Male Overt Homosexual," *Mattachine Review* (December 1957): 33–40; "Dr. Blanche Baker Challenges—Accept Yourself," *Ladder* (May 1957): 6.

57. *Mattachine Review* (February 1956): 28, and quoted in Bayer, *Homosexuality and American Psychiatry,* 78. Albert Ellis, "Are Homosexuals Necessarily Neurotic?" *ONE Magazine* (April 1955): 8–12; idem, "On the Cure of Homosexuality," *Mattachine Review* (November–December 1955): 7–9; idem, "The Use of Psychotherapy with Homosexuals," *Mattachine Review* (February 1956): 16–27. For excerpts of Ellis's views in the *Mattachine Review* and *ONE Magazine,* see Kepner, *Rough News,* 309–29.

58. Ken Burns, "The Homosexual Faces a Challenge," *Mattachine Review* (August 1956): 24; Edmund Bergler, *Homosexuality: Disease or Way of Life?* (New York: Hill & Wang, 1956). For a review to the reactions to Bergler in the homophile journals, see Bayer, *Homosexuality and American Psychiatry,* 78–80. On Bergler and his attack on Kinsey, see Terry, *American Obsession,* 308–14.

59. See D'Emilio, *Sexual Politics,* 129–48, for an extensive discussion of the social trends of the 1960s and their impact on the homophile movement.

60. William S. Burroughs, *Naked Lunch* (New York: Grove Press, 1959); John Rechy, *City of Night* (New York: Grove Press, 1963); James Baldwin, *Another Country* (New York: Dial Press, 1962); Mary McCarthy, *The Group* (New York: Harcourt Brace & World, 1963); Jess Stearn, *The Sixth Man* (New York: Macfadden Books, 1962), quote on dust jacket of paperback edition; idem, *The Grapevine* (Garden City, N.Y.: Doubleday, 1964). In writing *The Sixth Man,* Stearn interviewed psychiatrist George W. Henry and cited Henry's views about the need for homosexuals to fit into society. Henry's associate, Alfred A. Gross, wrote the foreword and although cautioning that "it is not necessary to agree with what he has to say," praised Stearn for his contribution to the "popular understanding" of male homosexuality (*The Sixth Man,* viii). On Henry and Gross, see chapter 5. On the changing trends in gay American literature, see Byrne R. S. Fone, *A Road to Stonewall: Male Homosexuality and Homophobia in English and American Literature, 1750–1969* (New York: Twayne, 1995), 249–78; on the changing trends in film representation, see Vito Russo, *The Celluloid Closet,* 2nd ed. (New York: Harper & Row, 1987), 62–179.

61. On the Wolfenden Report, see Weeks, *Coming Out,* chaps. 14, 15.

62. For the background and activist career of Kameny, see D'Emilio, *Sexual Politics,* 150–57; "Frank Kameny," in *The Gay Crusaders,* ed. Kay Tobin and Randy Wicker (New York: Paperback Library, 1972), 89–134; Frank Kameny, "The Very Mad Scientist," in *Making History,* ed. Marcus, 93–103; Charles Kaiser, *The Gay Metropolis: 1940–1996* (New York: Houghton Mifflin, 1997), 138–41; Dudley Clendinen and Adam Nagourney, *Out for Good: The Struggle to Build a Gay Rights Movement in America* (New York: Simon & Schuster, 1999), 112–14.

63. Cited in D'Emilio, *Sexual Politics,* 152.

64. On Wicker, see ibid., 158–60.

65. Barbara Gittings and Kay Lahusen, "The Rabble Rousers," in *Making History,* ed. Marcus, 120.

66. Franklin E. Kameny, "Gay Liberation and Psychiatry," in *Homosexual Dialectic,* ed. McCaffrey, 189. This article was based on speeches Kameny made in the mid-1960s.

67. Ibid.; Frank E. Kameny, "Does Research into Homosexuality Really Matter?" *Ladder* (May 1965): 14–20.

68. Kameny, "Research," 14; emphasis in original.

69. Kameny's position was rebutted in Florence Conrad, "Research Is Here to Stay, *Ladder* (July–August 1965): 15–21. Conrad was the DOB's director of research. Also see Bayer, *Homosexuality and American Psychiatry,* 81–83; Soares, "The Purloined *Ladder,*" 35–39.

70. Quotes cited in D'Emilio, *Sexual Politics,* 163–64; emphasis in original.

71. Ibid., 164–65.

72. Frank Kameny to Charles Kaiser, 19 December 1995, cited in Kaiser, *Gay Metropolis,* 142.

73. D'Emilio, *Sexual Politics,* 165.

74. On the Mattachine elections, see Martin Duberman, *Stonewall* (New York: Dutton, 1993), 108–9. In the mid-1960s Ruitenbeek and fellow psychoanalyst Ernest van den Haag, as well as psychiatrist George Weinberg, were significant supporters of the homophile challenge to the medical model. In speeches to homophile groups, they attacked the ethical abuse inherent in the therapeutic efforts of psychiatrists and psychoanalysts to cure homosexuals—see Bayer, *Homosexuality and American Psychiatry,* 86–87. Weinberg also coined the term "homophobia," which he defined as the fear of being in close proximity with homosexuals. See George Weinberg, *Society and the Healthy Homosexual* (New York: St. Martin's Press, 1972). In this book, he attacked the bias of psychoanalytic theory and practice and argued against the medical model. On issues about defining homophobia, see Gregory Herek, "On Homosexual Masculinity," *American Behavioral Scientist* 29 (1986): 563–77.

75. Cory [Sagarin], *Homosexual in America,* 228.

76. Ibid., 230–31. On Cory's work on lesbianism, see idem, *The Lesbian in America* (New York: Citadel Press, 1964). Sagarin chose his pseudonym to honor André Gide's *Corydon,* a philosophical defense of homosexuality. He added "Webster" to insure that another Donald Cory would not sue him. On the origins of Sagarin's pseudonym, see Martin Duberman, "Dr. Edward Sagarin and Mr. Cory: The 'Father' of the Homophile Movement," *Harvard Gay and Lesbian Review* (fall 1997): 7–14. On Gide, see Paul Robinson, *Gay Lives: Homosexual Autobiography from John Addington Symonds to Paul Monette* (Chicago: University of Chicago Press, 1999), 181–204.

77. Cory [Sagarin], *Homosexual in America,* 235.

78. On Nichols, see D'Emilio, *Sexual Politics,* 152; on Gittings, see Gittings and Lahusen, "The Rabble Rousers," 111; on Wynkoop, see Kaiser, *Gay Metropolis,* 125; on Prime-Stevenson and Lind, see chapter 2. Not all homosexual readers were enamored with Sagarin's book. Thomas Painter expressed his reactions to Sagarin's work, as well as his impressions after meeting Sagarin in 1962, in a letter to Wardell Pomeroy—Thomas Painter to Wardell B. Pomeroy, 5 May 1962, Journal (1962), Thomas Painter Papers, Kinsey Institute Archives, Indiana University. Painter was critical of Sagarin's lack of knowledge about male prosti-

tution. Moreover, he questioned Sagarin's skills as an interviewer who could obtain meaningful and accurate ethnographic material. In comparison with the rich detail and analysis in Painter's ethnographic work, Sagarin's material on gay life was sketchy. Out of 266 pages of text in *The Homosexual in America,* Sagarin devoted only 45 pages to the gay male subculture (language, cruising, bars, drag shows, and sexual relationships). On Painter, see chapters 6 and 7.

79. Kepner, *Rough News,* 9; Kaiser, *Gay Metropolis,* 125.

80. On Sagarin's life and career, see Duberman, "Dr. Sagarin." On Sagarin's association with Greenberg, see Kaiser, *Gay Metropolis,* 125, 130.

81. Cory [Sagarin], preface to *Homosexual in America,* xv.

82. Duberman indicates that the nearly fifty-year marriage was successful and marked by mutual devotion. See Duberman, "Dr. Sagarin."

83. Cory [Sagarin], *Homosexual in America,* 72–75, 181–92. Sagarin cited George W. Henry, *Sex Variants: A Study of Homosexual Patterns,* one-volume edition (New York: Hoeber, 1948), 1028, and Thompson, "Changing Concepts."

84. Cory [Sagarin], *Homosexual in America,* 206.

85. On Sagarin's views about marriage, see ibid., 200–10; on his views about homosexual love, ibid., 135–44. Sagarin did acknowledge that gay men could find long-term committed relationships, but it was difficult because of a number of factors. These included the internalized social hostility to homosexuality that was projected on to male partners, the psychological defenses involved in the need to seek multiple sex partners, and the fact that two men were not as natural a biological fit as opposite-sex partners. The last reason was symptomatic of the heterosexist bias inherent in parts of Sagarin's book. Sagarin referred to his gay relationship as, "a firm bond of friendship that has developed with a man who has been an inspiring person in my life" (ibid., xvi). He also, apparently, dedicated his book to his companion: "to Howard *A filosofia è necessario amore"* (ibid., v; emphasis in original).

86. Donald Webster Cory [Edward Sagarin], ed., *Homosexuality: A Cross Cultural Approach* (New York: Julian Press, 1956). Sagarin's essays dealt with the assimilation of heterosexual prejudices by homosexuals and the increasing social acceptance of homosexuals.

87. Donald Webster Cory [Edward Sagarin], *The Homosexual in America: A Subjective Approach,* 2nd ed. (New York: Castle Books, 1960), xxii.

88. Ibid., xxiii. Duberman indicates that Sagarin consulted Albert Ellis about his personal problems as well as his book. In Duberman's interview with Ellis, Ellis revealed that as a result of their few, informal sessions, Sagarin achieved more satisfying sex relations with his wife—see Duberman, "Dr. Sagarin," 11.

89. Cory [Sagarin], *Homosexual in America,* 2nd ed., xxv.

90. Albert Ellis, introduction to Cory [Sagarin], *Homosexual in America,* x–xi. Also see Donald Webster Cory [Edward Sagarin], introduction to *Homosexuality: Its Cause and Cure,* by Albert Ellis (New York: Lyle Stuart, 1965), 7–15. On Ellis's support for Kinsey, see Wardell B. Pomeroy, *Dr. Kinsey and the Institute for Sex Research* (1972; reprint, New Haven: Yale University Press, 1982), 298; James H. Jones, *Alfred C. Kinsey: A Public/Private Life* (New York: Norton, 1997), 590–91.

91. Albert Ellis, "Are Homosexuals Necessarily Neurotic?" in *Homosexuality: A Cross Cultural Approach,* ed. Cory [Sagarin], 412. Logically consistent with his argument, Ellis opined that exclusive heterosexuality was also neurotic.

He first expressed this audacious view in Albert Ellis, *The American Sexual Tragedy* (New York: Twayne, 1954). Ellis's support for bisexuality produced a fan in self-identified bisexual J. D. Mercer. Mercer, who preferred the label "ambisexual," published a book defending bisexuality and advocating reform of sex laws to decriminalize homosexual relations. See J. D. Mercer, *They Walk in Shadow: A Study of Sexual Variations with Emphasis on the Ambisexual and Homosexual Components and Our Contemporary Sex Laws* (New York: Comet Press Books, 1959).

92. Donald Webster Cory [Edward Sagarin] and John P. LeRoy [pseud.], *The Homosexual and His Society: A View from Within* (New York: Citadel Press, 1963), 209, 210. On LeRoy, whose real name was Barry Sheer, see Duberman, "Dr. Sagarin." On Henry's views, see chapter 5. In his book on lesbianism (Cory [Sagarin], *Lesbian in America*), Sagarin reiterated his position, arguing, "Some lesbians see themselves only as victims of hostility; some onlookers and specialists see them only as disturbed. The truth would seem to be found in a combination of both" (259).

93. Donald Webster Cory [Edward Sagarin], "After Twenty-Five Years: A Retrospective Foreword to the Reprint Edition," *The Homosexual in America: A Subjective Approach* (1951; reprint, New York: Arno Press, 1975), 9.

94. Quoted in D'Emilio, *Sexual Politics,* 167.

95. Ibid., 167.

96. Frank Kameny to Edward Sagarin, 7 April 1965, quoted in ibid., 167.

97. Duberman, *Stonewall,* 108–9.

98. Duberman, "Dr. Sagarin," 14; emphasis in original. On the Mattachine elections, see D'Emilio, *Sexual Politics,* 168. On Sagarin's writings, see Edward Sagarin, "Structure and Ideology in an Association of Deviants" (Ph.D. diss., New York University, 1966; reprint, New York: Arno Press, 1975); idem, *Odd Man In: Societies of Deviants in America* (Chicago: Quadrangle Books, 1969), especially chap. 4, "Homosexual: The Many Masks of Mattachine"; idem, "The Good Guys, the Bad Guys, and the Gay Guys: Survey Essay," *Contemporary Sociology* 2 (1973): 3–13. For a gay liberationist view on Sagarin, see John Kyper and Steven Abbott, "The Betrayal of Donald Webster Cory?" *Fag Rag/Gay Sunshine: Stonewall 5th Anniversary Issue* (summer 1974): 23. On Humphreys, see Laud Humphreys, *Tearoom Trade: Impersonal Sex in Public Places* (Chicago: Aldine, 1970).

99. D'Emilio, *Sexual Politics,* 172, 202.

100. Ibid., 198.

101. Quoted in Bayer, *Homosexuality and American Psychiatry,* 90–91.

102. Franklin E. Kameny, "Gay Is Good," in *The Same Sex: An Appraisal of Homosexuality,* ed. Ralph W. Weltge (Philadelphia: Pilgrim, 1969), 129–45.

103. For an overview of the accomplishments of the homophile movement in the 1960s, see D'Emilio, *Sexual Politics,* 176–219.

104. Student representatives quoted in Duberman, *Stonewall,* 172.

105. Socarides, quoted in D'Emilio, *Sexual Politics,* 216.

106. On the trends and events of the 1960s, see Todd Gitlen, *The Sixties: Years of Hope, Days of Rage* (New York: Bantam, 1987). On the contrast between the homophile movement and other liberation movements, see Duberman, *Stonewall,* 169–72; D'Emilio, *Sexual Politics,* 223–27.

107. Duberman, *Stonewall,* 171.

108. D'Emilio, *Sexual Politics,* 227–31.

109. Duberman, *Stonewall,* xv. On the Stonewall riot, see Clendinen and Nagourney, *Out for Good,* chap. 1.

110. GLF Statement of Purpose, 31 July 1969, quoted in D'Emilio, *Sexual Politics,* 234. Another influential statement of gay liberation thinking was Carl Wittman's 1970 "gay manifesto." See Carl Wittman, "Refugees from Amerika," in *Homosexual Dialectic,* ed. McCaffrey, 157–71. On the early gay liberation movement (1969–72), also see Dennis Altman, *Homosexual: Oppression and Liberation* (New York: Dutton, 1971); Donn Teal, *The Gay Militants* (New York: Stein and Day, 1971); *Out of the Closets: Voices of Gay Liberation,* ed. Karla Jay and Allen Young (New York: Douglas/Lynx, 1972); Adam, *Gay and Lesbian Movement,* 81–108; Clendinen and Nagourney, *Out for Good,* chaps. 1–10.

111. D'Emilio, *Sexual Politics,* 234–35; Adam, *Gay and Lesbian Movement,* 85–86.

112. On the Gay Activists Alliance, see Altman, *Homosexual,* 122–26; Adam, *Gay and Lesbian Movement,* 86–87; Duberman, *Stonewall,* 232–33; Clendinen and Nagourney, *Out for Good,* 76–80, 188–92.

113. Gary Alinder, "Gay Liberation Meets the Shrinks," and Chicago Gay Liberation Front, "A Leaflet for the American Medical Association," in *Out of the Closets,* ed. Jay and Young, 141–47; "GLF Pulls the Plug on Shock Therapy," *Advocate* (1970), reprinted in *Long Road to Freedom: The Advocate History of the Gay and Lesbian Movement,* ed. Mark Thompson (New York: St. Martin's Press, 1994), 38–39; D'Emilio, *Sexual Politics,* 235; Bayer, *Homosexuality and American Psychiatry,* 99–100.

114. Barbara Gittings and Kay Lahusen, "The Old Timers," in *Making History,* ed. Marcus, 213–27, quote by Gittings, 222; emphasis in original.

115. Quotes from the aversive conditioning and Bieber sessions in Alinder, "Gay Liberation," 143–44. On the Bieber session, also see Bayer, *Homosexuality and American Psychiatry,* 102–3.

116. Bayer, *Homosexuality and American Psychiatry,* 106. For an overview of the gay activists' confrontation with the APA, also see Clendinen and Nagourney, *Out for Good,* chap. 14.

117. Gittings and Lahusen, "Old Timers," 222–23.

118. *Advocate,* 26 May 1971, 3, quoted in Bayer, *Homosexuality and American Psychiatry,* 105.

119. On the Washington demonstration, see Clendinen and Nagourney, *Out for Good,* 203–5.

120. Bayer, *Homosexuality and American Psychiatry,* 107.

121. Ibid., 107–11; Gittings and Lahusen, "Old Timers," 222–23; Ellen Herman, *Psychiatry, Psychology and Homosexuality* (New York: Chelsea House, 1995), 97–99. On John Fryer, see Clendinen and Nagourney, *Out for Good,* 208.

122. Cited in Bayer, *Homosexuality and American Psychiatry,* 110.

123. Ibid., 110–11; Marmor, "Introduction"; idem, "Good Doctor." In his presentation, Marmor also referred to his forthcoming 1972 article—see Marmor, "Homosexuality."

124. Bayer, *Homosexuality and American Psychiatry,* 111.

125. "Homosexuality in the Male," 461. The series of position papers in the *International Journal of Psychiatry* 10 (1972) consisted of Richard Green,

"Homosexuality as a Mental Illness," 72–98; Marmor, "Homosexuality"; Martin Hoffman, "Philosophic, Empirical, and Ecological Remarks," 105–7; Charles W. Socarides, "Homosexuality—Basic Concepts and Psychodynamics," 118–25; Lawrence J. Hatterer, "A Critique," 102–4. On the position papers, also see Bayer, *Homosexuality and American Psychiatry,* 112–14. The study group originally met as the Task Force on Homosexuality of the New York County (Manhattan) District Branch of the APA. The district branch rejected the study group's report.

126. Bayer, *Homosexuality and American Psychiatry,* 115–16.

127. Ibid., 116–21; Siegelman, "Adjustment"; Marcel T. Saghir and Eli Robins, *Male and Female Homosexuality: A Comprehensive Investigation* (Baltimore: Williams & Wilkins, 1973).

128. Bayer, *Homosexuality and American Psychiatry,* 123–25; Lewes, *Psychoanalytic Theory,* 222; Saghir and Robins, *Male and Female Homosexuality.* Saghir and Robins's study was based on a sample of 146 nonpatient homosexual men and women, and also included a control sample of 79 heterosexual men and women.

129. Robert J. Stoller, Judd Marmor, Irving Bieber, Ronald Gold, Charles W. Socarides, Richard Green, and Robert L. Spitzer, "A Symposium: Should Homosexuality Be in the APA Nomenclature?" *American Journal of Psychiatry* 130 (1973): 1215. Spitzer's paper, "A Proposal about Homosexuality and the APA Nomenclature: Homosexuality as an Irregular Form of Sexual Behavior and Sexual Orientation Disturbance as a Psychiatric Disorder," ibid., 1214–16, was written after the APA meeting and included in the published form of the panel presentations.

130. When the *DSM-II* was revised as the *DSM-III,* in 1978, "sexual orientation disturbance" was changed to "ego-dystonic homosexuality." The latter category was removed from the psychiatric nosology in 1986—see Bayer, *Homosexuality and American Psychiatry,* 168–78, 208–18.

131. Bayer, *Homosexuality and American Psychiatry,* 127–34.

132. Robert Spitzer interview, *Advocate,* 8 May 1974, cited in Clandinen and Nagourney, *Out for Good,* 217; Bayer, *Homosexuality and American Psychiatry,* 134–38.

133. Cited in "The Vote that 'Cured' Twenty Million," *Advocate,* 1974, reprinted in *Long Road,* ed. Thompson, 104.

134. Cited in Bayer, *Homosexuality and American Psychiatry,* 138.

135. Cited in Herman, *Psychiatry,* 103.

136. Bayer, *Homosexuality and American Psychiatry,* 148; Marmor, "Good Doctor," 254. All three of the APA presidential candidates—Judd Marmor, Louis Jolyon West, and Herbert Modlin—were strong supporters of gay rights. Marmor was the most strongly identified with gay rights, which most likely played a role in his winning the election, held at the same time as the referendum. Two APA vice presidents also signed the NGTF-sponsored statement. NGTF's involvement in the referendum surfaced before the vote was taken. As a result, Socarides protested, claiming the NGTF's involvement was an unfair campaign practice. An ad hoc committee was set up to investigate and ruled against the charges of unethical campaign practices.

137. Bruce Voeller, "For Whom the Ballot Tolls," *Advocate,* 1974; reprinted in *Long Road,* ed. Thompson, 106.

138. Douglas C. Haldeman, "Sexual Orientation Conversion Therapy for Gay Men and Lesbians: A Scientific Examination," in *Homosexuality: Research Implications for Public Policy*, ed. John C. Gonsiorek and James D. Weinrich (Newbury Park, Calif.: Sage, 1991), 159.

139. Charles W. Socarides, *Homosexuality* (New York: Aronson, 1978); Joseph Nicolosi, *Healing Homosexuality: Case Stories of Reparative Therapy* (Northvale, N.J.: Aronson, 1993); Bayer, *Homosexuality and American Psychiatry*, 208–18.

140. Tom Musbach, "Frank Kameny 1925—American Astronomer and Activist," in *Gay and Lesbian Biography*, ed. Michael J. Tyrkus (Detroit: St. James Press, 1997), 261.

141. Hooker, "The Psychologist," 25.

142. "Awards"; *Changing Our Minds;* phone interview with Edwin Shneidman, 23 June 1998.

Epilogue

1. Adrienne Rich, foreword to *The Coming Out Stories,* ed. Julia Penelope Stanley and Susan J. Wolfe (Watertown, Mass.: Persephone Press, 1980), xii.

2. For overviews of the gay and lesbian movement since Stonewall, see Barry D. Adam, *The Rise of a Gay and Lesbian Movement*, rev. ed. (New York: Twayne, 1995), chaps. 5–9; John D'Emilio, *Sexual Politics, Sexual Communities: The Making of a Homosexual Movement in the United States, 1940–1970*, 2nd ed. (Chicago: University of Chicago Press, 1998), chaps. 12, 13, afterword.

3. Adam, *Gay and Lesbian Movement*, 96–104.

4. For analyses of the New Right in relation to the gay and lesbian movement, see John D'Emilio, *Making Trouble: Essays in Gay History, Politics, and the University* (New York: Routledge, 1992), 3–16; Didi Herman, *The Antigay Agenda: Orthodox Vision and the Christian Right* (Chicago: University of Chicago Press, 1997).

5. Stephen O. Murray, *American Gay* (Chicago: University of Chicago Press, 1996), chap. 4.

6. "Queer" as a label has also become a part of gay and lesbian studies in the form of queer theory. On queer theory, see Michael Warner, ed., *Fear of a Queer Planet: Queer Politics and Social Theory* (Minneapolis: University of Minnesota Press, 1993); Annamarie Jogose, *Queer Theory: An Introduction* (New York: New York University Press, 1996); Theo Sandfort, Judith Schuyf, Jan Willem Duyvendak, and Jeffrey Weeks, eds., *Lesbian and Gay Studies: An Introductory, Interdisciplinary Approach* (Thousand Oaks, Calif.: Sage, 2000).

7. On gay and lesbian studies, see D'Emilio, *Making Trouble,* 160–75; Jeffrey Escoffier, *American Homo: Community and Perversity* (Berkeley: University of California Press, 1998), 118–41.

8. On the Cameron studies and their use in public policy, see Gregory M. Herek, "Bad Science in the Service of Stigma: A Critique of the Cameron Group's Survey Studies," in *Stigma and Sexual Orientation: Understanding Prejudice against Lesbians, Gay Men, and Bisexuals*, ed. Gregory M. Herek (Thousand Oaks, Calif.: Sage, 1998), 223–55.

9. Douglas C. Haldeman, "Sexual Orientation Conversion Therapy for Gay Men and Lesbians: A Scientific Examination," in *Homosexuality: Research Im-*

plications for Public Policy, ed. John C. Gonsiorek and James D. Weinrich (Newbury Park, Calif.: Sage, 1991), 149–60.

10. Ibid.

11. For a summary of the research on gay and lesbian identity, see Richard Troiden, *Gay and Lesbian Identity: A Sociological Analysis* (New York: General Hall, 1988), chap. 4.

12. On racial and ethnic diversity, see Beverly Greene, ed., *Ethnic and Cultural Diversity among Lesbians and Gay Men* (Thousand Oaks, Calif.: Sage, 1997). On gay and lesbian youths, see Gilbert Herdt, ed. *Gay and Lesbian Youth* (New York: Harrington Park Press, 1989); Anthony R. D'Augelli, "Developmental Implications of Victimization of Lesbian, Gay, and Bisexual Youths," in *Stigma and Sexual Orientation,* ed. Herek, 187–210.

13. On the research on relationships, see Letitia Anne Peplau, "Lesbian and Gay Relationships," in *Homosexuality,* ed. Gonsiorek and Weinrich, 177–96. On gay and lesbian parenting, see Andrew McLeod and Isaiah Crawford, "The Postmodern Family: An Examination of the Psychosocial and Legal Perspectives of Gay and Lesbian Parenting," in *Stigma and Sexual Orientation,* ed. Herek, 211–22. On issues of gay and lesbian families, see Kath Westin, *The Families We Choose* (New York: Columbia University Press, 1991).

14. Geoffrey Haddock and Mark P. Zanna, "Authoritarianism, Values, and the Favorability and Structure of Antigay Attitudes," in *Stigma and Sexual Orientation,* ed. Herek, 82–107; Gregory M. Herek, preface to *Stigma and Sexual Orientation,* ed. Herek, viii–x.

15. On the interface between research on sexual orientation and public policy, see Sheila James Kuehl, "Seeing Is Believing: Research on Women's Sexual Orientation and Public Policy," *Journal of Social Issues* 56, no. 2 (2000): 351–59.

Abraham, Julie, 28
ACT UP, 267
Adam, Barry, 266
Addams, Jane, 10
adjustment therapy, 12, 22, 55
Adler, Alfred, 126–27, 137
AIDS, 266–67, 270
Al, 131
Alexander, Jeb, 7, 67
Alika, 207–8
All the Sexes (Henry), 102–3, 111–19, 228
Allport, Gordon W., 225
American Civil Liberties Union (ACLU),
    173, 243
American Law Institute, 241
American Medical Association, 254, 256
American Psychiatric Association (APA),
    2, 219, 234, 238, 256–61, 273
    Committee on Nomenclature, 259–60
    Task Force on Social Issues, 259
American Psychological Association, 228,
    263
*American Sexual Behavior and the Kinsey
    Report* (Ernst and Loth), 159
American Sociological Association, 252
anarchist movement, 34
androgynes, 25–26. *See also* homosexuals
Anger, Kenneth, 172–73
Anonymous, Dr. Henry. *See* John Fryer
Another Country (Baldwin), 241
antigay
    attitudes, 270
    violence, 267, 270
Association for Advancement of Behavior
    Therapy, 259
Augustin, 199
Autobiography of an Androgyne (Lind),
    23–24
Aymar, Brandt, 247

Baker, Blanche M., 240
Baker, Jack, 257
Baldwin, James, 241

Barnes, Leland A., 105
Bayer, Ronald, 260–61
Bazelon, David C., 236
Beach, Frank, 259
Beam, Lura, 37–38, 282 nn. 8, 11
Beekman, Gustave, 150
Beers, Clifford W., 39
Behavior Modification Conference, 256
Bell, Alan, 259
Benjamin, Harry, 188, 204–6, 216–17
Bently, Gladys, 10
berdache, 8
Bergler, Edmund, 240
Berkeley, Ruth P., 110
Berkman, Alexander, 17–18
Berryman, Mildred, 29–32, 280 n. 63
Bhavani, Kum-Kum, 92
Bieber, Irving, 111–12, 232–35, 260–61
Bieber, Toby B., 234
Bill, 182–84, 188, 193–94, 196, 199
birth control movement, 34, 37–38
bisexuals, 25, 41–42, 61–62, 140, 267,
    271
    female, 44, 78–80, 82–83, 85
    male, 62, 69, 232–33
Black, Algernon D., 105
Black Panther leaders, 255
Blackie, 128
Bloch, Iwan, 11
Bobby, 192, 199
Bonds, Caska, 61
Boston marriages, 10
Bromberger, Edgar, 104
Brown, Harold, 261
Bryant, Anita, 266
Bryant, Louise Stevens, 34, 37, 39, 283 n.
    16
Buffalo Bill, 221
Bullough, Bonnie, 31
Bullough, Vern L., 31
Burns, Ken, 240
Burroughs, William S., 241
Burton, Richard, 249

butch/femme, 76–77, 85, 113–15. *See also* feminine women; mannish women
Butler, Judith, 123
Byron, 23

Cadmus, Paul, 173
Caldwell, Donn, 220–21
Call, Hal, 174, 205, 239
Callow, Simon, 60
Cameron, Paul, 268–69
Carmine, 188
Carpenter, Edward, 13, 20–21, 28, 31, 158, 249
Casal, Mary, 28
Cercle Hermaphroditos, 26
Changing Our Minds, 264
Charlie P., 215
Chauncey, George, 3, 12, 62, 66, 68
Chicago Inventory of Beliefs (Stern), 223
Chuck, 189
City of Night (Rechy), 210, 241
The City and the Pillar (Vidal), 171
civil rights movement, 238, 242–43, 245, 251–54, 266
Civil Service Commission, 242
Clinton, Bill (president) 268
Committee for Research in Problems of Sex, 39, 161–62
Committee for the Study of Sex Crimes, 96
Committee for the Study of Sex Variants, 4–5, 34, 36, 39–40, 45–46, 94–95, 97–98, 101, 120, 122, 129–31
    objectives of the, 49–56
community mental health movement, 236
Comstock, Anthony, 24
Con, 186
Conrad, Joseph, 125
contrary sexual feeling, 12. *See also* homosexuality
conversion therapy, 262–63
Cook, Charles, 105
Cory, Donald Webster. *See* Edward Sagarin
Costello, Matty, 150–51, 183
Craigin, Elisabeth (pseud.), 28–29
criminal behavior, 98–99
Crisp, Quentin, 25
Cukor, George, 173
Cures (Duberman), 217
Cyrus, 215

Daughters of Bilitis (DOB), 174–75, 239, 244, 251, 254, 257

Davie, Maurice R., 130
Davis, Katharine Bement, 16–17, 37, 50, 94
Davis, Madeline, 85
Dellenback, Bill, 170
D'Emilio, John, 109, 175, 238, 240, 266
Depression, 42, 47, 128, 139, 147, 156
Dewey, Thomas E., 100
Diagnostic and Statistical Manual of Mental Disorders (DSM), 219, 238, 256–60
Diana (Frederics), 29
Dickinson, Robert Latou, 33–39, 42–43, 50–52, 54, 92–93, 122, 128–30, 132–35, 158–59, 165, 217, 271, 287 n. 49
Diethelm, Oskar, 101–2
Driscoll, Jean, 155
Duberman, Martin, 3, 217, 254–55
Duggan, Lisa, 14
Dunlap, Knight, 222

East Coast Homophile Organization (ECHO), 244
Eberhardt, John, 223–24, 234
Edward, 183, 186–89, 191–92, 201
Efrian, 199–201, 203–6, 210
ego-dystonic homosexuality, 262. *See also* sexual orientation disturbance
Either Is Love (Craigin), 29
Ellis, Albert, 159, 240, 249–50
Ellis, Havelock, 3, 7, 12, 14, 25, 30, 35, 46, 71, 119
emancipatory science, 1–2, 6, 219–20, 265, 269–73
empowerment, 92–93
Epistemology of the Closet (Sedgwick), 137
Erasmus, 23
Ernst, Morris L., 159
Exodus International, 269

Faderman, Lillian, 114
fairies, 9, 20, 27, 62–68, 71, 129, 139, 141, 151, 156. *See also* homosexuals
Falek, Betty, 106
family
    breakdown of the, 52, 54
    values, 266–68
Family Research Council, 268–69
The Female-Impersonators (Lind), 25, 27
feminine women, 30, 44, 75, 77–78, 81–82. *See also* butch/femme; mannish women
femininity, physical signs of, 42–43

feminist movement, 2, 9, 36, 90–91, 117, 266. *See also* women's movement
Ferris, G. N., 15
Finch, Will. *See* Thomas Painter
Fine, Reuben, 234
Flaherty, Jack, 127, 155
Fone, Byrne, 26–27
Ford, Clelland, 236, 259
Forer, Bertram R., 229
Forster, E. M., 125, 172
Foucault, Michel, 123
Fox, Miss, 150
Frank, Jerome D., 236
Frederics, Diana (pseud.), 28–29
Freedman, Alfred, 261
Freud, Sigmund, 12, 111, 119, 167
Fritz, Marjorie, 93
From, Sam, 219–21, 264
Fryer, John (pseud. Dr. Henry Anonymous), 258

Gagnon, John, 252
Gamble, Clarence, 38
Gamble, Sidney, 38, 40
Garber, Eric, 61
Garrett, Mary, 10
Gathorne-Hardy, Jonathan, 162, 165, 175
Gay Academic Union, 267
Gay Activists Alliance (GAA), 255, 257, 259–60
The Gay Agenda, 268
gay identity, 13, 137, 265–66, 269. *See also* homosexual identity; queer identity
gay and lesbian caucuses, 268
gay and lesbian liberation movement, 93, 110, 215, 219, 252–53, 255, 266–67, 269, 273. *See also* homophile movement; homosexual rights movement
gay and lesbian studies, 3, 6, 262, 267–73
gay and lesbian youths, 270
Gay, Jan, 5, 33–42, 46–47, 57, 59, 61, 88–89, 91, 93–94, 118, 128–29, 133, 159, 229, 244, 264, 270–72, 282 n. 7. *See also* Helen Reitman
Gay Liberation Front (GLF), 255–56
gay male communities, 8–10, 71, 225–27, 229–30
Gay-PA, 257
Gay, Zhenya, 93
Gebhard, Paul, 166, 195, 204, 207, 209–10, 216–17, 236
gender duality, 63, 76–77

Genet, Jean, 172
Gentry, Evelyn, 221. *See also* Evelyn Hooker
George, 127
George A., 220
George W. Henry Foundation, 5, 95, 104–11, 118–20
    Hartford chapter, 110
Gerric, 192, 201
Ghandi, 125
Gilbert, 211–16
Ginsberg, Allen, 172
Gittings, Barbara, 244, 247, 257–58
Gloria Bar & Grill, 49
Goethe, 24
Gold, Ronald, 260–61
Goldman, Emma, 34
Gordon, Stephen, 14
The Grapevine (Stearn), 241
Green, Richard, 260–61
Greenberg, Jac, 247
Grier, Barbara, 255
Gross, Alfred A., 5, 40, 47, 94–110, 118–22, 159, 264, 272
The Group (McCarthy), 241
Gus, 189
gynanders, 25. *See also* lesbianism

Haddock, Geoffrey, 270
Haldeman, Douglas C., 262, 269
Hall, Radclyffe, 14, 28, 76
Halleck, Seymour, 259
Hammond, William, 15
Haraway, Donna, 2
Hartland, Claude, 27–29, 57
Hatterer, Lawrence, 259
Hay, Harry, 109, 238
Hector, 199, 210
Heller, Louis B., 165
Helms, Alan, 217
Henry, George W., 5, 18, 33, 36, 39–55, 57–61, 66, 73–76, 85–90, 92–113, 115–20, 124, 130, 133–34, 141, 159, 228, 248–49, 264, 272, 285 n. 22, 286 n. 30, 299 n. 37, 300 n. 55
Herek, Gregory M., 268, 270
Herzog, Alfred W., 25, 159
heterosexist
    ideology, 267
    institutions, 267, 269
Hildreth, Harold, 234
Hirschfeld, Magnus, 3, 11–13, 19–22, 25, 28–31, 35, 39, 41, 46, 55, 64, 119, 141, 158, 264, 271
Hodges, Julian, 245–46, 251

Hoffman, Martin, 236, 259
homophile movement, 58, 108–10, 119,
    121–23, 169, 175, 202–3, 238–56,
    272–73. *See also* gay and lesbian lib-
    eration movement; homosexual
    rights movement
  radicalization of the, 110, 121, 238,
    240, 243–45, 251–56, 272
Homophile Studies, 237–39
homosexual adjustment, 55, 103–4, 107–
    11, 115
The Homosexual in America (Cory), 112,
    135, 210, 226–27, 242, 246–51
The Homosexual and His Society (Cory
    and LeRoy), 250
homosexual identity, 164, 168, 178, 203,
    231. *See also* gay identity; queer iden-
    tity
The Homosexual Matrix (Tripp), 170
homosexual men, underprivileged, 96–
    100, 103
homosexual preference, 69–70
homosexual rights movement. *See also* gay
    and lesbian liberation movement; ho-
    mophile movement
  in America, 35–36, 45–46, 48, 56–57,
    61, 91, 218, 265–67
  in England, 20, 31, 55
  in Germany, 3, 11, 19–20, 31, 55
homosexual subculture, 43, 57, 112–15,
    229, 241. *See also* Evelyn Hooker;
    Thomas Painter
homosexuality. *See also* contrary sexual
    feeling; lesbianism; sexual intermedi-
    acy; sexual inversion; Uranianism
  decriminalization of, 12, 19, 35–36, 45,
    56, 137, 157–58, 236–37, 241, 248.
    See also homosexual rights move-
    ment
  etiology of, 12, 25, 38–39, 43–44, 54,
    140–41, 164, 180, 232–33
  and gender inversion, 37–38, 44, 49,
    53–54, 62–68, 71–72, 89–90, 111,
    217. *See also* sexual inversion
  and pathology model, 2–5, 43, 56, 73,
    85–86, 105, 110, 136–37, 146, 158,
    219, 229, 232–38, 240, 242, 244–
    46, 248–51, 259–63, 271, 273
  prevention of, 45, 51, 54, 56, 111, 116–
    17, 237
  in prison, 17–18, 99–100
  psychiatric declassification of, 2–4, 242,
    256–60, 263, 265, 269
  psychiatric screening of, 100–2, 111.
    See also World War II draft

  as a social problem, 112, 115–18
  treatment of, 13, 39–40, 45, 51, 54–56,
    111, 115–16, 233, 237, 248
Homosexuality (Bergler), 240
Homosexuality (Cory), 249–50
The Homosexuality of Men and Women
    (Hirschfeld), 21
homosexuals. *See also* androgynes; fairies
  and sex researchers, 4, 8, 14–20, 36,
    55–57, 59, 75, 89, 94, 122–23,
    217
  types of, 22, 25
Hooker, Edward Niles, 221, 227, 229
Hooker, Evelyn, 5–6, 109, 144, 205–6,
    208–9, 217, 219–36, 239–40, 244–
    45, 252, 258–59, 263–64, 272–73.
    See also Evelyn Gentry
  on male homosexual subculture, 225–
    27, 229–31
  research by, 5, 223–35
hooks, bell, 1, 91
Howard, William Lee, 15
Humphreys, Laud, 252
Huncke, Herbert, 164
"husbands," 9, 27, 151, 155. *See also*
    fairies
hustlers. *See* male prostitution

Imre (Prime-Stevenson), 21
Indio, 193, 199–200, 210
Institute for Sexual Science, 11, 20, 35
The Intermediate Sex (Carpenter), 21
International Congress of Applied Psy-
    chology, 229
International Journal of Psychiatry, 259
The Intersexes (Prime-Stevenson), 19, 21
inversion. *See under* sexual
Isherwood, Christopher, 172, 174, 206,
    210, 225

Jeb and Dash (Russell), 7
Jennie June. *See* Earl Lind
Jesus, 125
Jim, 186–87
Jimmy F., 191
Johnson, Alan, 166
Johnson, David, 68
Jones, Cannon Clinton, 120
Jones, James H., 162, 165
Journal of Homosexuality, 268
Journal of Projective Techniques, 229
Julio, 197–98

Kahn, Eugen, 39–40, 50
Kahn, Samuel, 17

Kameny, Frank, 5–6, 219–20, 242–45, 248, 251–53, 256–58, 261–63
Kefauver, Estes, 173
Kelly, E. Lowell, 18
Kennedy, Elizabeth, 85
Kennedy, Stoddard, 126
kept boys, 132, 148, 154. *See also* male prostitution
Kertbeny, Karl Maria, 11, 13
Kiernan, James G., 15
ki-ki queens, 149, 155. *See also* male prostitution
Kinsey, Alfred C., 5, 47, 93, 103, 109, 120, 122–24, 133–35, 139–40, 158–85, 187, 189–90, 194–95, 198, 203, 207, 209, 217, 227, 239, 241, 249–50, 259, 263–64, 272–73
    and the homosexual community, 5, 169–75
    homosexual sex histories by, 162–64
    views on homosexuality by, 164–69
Kinsey, Clara Bracken McMillen, 161
Kinsey Institute, 5, 122, 137, 160, 170, 172–76, 185, 187, 194–95, 201, 216, 234, 239, 272
Kirstein, Lincoln, 171
Klopfer, Bruno, 223, 227
Kohler, Robert, 46
Krafft-Ebing, Richard von, 12, 16, 19, 22, 35, 54, 59, 83, 94, 167
Kuklick, Henricka, 46

Ladder, 239–40, 255
La Guardia, Fiorello, 95–96
Lahusen, Kay, 258
Laidlaw, Robert W., 118, 130
Lambert, Bill, 107
Laporte, Rita, 254
Laurence, Leo, 255
Legg, Dorr, 206, 237
Legman, Gershon, 92–93, 130, 132–34, 137–38, 178, 304 n. 37
Leitsch, Dick, 251–52
LeRoy, John P., 250
lesbian communities, 9–10, 83
lesbian feminism, 91, 266
lesbian identity, 13–14, 265–66, 269. *See also* butch/femme; feminine women; mannish women
lesbianism, 12, 37, 46, 115, 138, 246, 266. *See also* homosexuality
    and gender inversion, 13–14, 76–78, 80–81, 85
Leznoff, Maurice, 227
Lichtenstein, Perry, 19–20

life stories, 4–5, 33, 42–43, 56–61, 92–93, 218, 265, 269
    coming out in, 61–62, 69–73, 80–85, 93, 137, 265–66
    despair and resistance in, 87–92
    female, 75–86
    male, 61–75
    medicalized interpretation of, 73–75, 85–86
    sexual identities in, 61–69, 75–80
Lind, Earl (pseud. Jennie June; Ralph Werther), 19–21, 23–29, 31, 57, 59, 66, 135, 139, 147, 156, 159, 229, 247, 271
Littlejohn, Larry, 256–57
Llewellyn, Mary, 14
Loeb, Leo, 34
Loth, David, 159
Luis, 196–98
Lukas, Edwin, 105

Macbeth (Shakespeare), 60
Make-a-Picture-Story test (MAPS), 227
male prostitution, 23, 41–42, 47, 61–64, 69, 128, 147, 217, 291 n. 33. *See also* kept boys, ki-ki queens, Thomas Painter, wolves
mannish women, 13, 22, 29–30, 44, 75–78, 80–82, 85. *See also* butch/femme; feminine women
Manuel, 199–201
maricón, 197
Marmor, Judd, 229, 235–36, 258–61
Martin, Del, 257
masculine gay men, 44. *See also* queer men
masculinity-femininity (M-F) test, 18, 40, 42, 54, 98, 288 n. 62
masculinity, physical signs, 42
Mattachine Review, 239–40
Mattachine Society, 109–10, 172, 174–75, 205, 227, 238–40, 242–46
    New York chapter, 243–46, 251–52
    Washington chapter, 242–43, 245, 252
Maurice (Forster), 125
Mayer, E. E., 51
Mayne, Xavier. *See* Edward I. Prime-Stevenson
McCarthy, Mary, 241
McCarthyism, 57, 85, 106, 109, 135, 165, 175, 223–24, 238, 247
McMurtrie, Douglas C., 19
Meagher, John F., 19
mental hygiene movement, 39, 41, 53–56
Mentality and Homosexuality (Kahn), 17
Meyer, Adolf, 39, 53, 55

Meyer, Mortimer, 227
Midnight Cowboy, 215
Miles, Catharine Cox, 18, 40, 42, 54
Mitchell, Alice, 13–14, 76
Mizer, Bob, 173
molly houses, 8
Money, John, 236
Montagu, Ashley, 92
Motion Picture Production Code, 241
Muenzinger, Karl, 222
Murray, Stephen, 218, 267
muscle boys, 183, 188–89, 191–92, 217

Naked Lunch (Burroughs), 241
Napheys, George, 9
National Association for Research and
    Therapy of Homosexuality
    (NARTH), 262, 269
National Committee on Maternal Health,
    34, 36–39, 129
National Committee for Mental Hygiene,
    39
National Gay Task Force (NGTF), 261
National Institute of Mental Health
    (NIMH), 223–24, 234–38, 264
    Task Force on Homosexuality, 235–38,
    263
National Research Council, 39, 165
New Deal, 98–99
New Left, 254–55
New Right, 266–69, 271
New Women, 13
New York City Committee of Neuropsy-
    chiatric Societies, 101
New York State Liquor Authority, 48–49
Newton, Esther, 85
Nichols, Jack, 242, 247
Nicolosi, Joseph, 262
North American Conference of Ho-
    mophile Organizations (NACHO),
    252–54

obscenity statutes, 241
On Going Naked (Gay), 35
ONE, Incorporated, 237, 239, 242
ONE Institute of Homophile Studies,
    239
ONE Magazine, 107, 206, 239–40, 250
Oosterhuis, Harry, 19
O'Rourke, Willie, 128, 155

Painter, Carrie Stevens, 124, 127, 131
Painter, Henry McMahon, 124–27, 131,
    183
Painter, Sidney, 124, 131, 199, 201

Painter, Thomas (pseud. Will Finch), 5, 35,
    38–41, 47–49, 59–60, 90, 102, 108,
    122–60, 165, 169, 173, 176–218,
    227, 229–30, 244, 264, 270–72,
    303 n. 27
    Life Record of, 5, 173, 181, 196, 201,
    203, 206–7, 209–10, 214–16, 218
    on male homosexual subculture, 123,
    135, 137–46
    on male prostitution, 5, 38–40, 47, 123,
    126–32, 135, 137, 139–41, 145–57
Paresis Hall, 26
Parker, William (police chief), 208
pastoral counseling, 103, 106–7
pato, 197
Pentagon's Military Working Group, 268
Peter, 132, 186–87, 191, 199, 205
Plato, 23
Ploscowe, Morris, 236
Plummer, Ken, 218
Pomeroy, Wardell B., 122, 163, 169, 176,
    194–96, 201–2, 204–7, 209–10, 217,
    234, 259
Porter, 187–88
Prime-Stevenson, Edward I. (pseud. Xavier
    Mayne), 19–23, 25, 28–29, 31, 135,
    229, 247, 271
*The Problem of Homosexuality in Modern
    Society* (Ruitenbeek), 234–35
professionalization, medical and scientific,
    52–54
projective personality tests, 227
psychoanalysis, 53, 55, 111
Psychobiological Questionnaire
    (Hirschfeld), 35
Psychopathia sexualis (Krafft-Ebing), 12,
    16, 19
Puerto Rican culture, 193, 197–98, 200,
    217

Quaker Civil Readjustment Committee,
    102–6, 108, 118, 120, 297 n. 19
queer
    identity, 123, 199–200, 267. *See also*
    gay identity; homosexual identity
    men, 9, 62, 66–68, 71–72. *See also* mas-
    culine gay men
    politics, 267. *See also* Queer Nation
Queer Nation, 267

Rado, Sandor, 111, 235
Rapff, Sixte, 173–74
Raphael, 24
Raul, 201
Rechy, John, 210, 241

Reitman, Ben L., 34, 281 n. 5
Reitman, Helen, 34–35. *See also* Jan Gay
Renslow, Charles, 173
Rice, Thurman, 161
Rich, Adrienne, 265
Riecken, Henry W., 236
Robins, Eli, 259–60
Robinson, Kent, 256–57
Robinson, Victor, 29
Robinson, William J., 20, 29
Rockefeller Foundation, 165, 169, 177
Rodgers, Danny, 150–51, 153
Roger, 186–87, 191, 199
Roosevelt, Eleanor, 220
Roosevelt, Theodore, 125
Rorschach test, 98, 221, 227–28
Rorum, Ned, 171
Ruitenbeek, Hendrik M., 234–35, 245
Rusk, Dean, 245
Russell, Ina, 7

Sagarin, Edward (pseud. Donald Webster
    Cory), 109, 112, 135, 144, 159, 210,
    226, 229, 242, 246–52, 330 n. 85
Saghir, Marcel, 259–60
Salt Lake Bohemian Club, 10, 30
Salvation Army, 242
Sapir, Phillip, 234
Schwartz, Leonard, 133
Schwartz, May, 34
Schwartz, Mr., 49
Scott, Bruce, 243
Sedgwick, Eve K. 123, 137
Seidenberg, Robert, 258
sex offenders, 5, 40, 47, 95–100, 102–10
    treatment of, 97–100, 103–8
Sex and Personality (Terman and Miles),
    18–19
sex reformers, 36
sex survey, 16–17, 39
Sex Variants (Henry), 5, 33, 40–42, 46–
    47, 49–51, 55, 57–60, 64, 92–93,
    101–3, 111, 120, 124, 129–30, 133,
    141, 228, 272
sex variants study, 33, 36, 40–46, 50–51,
    55–57, 67, 91, 95–96, 118, 130
    objectives of research activists and par-
    ticipants, 46–49, 90
sexology, 11–14, 36, 54
sexual
    adjustment, 37, 51–52
    intermediacy, 3, 12–13, 22, 25, 39. *See
    also* homosexuality
    inversion, 12, 30, 53. *See also* homosex-
    uality

object-choice, 12, 52–53, 111
orientation disturbance, 2, 219, 260–
    62. *See also* ego-dystonic homosexu-
    ality
Sexual Behavior in the Human Male (Kin-
    sey), 171
Sexual Inversion (H. Ellis), 7
Sexual Inversion (Marmor), 258
Seymour, 188
Shakespeare, 23
Shaw, J. C., 15
Shawn, Ted, 171
Shepard, Matthew, 267
Shneidman, Edwin, 227, 264
Siegelman, Marvin, 235, 259
Silverstein, Charles, 259–60
Simon, William, 168
The Single Woman (Dickinson and Beam),
    37–38
The Sixth Man (Stearn), 241
Smith, Jack, 172
Smith, Mary Rozet, 10
Socarides, Charles, 234, 254, 259–62
Society for Individual Rights (SIR), 225
Society of Janus, 252
Society for the Prevention of Crime, 100,
    105
Spitzer, Robert, 259–61
Stearn, Jess, 241
Stern, George, 223
Steward, Sam, 170–71
Stoller, Robert, 260
The Stone Wall (Casal), 28
Stonewall (Duberman), 255
Stonewall riot, 215, 245, 253, 255,
    265
The Story of a Life (Hartland), 28
Strangers in Our Midst (Gross), 120
A Streetcar Named Desire (Williams), 60,
    172
student antiwar protests, 238, 254
Students for a Democratic Society, 254
Suddenly Last Summer (Williams), 204
Symonds, John Addington, 13, 21, 249
Szasz, Thomas, 235

Talking Back (hooks), 1
Tallmij, Billie, 175
Tearoom Trade (Humphreys), 252
Terman, Lewis M., 18–19, 40, 42, 54,
    278 n. 28
Terry, Jennifer, 42, 96
Thematic Apperception Test (TAT), 227
This Naked World (Gay), 35
Thomas, Cary, 10

Thomas, Edna, 60–61
Thompson, Clara, 118, 248
A Thousand Marriages (Dickinson and
    Beam), 37
Tolstoy, 125
Tommy, 173
Tony, 131–32, 187, 191, 199
Tony C., 196
transgendered community, 65, 267, 271.
    See also transsexual identity; trans-
    vestites
transsexual identity, 64, 267. *See also*
    transgendered community; transves-
    tites
transvestites, 41, 42, 61–62, 64–65, 88,
    289 n. 18. *See also* transgendered
    community; transsexual identity
The Transvestites (Hirschfeld), 64
Tripp, Clarence A., 103, 169–70, 174
Troiden, Richard, 269
Tucker, Luther, 129–31, 184

Uckerman, Ruth, 31
Ulrichs, Karl Heinrich, 11–12, 25, 149–41
Uranianism, 19. *See also* homosexuality
Urning and Urningin, 3, 11, 19

van den Haag, Ernest, 235
Veterans Benevolent Association, 109
Vicinus, Martha, 3
Vidal, Gore, 171, 210
Voeller, Bruce, 261
Voris, Ralph, 163–64

Wade, Otis, 173
Wade, Theodore, 155
Walker, Jimmy (mayor), 95
Wallace, Anthony F. C., 236
Walsh, David I., 150
Ward, Freda, 13–14
Waugh, Thomas, 188

The Well of Loneliness (Hall), 14, 28, 31–
    32, 76
Welles, Orson, 60
Wells, Herman B., 161
Wertham, Frederic, 104
Werther, Ralph. *See* Earl Lind
Wescott, Glenway, 172, 174
West Side Discussion Group, 251
Westermarck, Edward, 13
Westley, William A., 227
Westphal, Karl, 12
Wheeler, Monroe, 171–72
White, William Alanson, 55
Whitman, Howard, 104
Whitman, Walt, 23, 125
Wicker, Randy, 243–44
Wilder, Thornton, 172
Williams, Tennessee, 172, 204
Windham, Olivia, 61
Wolfenden Report, 110, 121, 237, 241
"wolves," 149, 156. *See also* male prostitu-
    tion
Woodstock, 215
women's movement, 266. *See also* feminist
    movement
Worden, Frederic, 224
World War II draft, 100–2. *See also* homo-
    sexuality, psychiatric screening of
Wright, Clifford A., 164
Wyman, Loraine, 124, 131
Wynkoop, William, 247

Yale University Christian Association,
    125–27, 184
Yayito, 197
Yerkes, Robert M., 222
Yolles, Stanley F., 235–37
Young Man from the Provinces (Helms),
    217

Zanna, Mark P., 270